For Sherry,

בהצלחה,

Richard Kalin

THE S. MARK TAPER FOUNDATION

IMPRINT IN JEWISH STUDIES

BY THIS ENDOWMENT
THE S. MARK TAPER FOUNDATION SUPPORTS
THE APPRECIATION AND UNDERSTANDING
OF THE RICHNESS AND DIVERSITY OF
JEWISH LIFE AND CULTURE

The publisher gratefully acknowledges the generous support of the Jewish Studies Endowment Fund of the University of California Press Foundation, which was established by a major gift from the S. Mark Taper Foundation.

Migrating Tales

Migrating Tales

THE TALMUD'S NARRATIVES AND
THEIR HISTORICAL CONTEXT

Richard Kalmin

UNIVERSITY OF CALIFORNIA PRESS

University of California Press, one of the most distinguished university presses in the United States, enriches lives around the world by advancing scholarship in the humanities, social sciences, and natural sciences. Its activities are supported by the UC Press Foundation and by philanthropic contributions from individuals and institutions. For more information, visit www.ucpress.edu.

University of California Press
Oakland, California

© 2014 by The Regents of the University of California

Library of Congress Cataloging-in-Publication Data

Kalmin, Richard Lee.
   Migrating tales : the Talmud's narratives and their historical context / Richard Kalmin.
      pages   cm.
   Includes bibliographical references and index.
   ISBN 978-0-520-27725-0 (cloth : alk. paper)
   ISBN 978-0-520-95899-9 (ebook)
   1. Talmud—Criticism, Narrative.   2. Narration in rabbinical literature.   I. Title.
   BM509.N37K35   2014
   296.1'2067—dc23
                                        2014002050

Manufactured in the United States of America

23 22 21 20 19 18 17 16 15 14
10 9 8 7 6 5 4 3 2 1

In keeping with a commitment to support environmentally responsible and sustainable printing practices, UC Press has printed this book on Natures Natural, a fiber that contains 30% post-consumer waste and meets the minimum requirements of ANSI/NISO Z39.48–1992 (R 1997) (*Permanence of Paper*).

For Les Lenoff, Richard Sacks, and Claudia Setzer
In Friendship

CONTENTS

Preface ix
Acknowledgments xvii
Manuscripts and Early Editions xxi

Introduction 1

1 · "Manasseh Sawed Isaiah with a Saw of Wood":
An Ancient Legend in Jewish, Christian, Muslim,
and Persian Sources 29

2 · R. Shimon bar Yohai Meets St. Bartholomew:
Peripatetic Traditions in Late Antique Judaism and
Christianity East of Syria 53

3 · The Miracle of the Septuagint in Ancient Rabbinic and
Christian Literature 80

4 · The Demons in Solomon's Temple 95

5 · Zechariah and the Bubbling Blood: An Ancient
Tradition in Jewish, Christian, and Muslim Literature 130

6 · Pharisees 164

7 · Astrology 175

8 · The Alexander Romance 200

Summary and Conclusions 236

Bibliography 241
General Index 269
Index of Primary Sources 275

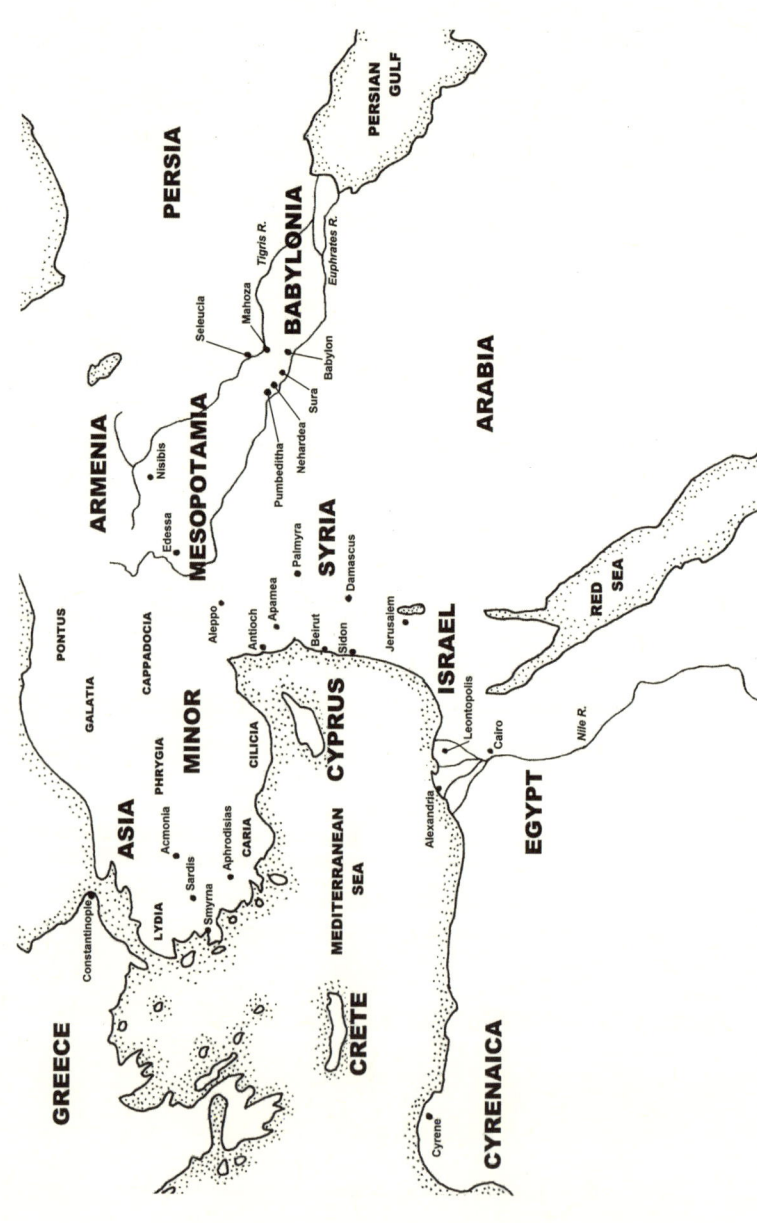

The Near East in late antiquity.

PREFACE

It is my hope that readers interested in the relationship between Jewish, Christian, and pagan literature and culture in late antiquity will be drawn to this book. The book is concerned with narratives that traveled from one culture to another, and how the meaning of these narratives changed from one literary and cultural context to another. These narratives are often very strange to the uninitiated ear; this preface therefore attempts to define fundamental technical terminology and to locate the discussion geographically and chronologically (see the map).

This book focuses on the Babylonian Talmud (or "Bavli"), composed by rabbis who flourished under Sasanian Persian domination (ca. 224–651 C.E.). These rabbis lived between the Tigris and Euphrates Rivers, in what corresponds to modern-day southwest Iraq, between the third and sixth or seventh centuries C.E. While two Talmuds survived from late antiquity (see below), the Bavli is the primary subject of this study.

The rabbis, primarily on the basis of their knowledge of Torah, competed with other groups and individuals for authority over the Babylonian Jewish community, although the precise extent of the authority of any of these competing groups is by no means clear. Precisely what the rabbis meant by "Torah" is a complex question, although it certainly included expertise in traditional rabbinic learning (see below) and scriptural interpretation, as well as a variety of other subjects, such as astrology, dream interpretation, and the ability to control demons.

This book focuses to a lesser extent on the Palestinian Talmud (or "Yerushalmi"), composed by another major community of rabbis, who flourished in the land of Israel under Roman domination between the second and the late fourth or early fifth centuries C.E. Palestinian rabbis composed other major works that figure in this study (see below), whose relationship to the two Talmuds is a matter of scholarly dispute, but which seem to have been edited during the fifth and sixth centuries C.E.

Throughout this book, the term "Tannaim" refers to rabbis who flourished in Palestine between the first and the early third centuries C.E.,[1] and the term "Amoraim" refers to rabbis who flourished in Palestine and Babylonia between the early third and the late fourth centuries (in Palestine) and between the early third and the early sixth centuries (in Babylonia). This book follows the scholarly convention of introducing the names of Babylonian Amoraim with the honorific "Rav" ("master," "teacher") and the names of Palestinian Amoraim with the honorific "R.," an abbreviation for "Rabbi." We also follow scholarly convention by introducing the names of Tannaim, virtually all of whom were Palestinian, with the honorific "R." The different titles do not appear to indicate a difference in status, but rather reflect a phonetic difference between the western Aramaic spoken by Palestinian rabbis and the eastern Aramaic spoken by Babylonian rabbis.[2] Some rabbis, for reasons that are not entirely clear, have no honorific preceding their names, notably the prominent third-century Babylonian Amora Shmuel, and other individuals whose rabbinic status is in doubt, notably Hanina ben Dosa, are rabbinized in the Talmud by the addition of the honorific "R." introducing their names. If the honorific is well attested in the manuscripts of the Talmuds, we use it in our discussions, intending by it no claims regarding the biography of the individual, but only recognition of an attempt by the classical rabbis to depict a nonrabbi as "one of their own."

Some Talmudic material predates the destruction of the second Temple in 70 C.E., but this material derives from groups or individuals other than rabbis, since the earliest rabbis lived after the destruction of the Temple. Study of second Temple literature, for example, reveals that the Talmud contains a significant amount of pre–70 C.E. literature, but the Talmud does not explic-

---

1. Virtually all Tannaitic statements derive from Palestine, although a small number of Tannaim lived in Babylonia. See Yeshayahu Gafni, *Yehudei Bavel bi-Tekufat ha-Talmud: Hayyei ha-Hevrah ve-ha-Ruah* (Jerusalem: Zalman Shazar Center for Jewish History, 1990), pp. 68–91.

2. See Yohanan Breuer, "Gadol mei-Rav Rabbi, Gadol mei-Rabbi Rabban, Gadol mei-Rabban Shemo," *Tarbiz* 66, no. 1 (1997): 41–59, esp. pp. 53–56. Breuer argues that Eastern Aramaic dialects tended to drop vowels at the end of words (hence: Rav), whereas Western Aramaic retained them. The names of some rabbis, such as Rava, are formed via the contraction of the honorific, Rav, and the personal name, Abba. As a rule, however, the honorifics cited here suffice for my purposes.

itly distinguish this material from Tannaitic statements per se. In addition, much of this material has been rabbinized, that is, made to conform to rabbinic standards, such that it often tells more about the rabbis who transmitted it than about the prerabbinic figures who are its purported authors and protagonists.[3]

We will also refer to "anonymous editors" of the material preserved in both Talmuds.[4] Due to their anonymous character, the chronology of these editors and the material they composed is difficult to assess.[5] Some scholars claim that the anonymous material comprises the latest stratum of the Talmuds, while other scholars claim that it was produced contemporaneously with the material produced by the Amoraim. Throughout this book I make every effort to avoid taking a stand on this issue in the absence of concrete proof, since in my opinion, scholars too often base conclusions about the chronology of the text based on preconceived notions regarding the provenance of the anonymous material. Very often we will be able to assert responsibly only that the anonymous material postdates the latest Amoraic material in a given text.

The past half century or so of research, furthermore, has provided abundant evidence that attributions of statements to particular rabbis are often not trustworthy, hampering our efforts to date or locate even the attributed material. Throughout this book I make no assumptions about the chronology and geography of isolated attributed statements, since I take very

---

3. As numerous scholars have noted, the Bavli routinely rabbinizes nonrabbinic figures, for example, Jesus, Ashmedai (the king of the demons), Honi the Circle Drawer, and Hanina ben Dosa. See William Scott Green, "Palestinian Holy Men: Charismatic Leadership and Rabbinic Tradition," in *Aufstieg und Niedergang der römischen Welt* 2:19/2 (1979): 619–47; Baruch M. Bokser, "Wonder-Working and the Rabbinic Tradition: The Case of Hanina ben Dosa," *Journal for the Study of Judaism* 16 (1985): 42–92; Richard Kalmin, "Christians and Heretics in Rabbinic Literature of Late Antiquity," *Harvard Theological Review* 87, no. 2 (1994): 156–60; idem, "Holy Men, Rabbis, and Demonic Sages in Late Antiquity," in *Jewish Culture and Society under the Christian Roman Empire*, ed. Richard Kalmin and Seth Schwartz (Leuven: Peeters, 2003), pp. 234–45; and chapter 4.

4. For scholarly literature on the editorial character of the anonymous material in the Talmud, see Richard Kalmin, *Sages, Stories, Authors, and Editors in Rabbinic Babylonia* (Atlanta: Scholars Press, 1994), p. xiv, n. 2.

5. See, for example, Robert Brody, "Stam ha-Talmud ve-Divrei ha-Amoraim," in *Ha-Mikra ve-Olamo: Sifrut Hazal u-Mishpat Ivri u-Mahshevet Yisrael*, ed. Baruch Schwartz, Abraham Melamed, and Aharon Shemesh (Jerusalem: Ha-Igud ha-Olami le-Mada'ei ha-Yahadut, 2008), pp. 213–32; and Shamma Friedman, *Talmud Arukh: Bavli Bava Mezi'a VI* (New York: Jewish Theological Seminary, 1996), vol. 2, pp. 22–23.

seriously the possibility of pseudepigraphic attribution. Only if a statement conforms to well-documented patterns exhibited by rabbis known to have lived during the approximate time and place as the author of the statement do I tentatively assume that it is possible to draw chronological and geographical conclusions. As I noted in an earlier study,

> It is frequently possible to divide the Talmud into its constituent layers and reach significant conclusions about the literature, personalities, and institutions of the rabbis who flourished prior to the Talmud's final redaction. Material attributed to early rabbis often differs from that attributed to later rabbis; early material is at times even antithetical to the standards and norms of later generations.[6]

Even when we have this much proof of the layered nature of the Talmud, however, we must remain cognizant of the relatively fragile basis upon which our chronological and geographical conclusions rest, since these conclusions depend primarily on the internal evidence of the Talmuds, and only in rare instances on the chronology and geography of events documented in sources external to the Talmuds. Geonic chronicles sometimes provide a measure of confirmation of the internal Talmudic evidence. The historical value of the geonic chronicles is enhanced by the fact that the information in these works appears to be based in part upon authentic traditions deriving from earlier sources.[7] The geonic traditions are also problematic, however, due to the fact that they are preserved in works composed centuries after the final editing of the Talmuds.[8]

In case after case, however, we will find that Palestinian rabbinic material in the Bavli (that is, material in the Bavli attributed to Palestinian rabbis) conforms to patterns exhibited by material, both Jewish and non-Jewish, deriving from Palestine and from elsewhere in the eastern Roman provinces. We will also find that Babylonian material preserved in the Bavli (that is, material in the Bavli attributed to Babylonian rabbis) conforms to different patterns, providing significant evidence that at least in some cases the geo-

---

6. See Richard Kalmin, *Jewish Babylonia between Persia and Roman Palestine* (New York: Oxford University Press, 2006), p. 194, n. 58. See also the literature cited there, pp. 58–59.

7. See Yeshayahu Gafni, "Le-Heker ha-Khronologiah be-Igeret Rav Sherira Gaon," *Zion* 52 (1987): 1–24, reprinted in Gafni, *Yehudei Bavli*, pp. 239–65.

8. See, for example, David Goodblatt, *Rabbinic Instruction in Sasanian Babylonia* (Leiden: Brill, 1975), pp. 38–40.

graphical distinctions attested by the Talmud conform to historical reality. In addition, we will find in case after case that material in the Bavli attributed to Babylonian rabbis who lived between the fourth and the early sixth centuries C.E. conforms to the patterns exhibited by the Jewish and non-Jewish traditions deriving from the eastern Roman provinces, which constitutes significant evidence of a dramatic shift in the literature of rabbinic Babylonia as a result of cultural contacts with the Roman East. We will have much more to say about the implications of these cultural contacts, since the surprising importance of the Roman East in contributing to our understanding of post–third century developments of Babylonian rabbinic culture is the primary subject of this book.

Quotations from the Bavli are introduced throughout by a lowercase "b.," and quotations from the Yerushalmi are introduced by a lowercase "y." Other rabbinic works quoted throughout include several Tannaitic compilations deriving from Palestine, edited in the early third century C.E. Most prominent among these are the Mishnah and Tosefta, both of which are largely, although not exclusively, collections of legal statements. We introduce quotations from the Mishnah with a lowercase "m." and quotations from the Tosefta with a lowercase "t." Other Tannaitic compilations are characterized by scholars, with only partial appropriateness, as "halakhic midrashim," since they contain primarily (although far from exclusively) legal texts (halakhah) based on interpretation of the Bible (midrash). Other scholars refer to these compilations as "exegetical midrashim," since they follow, and explain, the biblical text verse by verse.[9] Most notable among these compilations are Mekhilta de-R. Yishmael (based on the book of Exodus), Mekhilta de-R. Shimon bar Yohai (also based on Exodus), Sifra (based on Leviticus), Sifrei Bemidbar (based on Numbers), and Sifrei Devarim (based on Deuteronomy). These compilations contain primarily Tannaitic material and their editing is conventionally assigned to the third century C.E. We also quote frequently from most of the "Amoraic," "aggadic,"[10] or "homiletical" midrashim:

---

9. See Avigdor Shinan, "The Late Midrashic, Paytanic, and Targumic Literature," in *The Cambridge History of Judaism*, vol. 4, *The Late Roman-Rabbinic Period*, ed. Steven T. Katz (Cambridge: Cambridge University Press, 2006), p. 685.

10. I am well aware that the term "aggadic" as a synonym for "nonlegal" is problematic in this context, first because the lines separating "aggadah" and "halakhah" have been shown by scholars to be more porous than has traditionally been thought, and second because the so-called halakhic midrashim also contain much aggadah. Once again I use the term for the sake of convenience, while remaining cognizant of its limitations.

Bereshit Rabbah (based on Genesis), Vayikra Rabba (based on Leviticus), Pesikta de-Rav Kahana (based on the weekly Torah reading), Eikhah Rabbah (based on Lamentations), the first seven chapters of Esther Rabbah, and Kohelet Rabbah (based on Ecclesiastes). While these latter compilations exclusively quote Tannaim and Amoraim, the editing of most of these texts is conventionally dated later than that of the Yerushalmi.[11] This does not necessarily mean that all texts in the homiletical midrashim reflect a later stage in the development of traditions than those found in the Yerushalmi, in the same way that Tannaitic statements (or "Baraitot") found in the Talmuds do not necessarily reflect a later stage in the development of traditions than those found in Tannaitic compilations. While they are often later, this should not be assumed to be so uncritically, and every case needs to be examined on its own merits.

Much of the Bavli is a commentary on the Mishnah. It would be a gross oversimplification, however, to characterize the Bavli as a mere commentary on the Mishnah, since frequently the Bavli's discussions are based on scripture, Baraitot, or Amoraic statements, or consist entirely of sources whose connection to the Mishnah is fragile or artificial.[12]

The Bavli contains legal pronouncements on civil, criminal, and ritual matters. It also contains sententious sayings, advice, dream interpretations, magical incantations, medical cures, polemics, folk tales, fables, legends, scriptural interpretations, legal case reports, and numerous other literary genres. Much more so than Palestinian rabbinic compilations, the Bavli is encyclopedic in character, meaning that it contains many more varieties of rabbinic literature than roughly contemporaneous Palestinian compilations.[13] The Bavli, for example, is much richer in nonlegal scriptural commentary (aggadic midrash) than the Yerushalmi, which is more narrowly focused on law and Mishnah commentary. Apparently, the relatively narrow focus of the Yerushalmi is due in part to the fact that compilations of aggadic midrash circulated in Palestine, in contrast to the situation in Babylonia. In Babylonia, aggadic midrash survived in the context of a compilation only if it was incorporated into the Bavli. In Palestine, in contrast, there was more specialization, with midrashic compilations as the primary repositories of

---

11. Shinan, "Midrashic, Paytanic, and Targumic Literature," pp. 685–90.
12. David Rosenthal, "Arikhot Kedumot ba-Talmud ha-Bavli," in *Mehkerei Talmud*, ed. David Rosenthal and Yaakov Sussmann (Jerusalem: Magnes Press, 1990), vol. 1, pp. 155–204.
13. See Jacob Neusner, *Judaism: The Classical Statement: The Evidence of the Bavli* (Chicago: University of Chicago Press, 1986), pp. 94–114 and 211–40.

aggadic scriptural commentary, and the Yerushalmi as the primary repository of law and Mishnah commentary.[14]

There is no critical edition of the entire Bavli that takes into account all the manuscripts, not to mention the extensive quotations in the early medieval writers, though portions have been so treated. The *textus receptus* (received text) is the edition issued by the Widow and Brothers Romm, Vilna 1880–86 (the "Vilna Shas," often reprinted). This edition is ultimately derived from the first printed edition issued by Daniel Bomberg in Venice (1520–23), the folio numbers of which (for example, 59a) are still used for purposes of reference.

Michael Krupp lists sixty-three manuscripts of the Babylonian Talmud,[15] ranging in date from the twelfth to the seventeenth century and ranging in size from a few leaves to the entire Talmud. Some of the oldest fragments, however, are from the Cairo Genizah, some of which predate 1000 C.E. Ms Munich 95 is the only complete manuscript of the Bavli, and even it is missing a few pages. Medieval rabbinic authors are also a crucially important source of variant readings, since many of these authors predate our earliest Talmud manuscripts.

The Saul Lieberman Institute for Talmudic Research at the Jewish Theological Seminary of America in New York maintains a computerized databank of Talmudic manuscripts and Genizah fragments. The goal of this project is to transcribe, in a searchable format, all extant manuscripts and Genizah fragments. In addition, the Jewish National and University Library in Jerusalem and the Hebrew University's Department of Talmud maintain an online databank of Talmudic manuscripts (http://jnul.huji.ac.il/dl/talmud). Still of tremendous importance is the work of Rafael Rabbinovicz, for his sophisticated discussions of manuscript variants and of variant readings preserved in the works of medieval commentators and anthologizers of the Bavli.[16] The Institute for the Complete Israeli Talmud is publishing a critical edition (Herschler et al., eds., 1972–). So far four full tractates have appeared (Ketubot, Sotah, Nedarim, Yevamot) and part of a fifth (Gittin).

---

14. See Avraham Goldberg, "The Babylonian Talmud," in *The Literature of the Sages: Oral Torah, Halakha, Mishna, Tosefta, Talmud, External Tractates,* Compendia Rerum Iudaicarum ad Novum Testamentum, pt. 1, sec. 2, vol. 3, edited by Shmuel Safrai (Assen: Van Gorcum, 1987), p. 336.

15. Michael Krupp, "Manuscripts of the Babylonian Talmud," in *The Literature of the Sages,* ed. Safrai, pp. 351–61.

16. Rafael Rabbinovicz, *Dikdukei Soferim: Variae Lectiones in Mischnam et in Talmud Babylonicum,* 12 vols. (Munich, 1867–97; Jerusalem: Ma'ayan ha-Hokhmah, 1960).

ACKNOWLEDGMENTS

This book benefited greatly from the support of several institutions and foundations. An NEH fellowship for the academic year 2013–14 enabled me to complete several chapters that existed only in outline form and to put the finishing touches on several others. I am grateful to the Jewish Theological Seminary, Arnold Eisen, Alan Cooper, Marc Gary, and Steven Garfinkel, who devised an imaginative plan that enabled me to accept the fellowship. It is also my pleasure to thank Ismar Schorsch of the Jewish Theological Seminary, under whose leadership I was given the freedom and support to pursue my scholarly endeavors for two very full decades. With their professionalism, enthusiasm, and good humor, Eric Schmidt, Jessica Moll, Robert Demke, Maeve Cornell-Taylor, and Aimee Goggins of the University of California Press made the process of publication a delightful one. As usual, Adam Parker expertly compiled the indices, and the finished product reflects his intimate knowledge of the field.

A fellowship and a Visiting Professorship at the Frankel Center for Advanced Judaic Studies at the University of Michigan during the winter semester of 2010 enabled me to revise chapter 5 and to write chapter 2. I thank Anita Norich and Joshua Miller, the leaders of the Frankel Center's group on Jewish Languages, for creating an atmosphere of collegiality and intellectual creativity, and I also thank Deborah Dash Moore, director of the Frankel Center, for extending to me the invitation to participate in the group.

The Horace W. Goldsmith Visiting Professorship at Yale University during the fall semester of 2012 gave me the opportunity to try out my theories on a live audience. I am happy to thank Steven Fraade, Christine Hayes, Hindy Najman, and Aaron Butts for making me feel at home at Yale. I also thank Tully Harcsztark and Freda Kleinburd for making the SAR High School library such an inviting place to work during the final stages of writing. My research assistant, Bernie Hodkin, checked and double-checked the footnotes of chapters 1–5 and helped me compile the bibliography, and *aharon, aharon haviv*, I thank Rachel Kalmin for expertly drawing the map.

I am pleased to thank several scholars who read and critiqued all or part of the manuscript and contributed numerous helpful comments and criticisms. Moulie Vidas and Isaiah Gafni read the manuscript for the University of California Press and took their work extremely seriously. They graciously revealed their identities to me and, in addition to their copious written comments, they met with me face to face for detailed discussion of additional issues. Judith Hauptman and Geoffrey Herman read the entire manuscript; Beth Berkowitz read chapters 1, 2, and 4; Maren Niehoff read chapter 2; Adam Becker, Alyssa Gray, and Kristen Lindbeck read chapter 1, and Alon Ten-Ami read chapter 4. The responsibility is mine alone for any remaining errors of fact or judgment.

In addition, I read an earlier version of chapter 1 at a conference on "Talmudic Archaeology: The Archaeology of the Babylonian Talmud from the Specific Perspective of Babylonia," sponsored by the Institute for Jewish Studies at the University College London; before the Talmud and Ancient Jewish literature faculty of Tel Aviv University in 2009; at a workshop on Jewish Languages in my capacity as a faculty fellow at the University of Michigan in the winter semester of 2011; and at the Syriac Literature and Interpretation of Sacred Texts section of the November 2012 SBL conference in Chicago. I am grateful to the participants in these conferences and audiences for these lectures for their helpful feedback.

I read an earlier version of chapter 2 at a colloquium sponsored by the University of Michigan's Frankel Center for Judaic studies during the winter semester of 2010 and am delighted to thank the participants for their helpful remarks. I read another version at the SBL conference in San Francisco in November 2011, and benefited greatly from comments by Steven Fraade and Maren Niehoff. I am also pleased to thank Pierluigi Piovanelli of the University of Ottowa and Ilaria Ramelli of Catholic University of the Sacred Heart, Milan, for help with the Christian traditions about Bartholomew the apostle, and Adam Becker of New York University for help with Arabic literature.

Chapter 1 is a revised version of "'Manasseh Sawed Isaiah with a Saw of Wood': An Ancient Legend in Jewish, Christian, Persian, and Arabic

Sources," in *Talmudic Archaeology,* ed. Mark Geller (Boston: Brill, forthcoming). Chapter 3 is a revised version of "The Miracle of the Septuagint in Ancient Rabbinic and Christian Literature," in *"Follow the Wise": Studies in Jewish History and Culture in Honor of Lee I. Levine,* ed. Zeev Weiss, Oded Irshai, Jodi Magness, and Seth Schwartz (Winona Lake, IN: Eisenbrauns, 2010), pp. 239–51. Chapter 5 is a revised and abbreviated version of Richard Kalmin, "Zechariah and the Bubbling Blood: An Ancient Tradition in Jewish, Christian, and Muslim Literature," in *Jews and Christians in Sasanian Babylonia,* ed. Geoffrey Herman (Piscataway, NJ: Gorgias Press, forthcoming). Chapter 6 is a revised and abbreviated version of Richard Kalmin, "The Pharisees in Rabbinic Literature," *Sidra* 24–25 (2010): vii–xxviii (the issue was edited by David Henshke). Chapter 7 is a revised version of Richard Kalmin, "A Late Antique Babylonian Rabbinic Treatise on Astrology," in *Shoshannat Yaakov: Jewish and Iranian Studies in Honor of Yaakov Elman,* ed. Steven Fine and Samuel Secunda (Leiden: Brill, 2012). I thank the editors and publishers of these collections for permission to publish revised versions of these studies.

This book would have remained stillborn if not for the love and support extended to me by friends and family members too numerous to mention. I hope I am not offending anyone too egregiously by making special mention of the following people: Lester Lenoff, Richard Sacks, Freda Kleinburd, David Wasserman, Claudia Setzer, Judy Matthews, Maren Niehoff, Seth Schwartz, Jeffrey Miller, Deborah Hamm, Beth Berkowitz, Maud Kozodoy, Judith Hauptman, Shuly Schwartz, Carol Bakhos, Marjorie Lehman, and Barry Dov Katz. It is no exaggeration to say that I owe my life to these people.

MANUSCRIPTS AND EARLY EDITIONS

Unless otherwise indicated, citations of the Mishnah follow Albeck's edition; citations of the Tosefta follow Lieberman's or Zuckermandel's edition; citations of the Mekhilta de-R. Yishmael follow the Horovitz and Rabin edition; citations of the Mekhilta de-R. Shimon bar Yohai follow the edition of Epstein and Melamed; citations of the Sifra follow the Weiss edition; citations of Sifrei Bemidbar follow the Horowitz edition; citations of Sifrei Devarim follow the Finkelstein edition; citations of Midrash Tannaim follow the Hoffman edition; citations of the Yerushalmi follow the Venice edition; citations of Bereshit Rabbah follow the edition of Theodor and Albeck; citations of Vayikra Rabbah follow the Margaliot edition; citations of Pesikta de-Rav Kahana follow the Mandelbaum edition; and citations of the Bavli follow the standard Romm printed edition.

Mishnah: Hanokh Albeck, ed., *Shishah Sidrei Mishnah*, 6 vols. (Tel Aviv: Devir, 1957–59).
Tosefta: Saul Lieberman, ed., *The Tosefta*, 5 vols. (Jerusalem: Jewish Theological Seminary, 1955–88); M. S. Zuckermandel, ed., *Tosefta, Based on the Venice and Vienna Codices* (Jerusalem: Wahrmann Books, 1970).
Mekhilta de-R. Yishmael: H. S. Horovitz and I. A. Rabin, eds., *Mekhilta de-R. Yishmael,* 2nd ed. (Jerusalem: Wahrmann Books, 1970).
Mekhilta de-R. Shimon bar Yohai: Y. N. Epstein and E. Z. Melamed, eds., *Mekhilta de-R. Shimon bar Yohai* (Jerusalem: Mekitzei Nirdamim, 1955).
Sifrei Bemidbar: H. S. Horovitz, ed., *Sifrei Bemidbar,* 2nd ed. (Jerusalem: Wahrmann Books, 1966).
Sifrei Devarim: Louis Finkelstein, ed., *Sifrei al Sefer Devarim,* 2nd ed. (New York: Theological Seminary, 1969).

Midrash Tannaim: David Hoffman, ed., *Midrash Tannaim zu Deuteronomium* (Berlin, 1908–09).

Yerushalmi (Palestinian Talmud): Ms. Leiden, Scaliger no. 3 (Or. 4720). Facsimile edition with introduction by Saul Lieberman: Jerusalem: Kedem, 1971. Published with corrections and additions and an introduction by Yaacov Sussmann: Jerusalem: Ha-Academi'ah le-Lashon ha-Ivrit, 2001. First printed edition, based upon the Leiden ms: *Talmud Yerushalmi,* Venice: Bomberg, 1523–24. Facsimile edition: Berlin: Sefarim, 1925.

Bereshit Rabbah: J. Theodor and Hanokh Albeck, eds., *Midrash Bereshit Rabbah,* 2nd ed. (Jerusalem: Wahrmann Books, 1965).

Vayikra Rabbah: Mordechai Margaliot, ed., *Midrash Vayikra Rabbah* (New York: Jewish Theological Seminary, 1993).

Pesikta de-Rav Kahana: Bernard Mandelbaum, ed., *Pesikta de-Rav Kahana: A Critical Edition* (New York: Jewish Theological Seminary, 1962).

Babylonian Talmud (Bavli): Standard printed edition: *The Babylonian Talmud* (Vilna: Romm, 1880–86).

Introduction

IN RECENT YEARS SCHOLARS HAVE made great progress in situating rabbinic narratives in their late antique cultural context. They have enriched our understanding of rabbinic narratives by reading them against the background of second Temple Jewish literature, the full gamut of classical rabbinic literature, and contemporaneous non-Jewish literatures and cultures. The present book attempts to add depth and nuance to this scholarship by reading several rich rabbinic narratives against the background of nonrabbinic literature of late antiquity and the early Middle Ages, most of it Christian in origin. In brief, this book argues that Christian and pagan literature from the Roman East was a crucially important hermeneutical key to the interpretation of late antique Babylonian rabbinic literature. My major area of interest is rabbinic Babylonia viewed through the prism of eastern provincial Roman Christian and pagan literature, but Babylonian rabbinic literature and its relationship to Christian and pagan literature east of Syria will also be an important concern. The book argues that it is not enough for scholars to find parallels between Babylonian rabbinic literature and Persian literature, for example, and to consider their work done. Rather, their work is only beginning, since it is necessary to examine all of the possibly relevant contexts, given the limits of our present knowledge, to determine whether there is something special about the connection between Persia and the Bavli, or whether the commonality is symptomatic of late antiquity in general, or of ancient religion east of Byzantium, or the like. In fact, we will find in the material examined in this study (1) surprisingly strong connections between Babylonian rabbinic culture and the culture of the eastern Roman provinces, as well as to a lesser extent (2) the emerging but never fully realized cultural unity that was beginning to form in Mesopotamia, eastern Syria, and Armenia.¹

THE BAVLI'S MESOPOTAMIAN, EASTERN PROVINCIAL ROMAN, AND PERSIAN CONTEXTS

New and refined methodologies have facilitated our understanding of the degree to which the Babylonian Talmud was situated in a Mesopotamian, eastern provincial Roman, indigenous Babylonian, Armenian, and Persian cultural context,² although there remain substantive disagreements about the extent and meaning of parallels between rabbinic and nonrabbinic literature

---

1. See, for example, J. B. Ward-Perkins, "The Roman West and the Parthian East," *Proceedings of the British Academy* 51 (1985): 174–99; Fergus Millar, *The Roman Near East, 31 BC–AD 337* (Cambridge, MA: Harvard University Press, 1993), p. 481: "Like Palmyra, the whole region from the Euphrates to the Tigris was now 'Roman,' 'Greek,' and 'Syrian' at the same time," and p. 502, where he refers to the "cultural unity of the Fertile Crescent"; Garth Fowden, *Empire to Commonwealth: Consequences of Monotheism in Late Antiquity* (Princeton: Princeton University Press, 1993), pp. 12–36; Maurice Sartre, *The Middle East under Rome*, trans. Catherine Porter and Elizabeth Rawlings (Cambridge, MA: Harvard University Press, 2005), pp. 318, 365–66; and Kalmin, *Jewish Babylonia*, p. 5. This point should not be understood as an attempt on my part to gloss over the very real and pronounced distinctions between the cultures that flourished within this vast territory. See, for example, Millar, *The Roman Near East*, pp. 492–93 and 510.

2. Regarding Mesopotamia and the Roman East, see the literature cited below. Regarding Persia, see, for example, Jonas Greenfield, "Ratin Megusha," in *Exploring the Talmud*, vol. 1, *Education*, ed. Haim Z. Dimitrovsky (New York: Ktav, 1974), pp. 272–76; Shaul Shaked, *Dualism in Transformation: Varieties of Religion in Sasanian Iran* (London: School of Oriental and African Studies, 1994); Richard Kalmin, *The Sage in Jewish Society of Late Antiquity* (London: Routledge, 1999); Geoffrey Herman, "Ahasuerus, the Former Stable-Master of Belshazzar and the Wicked Alexander of Macedon: Two Parallels between the Babylonian Talmud and Persian Sources," *Association for Jewish Studies Review* 29, no. 2 (2005): 283–97; and idem, *A Prince without a Kingdom* (Tübingen: Mohr/Siebeck, 2012), pp. 74–76, 82–92, 150–56, 161, 202–9, 215–17, 221–22, and 239–57; Yaakov Elman, "Middle Persian Culture and Babylonian Sages: Accommodation and Resistance in the Shaping of Rabbinic Legal Tradition," in *The Cambridge Companion to the Talmud and Rabbinic Literature*, ed. Charlotte E. Fonrobert and Martin S. Jaffee (Cambridge: Cambridge University Press, 2007), pp. 165–97; Shai Secunda, "Reading the Bavli in Iran," *Jewish Quarterly Review* 100, no. 2 (2010): 310–42; and idem, *The Iranian Talmud: Reading the Bavli in Its Sasanian Context* (Philadelphia: University of Pennsylvania Press, 2013), passim; as well as the articles collected in Carol Bakhos and Rahim Shayegan, eds., *The Talmud in Its Iranian Context* (Tübingen: Mohr/Siebeck, 2010). Regarding Armenia, see Geoffrey Herman, "The Story of Rav Kahana (BT Baba Qamma 117a–b) in Light of Armeno-Persian Sources," in *Irano-Judaica*, vol. 6, *Studies Relating to Jewish Contacts with Persian Culture*

and how these parallels came about. Are the parallels that scholars have found real parallels, and if so, are they indications of influence or of creative appropriation? Are they symptomatic of late antiquity in general, or are they the result of similar cultures manifesting similar phenomena at comparable stages of development? Are the rabbis responding polemically to neighboring groups, are they reading their literature and hearing their oral traditions, or are we dealing with folkloristic motifs that transcend the boundaries of individual cultures? The Bavli has figured prominently in scholarly discussions, since the Bavli was particularly open to traditions and motifs deriving from the literatures and cultures of contemporaneous religious groups, but Palestinian rabbinic literature is also of crucial concern.[3]

This book is not a systematic examination of all of the evidence, which at this point is impossible, but rather a close reading of several texts that have not yet received the attention they deserve or have not yet been fully understood. I will argue that it is sometimes possible to prove that Babylonian rabbis were responding to texts and religious trends in Christian Mesopotamia, as well as to those of other Christian communities east of Syria, but that in many cases it is at least as likely, and sometimes more likely, that the relevant connection was between Jewish Babylonia and the Roman East.[4] In other words, I argue that while Christians and Jews east of Syria shared texts and behaviors in common, scholars have neglected to consider an alternative explanation: the possibility that they appropriated texts and modes of behavior from a common source—the eastern provinces of the Roman Empire.

It may seem counterintuitive to argue that similarities between Jews and Christians of Mesopotamia[5] sometimes derived from cultural connections

---

throughout the Ages, ed. Shaul Shaked and Amnon Netzer (Jerusalem: Yad Yizhak Ben-Zvi, 2008), pp. 53–80; and chapter 2 of this book.

3. See also, for example, Martha Himmelfarb, "The Mother of the Messiah in the Talmud Yerushalmi and Sefer Zerubbabel," in *The Talmud Yerushalmi and Graeco-Roman Culture,* vol. 3, ed. Peter Schäfer (Tübingen: Mohr/Siebeck, 2002), pp. 369–89; and Peter Schäfer, *The Jewish Jesus: How Judaism and Christianity Shaped Each Other* (Princeton: Princeton University Press, 2012), pp. 214–35.

4. See also the comments of Catherine Hezser, *Jewish Travel in Antiquity* (Tübingen: Mohr/Siebeck, 2011), pp. 312–13.

5. David Bundy, "Early Asian and East African Christianities," in *Cambridge History of Christianity,* vol. 2, *Constantine to ca. 600,* ed. A. Casiday and F. W. Norris (Cambridge: Cambridge University Press, 2008), pp. 131–35, observes that in addition to the densely populated Christian communities in northern Mesopotamia (notably Edessa and Nisibis), southern Mesopotamia, where the rabbis lived, was home to large and important Christian communities during late antiquity. See also Shaul Shaked, "A Persian House of Study, a King's

that the two neighbors formed independently with individuals and groups from the geographically distant eastern Roman provinces. Closer examination, however, establishes the likelihood of this theory as an explanation of some of the evidence. For example, several statements recorded in the Bavli about Jesus of Nazareth appear to have reached Babylonia from the eastern Roman provinces rather than from the New Testament, as it had been translated into Syriac and was available to late antique Mesopotamian Christians. For example, the second-century-C.E. pagan philosopher Celsus relates Jesus's life story as follows: Jesus fabricated the story of his birth from a virgin, Mary's husband drove her away because she was an adulteress, and the real father of Jesus was a soldier named Panthera. Mary wandered in disgrace and gave birth to Jesus in secret. Because Jesus was poor he worked as a laborer in Egypt and there he learned the magical arts. Jesus returned to Palestine full of arrogance because of his skill as a magician, going so far as to call himself God. Like Celsus but unlike the New Testament, the Bavli refers to Jesus as the son of a certain Panthera/Pandera, who was his mother's

---

Secretary: Irano-Aramaic Notes," *Acta Orientalia Academiae Scientiarum Hungaricae* 48 (1995): 171–86, who accepts the understanding of Jacob Levy, *Wörterbuch über die Talmudim und Midraschim* (Berlin: Benjamin Harz, 1924), vol. 3, p. 432, that the term *Bei Nizrefei* in Bavli Shabbat 116a refers to a place of interreligious disputations between Christians and other religious groups, including rabbis who chose to attend such gatherings. Adam Becker, *Fear of God and the Beginning of Wisdom: The School of Nisibis and the Development of Scholastic Culture in Late Antique Mesopotamia* (Philadelphia: University of Pennsylvania Press, 2006), p. 80, writes that "the members of the [Christian] School maintained their distance from the larger community." See also pp. 13, 86–87, and 95 there. Becker (on pp. 14–15 and 204–9) describes study as a ritual and a religious act, in fact, as "the" religious act par excellence, of the Christians who studied at the School of Nisibis. As I argued in Kalmin, *Jewish Babylonia*, pp. 8–9 and 19–36, late antique Babylonian rabbis share both of these characteristics. It is difficult to claim that one group derived these characteristics from the other, since other Mesopotamian Christians, notably monastics, did not share the emphasis on study of their coreligionists at the School, and for many Christians the School was the first step on the way to the monastic way of life. See Becker, *Fear of God*, pp. 169–97. See also p. 205, for Barhadbesabba's description of Narsai's study habits, in which asceticism and study were fully fused. See also Geoffrey Herman, "Rashut ha-Golah be-Vavel bi-Tekufat ha-Talmud," PhD diss., Hebrew University, 2005, pp. 281–89, 295–96, 300–301, 304, 306, n. 1510, 309–19, and the English summary on p. xvi there. On p. 283, Herman explains the similarities between the Christian *catholicos* and the Jewish *rosh golah* (exilarch) as the result of "a common political reality and a common Scripture," rather than positing interaction between the two communities. For additional discussion of commonalities between the Jewish and Christian communities in Mesopotamia, see Herman, *Prince without a Kingdom*, pp. 12–16, 19–20, 51–55, 117–32, 150–54, 175–78, 202–3, 211, 215–16, and 230–34; and Secunda, *Iranian Talmud*, pp. 17–23, 36–38, 54–55, 157–60, 165–68, and 179.

lover rather than her husband. Like Celsus but unlike the New Testament, the Bavli combines its account of Jesus's illegitimate birth with claims about his visit to Egypt, where he learned to practice magic. Further linking the Bavli and Celsus is the fact that Celsus presents the charges against Jesus as deriving from an unnamed Jew, making it likely that both Celsus and the Bavli derive their information from the same Jewish source, and since Celsus flourished in Alexandria it is likely that the Bavli also received these traditions from a Jewish source circulating in the eastern Roman provinces.[6]

In one significant sense, it makes little difference whether the Bavli incorporated Christian, pagan, or nonrabbinic Jewish sources directly from the Roman East, or did so from Rome via Christian, pagan, or nonrabbinic Jewish Mesopotamia. This is so because in either event, we have important new information about the diverse source material that went into the formation of the Babylonian Talmud, and about the significance of literature that much previous scholarship deemed unimportant in understanding the formation of the Bavli. In another sense, however, it is very important to know whether a tradition reached the Bavli from the Roman East or from Mesopotamia, since deciding this issue teaches us about the history of the period and about the channels through which literature from diverse cultures traveled in late antiquity. To what extent were the Christian and Jewish communities of northern and southern Mesopotamia culturally linked, or was rabbinic Babylonia part of the Roman East to a greater extent than most scholars imagined, and if the latter is true, how did it happen?

We will find that the evidence examined in this study suggests that material in the Bavli is paralleled a good deal more frequently by sources deriving from the Roman East than from Christian or pagan Mesopotamia. The present study, therefore, builds on the findings of my previous book, *Jewish Babylonia between Persia and Roman Palestine,* according to which Jewish Babylonia and Christian Mesopotamia underwent similar processes of eastern provincial Romanization beginning in the fourth century C.E., in part the result of events of the mid-third century C.E., when Shapur I of Persia invaded deep into Roman territory and transplanted thousands of Jews, Christians, and pagans from the Roman East and settled them in

---

6. See Richard Kalmin, "Jesus in Sasanian Babylonia," review essay of Peter Schäfer, *Jesus in the Talmud, Jewish Quarterly Review* 99, no. 1 (2008): 107–12.

Mesopotamia and western Persia.[7] At least in part as a result of these dramatic events of the mid-third century, the Jewish and Christian communities of Mesopotamia experienced an influx of literature and modes of behavior deriving from the eastern Roman provinces beginning in the fourth century, a phenomenon that removes the necessity, in the absence of supporting evidence, of viewing commonalities between the Jews and Christians of Mesopotamia as the result of contact between these groups within Mesopotamia.[8] This pattern of forced resettlement repeated itself later in the Sasanian period, under Shapur II, Kavad I, Khusrau II, and particularly during the reign of Khusrau I (531–579 C.E.), who founded Veh Antioch Khusrau (Khusrau's City of Antioch) close to Ctesiphon and thus in close proximity to the Babylonian rabbis,[9] populating it with deportees from Antioch when he sacked the city in 542 C.E.[10]

---

7. See, for example, Shapur's inscription on the Ka'ba-I Zardusht at Naqsh-i Rustam near Persepolis, translated by Josef Wiesehöfer, *Ancient Persia from 550 BC to 65 AD*, trans. Azizeh Azodi (London: Tauris, 1996), p. 155; D. N. Mackenzie, "Kerdir's Inscription," in *Iranische Denkmäler*, fasc. 13, "The Sasanian Rock Reliefs at Naqsh-i Rustam" (Berlin: Dietrich Reimer, 1989), pp. 43–44 (synoptic text in translation), 55 (transcription), 65 (commentary); Ammianus Marcellinus 20.6.7; and Procopius, *Persian Wars* 2.9.15–16. See also J. M. Fiey, *Jalons pour une histoire de l'église en Iraq* (Leuven: Secrétariat du Corpus SCO, 1970), pp. 57 and 60, n. 83; M.-L. Chaumont, *La christianisation de l'empire iranien des origenes aux grandes persécutions du IVᵉ siècle* (Leuven: Peeters, 1988), pp. 56–84 and 88–89; Herman, *Rashut ha-Golah*, p. 287 and the literature cited in n. 1396 there.

8. The phenomenon of the *nahotei*, rabbis who traveled between Palestine and Babylonia carrying Palestinian rabbinic traditions and reporting them to the Babylonian rabbis (and, rarely, vice versa [see Aharon Oppenheimer, "Contacts between Eretz Israel and Babylonia at the Turn of the Period of the *Tannaim* and the *Amoraim*," in *Between Rome and Babylon* (Tübingen: Mohr/Siebeck, 2005), p. 419 and n. 7 there]), also helped forge a connection between the two communities. Alyssa Gray, *A Talmud in Exile: The Influence of Yerushalmi Avodah Zarah on the Formation of Bavli Avodah Zarah* (Providence, RI: Brown University Press, 2005), pp. 5–7 and passim, argues convincingly, however, that the *nahotei* transmitted only individual traditions shared by the two Talmuds and cannot be credited with transmitting the deepest structures linking the two Talmuds, for example, complicated discussions and even complicated discussions that are themselves linked together in a particular order. In addition, Oppenheimer, "Contacts between Eretz Israel and Babylonia," p. 418, notes that "the activity of the *nahotei* was actually concentrated in the period between the end of the third century and the first decades of the fourth century." Taking account of the activity of the *nahotei*, therefore, complements rather than contradicts an explanation based on Shapur's conquests.

9. See, for example, Beate Dignas and Engelbert Winter, *Rome and Persia in Late Antiquity: Neighbors and Rivals* (Cambridge: Cambridge University Press, 2007), pp. 261–63.

10. Procopius, *The Persian Wars* 2.6.1–9.7, 9.14–18; and Theophylact Simocatta 5.6.10. See also Michael G. Morony, *Iraq after the Muslim Conquest* (Princeton: Princeton University

This contention, of course, should not be understood as a denial on my part of the fact that western Persia, eastern Syria, and Mesopotamia appropriated much material from the Greek and Roman world during the centuries prior to the conquests of the Persian kings. Such a denial would contradict the well-established cultural impact of the conquests of Alexander the Great on this part of the world. Rather, our claim is that there were ebbs and flows in the relationship between the Roman East and the Persian West, and the third century C.E. began one important era when the relationship between the two localities was particularly close, and the results of this closeness are visible in the literature of the Babylonian rabbis beginning in the fourth century.

Press, 1984), pp. 266–67; S. N. C. Lieu, "Captives, Refugees and Exiles: A Study of Cross-Frontier Civilian Movements and Contacts between Rome and Persia from Valerian to Jovian," in *The Defence of the Roman and Byzantine East*, ed. P. Freeman and D. Kennedy (Oxford: B. A. R., 1986), pp. 495 and 499–500; A. D. Lee, *Information and Frontiers: Roman Foreign Relations in Late Antiquity* (Cambridge: Cambridge University Press, 1993), pp. 17–18 and 51; Erich Kettenhofen, "Deportations II: In the Parthian and Sasanian Period," *Encyclopaedia Iranica*, www.iranicaonline.org/articles/deportations#pt.2. See also Michael G. Morony, "Population Transfers between Sasanian Iran and the Byzantine Empire," in *Convengo Internazionale La Persia e Bisanzio, Roma: 14–18 ottobre 2002* (Rome: Accademia Nazionale dei Lincei, 2004), pp. 161–79; and Matthew P. Canepa, *The Two Eyes of the Earth: Art and Ritual of Kingship between Rome and Sasanian Iran* (Berkeley: University of California Press, 2009), pp. 21–33; and idem, "Distant Displays of Power: Understanding Cross-Cultural Interaction among the Elites of Rome, Sasanian Iran, and Sui-Tang China," in *Theorizing Cross-Cultural Interaction among the Ancient and Early Medieval Mediterranean, Near East and Asia*, ed. Matthew P. Canepa, *Ars Orientalis* 38 (2010)1 138 39. For additional historical factors that might have contributed to Babylonian rabbinic appropriation of literature and ideas from the Roman East in the sixth and seventh centuries, see Gray, *A Talmud in Exile*, pp. 199–234. In addition, trade routes and traveling merchants certainly served as an important conduit of ideas as well as material goods (see, for example, Hezser, *Jewish Travel in Antiquity*, pp. 360, 364, 438–39). There is little archaeological evidence of routine trade between the two empires, as noted by J. Lang, P. T. Craddock, and St. J. Simpson, "New Evidence for Early Crucible Steel," *Journal of the Historical Metallurgy Society* 32, no. 1 (1998): 11: "Sasanian trade and foreign relations appear to have been carefully regulated. There is no surviving historical evidence for the widespread import of Far Eastern or Roman/Byzantine goods into the Sasanian Empire, or vice versa. Indeed, surface surveys in northern Mesopotamia suggest that the markedly different distributions of Sasanian and Roman finds correspond closely to the political limits of the respective Empires." Manfred Raschke, "New Studies in Roman Commerce with the East," *Aufstieg und Niedergang der römischen Welt* 2.19/2 (1978), p. 677, however, insists correctly that "the volume of discovered archaeological material . . . is not a reliable index for the briskness of trade," noting that while a vigorous trade exchange existed between Rome and India, few Indian artifacts have been discovered in the Roman Empire.

In addition, however, the present book, through close readings of several fascinating rabbinic stories, argues that on rare occasions it is possible to demonstrate a cultural connection between the neighboring Mesopotamian Jewish and Christian communities,[11] as well as a cultural connection between rabbinic Babylonia and Christian Armenia, a province to the north and west of Mesopotamia. Earlier generations of scholars of Judaism tended to underestimate the importance of late antique Mesopotamian Christianity, going so far as to claim that this locality was virtually Christian-free, especially compared to the situation in contemporaneous Roman Palestine.[12] At the other extreme, more recent scholars, for example, Daniel Boyarin in *Socrates and the Fat Rabbis,* contend that a crucially important feature of Babylonian rabbinic discourse was mediated to Babylonian rabbis via Mesopotamian Christians.[13] Peter Schäfer, in *Jesus in the Talmud,*[14] claims that Babylonian Jews obtained intimate knowledge of the New Testament via the

---

11. See also Peter Brown, "The Diffusion of Manichaeism in the Roman Empire," *Journal of Roman Studies* 59 (1969): 101–5; Nina Garsoïan, "Byzantium and the Sasanians," in *Cambridge History of Iran,* vol. 3, pt. 1, ed. Ehsan Yarshater (Cambridge: Cambridge University Press, 1983), pp. 568–75; Fowden, *Empire to Commonwealth,* pp. 136–37; Millar, *The Roman Near East,* pp. 7–21; and Elizabeth K. Fowden, *The Barbarian Plain: Saint Sergius between Rome and Iran* (Berkeley: University of California Press, 1999), pp. 2, 139, and passim (for example, p. 55, where she employs the locution "from the Syro-Mesopotamian perspective"). On p. 143, however, she emphasizes "the diversity of the Syro-Mesopotamian ... sphere."

12. See the critique of Adam Becker, "Beyond the Spatial and Temporal 'Limes': Questioning the 'Parting of the Ways' outside the Roman Empire," in *The Ways That Never Parted: Jews and Christians in Late Antiquity and the Early Middle Ages,* ed. Adam Becker and Annette Yoshiko Reed (Tübingen: Mohr/Siebeck, 2003), pp. 373–92; and Becker, *Fear of God,* p. 18 and the references cited at p. 219.

13. Daniel Boyarin, *Socrates and the Fat Rabbis* (Chicago: University of Chicago Press, 2009), pp. 133–91, esp. pp. 133–40.

14. Peter Schäfer, *Jesus in the Talmud* (Princeton: Princeton University Press, 2007). See also Schäfer, *Jewish Jesus,* pp. 70–85, p. 287, n. 41, and pp. 125–49. For further discussion of the reception of the New Testament in the Babylonian Talmud, see, for example, Moshe Halbertal and Shlomo Naeh, "Ma'ayanei ha-Yeshuah: Satirah Parshanit u-Teshuvat ha-Minim," in *Higayon le-Yona: Hebetim Hadashim be-Heker Sifrut ha-Midrash, ha-Aggadah, ve-ha-Piyyut li-Kevodo shel Professor Yona Fraenkel,* ed. Joshua Levinson, Yaakov Elbaum, and Galit Hasan-Rokem (Jerusalem: Magnes Press, 2006), pp. 179–97; Aaron Amit, "A Rabbinic Satire on the Last Judgment," *Journal of Biblical Literature* 129 (2010): 679–97; Holger Zellentin, *Rabbinic Parodies of Jewish and Christian Literature* (Tübingen: Mohr/Siebeck, 2011), pp. 137–66; and Shaye J.D. Cohen, "Antipodal Texts: B. Eruvin 21b–22a and Mark 7:1–23 on the Tradition of the Elders and the Commandment of God," in *Envisioning Judaism: Studies in Honor of Peter Schäfer on the Occasion of his Seventieth Birthday,* ed. Ra'anan Boustan, Klaus Herrmann, Reimund Leicht, Annette Yoshiko Reed, and Giuseppe Veltri (Tübingen: Mohr/Siebeck, 2013).

Diatessaron,¹⁵ a Syriac harmony of the Gospels, which was available to Mesopotamian Christians in late antiquity, which Babylonian rabbis would have been able to understand due to the similarity between Syriac and Babylonian Jewish Aramaic.¹⁶

While I find much to admire about Boyarin's and Schäfer's books, on the issue of concern to me here I argue that their claims are overly sweeping and not yet justified by the available evidence. In my estimation, given the present state of our knowledge, it is premature to be asking whether or not there was a *close* cultural connection between Mesopotamian Jews and Christians, but rather we should be accumulating examples illustrating *any sort of* a cultural connection between them, which will hopefully provide methodological models for future research. What allows us to determine with reasonable certainty that Mesopotamian and Armenian Christianity had an impact on Babylonian rabbis, when it is likely that the rabbis were reacting to the Christianity more familiar to us from the eastern provinces of the Roman Empire? In an article published fifteen years ago, Shlomo Naeh demonstrated that the key to the interpretation of a story in the Babylonian Talmud¹⁷ is to be found in its use of a word, *heruta,* which means both sexual license and sexual restraint in Mesopotamian Christian literature composed in Syriac, but which is otherwise unattested in these senses in the Babylonian Talmud and in Babylonian Jewish Aramaic. Naeh posited that the story's use of this term presupposed Babylonian rabbinic knowledge of a significant aspect of Mesopotamian Christian culture,¹⁸ a conclusion I find utterly persuasive. The question, however, is the extent to which this instance of

---

15. The *Diatessaron* was a harmonization of the Gospels created by Tatian in approximately 170 C.E., which may have been written in Syriac in the Syrian East. Any efforts on our part to draw conclusions based on the *Diatessaron* are hampered, but by no means rendered impossible, by the fact that none of the texts used as the basis of these reconstructions predates the fourth century. See William L. Peterson, *Tatian's Diatessaron: Its Creation, Dissemination, Significance, and History in Scholarship* (Leiden: Brill, 1993), pp. 5–6 and 35–45.

16. See, for example, Adam Becker, "The Comparative Study of 'Scholasticism' in Late Antique Mesopotamia: Rabbis and East Syrians," *Association for Jewish Studies Review* 34, no. 1 (2010): 98–99.

17. B. Kiddushin 81b.

18. Shlomo Naeh, "Freedom and Celibacy: A Talmudic Variation on Tales of Temptation and Fall in Genesis and Its Syrian Background," in *The Book of Genesis in Jewish and Oriental Christian Interpretation,* ed. Judith Frishman and Lucas van Rompay (Leuven: Peeters, 1997), pp. 73–89.

Babylonian rabbinic acquaintance with Syriac Christian culture is the exception or the rule.[19]

The present book will not provide a systematic answer to this question, but hopefully it will sensitize readers to the issue of what Babylonian rabbis knew and did not know about Christian and pagan literature deriving from the Roman East, and the extent to which we are able to say at present that the literature and culture of the Christian and pagan communities east of Syria did or did not impinge on the rabbis, and vice versa. At what period of their history did Babylonian rabbis become cognizant of Christianity and what were their attitudes toward it? To what extent did Babylonian rabbis relate polemically to Christianity (à la Yuval in *Two Nations in Your Womb*,[20] and Schäfer in *Jesus in the Talmud*) and to what extent did they relate to it in more subtle ways (à la Boyarin in *Border Lines*[21]).

This book, therefore, adds to our knowledge of the relationship between Judaism and Christianity during their formative periods, and demonstrates that it is a gross oversimplification to say that the two religions were implacably hostile to each other. Hostility there certainly was, and we will find clear examples of it in the literature studied in the pages that follow, but we will also find clear examples in which the literature attests to permeable boundaries between the literatures produced by some of the elite representatives of the two religions, and likewise to clear cases in which the rabbis use Christians and Christianity as "a tool to think with."[22]

---

19. For other literature on the subject, see Becker, "The Comparative Study of 'Scholasticism' in Late Antique Mesopotamia," pp. 91–113; Naomi Koltun-Fromm, *Jewish-Christian Conversation in Fourth-Century Persian Mesopotamia* (Piscataway, NJ: Gorgias Press, 2011); Michal Bar-Asher Siegal, "Hafikhat Rav le-Nazir: Ha-Reka le-Masoret R. Shimon bar Yohai ba-Me'arah," *Zion* 76, no. 3 (2011): 279–304; eadem, *Early Christian Monastic Literature and the Babylonian Talmud* (Cambridge: Cambridge University Press, 2014); Reuven Kiperwasser and Serge Ruzer, "Zoroastrian Proselytes in Rabbinic and Syriac Christian Narratives: Orality-Related Markers of Cultural Identity," *History of Religions* 51, no. 3 (2012): 197–218, and the literature cited on p. 197, n. 2 there; and Moulie Vidas, "Greek Wisdom in Babylonia," in *Envisioning Judaism*, ed. Boustan, 1:287–305.

20. Israel Yuval, *Two Nations in Your Womb: Perceptions of Jews and Christians in Late Antiquity and the Early Middle Ages*, trans. Barbara Harshav and Jonathan Chipman (Berkeley: University of California Press, 2006).

21. Daniel Boyarin, *Border Lines: The Partition of Judaeo-Christianity* (Philadelphia: University of Pennsylvania Press, 2004). It needs to be borne in mind, however, that "subtlety" is not necessarily synonymous with "truth."

22. For earlier studies that came to similar conclusions, see, for example, Boyarin, *Socrates and the Fat Rabbis*, passim; and Schäfer, *Jewish Jesus*, pp. 1–2 and passim.

My earlier book, *Jewish Babylonia between Persia and Roman Palestine*, dedicated a lot of attention to Babylonian rabbinic appropriation of the literature and modes of behavior of Palestinian rabbis. The present book, in contrast, argues that the motifs and ideas appropriated by the Bavli often originated in nonrabbinic, even non-Jewish sources. Because the Talmud readily concedes its Palestinian rabbinic sources but strongly tends to conceal most instances of its appropriation of nonrabbinic or non-Jewish sources, this focus is much more striking and significant. Second, while the earlier book focused on general dispositions—for example, the relations of rabbis to nonrabbis—the present book focuses on very specific narrative details. This shift in focus, I believe, makes for a more compelling argument.[23] We can perhaps imagine how cultures not in contact with one another could develop the broad tendencies discussed in the previous work; but the shared motifs, stories, and sources discussed in the present work are so specific that I believe we must posit an actual historical connection, either direct or indirect, between the cultures that preserve them.

In addition, the fact that in case after case we encounter the same pattern: clusters of unusual motifs in early literature from the Roman East paralleled in later Mesopotamian literature, and even later in Persian literature, makes it unlikely that the three literatures happened to incorporate the same folk motifs. Were we dealing with a folk literary phenomenon, we would expect the commonalities to be more haphazard, with some parallel motifs observable earlier in Mesopotamia than in Rome, or earlier in Persia than in Rome, and the like. The fact that the patterns are so consistent makes it likely we are dealing with cultural connections and historical processes rather than the coincidental and ahistorical incorporation of folk motifs that transcended cultural boundaries.

PROPER DATING OF RABBINIC TRADITIONS AND THE IMPORTANCE OF ATTRIBUTIONS

Attention to attributions, to the names of the rabbis credited with authorship of traditions within, or comments upon, rabbinic narratives, will prove to be

---

23. See also Shaye J. D. Cohen, "Patriarchs and Scholarchs," *Proceedings of the American Academy of Jewish Research* 48 (1981): 57–85, esp. p. 85; and Schäfer, *Jewish Jesus*, pp. 37–54, 68–102, and passim.

a significant, albeit by no means foolproof, mode of access to sources deriving from different times and geographical locations.[24] It goes without saying that attentiveness to attributions and entertaining the possibility that they provide useful chronological evidence is not the same as assuming until proven otherwise that they are accurate or that they enable us to produce full-blown biographies of rabbinic personalities,[25] a methodology I utterly reject.[26]

In the present study, attention to attributions will serve primarily to confirm my conclusion in earlier research that the fourth century marks the beginning of a significant turning point in Babylonian Jewish history, a development we would have missed had we assumed without further ado that attributions of statements to particular rabbinic authors are worthless as historical evidence. At several points in this study we will encounter the pivotal role of the fourth century as a transitional period in Babylonian Jewish history and literature, in contrast to the claims of other scholars that significant changes are not discernible until the sixth or seventh century.[27] Correct dating of rabbinic traditions is not simply a matter of antiquarian concern, since inevitably we will fail to understand the Jewish experience of late antiquity if we improperly date rabbinic materials, the most abundant historical source for the period. If the relevant Jewish sources turn out to derive from the sixth or seventh century, the period of the Bavli's final redactors, then obviously our understanding of late antique Jewish history and literature needs to be revised.

FROM GREEK IN THE ROMAN EAST TO HEBREW AND ARAMAIC IN RABBINIC BABYLONIA

In analyzing cultural transfers between texts that have survived only in Greek in the Graeco-Roman world and in Aramaic in Mesopotamia, we face

---

24. See, for example, Kalmin, *Jewish Babylonia*, 149–67; and idem, "The Formation and Character of the Babylonian Talmud," in *The Cambridge History of Judaism*, vol. 4, *The Late Roman-Rabbinic Period* (Cambridge: Cambridge University Press, 2006), pp. 840–42.

25. See, for example, Louis Finkelstein, *Akiba: Scholar, Saint, and Martyr* (1936; New York: Atheneum, 1970). Virtually no serious scholar nowadays would advocate such an approach.

26. For just such a misinterpretation of my position, including misquotations and quotations of my words out of context, see Adiel Schremer, review of Kalmin, *The Sage in Jewish Society of Late Antiquity*, *Zion* 60, no. 2 (2000): 229–35. See also my response: Kalmin, "'Mekorot Arzi'yisre'elim' u-'Mekorot Bavli'im,'" *Zion* 66, no. 2 (2001): 227–30.

27. See, for example, Jeffrey L. Rubenstein, *The Culture of the Babylonian Talmud* (Baltimore: Johns Hopkins University Press, 2003), pp. 2–9 and 31–35; and Boyarin, *Border Lines*, p. 5.

the difficult question of theorizing how these shared early traditions made their way from the Roman East to Mesopotamia, given the linguistic and cultural barriers between the Christian and Jewish communities in the two localities. How might we account for these parallels, given the fact that the *Testament of Solomon*, for example, was composed in Greek,[28] and Babylonian rabbis certainly knew no Greek? One possibility is that the Greek traditions that eventually reached the *Testament of Solomon* derive from Hebrew or Aramaic originals, or were translated from an original Greek text into Hebrew or Aramaic by bilingual Palestinian Jews or Christians. The traditions in Greek were incorporated into the *Testament of Solomon*, and into the Bavli in Hebrew or Aramaic.

Alternatively, Fergus Millar's theory of the penetration of Greek along with Syriac deep into Mesopotamia[29] explains how Greek traditions from the Roman East reached the Bavli via the medium of Syriac. According to this theory, the *Testament of Solomon*'s Greek traditions reached or approached Mesopotamia and were translated along the way into Syriac, a dialect of Aramaic that, as noted, Babylonian rabbis probably understood.[30]

For our purposes, the differences between these two theories are not critical, since according to both scenarios the traditions traveled from the Roman East to Mesopotamia. As a result, even if the specific texts incorporated into the *Testament of Solomon*, for example, did not reach the Bavli, but rather similar but not identical texts independently reached the *Testament of Solomon* on the one hand and the Bavli on the other, we have shown the

---

28. D. C. Duling, introduction to *Testament of Solomon*, in *The Old Testament Pseudepigrapha*, vol. 1, *Apocalyptic Literature and Testaments*, ed. James H. Charlesworth (Garden City, NY: Doubleday, 1983), p. 939. For more on the *Testament of Solomon*, see chapter 4.

29. Fergus Millar, "A Rural Jewish Community in Late Roman Mesopotamia, and the Question of a 'Split' Jewish Diaspora," *Journal for the Study of Judaism* 42 (2011): 351–74. See also Wiesehöfer, *Ancient Persia*, p. 203.

30. See n. 16. Millar, "A Rural Jewish Community in Late Roman Mesopotamia," p. 371, in contrast to other scholars, is not convinced of the rabbis' ability to understand Syriac. Even Millar, however, is convinced that the Jews of Sasanian Babylonia "communicated with the gentile pagans and Christians inhabiting the same area" in "some variety of Aramaic." See ibid., pp. 371–72. Even if we accept Syriac as the key to this cultural transfer, we have no clear evidence of a linkage between the Christian and Jewish communities of Mesopotamia when confronted with a text in Greek from the Roman East that somehow made the journey to rabbinic Babylonia, since we cannot be sure where the translation into Syriac took place. It might have happened anywhere in the vast territory between Syria and eastern Mesopotamia, where Syriac and Greek coexisted as literary languages.

importance of the Roman East as a source of the literature of late antique Mesopotamia. This is so because in case after case we find close parallels between clusters of motifs and traditions found in compilations preserved only in the Roman East and in Mesopotamian literature, and it is unlikely that in most of these cases the two literatures derived the shared material from an ancient text composed in another locality, for example, India, but no record of this third text survives.

In any event, we will find that one or possibly two of the traditions examined in detail in this study indicate a connection between Jewish and Christian Mesopotamia, and another indicates a connection between Babylonian rabbis and Armenia, but it is as yet unclear whether or not these connections qualify as "close." In my estimation even this limited conclusion is significant, since it is so difficult to contextualize late antique literatures east of Syria, because they strongly tend to convey the impression of having been formed in total isolation. As noted, parallels between Christian and pagan literatures from the Roman East on the one hand and the Bavli on the other will be substantially more common.

BABYLONIAN MAGIC BOWLS

Since the focus throughout is on narratives, this book has no systematic discussion of the Aramaic magic bowls, which date from the fifth to the eighth centuries and have been found only in Iraq and western Iran. Many of them appear to have been written by Jews,[31] but the clients of the bowls were probably non-Jews as well as Jews.[32] These bowls are a likely source of information about contacts between Jews and Christians of Mesopotamia and western Persia, and I hope to examine this topic in detail in a future study, when the focus is broadened to include nonnarrative material and understanding of the bowls has progressed to the point where answers to basic questions about

---

31. See, for example, S. A. Kaufman, "A Unique Magic Bowl from Nippur," *Journal of Near Eastern Studies* 32 (1973): 173; Joseph Naveh and Shaul Shaked, *Amulets and Magic Bowls* (Jerusalem: Magnes Press, 1985), pp. 16–18, 158–60; Gafni, *Yehudei Bavel*, pp. 172–76; Christa Müller-Kessler, "The Earliest Evidence for Targum Onqelos from Babylonia and the Question of Its Dialect and Origin," *Journal for the Aramaic Bible* 3 (2001): 193; and Dan Levene, *A Corpus of Magic Bowls: Incantation Texts in Jewish Aramaic from Late Antiquity* (London: Kegan Paul, 2003), pp. 11, 83–84, 87.

32. See, for example, Gafni, *Yehudei Bavel*, pp. 172–76, and the references cited in n. 125 on p. 174.

the meaning of the texts and the identities of the practitioners and the clients are on a much surer footing.

LATE ANTIQUE RABBINIC NARRATIVES: ANTHOLOGIES OR COHERENT DISCOURSES OR BOTH?

Since my approach to the issue of contextualizing the Bavli is primarily via narratives, I will evaluate and critique an important feature of the hermeneutical methods of other scholars who focus on narratives. I will argue that some scholars have overestimated the work of later Talmudic editors in homogenizing earlier narrative chains and producing coherent discourses with a consistent message and authorial voice.[33] Certainly later editorial activity needs to be taken into account, but the contribution of earlier generations sometimes remains visible to a degree that these scholars have underestimated. This insight sometimes leads to conclusions that differ dramatically from those of other scholars, since the degree to which we read a text as the product of an active author or editor molding earlier traditions in accordance with a preconceived design, as opposed to viewing it as an anthology subjected to relatively minimal editorial intervention, will have a significant impact on its interpretation.

One mode of access to the diverse sources that comprise rabbinic narratives will be attentiveness to language switching from Hebrew to Aramaic

---

33. Compare, for example, Jeffrey L. Rubenstein, "Talmudic Astrology: *Bavli Šabbat* 156a–b," *Hebrew Union College Annual* 78 (2007): 109–48, where he refers to b. Shabbat 156a–b as a "sustained composition" on p. 111, with my discussion of the same material, which I characterize as a "miscellany" in chapter 7. Compare Rubenstein's formulation in *Stories of the Babylonian Talmud* (Baltimore: Johns Hopkins University Press, 2010), p. 178: "As scholars have noted, a significant concern of the redactors was to systematize and synthesize earlier halakhic traditions, to eliminate contradictions and provide more general and abstract formulations. [In b. Shabbat 156a–b], I suggest, they engage in a similar activity in the aggadic and theological realm, drawing on inconsistent Amoraic traditions about astrology and trying to work out a grand synthesis. And they do an admirable job, presenting both sides of the issue, offering a more general formulation, and concluding with a type of compromise." See also Daniel Boyarin, *Carnal Israel: Reading Sex in Talmudic Culture* (Berkeley: University of California Press, 1990), pp. 197–225 and passim; and Jeffrey L. Rubenstein, *Talmudic Stories: Narrative Art, Composition, and Culture* (Baltimore: Johns Hopkins University Press, 1999), pp. 105–38 and passim. A notable exception is Schäfer, *Jewish Jesus,* passim, who pays careful attention to geographical markers in the rabbinic sources throughout his book.

and back again. "Language switching," or "code switching," is the alternating use of different languages, dialects, or registers of a single language in conversation or in a literary text.[34] Scholars have long noted the significance of the alternating use of Hebrew and Aramaic in the Talmudic *sugya*,[35] the basic unit of Talmudic discourse, which consists primarily[36] of legal traditions and discussions. When a single statement in a *sugya* comprises both Hebrew and Aramaic, the statement is often divisible into an early core and a later explanatory addition, particularly in the presence of other signs of editorial tampering.[37] However, scholars often claim that there is usually no rhyme or reason to the distribution of diverse languages within narratives. Other scholars claim that the text sometimes oscillates between Hebrew and Aramaic in conformity with the needs of the narrative,[38] to make a statement, for example, about a particular character and his or her relationship, hierarchical or otherwise, to other characters. I will argue that language switching not only serves the needs of the narrative, but is also at times more fundamentally one of several indications that later editors have added material from a different source to a preexisting narrative, or have combined narratives from diverse sources. As we shall see in detail in chapters 2 and 5, this observation has important implications for the study of ancient Judaism.

It will be helpful to examine one narrative in some detail, since this narrative illustrates both our claim regarding the importance of language switching and our claims regarding the impact of Christianity in the Roman

---

34. Reem Bassiouney, *Arabic Sociolinguistics: Topics in Diglossia, Gender, Identity, and Politics* (Washington, DC: Georgetown University, 2009), pp. 28–87.

35. See, most notably, Shamma Friedman, "Al Derekh Heker ha-Sugya," in *Perek ha-Ishah Rabbah ba-Bavli* (Jerusalem: Jewish Theological Seminary, 1978), pp. 25–26. A *sugya* is a unit of Talmudic discourse, consisting, for example, of a legal opinion or the interpretation of a tradition, and this opening statement becomes the subject of analysis, typically via a sequence of objections and responses or questions and answers, which can go on for a single line or several folios.

36. But not exclusively. See, for example, b. Kiddushin 39b.

37. Friedman, "Al Derekh Heker ha-Sugya," pp. 25–26.

38. See, for example, Eliezer Margaliot, "Ivrit ve-Aramit ba-Talmud u-va-Midrash," *Leshonenu* 27/28 (1963–64): 20–33; Avigdor Shinan, "Ivrit ve-Aramit be-Sifrut Beit-ha-Keneset," *Tura* 1 (1999): 224–32; Burton Visotzky, *Golden Bells and Pomegranates: Studies in Midrash Leviticus Rabbah* (Tübingen: Mohr/Siebeck, 2002), pp. 41–47; and Joseph Yahalom, "Angels Do Not Understand Aramaic: On the Literary Use of Palestinian Aramaic in Late Antiquity," *Journal of Jewish Studies* 47 (1996): 39–40. See also Yonatan Ben-Dov, "Ha-Ketivah ba-Aramit u-va-Ivrit be-Megilot Qumran u-va-Sefarim ha-Hizonim: Ha-Reka ba-Olam he-Atik ve-ha-Hipus Ahar Samkhut Yehudit Ketuvah," *Tarbiz* 78, no. 1 (2008): 27–60, esp. pp. 38–40.

East on Babylonian rabbis.[39] This example of language switching, found in b. Gittin 58a, may be the work of later Babylonian editors responding to the rise of Christianity in Roman Palestine:

> [Hebrew:] Said Rav Yehudah said Rav, "What is the meaning of the verse, 'And they oppress a man and his house, a man and his inheritance' (Mic 2:2)?
>
> "It once happened that a man laid eyes on the wife of his master; [Aramaic:] he was a carpenter's apprentice. [Hebrew:] One time his master needed to borrow money.
>
> "[The apprentice] said to [the master], 'Send your wife to me, and I'll lend her the money.'
>
> "[The master] sent his wife to him. She stayed with [the apprentice] for three days.[40]
>
> "[The apprentice] went ahead and came to [the master].[41]
>
> "[The master] said to [the apprentice], 'My wife, who I sent to you, where is she?'
>
> "[The apprentice] said to him, 'I sent her off immediately,[42] but I heard that the boys abused her on the road.'
>
> "[The master] said to the [apprentice], 'What shall I do?'
>
> "[The apprentice] said to him, 'If you listen to my advice, divorce her.'
>
> "[The master] said to him, 'Her marriage settlement is large.'

---

39. See also the discussion of b. Sanhedrin 19a-b in the appendix in this chapter.

40. See Meyer Feldblum, ed., *Dikdukei Soferim, Massekhet Gittin* (New York: Horeb, 1966), notes on line 46.

41. To preserve the ambiguity of the Hebrew story, we should translate simply, "The man went ahead and came to him," according to which it is unclear who "went ahead" and who he "came to." The material in brackets, however, reflects the fact that it is unlikely that the master is referred to, since the Hebrew word *kadam* implies that the subject of the verb did something ahead of schedule, and after three days of waiting and doing nothing it is inappropriate to characterize the master's appearance at the house of the apprentice as "ahead of schedule." It is likely, therefore, that the apprentice is the intended subject of the verb *kadam*. Even if the master is the intended subject, however, his behavior in waiting three days before inquiring about his wife is outrageous and worthy of condemnation.

42. The word "immediately" *(le-altar)* is also Aramaic. See Michael Sokoloff, *A Dictionary of Jewish Babylonian Aramaic of the Talmudic and Geonic Periods* (Ramat-Gan, Israel: Bar-Ilan University Press, 2002), pp. 136–37. In a text like the Bavli, imperfectly transmitted over many centuries, it is not at all surprising to find occasional examples of language switching that are not readily explicable as meaningful or indicative of the hand of a later author or editor.

"[The apprentice] said to him, 'I'll lend you the money, and you pay her marriage settlement.'

"[The master] got up and divorced her, and [the apprentice] went and married her. When the time came and [the master] had no money to pay him, he said to him, 'Come and work off your debt.'

"So they sat, eating and drinking, and [the master] stood and poured for them. And tears fell from [the master's] eyes into their wine cups, and at that moment the verdict was sealed."[43]

To determine the story's significance, it will be helpful to explicate the storyteller's attitudes toward the characters. Clearly the apprentice is wicked, since he lusts after the wife of another man and lies about her having been raped, tricking the husband into divorcing her so he can marry her himself. An important part of the story's message is the immense significance of routine interactions between people that lead to hurt feelings, such as the master's tears when he realizes he is now the underling, reduced to serving his former servant and his former wife.

An even more important key to the story's significance is the character of the master. Yonah Fraenkel claims that the story contrasts the wicked, crafty, and successful apprentice to the innocent, naïve, and unfortunate master, and presents the destruction of the Temple as the result of the victimization of the innocent by the wicked. Perhaps part of what leads Fraenkel to interpret in this fashion is the fact that the story is cited, apparently by Rav Yehudah quoting Rav, as illustrating the verse, "And they oppress a man and his house, a man and his inheritance" (Mic 2:2), which leads to the expectation that the story depicts a straightforward account of evil pitted against good in which the apprentice oppresses the master and his wife, since a wife is routinely referred to as a man's "house" in rabbinic literature. It is difficult to place too much emphasis on the actions of the wife since it is unclear how much choice she has to resist her fate. True, she did not have to agree to marry the wicked apprentice, and she seems perfectly willing to be with whoever has the upper hand at any given time. However, we should pause before concluding that the storyteller harshly condemns her, since he may have been of the opinion that a woman without a husband, particularly one concerning

---

43. For earlier discussions of this story, see Yonah Fraenkel, *Darkhei ha-Aggadah ve-ha-Midrash* (Givatayim, Israel: Yad La-Talmud, 1991), pp. 241–42, 250, 260–61, and 271; and Richard Kalmin, "The Modern Study of Ancient Rabbinic Literature: Yonah Fraenkel's Darkhei ha'aggadah vehamidrash," *Prooftexts* 14 (1994): 190–93 and 196–97.

whom rumors circulated that she had been raped, would have been in an extremely vulnerable position in ancient Jewish society.

The master, however, is a different story. Despite Fraenkel's claim to the contrary, and despite the verse quoted by Rav that the story supposedly illustrates, the master is anything but innocent. He sends his wife to the house of another man to transact business for him. Three days go by and she hasn't returned home, yet the master fails to visit the apprentice and inquire as to her whereabouts. The apprentice goes to the master[44] and tells him she has been raped, and without bothering to corroborate the story the master immediately contemplates divorce. His only thought is to the size of his wife's marriage settlement, although it is his fault she was out on the road alone, and as far as he knows his wife did nothing wrong.

The story, therefore, describes what happens when society's masters lack the moral strength to stand up to the evil of their underlings. The less-than-perfect fit between the verse quoted by Rav and the story is not a serious objection against this understanding of the master's character, since a wicked man can also be a victim of oppression, and this oppression can be a factor contributing to society's collapse.[45] The story depicts a stupid and wicked master allowing his wicked apprentice to gain the upper hand. When masters are evil, claims the story, and society's customary roles are reversed, when the masters become the servants and vice versa, God's "edict of destruction" is sealed, that is, society is ready to collapse under the weight of its own evil. God's punishment is simply the final seal placed on something that the community already brought upon itself. In contrast to the Bible, which tends to conceive of human sin and God's punishment as separate entities, this story views God as virtually inactive, simply allowing the Jews to bring about their own ruin. God declares a final halt to the proceedings, deciding only when the final curtain is ready to be brought down.

The story occupies us in the present context, however, because of language switching between Hebrew and Aramaic, which I will argue may be evidence of the preoccupation of later Babylonian editors with the increasingly dominant role played by Christianity in Roman Palestine. As we will see several times in this study, the later Babylonian editors formulate in Aramaic their

---

44. See n. 41.
45. It is also possible that the original answer to Rav's question about the meaning of the verse from Micah has not been preserved, and the story was added later to answer Rav's question. As often happens with composite texts, the fit between the various component parts is less than perfect.

later additions to an earlier Hebrew source, very likely for the simple reason that Aramaic increasingly eclipsed Hebrew in the later layers of Talmudic discourse.

In a story so sparse in detail, the curious identification of the apprentice as a carpenter stands out. The phrase identifying him as such is most likely a later addition, as Fraenkel already noted, since it is the only Aramaic in an otherwise Hebrew story. What is the purpose of this addition?

Fraenkel, consistent with his tendency elsewhere, interprets the phrase solely in terms of the closed universe of the story itself, rather than as a reference to a historical phenomenon outside of the story. In Fraenkel's view, the phrase serves to clarify the relationship between the story's protagonists, to explain that we are dealing with an artisan and his apprentice rather than a Torah scholar (a rabbi) and his disciple.

Alternatively, however, the Aramaic addition perhaps reads the story as an allegory about the relationship between Christianity and Judaism. The carpenter's apprentice is perhaps Jesus, representing Christendom, the master is the Jewish people, and the wife, perhaps, represents apostate Jews (although perhaps the allegory was not fully worked out and not every character stands for something or someone in particular). According to this interpretation, the story views with alarm the increasing success of Christianity among the Jewish people in the land of Israel. A later Babylonian glossator took a story that tried to explain a painful and perplexing ancient event (the destruction of the Temple), and gave it a stunning contemporary relevance.

CONTEXTUALIZING THE BAVLI

In emphasizing the importance of eastern provincial Rome and, to a lesser extent, Christianity east of Syria in contextualizing the Babylonian Talmud, my book challenges the claims of some scholars regarding the essential importance of Persia as by far the most important hermeneutical key to understanding Jewish Babylonia, to the virtual exclusion of all other factors.[46] The Persian context is undoubtedly significant, and in fact is often absolutely essential to proper understanding of the Babylonian Talmud, but it is only one of many factors that need to be taken into account. In fact, most

---

46. See, most notably, the recent publications of Yaakov Elman, for example, the article cited in n. 2.

of the traditions analyzed in detail throughout this book reached Persian culture at a very late stage of development, too late to have had any impact on the culture of late antique Babylonian Jews.

The claim that traditions from the Roman East make an appearance in the Bavli will be supported time and time again throughout this book. Chapter 1, for example, shows this to be the case with regard to motifs deriving from a Christian pseudepigraphic text from the late first or early second century and the Church Fathers from the third century, attested by a fourth-century Babylonian rabbi in the Bavli. Chapter 2 shows that the name of a demon depends on knowledge of New Testament traditions about Jesus's apostles, although we have no way of ascertaining whether these traditions reached the Bavli from the Roman East or from Mesopotamian Christians. Chapter 3 likewise leaves open the question of whether a parallel between Talmudic and Christian traditions reached the Bavli from the Roman East or from Christian Mesopotamia, although once again it is clear that the parallel reached the Talmud during the latter part of its formation, in the early fifth century or later. Chapter 4 demonstrates the penetration into the Bavli of Christian traditions from the Roman East, although we are unable to pin down even approximately when this took place. Chapter 5 demonstrates that the flow of traditions from rabbinic Palestine to rabbinic Babylonia is part of a larger process of the transfer of nonrabbinic traditions from the Roman East to localities east of Syria. Chapter 6 demonstrates that traditions about the Pharisees in the Bavli likewise derive from the Roman East and were independently incorporated into the New Testament and the Bavli. Chapter 7 attempts to show that traditions about astrology reached the Bavli from the Roman East, including Roman Mesopotamia, although we will be unable to determine whether the shared traditions reached rabbinic Babylonia from a specific source or as common knowledge attached to no particular ethnic or religious group. While we will find several very specific parallels between the Roman East and the Bavli, it is premature to discount Zoroastrian Persia as a source for at least some of the Bavli's variegated attitudes. Finally, chapter 8 demonstrates that the Alexander Romance, composed in the Roman East in approximately the third century C.E. but comprising many earlier sources, was incorporated into the Bavli but left virtually no traces in Palestinian rabbinic literature, as is true of most of the narratives examined in this book.

It is unlikely that the Bavli drew all or most of these sources from Palestinian rabbis, due to the regularity with which we would have to resort to the hypothesis that these supposed Palestinian rabbinic texts somehow did not survive in Palestinian compilations, but only survived in the Bavli.

In each instance of cultural appropriation, part of our challenge will be to describe the diverse ways in which the motifs incorporated into the Bavli were transformed in their new contexts, changed in accordance with the local Babylonian Jewish environment.

One significant implication of my conclusions regarding the nonrabbinic and even non-Jewish provenance of many traditions in the Babylonian Talmud is that, when the Bavli designates a tradition as Palestinian, we should not assume that if we can find no parallel to the tradition in a Palestinian rabbinic compilation we must conclude that the tradition is a Babylonian invention. While many purported Palestinian traditions in the Bavli *were* in all likelihood Babylonian inventions, my work demonstrates that, at least in some cases, other explanations should be sought to the problem of the absence of Palestinian rabbinic parallels to ostensibly Palestinian traditions in the Babylonian Talmud. We must take seriously the possibility that the tradition derived from nonrabbinic sources, whether Jewish or non-Jewish, Mesopotamian or eastern provincial Roman, and that the tradition was rabbinized by the Babylonian rabbis, minimally via its designation as a Palestinian rabbinic tradition, which accompanied or made possible its inclusion within the Bavli. For example, the absence of the above-mentioned traditions about Jesus from Palestinian rabbinic compilations is not proof that these traditions were a Babylonian rabbinic invention; instead, it is one of many manifestations of the Bavli's tendency to incorporate nonrabbinic material from the Roman East and to rabbinize it. Here we have clear nonrabbinic antecedents of the Bavli's traditions, which it presents as Palestinian rabbinic traditions, one of many indications that scholars should hesitate before making generalizations about the frequency of Babylonian rabbinic invention of material, simply because of the silence of Palestinian rabbinic compilations.

In addition, recent scholarship arguing that Hekhalot literature originated in Babylonia rather than Palestine perhaps needs to be reevaluated in light of the findings of the present book.[47] The possibility that this literature originated in Palestine and only subsequently traveled to Babylonia needs to be examined carefully, which may necessitate a revision of conclusions that

---

47. See, for example, Ra'anan S. Boustan, "The Study of Hekhalot Literature: Between Mystical Experience and Textual Artifact," *Currents in Biblical Research* 6 (2007): 130–60, and the literature cited there; and Schäfer, *Jewish Jesus*, pp. 70–94.

scholars have drawn about the variegated nature of the culture of the Babylonian Jews.⁴⁸

APPENDIX

A story in b. Sanhedrin 19a–b further exemplifies our claim regarding the importance of attentiveness to language switching for understanding the composite nature of rabbinic narratives, which sometimes leads to important conclusions about the literature and culture of the rabbis of late antiquity:⁴⁹

(1) [Aramaic:] *The slave of King Yannai killed someone.*

(2) [Hebrew:] Shimon ben Shetach said to the sages, "Examine him and let us judge him."

(1a) [Aramaic:] *They said to [King Yannai], "Your slave killed someone."*

[The king] sent [the slave] to them.

[The sages] sent [to the king], "You should also come here. [Hebrew:] 'The testimony must be in the presence of the owner' (Ex 21:29), said the Torah. Let the owner of the ox come and stand with his ox."⁵⁰

[Aramaic:] *[The king] came and sat.*⁵¹

(2a) [Hebrew:] Shimon ben Shetach said to him, "King Yannai, stand up and let them testify against you. Not before us do you stand, but before He who

---

48. See also the debate regarding the provenance of *Toledot Yeshu:* Willem F. Smelik, "The Aramaic Dialect(s) of the Toldot Yeshu Fragments," *Aramaic Studies* 7 (2009): 39–73; and Michael Sokoloff, "The Date and Provenance of the Aramaic *Toledot Yeshu* on the Basis of Aramaic Dialectology," in *Toledot Yeshu ("The Life Story of Jesus") Revisited*, ed. Peter Schäfer, Michael Meerson, and Yaakov Deutsch (Tübingen: Mohr/Siebeck, 2011), pp. 13–26.

49. In the translation of the story, the Aramaic sections are rendered in italics, while the Hebrew sections are in Roman characters. For an earlier version of the ensuing discussion, see Richard Kalmin, "Language Switching," in *Critical Terms in Jewish Language Studies*, Frankel Institute Annual 2011:18–20.

50. See *Sifrei Devarim*, ed. Finkelstein, *Piska* 190, p. 230, where the identical law is derived from Deuteronomy 19:17.

51. This brief phrase, which forms the exact center of the narrative (see Zivya Kafir, "Yannai ha-Melekh ve-Shimon ben Shetach: Aggadah Amora'it be-Tahposet Historit," *Tura* 3 [1994]: 92–93), links the Hebrew and Aramaic sources that were combined to form the narrative. It is in Aramaic perhaps because of its later provenance, and later layers of Talmudic discourse are predominantly in Aramaic.

spoke and the world came into being, as it is said, 'And the two parties to the dispute shall stand before the Lord'" (Deut 19:17).

[Yannai] said to him, "Not as you say, but as your colleagues say."

He turned to the right and they pressed their faces to the ground. He turned to the left and they pressed their faces to the ground.

Shimon ben Shetach said to them, "Deep thinkers are you? Let the Master of thoughts come and punish you."

Immediately [the angel] Gabriel came and struck them to the ground and they died. At that moment they said, "A king neither judges nor is he judged; he neither testifies nor is he testified against" (m. Sanhedrin 2:2).

This story presents several interpretive problems, including the question of why the text alternates between Aramaic and Hebrew. Part of the answer lies in the story's composite character. In the Aramaic material, the issue is the murder committed by the slave of King Yannai, and the requirement of the king to come to court along with his slave. In the Hebrew sections, however, the slave disappears and the king is suddenly on trial, and the issue is the king's refusal to stand in court. In addition, in the Aramaic material there is no mention of Shimon ben Shetach, but only of unnamed judges who insist that the king come to court, while Shimon ben Shetach dominates in the Hebrew sections and the other judges are totally passive.[52] The switch from Aramaic to Hebrew in part 1a is probably due to the fact that the midrash quoted by Shimon ben Shetach has a Tannaitic provenance.[53]

The Aramaic material parallels Josephus's account of Herod's trial for murder, and the Hebrew sections parallel a tradition mentioned in *Sifrei Zuta Devarim,* an ancient rabbinic compilation recently reconstructed by Menahem Kahana from a Judeo-Arabic commentary by the Karaite author Yeshuah.[54] B. Sanhedrin 19a–b, therefore, is a combination of two narrative fragments, one Aramaic and the other Hebrew. The two narrative fragments, neither of which tells a complete story as currently formulated, have been imperfectly stitched together and a new composition is the result.

---

52. Jacob Neusner, *The Rabbinic Traditions about the Pharisees before 70,* part 1, *The Masters* (1971; Atlanta: Scholars Press, 1999), p. 115, makes note of the language switching but claims that the narrative is smooth and indivisible into component sources.

53. See also part 2a, where Shimon ben Shetach's next midrash, also based on Deuteronomy 19:17, is the very next statement in *Sifrei Devarim.*

54. Menahem Kahana, *Sifrei Zuta Devarim* (Jerusalem: Magnes, 2002), pp. 282–86.

Josephus's account of Herod's trial for murder reads as follows:[55]

Having heard these arguments, Hyrcanus was persuaded. And his anger was further kindled by the mothers of the men who had been murdered by Herod, for every day in the temple they kept begging the king and the people to have Herod brought to judgment in the Synhedrion for what he had done. Being, therefore, moved by those pleas, Hyrcanus summoned Herod to stand trial for the crimes of which he had been accused. Accordingly, after he had settled his affairs in Galilee as he thought was to his best interests, because his father had advised him not to enter the city as a private individual but with the security of a bodyguard, he came with a troop sufficient for the purposes of the journey, and that he might not appear too formidable to Hyrcanus by arriving with a larger body of men and yet not be entirely unarmed and unprotected; and so he went to his trial. However Sextus, the governor of Syria, wrote to urge Hyrcanus to acquit Herod of the charge, and added threats as to what would happen if he disobeyed. The letter from Sextus gave Hyrcanus a pretext for letting Herod go without suffering any harm from the Synhedrion; for he loved him as a son. But when Herod stood in the Synhedrion, with his troops, he overawed them all, and no one of those who had denounced him before his arrival dared to accuse him thereafter; instead there was silence and doubt about what was to be done. While they were in this state, someone named Samaias, an upright man and for that reason superior to fear, arose and said, "Fellow councilors and King, I do not myself know of, nor do I suppose that you can name, anyone who when summoned before you for trial has ever presented such an appearance. For no matter who it was that came before this Synhedrion for trial, he has shown himself humble and has assumed the manner of one who is fearful and seeks mercy from you by letting his hair grow long and wearing a black garment. But this fine fellow Herod, who is accused of murder and has been summoned on no less grave a charge than this, stands here clothed in purple, with the hair of his head carefully arranged and with his soldiers round him, in order to kill us if we condemn him as the law prescribes, and to save himself by outraging justice. But it is not Herod whom I should blame for this or for putting his own interests above the law, but you and the king, for giving him such great license. Be assured, however, that God is great, and this man, whom you now wish to release for Hyrcanus's sake, will one day punish you and the king as well." And he was not mistaken in either part of his prediction. For when Herod assumed royal power, he killed Hyrcanus and all the other members of the Synhedrion with the exception of Samaias. Him he held in the greatest honor, both because of his uprightness and because when the city was later besieged by Herod and Sossius, he advised the people to admit Herod, and

---

55. Josephus, *Antiquities* 14.168–177. See also Josephus, *Jewish War* 1.204–212.

said that on account of their sins they would not be able to escape him. And of these events we shall speak in the proper place.

Now when Hyrcanus saw that the members of the Synhedrion were bent on putting Herod to death, he postponed the trial to another day, and secretly sent to Herod, advising him to flee from the city, for in that way, he said, he might escape danger.

Both Josephus's and the Bavli's Aramaic section of the story depict a trial of murder, and the identification of the murderer as "the slave of King Yannai" is in line with Herod's identification as the slave of the Hasmoneans in a lengthy story in b. Baba Batra 3b–4a, one of the very few times that the Bavli refers to Herod by name and by far the most extensive treatment of him in rabbinic literature. In both Josephus and b. Sanhedrin 19a–b the murderer makes an intimidating appearance in court and is confronted by a single heroic judge, who berates the other judges for their failure to stand up to the perpetrator. In both Josephus and the Bavli the cowardly judges die as punishment for their cowardice and the heroic judge is the only member of the court to remain alive. And as is also typically the case with parallels between the Bavli and Josephus, the Josephan narrative is clearly a later insertion into Josephus's main text, interrupting and contradicting the narrative flow and missing from Josephus's earlier version of events in the *Jewish War*.[56]

Certainly there are differences between the accounts in the Bavli and in *Antiquities,* but the most significant of these differences are attributable to the fact, noted above, that the Hebrew section of the Bavli's account is paralleled by a source preserved in *Sifrei Zuta Devarim,* which does not survive in its entirety, but is paraphrased by Yeshua:

> And they said about the matter, "'And the two men [that is, the litigants] shall stand' (Deut 19:17), even a king and a commoner." And they brought a lengthy story about Yannai the king, regarding a legal case he had with a poor man before Shimon ben Shetach.[57]

Both in the Hebrew section of the Bavli's account and in *Sifrei Zuta Devarim,* the text depicts King Yannai and Shimon ben Shetach but no

---

56. See, for example, Cohen, "Parallel Historical Traditions," pp. 12–13; and Kalmin, *Jewish Babylonia,* pp. 167–68.

57. Kahana, *Sifrei Zuta Devarim,* p. 282. See also *Tanhuma,* ed. Buber, *Shoftim* 6, p. 30. See also Kahana, *Sifrei Zuta Devarim,* p. 283, n. 1.

other judges, the king is a litigant, and the issue is the requirement of the king to stand in court.

What do the Babylonian rabbinic storytellers accomplish by combining these originally independent accounts? One significant result is the creation of a dramatic confrontation between Shimon ben Shetach and King Yannai, with Shimon ben Shetach portrayed as a hero and King Yannai as a villain, in keeping with their characterization elsewhere in the Bavli, and in keeping with the Bavli's tendency to portray Hasmonean kings negatively. The result of the clash between king and sage is the law of m. Sanhedrin 2:2—"The king neither judges nor is he judged"—since Shimon ben Shetach is ultimately too heroic for his standard of conduct to be applicable to the rest of humanity. In Palestinian rabbinic compilations, Hasmonean characters are portrayed either neutrally or positively,[58] making it likely that the provocative king portrayed in b. Sanhedrin represents the work of Babylonian storytellers rather than an original part of the Palestinian midrashic compilation *Sifrei Zuta Devarim*, from which the Bavli drew.

In other words, the Babylonian storytellers who combined these two sources pitted Shimon ben Shetach, a prerabbinic sage who Babylonian rabbis adopted as one of their spiritual ancestors, against King Yannai, who served as the prototypical wicked Hasmonean king. The motivation for the Bavli to create such a narrative might stem from contemporaneous societal concerns. We learn elsewhere in the Bavli of an attempt by Babylonian rabbis to discredit self-proclaimed descendants of the Hasmoneans, who claimed the right to lead the Babylonian Jewish community on the basis of their superior genealogy. Babylonian rabbis responded to the fact that some Jews, hundreds of years after the Hasmonean dynasty ostensibly came to an end in the land of Israel, claimed descent from Hasmonean royalty and used this claim to enhance their position in Babylonian Jewish society. The story and the larger context in which it is embedded support the theory that Babylonian rabbis opposed this claim, and that they supported instead the claims of the exilarch to rule Babylonian Jewish society on the basis of descent from King David. The Yannai/Shimon ben Shetach story is one of several Babylonian sources that reflect a political decision on the part of the rabbis, a choice between rival dynasties.[59]

The Babylonian storytellers who pitted Shimon ben Shetach against King Yannai claimed that m. Sanhedrin 2:2 excludes Hasmonean kings from the

---

58. Kalmin, *The Sage in Jewish Society,* pp. 61–67, 135–38.
59. Ibid.

judicial system to avoid disasters such as the one described in the story. Davidic kings, however, were not subject to the Mishnah's exclusion of kings from the judicial system, since they could be counted on to judge and testify honestly and to refrain from taking revenge on those who judged or testified against them. According to the Babylonian storytellers who combined these sources, therefore, exilarchs could participate as judges and litigants in the judicial system, but those claiming Hasmonean royal lineage could not.

Attention to language switching in Talmudic narratives, therefore, facilitates recovery of the diverse sources that compose the Talmudic text and a greater appreciation of the role of ancient editors in manipulating these diverse sources to create something new.

The above discussion also further exemplifies my claim that nonrabbinic texts from the eastern Roman provinces routinely make their first literary appearance in the Bavli beginning in the fourth century. The proof that this text was incorporated into the Bavli during or after the fourth century is provided by the fact that the narrative is quoted in b. Sanhedrin 19a–b as part of an argument based on a statement either by Rav Yosef or by Rav Papa, Amoraim of the early and later fourth century, respectively.[60] The Josephan[61] text examined above has no parallel in Palestinian rabbinic literature, and this case is another example of literature, motifs, and modes of behavior from the Roman East that provide evidence of a shift in the culture of Mesopotamia and neighboring provinces beginning in this period.[62]

---

60. See Kahana, *Sifrei Zuta Devarim*, p. 285, n. 33.
61. Or Josephus-like. See Kalmin, *Jewish Babylonia*, pp. 149–72, esp. pp. 167–68.
62. Kalmin, *Jewish Babylonia*, pp. 3–10 and 188–94.

ONE

"Manasseh Sawed Isaiah with a Saw of Wood"

AN ANCIENT LEGEND IN JEWISH, CHRISTIAN, MUSLIM, AND PERSIAN SOURCES

THIS CHAPTER EXEMPLIFIES OUR CLAIM in the introduction (1) that the fourth century began a period of eastern provincial Romanization of Jewish Babylonia, and (2) that the Jews and Christians of late antique Mesopotamia were culturally linked, although at present we are unable to determine how close these linkages were. So close is the relationship in this one case that a story told in a Syriac Christian source holds the hermeneutical key to the interpretation of a Babylonian rabbinic story, or vice versa, since the two stories utilize the same constellation of motifs and themes to teach strikingly similar lessons. This commonality does not necessarily indicate that the rabbis borrowed these motifs from the Mesopotamian Christians, or vice versa, although neither possibility is out of the question. Rather, it is one small but significant demonstration that the literature of the two groups formed part of a common cultural sphere, although the differences between the motifs and how they are utilized are potentially as interesting as the similarities. Analysis of this narrative reveals no indication of polemical interaction between the two communities.

This chapter approaches these issues via examination of the Babylonian Talmudic story of Manasseh's execution of Isaiah against the background of Christian, Jewish, Arabic, and Persian literature from the first to the eleventh centuries. The Bavli's version of the tradition depicts Moses as superior to the prophet Isaiah in response to other ancient depictions, notably by Christians, of Isaiah as Moses's superior. In addition, the Bavli's version of the tradition perhaps uses Isaiah (in Hebrew, Yeshayahu) as a stand-in for Jesus (in Hebrew, Yeshu), depicting Isaiah as executed according to God's will with the aid of a tree, for the crime of casting aspersions on the Israelite people. In evaluating this hypothesis, it is important to bear in mind that ancient Christians attempting to prove Jesus's messianic status quoted Isaiah's prophecies more frequently than those of any other biblical prophet. It is even more important to bear in mind that biblical words formed from the Hebrew root *yud, shin, ayin,* the basic components of Isaiah's Hebrew name, are routinely interpreted by the early Church fathers, including Church fathers who flourished in Palestine, as references to the Christian messiah, Jesus.[1] Also striking is the fact that Origen and Jerome, Church Fathers who flourished in Palestine, attributed precisely such a scriptural interpretation to a Jewish Christian[2] and a "semi-Christian"[3] respectively, and if the claims of these Church Fathers are reliable, we can easily understand how the Babylonian rabbis would have had access to them.[4] It is, therefore, not at all surprising that the rabbis should have viewed Isaiah as a stand-in for Jesus.

The Bavli's account also emphasizes God's continued close relationship with the Jewish people, insisting that Moses was correct when he said that God is available to the Jewish people whenever they call upon Him, in the face of claims by competing groups that God had abandoned the traditional people of Israel. While it is likely that the Bavli is responding in part to Christian claims against Judaism and the Mosaic revelation, this chapter takes pains not to overemphasize the Talmud's exclusive focus on Christianity. Examination of the full range of relevant traditions from the first to the eleventh centuries will reveal that closely related ideas were also expressed in the literature of other groups, including the literature of Jews produced at other times and in other localities.

THE *ASCENSION OF ISAIAH*

The sections of the *Ascension of Isaiah* that form the basis for our discussion (that is, those that have the closest parallels to rabbinic traditions)

---

1. See, for example, Halbertal and Naeh, "Ma'ayanei ha-Yeshua," in *Higayon le-Yonah,* pp. 186–90.

2. G. Merkati, "Un supposto framento di Origene," *Revue Biblique* 7 (1910): 76–79, cited by Halbertal and Naeh, "Ma'ayanei ha-Yeshua," p. 188, nn. 49–51.

3. *Hieronymi Presbytery Opera,* pars I,6, *Commentarii in Prophetas Minores.* Corpus Christianorum, series Latina 76 A, p. 641, cited in Halbertal and Naeh, "Ma'ayanei ha-Yeshua," p. 188, n. 52.

4. Some scholars, in fact, argue that the Bavli parodies Christian exegesis that interprets abstract nouns in the Bible as designations of the Christian messiah, and even engages in it periodically, choosing to identify as the messiah other figures besides the Christian messiah. See Halbertal and Naeh, "Ma'ayanei ha-Yeshua," pp. 190–97.

describe Manasseh's execution of Isaiah and relate the reasons for his execution:[5]

Ascension 1:7–10:

> Isaiah said to Hezekiah the king... "And Sammael Malkira [that is, Satan][6] will serve Manasseh and will do everything he wishes, and [Manasseh] will be a follower of Beliar [that is, Satan] rather than of me. He will cause many in Jerusalem and Judah to desert the true faith, and Beliar will dwell in Manasseh, and by his hands I will be sawn in half."

Ascension 3:6–10:

> And Belkira[7] [a Samaritan false prophet] accused Isaiah and the prophets who [were] with him, saying, "Isaiah and the prophets who [are] with him prophesy against Jerusalem and against the cities of Judah that they will be laid waste, and also [against] Benjamin that it will go into captivity, and also against you, O lord king, that you will go [bound] with hooks and chains of iron (2 Chr 33:11). But they prophesy lies against Israel and Judah. And Isaiah himself has said, 'I see more than Moses the prophet.' Moses said, 'There is no man who can see the Lord and live' (Ex 33:20). But Isaiah has said, 'I have seen the Lord, (Isa 6:1) and behold I am alive.' Know, therefore, O king, that they [are] false prophets. And he has called Jerusalem Sodom, and the princes of Judah and Jerusalem he has declared [to be] the people of Gomorrah."

---

5. The translation below is that of Michael A. Knibb, trans. and intro., "Martyrdom and Ascension of Isaiah," in *The Old Testament Pseudepigrapha*, vol. 2, ed. James H. Charlesworth (Garden City, NY: Doubleday, 1983), pp. 156–76. Compare the translations of Erling Hammershaimb, "Das Martyrium Jesajas," vol. 2, pt. 1, *Jüdische Schriften aus hellenistisch-römischer Zeit*, ed. Werner Georg Kümmel and Christian Habicht (Gütersloh: Gerd Mohn, 1973), pp. 23–32; and J. M. T. Barton, "The Ascension of Isaiah," in *The Apocryphal Old Testament*, ed. H. F. D. Sparks (Oxford: Clarendon Press, 1984), pp. 784–94. The most complete edition is that of R. H. Charles, *The Ascension of Isaiah* (London: Adam and Charles Black, 1900), pp. 83–148. See also Emil Schürer, *The History of the Jewish People in the Age of Jesus Christ*, vol. 3, pt. 1, rev. and ed. Geza Vermes, Fergus Millar, and Martin Goodman (Edinburgh: T & T Clark, 1986), p. 336, n. 2.

6. Sammael Malkira and Beliar appear to be synonymous appellations of Satan. George W. E. Nickelsburg, "Stories of Biblical and Early Post-Biblical Times," in *Jewish Writings of the Second Temple Period: Apocrypha, Pseudepigrapha, Qumran Sectarian Writings, Philo, Josephus*, section 2, ed. Michael E. Stone (Compendia Rerum Iudaicarum ad Novum Testamentum; Assen: Van Gorcum, 1984), p. 52, n. 107, writes that "the Martyrdom is notable for its many names for the chief demon or demons." (In much scholarship about the *Ascension of Isaiah*, the first six chapters are referred to as the *Martyrdom of Isaiah*.)

7. There are many variants of this name, even within individual manuscripts. See Knibb, "Martyrdom and Ascension," pp. 151–52; and Schürer, *History of the Jewish People*, p. 336, n. 3.

Ascension 5:1–2:

> Because of these visions, therefore, Beliar was angry with Isaiah, and he dwelt in the heart of Manasseh, and he sawed Isaiah in half with a wood saw.[8] And while Isaiah was being sawed in half....

Ascension 5:6–7

> And he said this to him when he began to be sawed in half. And Isaiah was in a vision of the Lord, but his eyes were open, and he saw them....

Ascension 5:11:

> And they seized Isaiah the son of Amoz and sawed him in half with a wood saw....

Ascension 5:13–16:

> And to the prophets who (were) with him he said before he was sawed in half, he did not cry out, or weep, but his mouth spoke with the Holy Spirit until he was sawed in two. Beliar did this to Isaiah through Belkira and through Manasseh, for Sammael was very angry with Isaiah from the days of Hezekiah, king of Judah, because of the things that he had seen concerning the Beloved,[9] and because of the destruction of Sammael that he had seen through the Lord, while Hezekiah his father was king. And he did as Satan wished.

Ascension 11:41:

> Because of these visions and prophecies Sammael Satan sawed Isaiah the son of Amoz, the prophet, in half by the hand of Manasseh.

We cannot be sure where and when the story of Manasseh's murder of Isaiah originated, but the earliest attestation of it is evidently in the *Ascension of*

---

8. Michael A. Knibb, "The Martyrdom of Isaiah," in *Outside the Old Testament*, ed. M. de Jonge (Cambridge: Cambridge University Press, 1985), p. 191, notes that the phrase "a wood saw" means "a saw to cut wood," but that in some works based on the *Ascension* it was understood to mean "a saw made out of wood." See Gary G. Porton, "Isaiah and the Kings: The Rabbis on the Prophet Isaiah," in *Writing and Reading the Scroll of Isaiah*, ed. Craig C. Broyles and Craig A. Evans (Leiden: Brill, 1997), vol. 2, p. 713, n. 44, for an intriguing explanation of the *Ascension*'s choice of a saw as the instrument of Isaiah's punishment.

9. "The Beloved" is apparently the *Ascension*'s term for Christ.

Isaiah.[10] While there is no unanimity on the subject, most scholars today date the *Ascension of Isaiah* to the end of the first and the beginning of the second century C.E.[11] It is also not entirely clear where the *Ascension* was authored, although according to the consensus of scholars it derives from western Syria or Palestine, and several scholars express a cautious preference for the latter.[12] This scholarly consensus makes it likely that the legend of Manasseh's murder of Isaiah originated in the eastern provinces of the Roman Empire, a conclusion supported by the fact that crucial aspects of the legend are also attested by several second- and third-century Church Fathers from the Greek and Roman world.[13] These facts will be crucial for establishing our claim that the legend originated in the Roman East, and traveled from there to Mesopotamia and Persia in subsequent centuries.

THE LEGEND IN THE BAVLI

The most extensive rabbinic parallel to the *Ascension*'s legend of Manasseh's execution of Isaiah, in b. Yevamot 49b–50a, reads as follows:

10. See also Hebrews 11:37.
11. Robert G. Hall, "*The Ascension of Isaiah:* Community Situation, Date, and Place in Early Christianity," *Journal of Biblical Literature* 109, no. 2 (1990): 300–306. See his summary of scholarly dating on p. 300. See also idem, "Isaiah's Ascent to See the Beloved: An Ancient Jewish Source for the *Ascension of Isaiah?*" *Journal of Biblical Literature* 113, no. 3 (1998): 463. See n. 2 there for references to earlier scholarship on the question of a preexisting *Martyrdom* source.
12. See, for example, Jan Dochhorn, "Die Ascensio Isaiae," in *Jüdische Schriften aus hellenistisch-römischer Zeit,* vol. 6, pt. 1, *Unterweisung in erzählender Form,* ed. Gerbern S. Oegema (Gütersloh: Gütersloher Verlagshaus, 2005), pp. 27–28. See also the literature cited on p. 28, n. 40.
13. For example, Justin, *Dialogue with Trypho* 120.5; and Tertullian, *De patientia* 14.1; and *Scorpiace* 8.3, mention that Isaiah was killed by being sawn in two. This form of execution may also be alluded to by the *Paraleipomena of Jeremiah* 9:19–21, a Christian work of the first third of the second century C.E. See Michael A. Knibb, "Isaianic Traditions in the Apocrypha and Pseudepigrapha," in Broyles and Evans, *Writing and Reading the Scroll of Isaiah,* vol. 2, p. 647. For the text and a translation of the *Paraleipomena,* see Robert A. Kraft and Ann-Elizabeth Purintum, *Paraleipomena Jeremiou* (Missoula, MT: SBL, 1972), pp. 46–47. See also R. Thornhill, "The Paraleipomena of Jeremiah," in *The Apocryphal Old Testament* (Oxford: Clarendon, 1984), p. 833. For further discussion of patristic use of the story of Isaiah's martyrdom, see Schürer, *History of the Jewish People,* vol. 3, pt. 1, pp. 338–40; Enrico Norelli, *Ascension du prophète Isaïe* (Turnhout: Brepols, 1993), pp. 23–29; and Dochhorn, "Die Ascensio Isaiae," pp. 12–13 and 29. See also n. 23 below for patristic attestations of the tradition that Isaiah was killed because he contradicted Moses and also because he uttered harsh prophecies against the Israelites.

(A) A Tanna recited: Shimon ben Azai says, "I found a scroll of genealogical records in Jerusalem and in it was written, 'So-and-so is a *mamzer*[14] from a married woman.' ... and in it was written, 'Manasseh killed Isaiah.'"

(B) Said Rava,[15] "He judged him and killed him."

(C) [Manasseh] said to [Isaiah], "Moses your rabbi said, 'For man may not see Me and live' (Ex 33:20); but you said, 'I saw the Lord seated on a high and lofty throne' (Isa 6:1). Moses your rabbi said, '[For what great nation is there that has a god so close at hand] as is the Lord our God whenever we call upon Him?' (Deut 4:7); but you said, 'Seek the Lord while He can be found' (Isa 55:6). Moses your rabbi said, 'I will let you enjoy the full count of your days' (Ex 23:26); but you said, 'And I will add 15 years to your life'" (2 Kgs 20:6).

(D) Said Isaiah, "I know that he will not accept whatever I say to him. If I say[16] [that is, respond] to him I will make him an intentional murderer."

---

14. This word is frequently, and inadequately, translated as "illegitimate child." It designates the legal status of a child born of a forbidden sexual union between two Jews. The nature and severity of the prohibited sexual union are the subject of debate in rabbinic sources. It is tempting to understand "So-and-so" (*Ish Ploni* in Hebrew) as a coded reference to Jesus, although as far as I have been able to determine, the second item on Shimon ben Azai's list, "Eliezer ben Yaakov's teachings are few but clean," has no connection to Jesus or Christianity, reducing the likelihood that the first item on the list, in the absence of compelling proof, should also be interpreted in this fashion.

15. *Dikdukei Soferim ha-Shalem:* Yevamot, ed. Avraham Liss (Jerusalem: Ha-Makhon ha-Yisre'eli ha-Shalem, 1988), notes on line 7 and n. 29, records versions with Rabbah *(reish, bet, hei)* instead of Rava *(reish, bet, alef)*. (For differences between these names, see Shamma Friedman, "Ketiv ha-Shemot 'Rabbah' ve-'Rava' ba-Talmud ha-Bavli," *Sinai* 55 [1992]: 140–64; and Kalmin, *Sages, Stories, Authors, and Editors,* pp. 175–92. If Rabbah, the conventional designation of the earlier, Pumbeditan rabbi, authored this statement, it dates from the early fourth century rather than the mid-fourth century, but this minor chronological difference has no significant impact on my conclusions.) In addition, one version reads Rav and another has a *reish* followed by a punctuation mark indicating that the *reish* is an abbreviation. Obviously my claim about a fourth-century dating of this statement in the Bavli depends on the rejection of the reading "Rav," found in only one manuscript. It is easy to see how a scribe could have mistakenly abbreviated the name "Rava" to "Rav," a scribal phenomenon encountered frequently in manuscripts and medieval testimonia of the Talmud. Absolute certainty on the question of the correct reading of the name, however, is obviously unattainable.

16. Mss Cambridge-Add. 3207, Oxford Opp. 248 (367), Munich 141, and Moscow-Guenzburg 1017 do not have the verb "say" twice in part D (" ... whatever I *say* to him. If I *say* to him ... "). Even according to these versions, however, Isaiah's "saying" is of central importance in this narrative.

(E) Isaiah said [God's] name and was swallowed by a cedar tree.[17] [The corner of his blue fringe remained outside.][18]

They brought the cedar tree and they sawed it.[19] When he reached [Isaiah's] mouth, he died, because [Isaiah] said, "And I live among a people of unclean lips" (Isa 6:5).

(F) Nevertheless, the verses [cited in part C] contradict one another.

(G) "I saw the Lord" (Isa 6:1), as it is taught [in a Baraita], "All of the prophets looked in a speculum that does not shine; Moses our rabbi looked in a speculum that shines." "Seek the Lord while He can be found" (Isa 55:6); this verse refers to an individual, the other verse (Deut 4:7) refers to the community.

(H) Regarding an individual, when [can God be found]?

(I) Said Rav Nahman said Rabbah bar Abuha, "These are the ten days between Rosh Hashanah and Yom Kippur."

What is the relationship between the Bavli's and the *Ascension*'s portrayal of Isaiah's execution by Manasseh? Certainly the authors of the *Ascension* and Bavli Yevamot responded in part to biblical and second Temple texts (see below), but it is no less certain that either (a) the Babylonian rabbis drew upon the traditions preserved in the *Ascension,* or (b) both the Bavli and the *Ascension* drew upon a common fund of preexisting source material. Suffice it to say in the present context that the Bavli's and the *Ascension*'s accounts differ in significant respects, with the *Ascension,* for example, saying nothing about Isaiah being swallowed by a tree, and the Bavli making no mention of Satan or the Beloved, to name only a few of the most obvious differences.[20]

---

17. B. Sanhedrin 101a describes Rav Yizhak bar Yosef swallowed by a cedar tree as a result of the malevolent action of demons. See also *Bereshit Rabbah* 15:7, ed. Theodor and Albeck, pp. 140–41. Porton, "Isaiah and the Kings," vol. 2, p. 703, observes that according to the Yerushalmi's version of the story of Isaiah's being swallowed by a tree, "one could argue that the tree captured Isaiah for the king's men." The tree in the Bavli's version of the story, however, is clearly doing the will of Isaiah.

18. Mss Cambridge-Add. 3207 and Moscow-Guenzburg 594 both record the sentence that I have placed in brackets, according to which the Bavli's version of the cedar tree episode more closely resembles that of the Yerushalmi. The same reading is found in the first printed edition of Rabenu Bahai, although he reads *kotza* instead of *karna*. See Sokoloff, *Dictionary of Jewish Babylonian Aramaic,* p. 1001, s.v., *kotza*.

19. See *Dikdukei Soferim ha-Shalem:* Yevamot, ed. Liss, notes on line 13 and n. 58.

20. It would be a simple matter to mention other differences between the Bavli's and the *Ascension*'s accounts of the legend. See, for example, Porton, "Isaiah and the Kings," pp. 712–14.

The most obvious similarity between the accounts in the Bavli and the *Ascension* is the depiction of Manasseh killing Isaiah by sawing him in half. Equally significant, however, is the fact that the *Ascension* and the Bavli depict the execution as the result of specific accusations brought by Manasseh against Isaiah, one of which is identical in the two accounts. To be specific, according to both accounts Manasseh's charge that Isaiah claims, in contradiction to Moses, to have seen "the Lord seated on a high and lofty throne" (Isa 6:1) provoked outrage and led to his execution. According to the *Ascension* no less than according to the Bavli, therefore, it is appropriate to say that "[Manasseh] judged [Isaiah] and killed him,"[21] although these exact words are recorded only in the Bavli's account.

Rava, the mid-fourth-century Babylonian rabbi who authored the statement "[Manasseh] judged [Isaiah] and killed him," clearly knows at least some of the material that the Bavli shares in common with the *Ascension*.[22] Rava clearly knows that "Manasseh killed Isaiah" (part A). He might also know the accusations against Isaiah (part C), since the contradictions between Moses and Isaiah are the basis upon which Manasseh judges Isaiah. Rava might not know all three accusations, but it is likely that he knows the first one ("Moses your master said, 'For man may not see Me and live' [Ex 33:20]; but you said, 'I saw the Lord seated on a high and lofty throne' [Isa 6:1]"), given that it is well attested in antiquity, since it is found already in the *Ascension of Isaiah* and in the writings of several early Church Fathers. According to Origen, for example: "They say that Isaiah was cut apart by the people, as one who depraved the law and spoke beyond what Scripture authored. For Scripture says, 'No one shall see My face and live,' but he says, 'I saw the Lord of Hosts.' Moses, they say, saw Him not, and you saw Him! And for this cause they cut him apart and condemned him as impious."[23] It

---

21. Mauro Pesce, "Presupposti per l'utilizzazione storica dell'*Ascensione di Isaia*," in *Isaia, il diletto e la Chiesa: Visione ed esegesi profetica cristiano-primitiva nell'Ascensione di Isaia*, ed. Mauro Pesce (Brescia: Paideia, 1983), pp. 40–45.

22. See Kalmin, *Jewish Babylonia*, pp.15–17 and 196, on the subject of the limited reliability of attributions of statements to particular rabbis in the Bavli, or at least to particular chronological layers.

23. Origen, *Homiliae in Isaiam* 1.5 (Griechischen christlichen Schriftsteller 33.247). See also Jerome, *Commentarii in Isaiam* 1.1.10 (Corpus Christianorum, series Latina 73.16); Didymus, *Commentarius in Psalmos* 34.19 (Tura-Papyrus III.218.3–14 [Papyrologische Texte und Abhandlungen 8.354–357]); and *Pseudo-Chrysostum, Opus Imperfectum* in Matthaeum, Homily 33 to Matthew 19.20, edited by J. P. Migne, Patrologiae cursus completes, series Graeca 56.808 (Paris, 1859).

is also possible, of course, that the three accusations against Isaiah postdate Rava in this context and were placed here to elaborate on his brief remark.

It is unclear whether or not the Bavli's account of the sin that actually caused Isaiah's death (part E: "When he reached [Isaiah's] mouth, he died, because [Isaiah] said, 'And I live among a people of unclean lips'") owes anything to earlier versions of the legend. The Bavli's explanation for Isaiah's death is similar but not identical to the reason given in the *Ascension,* since in the *Ascension* Satan becomes furious because of Isaiah's prophecies about (a) the wickedness of Jerusalem and the princes of Judah and Jerusalem, and (b) the destruction that awaits Jerusalem and the cities of Judah. According to *Ascension* 3:6–10, Isaiah's prophecies are of catastrophes that will befall Israel and the king, and Isaiah also angers Manasseh because "he has called Jerusalem Sodom, and the princes of Judah and Jerusalem he has declared [to be] the people of Gomorrah." So it would appear that for the author of the *Ascension,* part of Isaiah's "crime" (according to Beliar [= Satan] and his minions) was his denunciation of the Israelites. The Bavli is unique among all extant versions of the Isaiah legend, however, in characterizing as Isaiah's crime his assertion that he dwells among a people of unclean lips, and in making his punishment measure for measure.

Rava's claim that Manasseh "judged him and killed him" and the accusations against Isaiah that follow (parts B–C) compose a surprisingly sympathetic, or at least ambiguous, portrayal of Manasseh.[24] M. Sanhedrin 10:2 contains a Tannaitic dispute about whether or not Manasseh fully repented and thereby inherited a portion in the world to come, and Bavli Yevamot may reflect the opinion that the king did repent. Contributing to this sympathetic or less than clearly negative portrayal is the fact that Bavli Yevamot portrays Manasseh as innocent of murder, since Isaiah deliberately says nothing in response to Manasseh's charges. Manasseh's objections against Isaiah are serious and demand a response, however, as indicated by the fact that the Bavli's anonymous editors (parts F–H) feel the need to respond to them.

Perhaps in tension with this idea of a sympathetic or ambiguous portrayal of Manasseh is the fact that the king consistently refers to Moses as "your [that is, Isaiah's] rabbi," implying that he is not his own (that is, Manasseh's) rabbi, thus reading himself out of the rabbinic movement. In addition, Isaiah

---

24. See Alberdina Houtman, "The Targumic Versions of the 'Martyrdom of Isaiah,'" in *Studies in Hebrew Literature and Jewish Culture,* ed. Martin F. J. Baasten and Reinier Munk (Dordrecht: Springer, 2007) p. 200, who reads the Bavli's portrayal of Manasseh as sympathetic.

in part D definitely presupposes a less than fully repentant Manasseh, since Isaiah is certain that Manasseh will not listen to reason and will kill him even if he satisfactorily responds to his objections, and will thereby be rendered an intentional murderer. The fact that Isaiah expresses his certainty, however, does not guarantee that he is correct, and in the ensuing discussion I argue that the author of the story in the Bavli probably does not share Isaiah's clearly negative opinion of the king.

Support for this interpretation emerges when we examine the importance in the story of motifs of speech and the mouth. Everything that happens in the story is effectuated through speech, casting doubt on Isaiah's claim that nothing he would have said would have had any effect on Manasseh. After all, his words have all kinds of effects. He "says" God's name, which causes him to be swallowed by a tree (although his *tsitsit* are showing, revealing his hiding place, suggesting that God wants him to receive his just deserts, that is, his punishment for having insulted the Israelites). In addition, Isaiah "said," "I live among a people of unclean lips," which is the sin for which he is punished with death, and his death is via his mouth. He "said" things that appear to contradict what Moses "said," which gets him into trouble with the king and causes his death. And as a prophet, when he says God's word he puts it into effect. Perhaps Isaiah is punished not only because of what he said, but also because of what he refrained from saying, namely, the reasons why his (Isaiah's) words do not contradict those of Moses. In addition, when Isaiah says that he chooses to die rather than make the king guilty of premeditated murder, perhaps we are meant to be unsympathetic, in line with the rabbis' tendency in the Bavli to view with suspicion those who prefer martyrdom to escaping with their lives by means of subterfuge. Rabbinic traditions in the Bavli frequently favor the trickster who saves his life and avoids a noble death to the "hero" who chooses martyrdom.[25]

Also of critical importance for understanding the Bavli's discussion is the Syriac *Acts of Sharbil,* probably written in the fourth or fifth century in Edessa, a city in northern Mesopotamia,[26] not far from the Babylonian rab-

---

25. Daniel Boyarin, *Dying for God: Martyrdom and the Making of Christianity and Judaism* (Stanford: Stanford University Press, 1999), pp. 42–66, 162–73, and n. 11, pp. 175–76, observes that many rabbinic traditions favor the trickster over the hero who chooses a noble death, but he does not point out the distinction between traditions in the Bavli and traditions in Palestinian rabbinic compilations. I hope to expand upon this point in further research.

26. See H. J. W. Drijvers, *Cults and Beliefs at Edessa* (Leiden: Brill, 1980), pp. 35, 40, 43, and 181; and Susan Ashbrook Harvey, "The Edessan Martyrs and Ascetic Tradition,"

bis. In this Christian text, like the Bavli's text, we find the motifs of (a) the hero judged and executed by being sawn in two, (b) his death coming about because of a crime of speech, and (c) the crucial importance of the hero's mouth in his measure-for-measure punishment:[27]

> And suddenly the curtain was drawn back again, and the judge cried aloud and said, "As regards this Sharbil, who was formerly priest of the gods, but has turned this day and renounced the gods, and has cried aloud, 'I am a Christian,' and has not trembled at the gods, but has insulted them; and, further, has not been afraid of the emperors and their command; and, though I have bidden him sacrifice to the gods according to his former custom, has not sacrificed, but has treated them with the greatest insult: I have looked into the matter, and decided, that towards a man who does these things, even though he were now to sacrifice, it is not fit that any mercy should be shown; and that it is not fit that he should any longer behold the sun of his lords, because he has scorned their laws. I give sentence that, according to the laws of the emperors, a strap be thrust into the mouth of the insulter, as into the mouth of a murderer, and that he depart outside of the city of the emperors with haste, as one who has insulted the lords of the city and the gods who hold authority over it. I give sentence that he be sawn with a saw of wood,[28] and that, when he is near to die, then his head be taken off with the sword of the executioner."
>
> And at the same moment the strap was suddenly thrust into his mouth, and the executioners seized him.... And they offered him some wine to drink, according to the custom of murderers to drink. But he said to them, "I will not drink, because I wish to feel the saw with which you saw me, and the sword which you push over my neck...."
>
> They brought carpenters' instruments and thrust him into a wooden vise, and tightened it upon him until the bones of his joints creaked with the pressure, then they put upon him a saw of iron, and began sawing him asunder; and, when he was just about to die, because the saw had reached his mouth, they smote him with the sword and took off his head, while he was still squeezed down in the vise.[29]

---

in *V Symposium Syriacum, 1988*, ed. René Lavenant (Rome: Pont. Institutum Studiorum Orientalium, 1990), p. 197.

27. Regarding the *Acts of Sharbil*, see Millar, *The Roman Near East*, pp. 464 and 486–87. See also Drijvers, *Cults and Beliefs at Edessa*, pp. 33 and 35; and Harvey, "Edessan Martyrs," p. 195.

28. Note the use of the same phraseology as in the *Ascension of Isaiah* 5:2.

29. For this translation I consulted *The Acts of Sharbil*, in *Ancient Syriac Documents*, trans. and ed. William Cureton (1864; Amsterdam: Oriental Press, 1967), pp. 58–60 (see the Syriac text on pp. 59–61); and in *The Ante-Nicene Fathers*, ed. Alexander Roberts and James Donaldson, rev. ed. A. Cleveland Coxe, vol. 8; and in *Memoirs of Edessa, and Other Ancient*

In the Bavli's story the protagonist dies when they reach his mouth and in the story of Sharbil the executioners lop off his head when they reach the mouth, so the motif does not play out exactly the same in the two contexts, but in both narratives the point is that the protagonist's mouth plays a crucial role in the "crime" that leads to his execution, and in the working out of the execution. In the Sharbil tale the executioners make the point that their victim's crime was that of "insulting the gods" by "crying aloud, 'I am a Christian,'" the standard climax of Christian accounts of late antique martyrology trials.[30] In the story of Isaiah's martyrdom in the Bavli, in contrast, the critical role of the mouth in the death of the martyr is not a sign of his saintliness and heroism, but rather a symbol of the sin he committed for which he is punished. While the precise relationship between the Christian and the rabbinic stories is difficult to determine at present, as is the significance of the difference between the way the motifs are utilized in the two literatures, the centrality of the motifs of speech and the mouth in the Sharbil tale supports my claim that these motifs are an important hermeneutical key to the meaning of the Bavli's story as well.

One might be inclined to see in Bavli Yevamot's high opinion of Moses and surprisingly low, or at least ambivalent, opinion of Isaiah an attempt to deliver the message that the power of the rabbi (Moses) is greater than that of the prophet (Isaiah). When we examine the passage more closely, however, we see that this explanation is unsatisfactory. First, Isaiah apparently knows how to answer Manasseh's objections; he just refrained from doing so. And as Manasseh says, Moses is Isaiah's *rav,* apparently proof that Isaiah is also a rabbi.[31] So the operative distinction is not rabbis versus prophets, but the specific figure of Moses (who is both a rabbi and a prophet) versus the specific figure of Isaiah (also both a rabbi and a prophet), probably viewed as paradigmatic of or superior to all other non-Mosaic prophets. Isaiah is Moses's inferior as a prophet: Moses saw clearly; Isaiah and other prophets did not. And

---

Syriac Documents: Acts of Sharbil, trans. B. P. Pratten (Grand Rapids, MI: Wm. B. Eerdmans, 1951), p. 684.

30. See, for example, Hugh Jackson Lawlor and John Ernest Leonard Oulton, trans. and ed., Eusebius, Bishop of Caesarea. *Ecclesiastical History and the Martyrs of Palestine* (London: Society for Promoting Christian Knowledge, 1927), vol. 1, p. 142; and J. Stevenson, *A New Eusebius: Documents Illustrative of the History of the Church to A.D. 337* (London: Society for Promoting Christian Knowledge, 1960), p. 42.

31. It is possible that the meaning is that Moses is Isaiah's "master" as a prophet. Still, the fact that the story credits Isaiah with the ability to resolve objections suggests that it views him as a rabbi.

Isaiah condemned the Israelites and Moses apparently did not. Isaiah is also lacking as a rabbi: Isaiah did not respond to the objections posed by the king, even though the situation demanded a response, and it is a rabbi's stock-in-trade to respond to objections posed against problematic traditions. Presumably this discussion is directed against those rabbis or nonrabbis, Jews or non-Jews, who favored Isaiah (and other prophets) over Moses himself.

The *Ascension of Isaiah* clearly favored Isaiah over Moses. According to the *Ascension,* Isaiah had visions of the Beloved, the seven heavens, the incarnation, and the resurrection, and therefore Isaiah clearly saw more than Moses. There may or may not have been direct dependence of the Bavli upon the *Ascension,* but even if there was not, and the two texts instead drew upon common sources, the *Ascension* gives us a good idea of the kinds of traditions and cultural tensions that provided the background of the Bavli's discussion.

Another important theme in Bavli Yevamot is the anonymous editorial claim (part G, responding to the objection in part C) that God is always responsive to petitions by the community of Israel. God has not abandoned the Jewish people, and even the individual Jew can always count on a sympathetic hearing from God during a critical time in the Jewish liturgical calendar, between Rosh Hashanah and Yom Kippur (part I). The God of Israel continues to have a special relationship with Jews, both individually and as a people.

Also crucial to the Bavli is the issue of the biblical prophets' condemnation of the Israelites. According to the Bavli, the only one responsible for the death of Isaiah is Manasseh, and as noted, even Manasseh may be portrayed as relatively benign. There is no hint in the Bavli that the Israelites are implicated in Isaiah's murder, and in fact Isaiah's death is described as deserved punishment for his harsh words about the Israelites. We will see that the parallel text in the Yerushalmi likewise blames only the king, but numerous voices in late antiquity and the early Middle Ages implicated the Israelites as well as (or instead of) the king. We saw above that the guilt of the Israelites for the death of Isaiah, and for much else besides, was an important concern of the *Ascension of Isaiah,* and Israelite guilt was likewise a central preoccupation of numerous other early Christian (and Jewish) authors.[32] We will also see that Tabarī, a Muslim historian writing in Baghdad in the ninth and

---

32. See the quotation of Origen above; and see Hans J. Schoeps, "Die jüdischen Prophetenmorde," in *Aus frühchristlicher Zeit: Religionsgeschichte Untersuchungen* (Tübingen: Mohr/Siebeck, 1950), p. 126; Odil Hannes Steck, *Israel und das gewaltsame Geschick des Propheten: Untersuchungen zur Überlieferung des deuteronomistischen Geschichtsbildes im Alten Testament, Spätjudentum und Urchristentum* (Neukirchen-Vluyn: Neukirchener

tenth centuries, cites a version of the story that blames the Israelites rather than the king for the murder of Isaiah. The issue of whether or not the biblical Israelites had been rejected by God on account of their sins or had maintained their status as God's special people was clearly a live one in antiquity and beyond. The absence of Israelite blame in both Talmuds could well be a rabbinic reworking of extant traditions that *did* blame the Israelites.

There are also specific traditions in *rabbinic* compilations that provide important background for Bavli Yevamot's discussion. It is likely that Bavli Yevamot had some of these traditions before it, but it is unlikely that the Bavli's narrative had *only* these traditions, since some motifs are found only in Bavli Yevamot and in nonrabbinic literature deriving from the eastern Roman provinces. As noted, only in Bavli Yevamot and the *Ascension of Isaiah* does Manasseh level specific charges against Isaiah, "judging him" for his objectionable prophecies; and only in the *Ascension,* the Church Fathers, and Bavli Yevamot is it explicit that one of the charges against Isaiah was that he contradicted Moses by claiming to have seen "the Lord seated on a high and lofty throne" (Isa 6:1).[33]

One rabbinic text that contains important parallels to the Bavli's version of the tradition of Isaiah's execution is found in y. Sanhedrin 10:2 (28c):

(A) [Mishnah:] Three kings and four commoners have no portion in the world to come. Three kings: Jeroboam, Ahab, and Manasseh.

R. Yehudah says, "Manasseh has a portion in the world to come, as it is said, 'Manasseh prayed to Him, and He granted his prayer, heard his plea, and returned him to Jerusalem to his kingdom'" (2 Chr 33:13).

They said to [R. Yehudah], "He returned him to his kingdom, but He did not return him to life in the world to come."

(B) [Talmud:] What did Manasseh do? . . .

(C) When Manasseh became king he ran after Isaiah. He wanted to kill him and [Isaiah] fled from before him. He fled to a cedar tree and the cedar tree swallowed him, except for the fringes of his cloak. They went and said before [Manasseh; that is, they told the king where Isaiah was hiding]. [Manasseh] said to them, "Go and saw the cedar tree." They sawed the cedar tree and blood was seen flowing.

Verlag, 1957); David Milton Scholter, "Israel Murdered Its Prophets: The Origins and Development of the Tradition in the Old Testament and Judaism," Doctor of Theology diss., Harvard Divinity School, 1980; and Barton, "Ascension of Isaiah," pp. 776–77.

33. See the patristic sources cited in n. 23.

In the Yerushalmi, therefore, Manasseh alone (along with the unnamed individuals whom he orders to saw the tree) murders the prophet, and the text supplies no motive for the king's actions. According to the Yerushalmi, the story explains only what Manasseh did to lose his portion in the world to come. The reference to "blood … seen flowing" at the end of part C is an allusion to 2 Kings 21:16, "Manasseh also shed much innocent blood," according to which the Yerushalmi portrays Isaiah as the innocent victim of the murderous king.

Support for this interpretation is provided by the fact that in the continuation, the Yerushalmi explicitly quotes and comments on 2 Kings 21:16:

> (D) But behold, it is written, "[Manasseh] also spilled much innocent blood until he filled Jerusalem [with blood] from end to end" [literally, "from mouth to mouth"] (2 Kgs 21:16). And is it possible for flesh and blood [that is, a human being] to fill Jerusalem with blood from end to end? Rather, [this verse refers to the fact] that he killed Isaiah, who was equal to Moses, about whom it was written, "Directly [literally, 'mouth to mouth'] I will speak to him" (Num 12:8).

This passage understands 2 Kings 21:16 to say that "Manasseh filled Jerusalem with the innocent blood of Isaiah," and it interprets the phrase "from mouth to mouth" as a reference to both Isaiah and Moses. The text does not specify how Isaiah was "equal to Moses," but the reference is probably to their close communication with God, since the phrase "mouth to mouth" refers to Moses's close communication with God in Numbers 12:8. Bavli Yevamot, which insists upon Moses's superior vision of and communication with God, is clearly responding to the idea reflected in the Yerushalmi passage, and in fact might be responding to this very passage itself. The Yerushalmi in this context is clearly less sensitive than the Bavli to the dangers involved in overestimating the importance of non-Mosaic prophets.

B. Sanhedrin 103b is another rabbinic text that helps us understand Bavli Yevamot:

> (A) "Moreover, Manasseh put so many innocent people to death that he filled Jerusalem [with blood] from end to end [literally, 'from mouth to mouth']—besides the sin he committed in causing Judah to do what was displeasing to the Lord" (2 Kgs 21:16).
>
> (B) Here [in Babylonia] they explained[34] that [Manasseh] killed Isaiah.

---

34. The verb *targimu* can mean "translated," "explained," or both. See Sokoloff, *Dictionary of Jewish Babylonian Aramaic*, pp. 1231–32. For discussion of the phrase *Hakha*

(C) In the west [that is, in Palestine] they said that [Manasseh] made an idol that was the weight of one thousand men, and every day he killed them all.

(D) The statement by Rabbah bar bar Hanah: "The life of one righteous person is equal to that of the entire world," which tradition does it follow?"

(E) It follows the one who said, "[Manasseh] killed Isaiah" [that is, part B].

Like the Yerushalmi passage above, the Bavli here claims that 2 Kings 21:16 refers specifically to Isaiah. And like the Yerushalmi, part of the Bavli's motivation is probably the phrase "mouth to mouth," which links this passage to the description of Moses in Numbers 12:8. The Yerushalmi and b. Sanhedrin 103b, therefore, maintain that Isaiah is the equal of Moses, and they do so by means of the phrase "mouth to mouth," which describes Moses's direct communication with God in Numbers 12:8. It is likely that Bavli Yevamot reacts against the evaluation of Isaiah vis-à-vis Moses found in b. Sanhedrin 103b, and it may be reacting against this specific text.[35] As noted, however, the probable dependence of Bavli Yevamot on Bavli Sanhedrin and the Yerushalmi does not negate the significance of the parallel between the *Ascension* and Bavli Yevamot, since only in the latter two texts does Manasseh execute Isaiah in response to the specific charge that he blasphemously claimed to have seen God and lived, in contradiction to Moses's explicit claim that such was impossible.

Targimu ("Here [in Babylonia] they explained") and the likelihood that *Targimu* in this expression means "explained" rather than "translated," see Richard Kalmin, "Targum in the Babylonian Talmud," in *Envisioning Judaism,* ed. Boustan, Herrmann, Leicht, Reed, and Veltri, p. 522.

35. *Pesikta Rabbati* and two manuscripts of *Targum Jonathan* on the Prophets also relate the story of Manasseh's murder of Isaiah. For discussion, see P. Grelot, "Deux tosephtas targoumiques inedites sur Isaie LXVI," *Revue Biblique* 79 (1972): 515–18; Barton, "The Ascension of Isaiah," p. 775; and Houtman, "The Targumic Versions of the Martyrdom of Isaiah," pp. 189–201. For the text of this Tosefta Targum, see Alexander Sperber, *The Bible in Aramaic,* 5 vols. (1959–73; Leiden: Brill, 1992), vol. 3, pp. 129–20; and Rimon Kasher, *Toseftot Targum la-Nevi'im* (Jerusalem: Ha-Igud ha-Olami le-Mada'ei ha-Yahadut, 1996), pp. 169–70. As noted, it is also likely that second Temple Jewish traditions were in the minds of the authors and editors of Bavli Yevamot. See, for example, the discussion of *Ben Sira* 48:17–25, especially 48:24–25, in Knibb, "Isaianic Traditions in the Apocrypha and Pseudepigrapha," p. 647. See also Jenny Labendz, "The Book of Ben Sira in Rabbinic Literature," *Association for Jewish Studies Review* 30, no. 2 (2006): 347–92, who observes that beginning in the late third century or early fourth, at least some Babylonian rabbis knew portions of *Ben Sira.* The Bavli may have been acquainted with *Ben Sira*'s portrayal of Isaiah, or comparable portrayals of the prophet elsewhere in second Temple literature, further fueling the polemical portrayal in Bavli Yevamot.

IRANIAN AND MUSLIM PARALLELS

Thus far we have analyzed Jewish and Christian versions of the legend of Manasseh's execution of Isaiah. Scholars have drawn attention, however, to several important parallels in other literatures, although there is little scholarly consensus concerning the relationship between these parallel versions. Larionoff argued in the late nineteenth century, for example, that several of the motifs preserved in the *Ascension* and in rabbinic literature derive from an ancient Iranian legend,[36] and James Russell, a prominent contemporary Iranologist, concurs.[37] Larionoff argued that a story in the *Avesta Yast* 19.49, dating from no later than the end of the Achaemenid period,[38] is the source of the Jewish, Christian, Arabic, and later Persian versions of the tradition. Russell notes the "striking resemblance" of the story of the martyrdom of Isaiah to the complex Iranian legend of the death of Yima, of which different and sometimes contradictory versions exist over a vast period, from the *Avesta* down to the tenth and eleventh century *Shahname,* also composed in Persia. Russell characterizes Yima as "the first king . . . and the first mortal," and says that "he becomes the king of the dead."[39] In Iranian literature Yima "is regarded as a great and creative monarch who sins through hubris, believing he is divine because his medicines have made men immortal."[40]

36. S. Larionoff, "Histoire du Roi Djemchid et des Divs," *Journal Asiatique* 14 (1889): 64–65. See also G. Beer, "Das Martyrium Jesajae," in *Die Apokryphen und Pseudepigraphen des Alten Testaments,* vol. 2, ed. E. Kautzsch (Tübingen: Mohr, 1900), pp. 122–23; and Valentin Nikiprowetzky, "Pseudépigraphes de l'ancien testament et manuscript de la mer morte," *Revue des Etudes Juives* 128 (1969): 12–13. Cf. M. Philonenko, *Pseudépigraphes de l'ancien Testament et Manuscrits de la Mer Morte,* vol. 1 (Paris: Presses Universitaires de France, 1967), p.10; and A. Caquot, "Bref commentaire du Martyre d'Isaîe," *Semitica* 23 (1973): 87–89.

37. James R. Russell, "The *Ascensio Isaiae* and Iran," in *Irano-Judaica,* vol. 3, ed. Shaul Shaked and Amnon Netzer (Jerusalem: Yad Izhak Ben-Zvi, 1994), pp. 63–69.

38. Gherardo Gnoli, "Questioni comparative sull'*Ascensione d'Isaia:* La tradizine iranica," in Pesce, *Isaia, il diletto e la Chiesa,* p. 125.

39. Russell, "*Ascensio Isaiae* and Iran," p. 64. For a discussion of Yima's ambiguous nature as partly good and partly evil, and the nature of his sin, see Shaul Shaked, "First Man, First King: Notes on Semitic-Iranian Syncretism and Iranian Mythological Transformations," in *Gilgul: Essays on Transformation, Revolution and Permanence in the History of Religions,* ed. Shaul Shaked, D. Schulman, and G. G. Stroumsa (Leiden: Brill, 1987), pp. 238–45.

40. Russell, "*Ascensio Isaiae* and Iran," p. 64. According to *Dadistan i denig* 38.19–20, for example, Jamshed (the Pahlavi form of the Avestan name Yima) was tricked by a demon into declaring himself the Creator; and in the Avestan *Videvdat* 2.1–19 and Pahlavi *Denkard* 8.44.3 he turns down the offer of the Good Religion to become immortal, preferring to be a great mortal monarch. See Russell, "*Ascensio Isaiae* and Iran," p. 65.

According to the *Avesta*, Yima's brother, Spityura, kills Yima by cutting him in two with the help of a three-headed monster, Azi Dahaka.

Larionoff's and Russell's theory is most likely incorrect, however. The only significant similarity between the Avestan and the later accounts is the fact that they all depict an important character's death by being cut in two. Gherardo Gnoli argued convincingly, however, that this similarity is of little significance, since the *Avesta* says that Yima was cut in pieces and not sawn in half, a conclusion confirmed by Bruce Lincoln's detailed philological study.[41] In Persian literature, the motif of sawing appears only in later texts, in all likelihood due to the spread of the motifs incorporated into the various versions of the story of the martyrdom of Isaiah.[42]

Virtually everything else about the *Avesta* and the later accounts is different. If we confine the discussion to comparison between the *Avesta* and the Bavli, Isaiah in the Bavli is a prophet who dies as punishment for the sin of speaking against his people, whereas Yima is a king who dies for some sin that in the *Avesta* (as opposed to some later Persian texts) is ill defined. King Manasseh judges and executes Isaiah for contradicting the words of Moses, for which he does not deserve death, while a three-headed serpent kills Yima in the Persian tale and it is unclear whether or not his death is undeserved. The serpent rules after Yima's death, which likewise has no parallel in the rabbinic tale.

As noted, however, there are many striking similarities between later Persian versions of the story of the execution of Yima and versions of the Isaiah story found in Jewish and Christian literature. There are also significant differences, however, and it is extremely difficult to describe the precise relationship between the various versions of the story. In the *History of King*

---

41. Gnoli, "Questioni comparative sull'*Ascensione d'Isaia*," p. 125; and Bruce Lincoln, "Pahlavi kirrenidan: Traces of Iranian Creation Mythology," *Journal of the American Oriental Society* 117, no. 4 (1997): 681–85. See also Arthur Christensen, *Les typos du premier Homme et du premier Roi dans l'histoire légendaire des Iraniens* (Leiden: Brill, 1934), vol. 2, pp. 71–74. There may be reasons to conclude that the *Ascension of Isaiah* is suffused with Iranian motifs (see Russell, "*Ascensio Isaiae* and Iran," pp. 65–67), but the execution by sawing is not one of them. Compare James Darmesteter, trans., *The Zend-Avesta*, vol. 23, in The Sacred Books of the East (Oxford: Clarendon Press, 1883), p. 297. See also *Bundahishn* 31.5; and E. W. West, trans., *The Bundahis*, vol. 5, in The Sacred Books of the East (Oxford: Clarendon Press, 1880), pp. 130–31. For the dating of this compilation, see D. N. Mackenzie, "Bundahisn," in *Encyclopaedia Iranica*, ed. Ehsan Yarshater (Boston: Routledge & Kegan Paul, 1990), vol. 4, pp. 547–49.

42. Christensen, *Les typos du premier Homme et du premier Roi*, p. 75; and Gnoli, "Questioni," pp. 125–26. See also Beer, "Das Martyrium Jesajae," vol. 2, pp. 122–123.

Jamshed and the Demon,⁴³ Jamshed (the Pahlavi version of the Avestan name Yima) is deposed by the man of serpents, Zohak (the Pahlavi version of the Avestan name Azi Dahaka). Zohak seizes Jamshed's throne, and the deposed king flees into the wilderness. After one hundred years, Ahriman (the evil god of Zoroastrianism) and Zohak come upon him in the wilderness and the good god causes a tree to open itself so that Jamshed can conceal himself inside. Ahriman and Zohak fail to find him until Iblis (= the devil in Islamic thought) informs them. They order the tree to be sawn in two, and after several failures they succeed on the third day in killing Jamshed. In the tenth and eleventh centuries *Shahname,* Zahhak (an Arabicized version of the name Azi Dahaka), who had entered into a covenant with the evil god Ahriman, discovers Jamshed on the shores of the Sea of China after one hundred years of hiding, and has him sawn in two. The *Shahname*'s version, significantly, lacks the motif of the tree.⁴⁴

Tabarī, a Muslim historian who wrote in Arabic in the ninth and tenth centuries, also records a closely related tradition:

> When Zedekiah, the aforementioned king of the Jews, passed away, the affairs of the Jews became confused. There was rivalry for the kingship. They killed one another to obtain it, and though their prophet Isaiah was among them, they did not turn to him nor did they listen to him. We heard that because they acted this way, God said to Isaiah, "Rise among thy people, let me send a revelation through you." When he rose, God inspired him. The prophet admonished them and filled them with fear about the vicissitudes of fate; he enumerated God's favors and fate's vicissitudes. As Isaiah finished his speech, they turned upon him to kill him, but the prophet fled from them. A tree that he passed split open, and he entered it. But Satan caught him and seized a fringe of his garment, which he showed to the pursuers. They set a saw across the middle of the tree and sawed through it, and Isaiah was sawed in two.

According to this version, therefore, the Israelites murder the prophet during a chaos-filled interregnum.⁴⁵

It is significant that Tabarī records the detail of a piece of Isaiah's cloak remaining outside the tree and giving away his hiding place. This detail

---

43. See Larionoff, "Histoire du Roi Djemchid et des Divs," pp. 64–65.

44. Ferdowsi, *Shahnameh: The Persian Book of Kings,* trans. Dick Davis (New York: Viking, 2006), pp. 12–13. Compare Russell, "*Ascensio Isaiae* and Iran," pp. 64–65.

45. *The History of al-Tabari,* vol. 4, *The Ancient Kingdoms,* trans. and annotated by Moshe Perlmann (Albany: SUNY Press, 1987), p. 41. See also ibid., p. 120, for a strikingly similar story about Jesus.

argues in favor of the versions that record the same detail in the Bavli, since Tabarī was from modern-day Iran, near the Caspian Sea, and lived in Bagdad, in close proximity to the Babylonian rabbis.[46] It is conceivable that Tabarī knows this detail, also found in the Yerushalmi, from his travels to Syria, Palestine, and Egypt, although in general Tabarī's accounts share much more in common with Babylonian than with Palestinian rabbinic literature.[47] As noted, the Muslim version, like the Christian, blames Isaiah's murder on the whole Jewish people, a charge that the Jewish versions deny.

THE RELATIONSHIP BETWEEN THE TRADITIONS

What is the relationship between the various versions of this legend? As noted, clearly there are many striking parallels between them, but there are also many significant differences. In the *Ascension* and in the later Persian legends the murder of the protagonist is accomplished with the help of Satan, or Satan's counterpart, the evil god Ahriman. Tabarī also records this detail, but it is not in the Talmuds or in the Syriac Christian *Acts of Sharbil* from the fourth or fifth centuries. Tabarī, the Persian *History of King Jamshed and the Demon*, and both Talmuds have the protagonist fleeing into a tree, but this motif is absent from both the *Ascension of Isaiah* and the *Shahname*. As noted, the surviving evidence does not make possible the reconstruction of an ur-text. We can, however, speak of the priority of traditions that originated in the Roman East, which subsequently traveled further east to Mesopotamia and Persia. The earliest attestation of the tradition east of the Roman Empire is in the Babylonian Talmud, apparently by Rava in the mid-fourth century C.E.

It is unlikely that we can reliably posit an original version of the story that had the detail of the protagonist hiding in a tree. Several scholars, unconvincingly in my view, argue on the basis of the specification of a "wood saw" that even those versions that lack a tree presume that Isaiah took refuge in a tree, which is why he died by being sawed in half.[48] In actuality, however, there is no need to posit a tree to explain Isaiah's death by sawing, since it can easily be

---

46. While Tabarī postdates the rabbis of the Talmud by several centuries, he is a contemporary of the Babylonian geonim, who also lived in Baghdad.

47. See also chapter 5.

48. See, for example, Knibb, "Martyrdom and Ascension of Isaiah," p. 151; and Craig A. Evans, "Scripture Based Stories in the Pseudepigrapha," in *Justification and Variegated Nomism*, vol. 1, *The Complexities of Second Temple Judaism*, ed. D. A. Carson, Peter T. O'Brien, and Mark A. Seifrid (Tübingen: Mohr/Siebeck, 2001), p. 60, n. 6.

argued that the author of the *Ascension* chose this form of execution because it serves the narrative's purposes quite well. For example, perhaps the *Ascension* chose death by sawing to emphasize the execution's gradual, gruesome quality, particularly appropriate for the depraved king, in whose heart dwells Satan himself. Sawing allows for a slow, painful death by torture, with a fully conscious victim, and it permits the drama of the scene to gradually unfold and emphasizes the greatness of Isaiah and the power of the Holy Spirit.

Literary accounts of execution by sawing are not plentiful in the ancient world, but they are not so rare that we need to create a missing tree in order to account for the motif.[49] For example, *Bereshit Rabbah* 65:22 contains the following tradition:[50]

> Yosi Mishitah, when the enemies [that is, the Romans] wanted to enter[51] the Temple Mount, they said, "Let one of them [that is, one of the Jews] enter first."
>
> They said to [Yosi Mishitah], "Enter. Whatever you bring out is yours."
>
> [Yosi Mishitah] entered and brought out the golden menorah.
>
> [The Romans] said to him, "It is not the way for a commoner to use this; rather, enter a second time and whatever you bring out is yours."[52]
>
> But he did not take it upon himself [to enter again].
>
> R. Pinhas said, "[The Romans] gave him [that is, they freed him from the obligation of] taxes for three years but he did not take it upon himself [to enter again]."
>
> [Yosi Mishitah] said, "Is it not enough that I angered my God one time, that I should anger Him another time?"
>
> What did [the Romans] do to him? They placed him on a sawhorse and sawed him.[53]

---

49. See also the *Acts of Sharbil*.
50. Ed. Theodor and Albeck, pp. 741–42, based on Genesis 27:27.
51. Ibid., p. 742, reads "to cause to enter."
52. The "joke" may be that the Romans, afraid of entering the Temple themselves, convince a Jew to enter by promising him that he can keep whatever he finds. Their plan is to confiscate whatever he brings out, inventing excuses until the Temple is completely looted by the hapless Jew. Unfortunately for the Romans, the plan does not succeed and they must plunder the Temple themselves, earning God's wrath.
53. See Richard Steiner, "Semitic Names for Utensils in the Demotic Word-List from Tebtunis," *Journal of Near Eastern Studies* 59, no. 3 (2000): 192; Michael Sokoloff, *Kitei Bereshit Rabba min ha-Genizah* (Jerusalem: Ha-Akademi'ah ha-Le'umit ha-Yisre'elit le-Mada'im, 1982), p. 152; and Theodor and Albeck, *Bereshit Rabbah*, p. 742. Steiner notes that "the same term appears in a proverb in *Genesis Rabba* 70, which loosely translated means

Elsewhere, Suetonius writes that "[Caligula] cut many people ... in two with a saw,"[54] and according to the Greek version of Amos 1:3, the Damascenes sawed asunder the Gileadite women.[55]

Further evidence for the claim that the account of Isaiah's martyrdom in the *Ascension* does not presuppose the detail of Isaiah's being swallowed up in a tree is the fact that no early Christian version of the story records this detail.[56] We would expect the motif to be more widespread in the Roman East if it were such an integral part of the Christian legend. Richard Bernheimer, for example, observes that in a fifth- or sixth-century artistic rendering of the martyrdom scene in El Bagawat in Egypt, Isaiah "stands on a rack while two executioners saw him in the middle."[57] Bernheimer further notes that Potamius, a fourth-century bishop of Lisbon, describes Isaiah's being sawn in half while standing "tall and splendid" and "in the immobile state of his unshaken body," while his torturers were bent back and twisted with the strain of their work. Such steadfastness presupposes that the motion of the saw was perpendicular, and Potamius informs us that the saw entered into the skull first, before it descended into the lower parts of the body. Bernheimer observes that this portrayal "gained literary acceptance" and eventually "became part of established medieval iconography."[58]

In any event, we see from this brief and incomplete survey that the motif of execution by saw is far from unprecedented in antiquity and the early Middle Ages.[59]

'even if you put a liar on a saw horse you'll never pin him down.'" See also Theodor and Albeck, *Bereshit Rabbah*, p. 816; and Sokoloff, *Kitei Bereshit Rabba min ha-Genizah*, p. 155. Steiner, "Semitic Names for Utensils," p. 152, further notes that "the proverb implies that the torture victim was completely immobilized."

54. *The Lives of the Caesars, Caligula* 27:3, pp. 448–49.
55. See also 2 Samuel 12:31 and 1 Chronicles 20:3.
56. See Porton, "Isaiah and the Kings," pp. 713–14, n. 45.
57. See Richard Bernheimer, "The Martyrdom of Isaiah," *Art Bulletin* 34, no. 1 (1952): 21. See also V. Bock, *Archéologie de l'Egypte chrétienne* (Paris, 1901), plate 21; A. M. Schwemer, *Studien zu den frühjüdischen Prophetenlegenden Vitae Prophetarum*, 2 vols. (Tübingen: Mohr/Siebeck, 1995–96), pp. 114–15; and Jan Willem van Henten and Friedrich Avemarie, *Martyrdom and Noble Death* (London: Routledge, 2002), p. 93.
58. Bernheimer, "The Martyrdom of Isaiah."
59. For more on the motif of killing by means of a saw, see the book of Susannah, chapter 13 of the Greek version of Daniel, NSRV version, vv. 54–59; H. Engel, *Die Susanna-Erzählung: Einleitung, Übersetzung und Kommentar zum Septuagint Text und zur Theodotion-Bearbeitung* (Freiburg: Universitätsverlag-Neukirchener, 1985), pp. 123–31; and Jan Willem van Henten, "The Story of Susanna as a Pre-Rabbinic Midrash to Dan. 1:1–2," in *Variety of Forms: Dutch Studies in Midrash*, ed. A. Kuyt, E. G. L. Schriver, and N. A. van

The vicissitudes of the motif of Satan's role in bringing about the death of the protagonist are also difficult to explain according to the ur-text model. As noted, this motif is present in the *Ascension,* in Ṭabarī, and in the early medieval Persian accounts, but it is missing from both Talmudic versions and from the *Acts of Sharbil.* It is possible that the Talmuds deliberately omitted Satan because of a desire on the authors' part to emphasize human responsibility and human agency, although there are certainly many cases when the rabbis assign to Satan a pivotal role in influencing or determining the motivations of a story's human characters.[60]

CONCLUSION

As noted, the precise relationships between the various versions of the story of Isaiah's execution are too complicated to disentangle with any degree of confidence. Nevertheless, a basic chronological and geographical picture emerges, such that it is possible to state in general terms that the chronological record of the various versions of the tradition is earlier in the Roman East than in Mesopotamia and Persia. As noted, the Yerushalmi was certainly composed in Palestine, and the *Ascension* also appears to have been composed there, although western Syria has also been proposed as a possible point of origin. The *Ascension* dates from the late first or early second century C.E., and the Yerushalmi was composed between the third and the early fifth centuries. The second- and third-century Church Fathers Justin, Tertullian, and Origen attest crucially important aspects of the tradition, and they all derive from the Greek and Roman world. The Bavli and the *Acts of Sharbil* attest many of the same motifs at approximately the same time and in the same part of the world: in northern and southern Mesopotamia in approximately the fourth or fifth centuries. The Muslim and Persian compilations that contain the tradition—the *History of King Jamshed and the Demon,* Ṭabarī, and the

---

Uchelen (Amsterdam: Publications of the Juda Palache Institute, 1990), pp. 1–14. All versions of the story of Manasseh's execution of Isaiah mention a saw as the means by which the execution is accomplished, so it is possible that the saw motif gave rise to the motif of Isaiah's being swallowed up in a tree. This progression is hardly inevitable, however, and it is also possible that the "saw" motif—in combination with the motif of hiding in a tree—led to "hiding in a tree and sawed in half." See n. 17 for other references in rabbinic literature to heroes hiding in or swallowed up by trees.

60. See, for example, the collection of stories in b. Kiddushin 81a–b. It would be a simple matter to multiply examples.

Shahname—were all composed in Persia and date from approximately the ninth to eleventh centuries. All of these facts, together with the fact that the Bavli, which contains traditions as old as the oldest traditions in the Yerushalmi, was completed approximately two centuries later than the Yerushalmi, make it likely that the tradition traveled from the Roman East to Mesopotamia and Persia.

Examination of the peregrinations of a cluster of literary motifs, therefore, confirms my claim that Jewish Babylonia increasingly became part of the eastern provincial Roman world beginning in the fourth century C.E., and that Mesopotamia and the eastern Roman provinces, and the territory in between, increasingly formed a cultural unity during the period under discussion. Significantly, we found that the Babylonian Talmudic account contained similarities to the accounts in the *Ascension* and in some Church Fathers from the Roman world attested in no other ancient or medieval compilation, including the Yerushalmi. The traditions examined in this chapter thus support my claim in the introduction that attitudes or specific traditions found in compilations deriving from the Roman East made a greater impression on Babylonian than Palestinian rabbis.

Finally, we found that one cluster of motifs achieved literary expression in Christian literature in close geographical and chronological proximity: fourth- or fifth-century Christian Edessa on the one hand and fourth-century rabbinic Babylonia on the other. This fact appears to indicate linkage between the literatures of the Jewish and Christian communities of Mesopotamia in late antiquity, since no record of this precise constellation of motifs is preserved in literature from Persia or from the Greek and Roman world. It is possible that these shared motifs are indicative of contact between the two communities in Mesopotamia itself during the Sasanian period, but minimally it indicates that they inhabit a common cultural sphere. Even if the shared motifs are not the result of direct contact, they nevertheless give us an idea of literary and conceptual linkages between the two communities, although we are far from being able to say precisely how close these linkages were or how frequent the patterns encountered in this example will turn out to be.

TWO

R. Shimon bar Yohai Meets St. Bartholomew

PERIPATETIC TRADITIONS IN LATE ANTIQUE
JUDAISM AND CHRISTIANITY EAST OF SYRIA

THIS CHAPTER ATTEMPTS TO FURTHER contribute to our understanding of the extent to which the Jews and Christians east of Syria impinged upon each other. It contains a detailed analysis of one case in which the Bavli responds to religious developments in Armenia, a Christian province to the north and west of Mesopotamia, in relatively close proximity to rabbinic Babylonia. The Bavli here also responds to traditions deriving from the New Testament, but it is unclear whether the Babylonian rabbis derive the New Testament traditions from Mesopotamian Christians or from the Roman East, and it is possible, in fact, that the rabbis derived this information in an informal manner from multiple channels, for example, via overheard conversations in the marketplaces or Christian preachers on the street.

This chapter also contributes to the study of language switching from Hebrew to Aramaic within a single rabbinic composition.[1] I will argue that in the narrative complex under study, language switching not only serves the needs of the narrative, but is also, and in fact is more fundamentally, one of several indications that later editors have added material from a different source. In the present instance, they have discarded an earlier version of the narrative's conclusion and substituted a different conclusion, one that makes subtle use of Christian traditions.

A narrative, or rather a narrative chain, in b. Meilah 17a–b will provide our mode of entry into these issues. For the sake of convenience, we will refer throughout to this narrative chain as "the compilation."

A word of warning is necessary, however, before we delve into the material: Lengthy stories in the Bavli are almost always the product of editors stitching

1. See the introduction.

together several originally independent traditions, and it is often possible to discern traces of originally independent traditions in places where the editing is imperfect and incomplete. In the compilation presently before us, however, rough edges are discernible in virtually every transition from one scene to the next. On the one hand we will argue that the compilation does exhibit several significant signs of sophisticated editing, but on the other hand it is undeniable that several striking signs of incoherence remain. This incoherence may be attributable in part to unique features of tractate Meilah, traditionally and with much justification referred to as one of the "unusual" tractates of the Talmud.[2] The reader should be prepared, therefore, for a strange and obscure text that will hopefully be rendered more intelligible as a result of the accompanying commentary.[3] The text is as follows:

(A, in Hebrew): R. Matya ben Heresh asked R. Shimon ben Yohai in Rome,[4] "What is the source [of the law that] the blood of reptiles is ritually impure?"

---

2. See, for example, David Goodblatt, "The Babylonian Talmud," in *The Study of Ancient Judaism*, vol. 2, *The Palestinian and Babylonian Talmuds*, ed. Jacob Neusner (New York: Ktav, 1981), p. 304.

3. For earlier discussion of this story, see, for example, I. Levi, "La légende chrétienne de Bartholomée dans le Talmud," *Revue des études juives* 8 (1884): 200–202; and idem, "Encore un mot sur la legende de Bartalmion," *Revue des études juives* 10 (1885): 66–73; J. Halevy, "Ben-Thymelion et Bartholomée," *Revue des études juives* 10 (1885): 60–65; Wilhelm Bacher, "La légende de l'exorcisme d'un démon par Simon b. Yohaï," *Revue des études juives* 35 (1897): 285–87; Zeev Jawitz, *Sefer Toldot Yisrael*, 3rd ed. (Tel Aviv, 1936), vol. 6, p. 319; John H. Gager, "The Dialogue of Paganism with Judaism: Bar Cochba to Julian," *Hebrew Union College Annual* 45 (1973): 92–93; Amnon Linder, *Ha-Yehudim ve-ha-Yahadut be-Hukei ha-Keisarit ha-Romit* (Jerusalem: Ha-Akademiyah ha-Le'umit ha-Yisre'elit le-Mada'im, 1983), p. 73; Gafni, *Yehudei Bavel*, p. 168; Eli Yasif, "Iyunim be-Sippurei Kishuf be-Aggadat Hazal," in *Sefer Yitshak Bakon*, ed. Aharon Komem (Beer-Sheva: Ben Gurion University, 1992), pp. 46–48; idem, *The Hebrew Folktale: History, Genre, Meaning* (Bloomington: Indiana University Press, 1999), pp. 154–55 and 497; Meir Bar-Ilan, "Gerush Shedim al Yedei Rabanim: Mashehu al Isukam shel Hakhmei ha-Talmud bi-Keshafim," *Da'at* 34 (1995): 21–24; Oded Bar, "Rabbi Shimon bar Yohai u-Mekomo be-Hayei ha-Hevrah," PhD diss., Tel Aviv University, 2002; Richard Kalmin, "Rabbinic Traditions about Roman Persecutions of the Jews: A Reconsideration," *Journal of Jewish Studies* 54, no. 1 (2003): 33–38; and Yuval Harari, *Ha-Kishuf ha-Yehudi ha-Kadum: Mehkar, Shitah, Mekorot* (Jerusalem: Mosad Bialik, 2010), pp. 311–12.

4. The word "Rome" was erased from later printed editions by scribes anxious to avoid the wrath of Christian censors, and the word *ir*, "town," was inserted in its place. Present printed editions read "the town [of Rome]," with the word "Rome" in brackets. Mss Oxford 370, Florence II-I-7, Munich 95, Vatican 119, and Vatican 120 all read simply, and correctly, "in Rome." See also *Shita Mekubezet*, n. vav.

[R. Shimon] said to him, "As Scripture says,[5] 'This is what is ritually impure for you'" (Lev 11:29).

[R. Matya ben Heresh's] students said to him, "Is the son of Yohai so wise?"[6]

[R. Matya ben Heresh] said to them, "It is a ready teaching in the mouth of R. Elazar bar R. Yosi."

(B, in Hebrew): One time[7] the kingdom decreed a decree that [the Jews] shall not observe the Sabbath nor circumcise their sons, and that they must have intercourse with menstruant women. R. Reuven ben Istrobli cut his hair in the style of a pagan[8] [so they would not recognize him as a Jew] and sat with them.

He said to them, "He who has an enemy, should [the enemy] become poor or rich?"

They said to him, "[He should become] poor."

He said to them, "If so, they should not do work on the Sabbath so that they will become poor."

They said, "He spoke well."[9]

And they annulled it.

---

5. "As scripture says" translates the phrase *de-amar kera*, which is a combination of Aramaic (the particle *de*) and Hebrew *(amar kera)*. While technically this combination of Hebrew and Aramaic is an exception to the generalization that language switching in this compilation follows consistent patterns, the fact is that in a text transmitted first orally and then in writing over a period of a millennium and a half it would be surprising if we did not find occasional phenomena that were not strictly speaking explicable on purely "scientific" grounds.

6. The printed text has a mixture of Hebrew and Aramaic *(hakhim lei)*, and apparently so do *Tosafot*, s.v. *hakhim*. Rashi, s.v. *Hakhim lo Ben Yohai*, has the entire phrase in Hebrew, as does *Rav Nissim Gaon* on b. Shabbat 63a. *Pseudo-R. Gershom*, and mss Oxford 370, Florence II-I-7, Munich 95, Vatican 119, and Vatican 120 read *Hakham lo Ben Yohai*, that is, also in Hebrew.

7. The printed edition reads, "For one time" *(she-pa'am ahat)*, with a preposition, *she-*, "for," strengthening the connection between part A and the continuation. This preposition, however, is missing from all of the manuscripts, according to which the connection between part A and what follows is weaker, and it is not even apparent that there is a connection until part E. The significance of this fact will be discussed below.

8. This hairstyle, referred to in rabbinic sources as *kumi*, is forbidden in t. Shabbat 6:1 (ed. Lieberman, p. 22), *Mekhilta de-Arayot* (Sifra, ed. Weiss, p. 86a), and b. Sotah 49b, and b. Baba Kamma 83a as one of the "ways of the Amorites."

9. The text reads *Taba'ut*. In the Babylonian Talmud, this word is only found in this composition. See Jastrow, *Dictionary*, p. 516, who records several usages in Palestinian compilations. See the discussion below.

He then said to them, "He who has an enemy, should he grow weak or strong?"

They said to him, "He should grow weak."

He said to them, "If so, let them circumcise their sons on the eighth day [so that] they become weak."

They said, "He spoke well."

And they annulled it.

He then said to them, "He who has an enemy, should he increase or decrease in number?"

They said to him, "He should decrease."

[He said to them], "If so, they should not have intercourse with menstruant women."

They said, "He spoke well."

And they annulled it.

(C, in Hebrew): They recognized that he was a Jew. They reinstituted [the decrees].

(D, in Hebrew): [The Jewish victims of the persecution] said, "Who should go and annul the decrees? Let R. Shimon ben Yohai go, for he is practiced in miracles. And after him who will go? R. Elazar bar R. Yosi."

R. Yosi[10] said to them, "If father Halafta were alive could you say to him, 'Give your son to be killed?'"

R. Shimon said to them, "If father Yohai were alive could you say to him, 'Give your son to be killed?'"

(E, in Aramaic): R. Yosi said to them, "I will go.[11] I am worried that R. Shimon will punish [my son]."[12]

(F, in Aramaic): [R. Shimon] took it upon himself not to punish [R. Elazar bar R. Yosi].

---

10. R. Yosi is the father of R. Elazar bar R. Yosi.

11. The printed edition reads *Ana azlin;* ms Oxford 370 reads *Azil ana;* and ms Vatican 120 reads *Ana azilna.* See also the following note.

12. I have translated according to the printed edition. The word *azlina* (and variants), translated here as "I will go," creates the expectation that R. Yosi will go in his son's place, which does not happen, and the word is missing in mss Florence II-I-7, Munich 95, and Vatican 119. The word makes sense, however, according to those versions that contain part F. See the discussion below.

Nevertheless, he punished him.[13]

(G, in Hebrew): When [R. Shimon and R. Elazar bar R. Yosi] walked along the road, this question was asked in their presence: 'What is the source [of the law that] the blood of a reptile is ritually impure?'"

R. Elazar bar R. Yosi twisted his mouth and said, "'This is what is ritually pure for you'" (Lev 11:29).

R. Shimon said to him, "From the twisting of your lips it is evident that you are a disciple of the wise *(talmid hakham)*. The son will not return to the father."[14]

Ben Thalamion[15] came out toward him.

[Ben Thalamion said], "Do you [plural] want me to go with you [plural]?"

R. Shimon cried and said, "An angel joined up with the maidservant of my father[16] three times, but I, not [even] one time. Nevertheless, let the miracle come."

---

13. Part F is found in ms Oxford 370 and Vatican 120. Part F, which mentions R. Shimon's promise not to harm R. Elazar bar R. Yosi, explains why R. Yosi let his son go on the journey despite his fear that R. Shimon would punish him. The alternative reading is (E, in Aramaic): R. Yosi said to them, "I am worried that R. Shimon will punish my son." This version lacks the phrase "I will go" in part E, and it also lacks part F entirely.

14. I have translated this passage according to the reading of *Rashi*, s.v. *Kibel alav; Tosafot*, s.v. *Al yahazor ha-ben ezel aviv; Pseudo-R. Gershom;* and mss Florence II-I-7, Munich 95, Vatican 120, and the printed edition. Ms Oxford 370 reads, "Rather *(Ela)*, the son will return in peace to the father"; and ms Vatican 119 reads, "He said to him, 'The son will return in peace to his mother.'" Without a doubt the readings of the latter two manuscripts are late scribal attempts to sanitize R. Shimon's behavior.

15. The printed text reads "Ben Thamalion," as do mss Oxford 370, Munich 95, Vatican 119, and Vatican 120. However, *Sefer Halakhot Gedolot, al pi mahadurat Venezia 308 u-she'ar defusim ve-kitvei yad;* two manuscripts of *Arukh ha-Shalem,* ed. Alexander Kohut (1878–92; Vienna: Menorah, 1926), vol. 2, p. 124 (see also Bernard Geiger, *Tosafot he-Arukh ha-Shalem* [Vienna: Alexander Kohut Memorial Foundation, 1937], pp. 95, 105); *Shitah Mekubetzet im Kuntres Acharon: Massekhet Meilah,* ed. Yaakov David Ilan (Benei Berak, Israel: Makhon Keneset ha-Rishonim, 1977), p. 106; and ms Florence II-I-7 read "Ben Thalamion" throughout. In addition, the Venice printed edition reads "Ben Thalamion" the first time the name is mentioned, and "Ben Thamalion" the next two times. If our claim is correct regarding the relationship between the Jewish and Christian traditions, the reading "Ben Thalamion" is preferable, although it is easy to see how a name might have become slightly garbled during the course of its transmission across cultural boundaries.

16. This is a reference to Hagar, the maidservant of Abraham. See the discussion of a parallel text in *Bereshit Rabbah* below.

(H, in Aramaic): [Ben Thalamion] went ahead and entered the body of the emperor's daughter. When he [singular, presumably referring to R. Shimon] arrived there, he said,

(I, in Hebrew): "Ben Thalamion, leave! Ben Thalamion, leave!"

(J, in Aramaic): And when they called to [Ben Thalamion], he came out and left.

[The emperor] said to them, "Ask for whatever you [plural] want. Enter the treasure house and take whatever you want."[17]

They found that letter [of decree]. They took it and ripped it up.

(K, in Aramaic): And this is what

(L, in Hebrew): R. Elazar bar R. Yosi said, "I saw it in Rome[18] and on it were several drops of blood."

ANALYSIS OF THE COMPILATION

Evidence of Rudimentary Editing

Several scholars have attempted to derive history from the above account's description of the Roman decrees against circumcision, Sabbath observance, and abstinence from sex with a woman who is impure by reason of menstruation. These scholars point out that the decrees against circumcision and the Sabbath are documented elsewhere in ancient literature,[19] and they claim that the "new" information supplied by this tradition is the Roman decree that Jewish men should have intercourse with women impure by reason of menstruation.

---

17. With minor variations, this is the reading of mss Oxford 370, Florence II-I-7, Munich 95, Vatican 119, and Vatican 120. The printed edition reads: "[The emperor] said to them, 'Ask for anything you want to ask for.' [The emperor] brought them into his treasure house to take whatever they wanted." See the discussion below.

18. See n. 4. We encounter the identical phenomenon here.

19. See *Mekhilta de-R. Yishmael,* ed. Horowitz and Rabin, p. 227; y. Avodah Zarah 3:1 (42c); *Vayikra Rabbah* 32:1, ed. Margaliot, p. 735; and *Kohelet Rabbah* 2:16; b. Shabbat 130a (twice); and b. Rosh Hashanah 19a (and parallel). See also t. Shabbat 15 (16): 19. In the case of circumcision, the Roman decree appears to be documented in Roman sources as well. See *Greek and Latin Authors on Jews and Judaism,* ed. Menahem Stern, 3 vols. (Jerusalem: Israel Academy of Sciences and Humanities, 1974), esp. vol. 2, p. 619 *(Scriptores Historiae Augustae),* and Stern's discussion on pp. 619–21. See also vol. 1, pp. 296, 300, 312 *(Strabo);* 415 *(Apion);* 442 *(Petronius);* 525–26 *(Martial);* and vol. 2, pp. 19, 26 *(Tacitus);* 102–3 *(Juvenal);* and 662–64 *(Rutilius Namatianus).*

To Peter Schäfer's cogent arguments against the historicity of the story's claim that the Romans coerced Jewish men to have intercourse with menstruant women, I would add that the matter of forced intercourse is mentioned only because it makes for a better story. Like Sabbath observance and circumcision, refraining from intercourse with menstruant women is a mitzvah that, using purely human logic, weakens the Jewish people. It decreases, think the storytellers, the ability of Jews to reproduce,[20] and permitting the Jews to observe this mitzvah would seem to be sound political strategy on the part of the Romans. The "joke" that the story's authors and audience share at the Romans' expense is that it is precisely by observing these mitzvot that the Jewish people keep their covenant with God and therefore guarantee their survival.

This narrative actually comprises several traditions that have been very imperfectly stitched together. The ensuing discussion attempts to show that some of these traditions originated as independent narratives, and others originated as exegetical traditions in Palestine that were "narrativized" during the course of their incorporation into the extended narrative in Bavli Meilah.

One originally independent narrative, part B above, interrupts part A, which mentions R. Shimon and R. Elazar bar R. Yosi, who are not mentioned again until part D. Part B is a self-contained unit, which ends when the Romans, tricked by R. Reuven ben Istrobli, annul the three decrees.

In part C, however, the Romans suddenly and anticlimactically recognize that R. Reuven is Jewish and reinstitute their decrees. The seams separating part B from the other sections are obvious, however, first because nothing happens to R. Reuven, who disappears from the narrative as abruptly as he first appeared.[21] In addition, in the continuation (parts C–L) there is no

---

20. It is possible, although not necessary, to understand the storytellers' logic as based on the fact that rabbinic law demands abstention from sex for seven "clean" days, that is, for a week after the woman stops menstruating, during which time it is actually possible for her to conceive.

21. It is also somewhat surprising that the Romans make no attempt to refute R. Reuven's arguments before reinstituting the decrees. They still think, apparently, that these three mitzvot weaken the Jewish people; why, then, do they prohibit them again simply because they discover that R. Reuven is Jewish? See also Aron Lezer, *Me'il Aharon* (Brooklyn: A. Lezer, 2004), s.v. *Hikiru bo she-hu Yehudi, Hehezirum*, pp. 344–45. Nevertheless, here it is possible to supply their motivation: now that they know that R. Reuven is Jewish, they also know that whatever he told them was the opposite of what they should do, without the need of specific refutations. This lacuna in the text might be a sign of imperfect editing, but it is also possible that it is a lacuna the audience can be expected to fill in on its own.

further mention of the specific Roman decrees that figure so prominently in part B. There is a nonspecific reference to "decrees" in part D and to a "letter" in part J,[22] but these references are overshadowed by (1) the complicated relationship between R. Shimon, R. Elazar bar R. Yosi, and R. Yosi, and (2) R. Shimon's encounter with Ben Thalamion. What had been a satirical story about a rabbi's cleverness in exploiting the Romans' inability to understand the importance of mitzvot becomes a brief interlude in a compilation that depicts its central character, R. Shimon, as alternatingly villainous and heroic, and resists and perhaps precludes attempts to derive from it a coherent message. On the one hand, R. Shimon commits the serious crime of failing to attribute a statement to its author (part A), and curses and almost kills R. Elazar bar R. Yosi when he feels himself insulted by what he thinks is the latter's breach of scholarly etiquette (part G). On the other hand, R. Shimon, together with R. Elazar bar R. Yosi, who inexplicably survives the curse, successfully intercedes on behalf of the Jewish people and annuls the Roman decrees rather than accepting riches from a grateful emperor.

The connection between the R. Shimon and R. Reuven stories, therefore, is clearly less than perfect. In addition, whoever joined the stories together made only the most perfunctory attempt to inject the issue of persecution into the R. Shimon story. In its early (hypothesized) context independent of the R. Reuven story, the R. Shimon story very likely followed the pattern of the narrative in b. Ta'anit 21a. According to this narrative, Nahum Ish Gamzu is chosen to bring a gift to the emperor because he is "practiced in miracles," and, like R. Shimon vis-à-vis the demon, Nahum Ish Gamzu is visited by a supernatural being (Elijah the Prophet). So impressed is the emperor by Nahum's gift that "he brought him into his treasure house" and filled his bag with jewels and precious stones.

In all probability, the R. Shimon story at an earlier stage similarly described the Jews sending R. Shimon to the emperor to win his favor by giving him a gift or performing some important service. A miracle worker must be sent because an encounter with the emperor is dangerous. Much good can result, but there is also the possibility of great misfortune should the emissary displease or offend the emperor, which in fact almost happens in the Nahum Ish Gamzu story until a miraculous intervention rescues the Jewish people from the wrath of the emperor and sends Nahum home with a vast fortune. It is likely that the R. Shimon story once ended like the

---

22. The "letter" referred to in part J contains the text of the emperor's decrees.

Nahum Ish Gamzu narrative, with the rabbis gaining access to the imperial treasury and carrying away a vast fortune. Whoever placed the story in its present context attributed to the rabbis a loftier motive. They could have asked for and received immense wealth, but all they asked for was cancelation of the evil decrees.

By positing that the R. Shimon story was originally an independent narrative, we explain the peculiar fact that in part J, the rabbis enter the emperor's treasure house and find there "the letter" containing the evil decrees. Obviously a letter of decrees has no business in a treasure house; instead, it belongs in the imperial archives. I suggest, therefore, that when the R. Shimon story was combined with the persecution narrative, it was linked only superficially to its new context. The detail of the treasure house remained; incongruously, the rabbis found there the text of the decrees rather than enormous wealth.

The composite nature of b. Meilah 17a–b is also indicated by the fact, noted above, that the character of R. Shimon is inconsistent from scene to scene. Part A criticizes him for plagiarism, for repeating without attribution a statement that R. Matya ben Heresh knows to derive from R. Elazar bar R. Yosi. Parts D–G also criticize R. Shimon, depicting him as unable to keep his word that he will not punish R. Elazar bar R. Yosi, and as ultimately cursing him: "The son will not return to his father." Some versions of Bavli Meilah lack part F,[23] according to which R. Shimon does not promise to refrain from punishing R. Elazar, but even according to these versions R. Shimon appears to be criticized for his intemperate behavior, coming perilously close to depriving a father of his beloved son, especially since the interaction between R. Shimon and R. Elazar bar R. Yosi throughout rabbinic literature reveals that the hierarchical relationship between them was ambiguous, such that R. Shimon was less than fully justified in his belief that R. Elazar bar R. Yosi should refrain from teaching in his presence.[24] R. Shimon is also criticized when he claims that the only sign of R. Elazar's wisdom is the twisting of his lips in an effort to disguise the

---

23. See n. 13.

24. There is a small amount of evidence in the vast corpus of rabbinic literature that R. Shimon is hierarchically superior to R. Elazar bar R. Yosi: see t. Gittin 1:4 (and Saul Lieberman, *Tosefta ki-Feshutah:* Seder Nashim [Jerusalem: Jewish Theological Seminary, 1973], vol. 8, pp. 785–86 [= b. Gittin 11a]); *Bereshit Rabbah* 60:8, ed. Theodor and Albeck, p. 650; and b. Berakhot 63b. In one tradition in the Bavli, however, R. Elazar bar R. Yosi is mentioned prior to R. Shimon and speaks before him (b. Shabbat 33a–b), suggesting that at least according to this one text, R. Elazar bar R. Yosi was the superior sage.

fact that he teaches Torah in the presence of his superior,[25] implying that his statement itself did not indicate his wisdom. R. Shimon's attempt to pass off the very same statement as his own gives the lie to this claim.

The interactions in Bavli Meilah, furthermore, perhaps suggest that while R. Shimon is R. Elazar's superior as a miracle worker,[26] R. Elazar bar R. Yosi is the superior Torah scholar, at least with respect to the tradition at issue in the present encounter, since R. Matya's reference to the plagiarized tradition as R. Elazar's "intellectual property" is borne out by events narrated subsequently. And while certainty on this subject is beyond our grasp, it appears that R. Elazar, unlike R. Shimon, is positively depicted as solicitous of the feelings of a fellow sage. This concern not to offend explains why he speaks with curled lips, indicative of an attempt to disguise the fact that he answers the question, an effort to make it appear as if the answer is coming from no one in particular. It bears emphasizing that R. Elazar does not introduce his quotation of Leviticus 11:39 with the formulaic "as it is said" *(she-ne'emar),* suggesting that he is not reporting a formal tradition but is merely imparting information, unlike R. Shimon, who did use this formula and made no attempt to conceal his authorship when he answered the same question with the same verse.[27]

R. Shimon the criticized figure becomes R. Shimon the comic figure later on in the compilation, when the demon, Ben Thalamion, offers to accompany the rabbis on their journey to the emperor and R. Shimon protests that even the "maidservant of my father" is accorded more honorable treatment at the hands of heaven. R. Shimon grudgingly acquiesces to the demon's help when he says, "Nevertheless, let the miracle come," providing an unexpected, ironic twist to his designation as "practiced in miracles." Ultimately, however, R. Shimon emerges as a heroic figure when he requests, and receives, as his reward the annulment of the decrees rather than personal gain. Had the story wished

---

25. As yet I have been unable to locate a usage of the phrasing "twisting of lips" *(akimat sefatayim)* that would shed light on the usage here. Elsewhere, the expression is used in halakhic discussions that deal with the issue of whether or not speech constitutes "action" in a case where action is required for halakhic consummation. Those who argue that speech is action base themselves on the fact that one "twists one's lips" when one speaks, which is a form of action.

26. And it is very likely for this reason that R. Elazar follows "after" R. Shimon on the journey to the palace: for the specific purpose of their journey, R. Shimon is the superior. In the version of the composition recorded in *Mafteah ha-Talmud le-Rav Nisim Gaon: Shabbat,* ed. David Metzger (Jerusalem: Makhon Lev Sameach, 1995), p. 22, the text reads, "And R. Elazar bar R. Yosi will go with him."

27. See Lezer, *Me'il Aharon,* s.v. *u-be-Sefer Amtahat Binyamin,* p. 355.

to present him as less heroic at this juncture, it could have depicted him asking for treasure together with the annulment of the decrees, but the story insists on the more heroic denouement. He goes from being criticized, to comic, to heroic in the span of a few brief scenes, and the motives for his transformations and the lessons they are intended to teach are difficult to discern.

The story exhibits other signs of incomplete or imperfect editing. The transition between the first installment of the R. Shimon story (part A) and the R. Reuven story (part B) is extremely abrupt. It is not at all clear what the connection is between part A and what follows, or even that there is a connection, until the account of the interaction between R. Shimon and R. Elazar bar R. Yosi in part G. Post-Talmudic copyists tried to smooth the connection by adding the preposition *she-*, "for," to part B, which serves as a signal to the reader to connect the continuation to what preceded, but this preposition is missing in all manuscripts and medieval testimonia and is clearly a late insertion.

Another strange feature of the compilation is the fact that it seems unable to decide whether or not R. Shimon killed R. Elazar bar R. Yosi. On the one hand, the narrator informs us that "Ben Thalamion came out toward him." On the other hand, Ben Thalamion says, "Do you [plural] want me to go with you [plural]." Later on, the narrator informs us that, "When he arrived there, he said, 'Ben Thalamion, leave! Ben Thalamion, leave!'" and apparently R. Shimon alone is speaking. Immediately afterward, however, the narrator informs us that, "When they [apparently R. Shimon and R. Elazar together] called to him, he came out." This uncertainty is due to the fact that R. Shimon curses R. Elazar bar R. Yosi with death, and throughout the Talmud the curse of a sage is always effective, all the more so in the present instance since the story identifies him as a miracle worker who inspires more fear than the Romans. Yet also throughout the Talmud, when a sage curses someone and the person dies as a result, the narrative routinely informs us of this fact, yet nowhere does the present narrative inform us that R. Elazar bar R. Yosi dies. Part L, furthermore, which quotes R. Elazar saying, "I saw it in Rome and on it were several drops of blood," is rendered totally incoherent unless we assume that R. Elazar somehow survived the curse, since otherwise he would have no way of knowing what was inside the emperor's treasury. The copyists, bewildered by the exception to the usual pattern, wavered from one sentence to the next.[28]

---

28. The copyists appear to have also been unnerved by the fact that after the curse, R. Elazar is not mentioned again by name in the body of the story, and it is only in an editorial comment affixed to the compilation that he is mentioned by name and given a speaking role.

Since we have no choice but to say that R. Elazar is still alive, however, we are left with a huge unanswered question: what became of R. Shimon's curse? If it was somehow reversed or rendered ineffective, the text should have informed us how this surprising reversal came about. This is such a significant lacuna in the text that it seems to me to justify the conclusion that part of the original text is missing at this point. As noted, we lack the original beginning of the R. Shimon/R. Elazar tale, since the text before us would have us believe that this tale is the continuation of the R. Reuven story, such that it is about the annulment of evil decrees, but we know that this is not the case because the R. Reuven story in part B is a self-contained unit and part C is a flimsy attempt to link the persecution story to the R. Shimon/R. Elazar tale in part D. According to this conclusion, the compilation does not supply the original reason for the rabbis' trip to visit the emperor. Since the original introduction to the R. Shimon/R. Elazar tale is missing, it is less radical to postulate that the text also does not provide us with its original conclusion.

If I am correct that the compilation's editors replaced the original conclusion with a newer conclusion, the one presently before us, we can explain why the text suddenly switches from Hebrew to Aramaic in part H. The text switches from Hebrew to Aramaic because the Aramaic portion of the text derives from a different source than the preceding Hebrew text, as is frequently the case throughout the Talmud when a new source intervenes. Prior to the concluding scene, the entire compilation is in Hebrew, with the exception of one line that is also suspect as a later addition to the Hebrew tale.

The original ending[29] of the story perhaps explained the strange coincidence of the appearance of Ben Thalamion right after R. Shimon's curse, perhaps explaining why Ben Thalamion offered to accompany R. Shimon, presumably as a substitute for the doomed R. Elazar. When R. Shimon called for a miracle, perhaps he originally called for the nullification of his curse, which he may have helped nullify by calling out, still in Hebrew: "Ben Thalamion, leave! Ben Thalamion, leave!" Alternatively, perhaps R. Shimon calls to the demon in Hebrew, in the midst of an Aramaic paragraph, since it makes sense that if one wishes to rule over a divine being, it is necessary to do so by means of words uttered in Hebrew, the language of holiness. R. Shimon's use of Hebrew, furthermore, might be in line with R. Yohanan's

---

29. Or, more precisely, an earlier version of the ending, since even this (hypothesized) earlier version is not necessarily the "original" version.

dictum in b. Shabbat 12b and b. Sotah 33a that "whoever makes a request in Aramaic, the ministering angels pay no attention to him, since the ministering angels do not understand Aramaic."[30]

Supporting the claim that the Aramaic parts of the story are later additions is the fact that the only places in the text where we find Aramaic are also the only places where we encounter additional signs of later provenance. Parts E and F, entirely in Aramaic, are evenly divided between manuscripts that read only: "R. Yosi said to them, 'I am worried that R. Shimon will punish my son,'" and those that read:

> (E, in Aramaic): R. Yosi said to them, "I will go. I am worried that R. Shimon will punish [my son]."
>
> (F, in Aramaic): [R. Shimon] took it upon himself not to punish [R. Elazar bar R. Yosi].
>
> Nevertheless, he punished him.

As noted, variations in the manuscripts and medieval testimonia are frequently a sign of later provenance,[31] increasing the likelihood that the switch from Hebrew to Aramaic is also a sign of lateness in the present context.[32]

And a section of part J, also in Aramaic, is unnecessarily wordy, another of Friedman's criteria for late provenance.[33] The text before us reads:

> (J, in Aramaic): "[The emperor] said to them, 'Ask for anything you want to ask for. Enter the treasure house and take whatever you want.'"

Given the usual verbal economy of Talmudic stories, including that of the Hebrew sections of the rest of this story, we would have expected simply:

> (J, in Aramaic): "[The emperor] said to them, 'Enter the treasure house and take whatever you want.'"

The superfluous clause "ask for anything you want to ask for," therefore, bears the signature of later provenance.

Finally, part K ("And this is what") is also in Aramaic, since it is an editorial introduction to a Hebrew statement attributed to R. Elazar several times

---

30. See Ben-Dov, "Ha-Ketivah ba-Aramit u-va-Ivrit," pp. 38–39.
31. Friedman, "Al Derekh Heker ha-Sugya," p. 30.
32. Ibid., pp. 25–26.
33. Ibid., p. 27.

in rabbinic literature, to the effect that "I saw it in Rome, and on it were several drops of blood." Parts K–L are not integral to the composition but are later editorial commentary based on the composition, which the editors indicate by phrasing part K in Aramaic.

Signs of Sophisticated Editing

Despite the fact that in several respects the compilation is a loose concatenation of poorly integrated individual scenes, it also exhibits several signs of unified editing. For example, to an extraordinary degree the text from start to finish emphasizes relationships between fathers and their children. All the references are positive, with fathers, including the Roman emperor, clearly depicted as caring deeply about their children. Further indicating the importance of this theme is the persistence with which the compilation describes the characters via their relationships to their fathers and vice versa. Already in part A, R. Shimon is referred to as "Ben Yohai" ("the son of Yohai"); in part D, R. Yosi refers to "father Halafta" and R. Shimon refers to "father Yohai"; part H refers to the "daughter of the emperor"; Hagar is referred to as "the maidservant of my father (Abraham)"; and even the demon in parts G–I is referred to as "Ben Thalamion" ("the son of Thalamion"). Along the same lines, R. Shimon's curse of R. Elazar bar R. Yosi in part G is phrased in terms of the father-son relationship ("The son will not return to the father"), and in part D, R. Yosi expresses intense concern for his son, according to some versions even offering to go on the dangerous mission in his son's place.[34] Even further, two of the three mitzvot prohibited by the Romans impact on the relationship between parents and children, between one generation and the next. Fathers are commanded to circumcise their sons, and observance of the laws of niddah, argues R. Reuven in part B, impacts on the ability of parents to reproduce. Finally, most of the references depict the relationship as fragile, with fathers on the brink of losing their children, or, in the case of the laws of niddah, of not having them to begin with.

In contrast to the relationships between parents and children, relationships between rabbis throughout the compilation are almost uniformly acrimonious. It is true that one of the most prominent features of stories in the

---

34. See, however, the discussion of manuscript variants in nn. 11–13. Our point remains the same according to the versions that do not read, "I will go," even though the expression of concern is less intense.

Talmud is the tension, competition, and conflict routinely depicted between rabbis. The pervasiveness of this theme, however, should not prevent us from appreciating its significance in this compilation, due to the stark contrast between the negative portrayal of relationships between rabbis and the highly positive depiction of relationships between parents and children, and perhaps even more so the relatively positive terms in which the text depicts relationships between Romans and Jews, and even between a demon and rabbis.

Several episodes illustrate these claims. In part A, in response to the question of his students ("Is the son of Yohai so wise?"), R. Matya ben Heresh answers that R. Shimon is not wise at all. Rather, he is guilty of passing off the learning of another rabbi as his own, an accusation confirmed in the continuation of the story (part G) and among the most serious offenses a rabbi can commit. Along the same lines, according to some versions of part D we learn that R. Yosi is more worried about how his son will fare in the company of R. Shimon than in the company of the Romans, a sentiment also borne out by events later in the story (part G). And finally, in part G, which depicts the interaction between R. Shimon and R. Elazar bar R. Yosi, we see again the abominable behavior of R. Shimon, who curses his colleague with death, in violation, according to some versions, of his explicit oath not to harm him. In addition, R. Elazar perhaps commits a serious breach of scholarly etiquette if he is indeed guilty of teaching in the presence of a superior sage.

In this compilation, furthermore, the rabbis engage in rabbinic learning only in parts A and G, where they pose a question requesting the biblical source of a halakhah and follow it up with a response. Each time they do so, they behave abominably and disaster strikes.[35] The rabbinic interaction in part A is followed immediately by the Roman persecution in part B, suggesting that the behavior of the rabbis led to divine punishment of the Jews via the action of the Romans. Along the same lines, the posing of the same question, followed by the same answer, leads to R. Shimon's curse of R. Elazar in part G, which is in turn followed immediately by the appearance of the demon, as if in direct response.

The relationships between rabbis look even worse when compared to the relationships between rabbis and Romans. The text depicts only cordial interaction between the Romans and R. Reuven, and while the Romans think R. Reuven is one of them, it is significant that the harmony between Jew and

---

35. In part D, R. Yosi and R. Shimon speak together, but they are not engaging in academic activity.

Roman contrasts starkly with the bitter animosity between rabbis. The Romans listen politely while R. Reuven speaks, approve of his arguments, and carry out his suggestions. They are not portrayed as thugs or murderers, but as reasonable people, whose Weltanschauung to be sure is different from that of the Jews, but whose perspective is portrayed sympathetically. The Romans wish to weaken their enemy, but the narrator delicately refrains from referring to this enemy by name. The audience of the story, furthermore, can be expected to supply the Jewish perspective, namely, that the performance of the prohibited mitzvot is crucially important, but the story itself only gives voice to the perspective of the Romans. Perhaps the desire of the narrator to portray harmonious relationships between the Romans and the rabbi explains why the narrator does not state explicitly that the Romans put R. Reuven to death, and perhaps we have a reason for R. Reuven's abrupt disappearance from the story. To tell us that R. Reuven was executed would fill a hole in the plot, but it would upset the picture the storyteller wishes to create of the relatively benign Roman people. The real anger and hatred in the story are expressed by the rabbis toward one another rather than by the Romans toward the Jews or vice versa. The only other Roman mentioned in the story is the emperor in the final scene, and his role is confined to expressing deep gratitude toward the sages for rescuing his daughter, and offering to fulfill their every wish.

Another unifying feature of Bavli Meilah is the motif of blood. The compilation opens and closes with blood, and blood features prominently in almost every scene. Part A opens with a question about the scriptural source for the halakhah about the blood of reptiles. In part B, two of the three prohibited mitzvot, circumcision and refraining from sex with menstruant women, directly involve blood. Part G repeats the halakhic question of part A, and the compilation's conclusion, part L, quotes R. Elazar's statement that "I saw it in Rome and on it were several drops of blood." According to Yonah Fraenkel, one of the significant characteristics of a well-constructed, artistic story is *Geschlossenheit*, "closedness," which is established by means of a motif that recurs at the beginning and end of a story and indicates clearly where it begins and ends.[36]

The appalling relationships between the rabbis also contrast with the helpful offer by the demon, Ben Thalamion, to accompany R. Shimon and R. Elazar on their journey to the emperor, apparently to assist in his own exor-

---

36. See, for example, Fraenkel, *Darkhei ha-Aggadah ve-ha-Midrash*, pp. 237 and 260.

cism.[37] Ben Thalamion, like the Romans, is depicted in surprisingly positive terms,[38] and an important point of the story, up until the sharp reversal in the final scene, appears to be the dramatic contrast between the rabbis' inability to get along with one another and the relative graciousness with which the other characters behave toward them.

THE MEILAH COMPILATION AND PARALLELS IN RABBINIC TEXTS

The authors and editors of Bavli Meilah incorporated into the text a wide array of rabbinic traditions. The ensuing discussion reviews two of the most

---

37. We should not unduly emphasize this point, however, since the Talmud's portrayal of Ben Thalamion's interaction with the rabbis is extremely brief. We should not fall victim to the surprising insistence of most Talmudic commentators, who base their interpretations of the interactions between the demon and the rabbis on post-Talmudic expansions of the Talmudic account. These scholars, apparently, were sensitive to the "gapped" character of the compilation, which was very likely an important factor in the development of these post-Talmudic expansions in the first place. To my mind, it is vital not to follow the lead of the medieval and modern commentators who "filled in" the gaps by reading into the Talmud's version the much more lavish, and in a certain sense (but only in a certain sense) much more satisfying, post-Talmudic details. See, for example, Rashi, s.v. *Ikem Piv* and *Al be-Vartei de-Keisar;* Tosafot, s.v. *Ilu* and *Amar* (and *Shitah Mekubetzet,* n. 22); *Pseudo-R. Gershom;* Levi, "Légende chrétienne de Bartholomée," pp. 200–2; Levi, "Encore un mot," pp. 66–73; Halevy, "Ben-Thymelion et Bartholomée," pp. 60–65; Bacher, "Légende de l'exorcisme," pp. 285–87; F. C. Conybeare, "Christian Demonology," *Jewish Quarterly Review* 9 (1897): 85; Yasif, *The Hebrew Folktale,* pp. 154–55; Dan Ben-Amos, *Folktales of the Jews: Tales from the Sephardic Dispersion* (Philadelphia: Jewish Publication Society, 2006), p. 246; Gideon Bohak, *Ancient Jewish Magic: A History* (Cambridge: Cambridge University Press, 2008), p. 96, n. 73; and Harari, *Ha-Kishuf ha-Yehudi,* pp. 311–12. Levi, "Légende chrétienne de Bartholomée," p. 200, n. 2, prefers the later, more expansive version in *Eyn Yaakov* because it is entirely in Hebrew. The version of the Talmud, he writes, is "an incoherent jumble of Hebrew and Aramaic." See also *Halakhot Gedolot,* ed. Ezriel Hildesheimer (Berlin, 1892), vol. 2, pp. 601–4; and *Bet ha-Midrasch,* ed. Adolph Jellinek, 3rd ed. (1853–79; Jerusalem: Wahrmann Books, 1967), part 4, pp. 117–19, and part 6, pp. 128–30. Ben-Amos, *Folktales,* pp. 246–47, however, characterizes several of the versions as late expansions of the Meilah text. Bar-Ilan, "Gerush Shedim," pp. 21–24, does not interpret the Talmudic account in light of the more expansive versions. He also observes correctly that the account in Jellinek's compilation was compiled after the Talmud's version.

38. It is important to acknowledge, however, that the portrayal of friendly, cooperative demons is not unprecedented both in world literature in general and in rabbinic literature in particular. See, for example, *Vayikra Rabbah* 24:3, ed. Margaliot, pp. 553–55; b. Berakhot 51a; and b. Pesahim 110a. See also Yasif, "Iyunim be-Sippurei-Kishuf be-Aggadat Hazal," pp. 41–42 and 46–49; and Harari, *Ha-Kishuf ha-Yehudi,* pp. 305–6 and 308–9.

important of these parallel texts, not to prove definitively that the authors and editors drew upon these specific texts, but to illustrate the kinds of traditions that probably form the background to our compilation and provide clues to its central message.

Bereshit Rabbah 60:8 preserves a particularly striking parallel:[39]

> R. Aha said, "The conversation of the slaves of the houses of the fathers is preferable to the Torah of the sons. The chapter dealing with Eliezer [the slave of Abraham] covers two or three columns [in the Torah scroll], and [his conversation] is not only recounted but repeated. But the [laws regarding the] reptile comprise the essence of Torah, and that its blood does not cause impurity like its flesh [we know] only via a superfluity of Scripture."
>
> "R. Shimon says, 'Impure *[Tamei],' 'The* impure *[ha-Tamei]'* (Lev 11:29).[40]
>
> "R. Lazar bar R. Yosi says, 'This *[Zeh],* **and** this *[ve-Zeh]'"* (Lev 11:29).[41]

The statements attributed to R. Shimon and R. Lazar bar R. Yosi (= the Bavli's R. Elazar bar R. Yosi) in *Bereshit Rabbah* are not identical to the statements attributed to them in Meilah. In Meilah they agree regarding the derivation of the law in question, and this agreement is a significant part of the engine that drives the plot, since, as noted, R. Matya ben Heresh faults R. Shimon for plagiarizing R. Elazar bar R. Yosi. In *Bereshit Rabbah,* in contrast, the two rabbis disagree over the precise scriptural superfluity that serves as the source of the law, although they agree that the superfluity is found in the opening words of Leviticus 11:29. It is easy to see how in the course of transmission the two opinions might have merged, since the difference between them is very slight, or how the opinions might have been altered slightly to fit the narrative or didactic purposes of the Bavli. What is of primary significance is the fact that we find coupled in a single tradition in *Bereshit Rabbah* two critically important building blocks of the composition in Meilah: the derivation, attributed to R. Shimon and R. Elazar bar R. Yosi, of the law regarding the impurity of the blood of reptiles, and a statement pointing out the striking fact that a slave of the patriarchs[42] was treated more honorably than two rabbis, even

---

39. Ed. Theodor and Albeck, p. 650, on Genesis 24:32. See also *Sifra Shemini Parsheta* 5:2.

40. See *Tosafot,* s.v. *vav,* on b. Menahot 51b. Apparently *Tosafot* there has a different version of R. Shimon's statement in *Bereshit Rabbah.*

41. For variants, see the notes in Theodor and Albeck, and *Arukh ha-Shalem,* ed. Kohut, s.v. *Sheretz,* vol. 8, p. 171.

42. In *Bereshit Rabbah* the slave referred to is Eliezer rather than the Bavli's Hagar, although this difference has no substantive effect on the tradition.

though the rabbis' words represent the "essence of Torah," which according to their system of values should clearly have priority.

A second motif in *Bereshit Rabbah* unmistakably makes an appearance in Bavli Meilah. I refer to a dispute between "the rabbis" *(Rabbanin)* and R. Yosi b'R. Hanina in *Bereshit Rabbah* 45:7 over the precise number of angels that Hagar encountered in the wilderness, calling to mind R. Shimon's reference in Bavli Meilah to the three times that angels appeared to "the maidservant of my father." In addition, statements by several rabbis follow in *Bereshit Rabbah*, all favorably comparing "the early ones" to "the later ones" or "the fathers" to "the sons,"[43] and these statements call to mind R. Shimon's complaint in Bavli Meilah about the superior visitation received by "the maidservant of my father." R. Hiyya, for example, states:

> Come and see what a difference there is between the early ones and the later ones. What did Manoah say to his wife? "We shall surely die for we have seen God" (Judges 13:22), while Hagar the maidservant saw five angels and she did not fear them.[44]

Bavli Meilah, therefore, in keeping with the Bavli's tendency elsewhere, constructs a narrative on the basis of nonnarrative material preserved in other contexts.[45] It will be interesting to see if comparable evidence of "narrativization" is discernible in cognate literatures in Mesopotamia or Persia in the centuries preceding the Muslim conquest, which would perhaps help us explain this difference between the Bavli and Palestinian rabbinic literature.

CHRISTIAN PARALLELS

I concluded above that a different source intervenes when the text switches from Hebrew to Aramaic in part J. This conclusion, of course, raises the

---

43. Ed. Theodor and Albeck, p. 455.

44. See also the statement attributed to R. Eliezer in *Mekhilta de-R. Yishmael Be-Shalah* 3, ed. Horowitz, p. 126; and to R. Elazar in *Mekhilta de-R. Shimon ben Yohai*, ed. Epstein, p. 78.

45. See also Joshua Levinson, "The Cultural Dignity of Narrative," in *Creation and Composition: The Contribution of the Bavli Redactors (Stammaim) to the Aggada,* ed. Jeffrey L. Rubenstein (Tübingen: Mohr/Siebeck, 2005), pp. 361–81; and Ra'anan Boustan, "The Spoils of the Jerusalem Temple at Rome and Constantinople: Jewish Counter-Geography in a Christianizing Empire," in *Antiquity in Antiquity: Jewish and Christian Pasts in the Greco-Roman World,* ed. Gregg Gardner and Kevin L. Osterloh (Tübingen: Mohr/Siebeck, 2008), pp. 354–56.

question of how the Hebrew story of the encounter between R. Shimon and R. Elazar bar R. Yosi originally ended. I suggested above a couple of possibilities, and the fact that a Bar Thalamion is depicted in *Pesikta Rabbati,* an early medieval Palestinian rabbinic compilation, as a person who loves to take oaths in order to obtain property that is not rightfully his may provide an additional clue.[46]

If we take Christian literature of late antiquity into consideration, another possible conclusion to our compilation presents itself. It appears that the rabbis shaped their portrayal of Ben Thalamion with Christian literature in mind, as shown by the fact that in early Arabic literature, the apostle Bartholomew is referred to as Ben Thalami. The form "Ben" in both rabbinic and Arabic literature, therefore, is evidently a Hebraized or Arabicized version of the Aramaic "Bar."[47] Perhaps Ben Thalamion, like his Christian namesake, the apostle Bartholomew,[48] was originally an exorcist, and when he first appeared in the Hebrew story he was offering to accompany Rabbi Shimon as a fellow exorcist on his way to the palace, in place of Rabbi Elazar,

---

46. See *Pesiqta Rabbati: A Synoptic Edition of Pesiqta Rabbati Based upon All Extant Manuscripts and the Editio Princeps,* vol. 1, ed. Rivka Ulmer (Atlanta: Scholars Press, 1997), pp. 540–41. Ms JTS 8195 and ed. Pr. 41a–b read "Bar Thalamion"; mss Parma 176, Vienna; Dropsie, and Casanata read "Bar Thamalion." See also b. Nedarim 25a, where basically the same story is told involving a "certain man" rather than Bar Thalamion. See also *Vayikra Rabbah* 6:3, ed. Margaliot, notes on p. 133. Perhaps the original (hypothesized) Hebrew story in Bavli Meilah concerned a human being, although it is difficult to determine how Ben Thalamion as he is portrayed in *Pesikta Rabbati* would advance the plot and bring it to a conclusion in Bavli Meilah. In addition, the parallel in b. Ta'anit 21a involves a supernatural being, Elijah, and based on this parallel we would also expect a supernatural being to intervene here. We should hesitate, however, to draw far-reaching conclusions on the basis of a single parallel.

47. See Giuseppe S. Assemani, *Bibliotheca Orientalis Clementino-Vaticana,* vol. 3, pt. 2 (Hildesheim: G. Olms, 2000), pp. 4–5, who quotes Mārī ibn Sulaymān (twelfth century) and 'Amr ibn Mattā (eleventh century). For the dates of these authors, see, for example, Robert G. Hoyland, *Seeing Islam as Others Saw It* (Princeton: Darwin Press, 1999), pp. 452–53, n. 251, who expresses a cautious preference for Bo Holmberg's dating of 'Amr ibn Mattā to the eleventh century, against the regnant dating of this Christian Arab author to the fourteenth century. See Bo Holmberg, "A Reconsideration of the Kitāb al-Maǧdal," *Parole de l'Orient* 18 (1993): 255–73. I thank Adam Becker for supplying me with these references. Levi, "Encore un mot," p. 66, observes that the Talmud's copyists frequently do not distinguish carefully between "ben" and "bar." In light of the Arabic parallel, however, we have no need to posit scribal carelessness.

48. See Levi, "Legendes Judeo-Chretiennes," pp. 200–2; and Levi, "Encore un mot," pp. 66–73; Halevy, "Ben-Thymelion et Bartholomée," pp. 60–65. Regarding the second-century Christian saint Abercius, who is said to have exorcised a demon from the body of the daughter of Marcus Aurelius, see Bacher, "Légende de l'exorcisme," pp. 285–87.

who was about to die because Rabbi Shimon cursed him. The Aramaic passage before us clearly envisages a demon, however, since Ben Thalamion enters the emperor's daughter and exits only when commanded by the miracle-working Rabbi Shimon.

How and when did Bartholomew, the colorless apostle who is no more than a name in the New Testament, become the subject of elaborate exorcism stories in later Christian tradition? Christian tradition identifies the apostles Bartholomew and Nathaniel, since Bartholomew is listed as an apostle after Philip in the three synoptic gospels[49] and Nathaniel is listed after Philip in the gospel of John, and John makes no mention of Bartholomew.[50] The Gospel of John's Nathaniel is a seeker of secrets, and so the Bartholomew of early Christian legend took on these same characteristics, which are already well attested in Gnostic revelatory dialogues and are fully narrativized in the fourth-century Greek composition *Questions (or Gospel) of Bartholomew* and the fourth- to ninth-century Coptic composition *Book of the Resurrection of Christ by Bartholomew, the Apostle*.[51] In the *Questions* the resurrected Christ gives Bartholomew a full lecture on demonology, but the apostle is not described as making any practical use of this knowledge.

There are two completely different accounts of Bartholomew's mission and passion in Christian literature. According to the version found in the Coptic, Arabic, and Ethiopic anthology of the *Apocryphal Acts of the Apostles*, Bartholomew's martyrdom takes place in the Egyptian oasis of al-Bahnasah, while in its Latin equivalent, erroneously attributed to the Babylonian bishop Abdias, the apostle is killed in India.[52] Interestingly, it is in *Pseudo-Abdias's*

---

49. Matthew 10:3; Mark 3:18; and Luke 6:14.

50. John 1:43–51. See *Écrits apocryphes sur les apôtres: Traduction de l'édition arménienne de Venise*, vol. 4, ed. Louis Leloir (Turnhout: Brepols, 1992), pp. 707–8; Matthias Zender, "Bartholomaeus," in *Lexicon des Mittelalters*, vol. 1 (Munich: Artemis, 1977), col. 1491; "Bartholomew," in *Oxford Dictionary of Saints*, ed. D. H. Farmer, 5th ed. (New York: Oxford University Press, 2004), p. 43; and Els Rose, *Ritual Meaning: The Apocryphal Acts and Liturgical Commemoration in the Early Medieval West, c. 500–1215* (Leiden: Brill, 2009), pp. 262–63.

51. See Dominique Alibert, M. Brossard-Dandre, and Simon Mimouni, "Actes Apocryphes des Apôtres de la collection dite du Pseudo-Abdias," in *Écrits apocryphes chrétiens*, vol. 2, ed. Pierre Geoltrain and Jean-Daniel Kaestli (Paris: Gallimard, 2005), vol. 2, p. 791; and Perluigi Piovanelli, "Bartholomew," "Bartholomew, Gospel [Questions] of," and "Bartholomew the Apostle, Book of the Resurrection of Christ by," in *The New Interpreter's Dictionary of the Bible*, ed. Katherin Doob Sakenfeld (Nashville, TN: Abingdon Press, 2006), 1:401–2.

52. The most recent edition is that of Max Bonnet, *Passio sancti Bartholomaei apostoli*, in *Acta apostolorum apocrypha* (Leipzig, 1891–1903), vol. 2.1, pp. 128–50. See the new French

text, probably compiled in France at the end of the sixth century C.E.,[53] that Bartholomew's extraordinary abilities as an exorcist are most prominent. The local deities are demons who take possession of the people, causing them sickness and curing them in exchange for sacrifices. Bartholomew appears on the scene and releases the people, including the daughter of Polymius the king, from demonic possession. Bartholomew rejects the king's grateful offer of gold and precious gifts, but instead initiates him into the mysteries of Christianity.[54] While we should be careful not to overstate the case, the parallels between the Latin Christian and the Aramaic Jewish stories are obvious.[55]

At first glance it seems improbable that there could be a relationship between *Pseudo-Abdias,* a western European tradition, and the rabbinic, Mesopotamian composition before us. Tantalizingly, Michael van Esbroeck has documented Bartholomew's importance in the Armenian Christian tradition beginning in the fourth century, that is, within the period of the

---

translation in Geoltrain and Kaestli, *Écrits apocryphes chrétiens,* vol. 2, pp. 789–808 and 873–99. For a discussion of the problems involved in working with the texts that compose this collection, and indeed whether they do compose a collection, see Rose, *Ritual Meaning,* pp. 21–22 and 28–42. On the apocryphal *Acts of Bartholomew* in particular, see Rose, *Ritual Meaning,* pp. 35 and 82–84.

53. See Alibert, Brossard-Dandre, and Mimouni, "Actes Aprocryphes d'Apôtres," in Geoltrain and Kaestli, *Écrits apocryphes chrétiens,* vol. 2, pp. 740–41; Rose, *Ritual Meaning,* pp. 21 and 82–84. Richard A. Lipsius, *Die apokryphen Apostelgeschichten und Apostellegenden,* 2 vols. (1883–90; Amsterdam: APA Philo Press, 1976), vol. 2.2, p. 71; and Walter A. Elwell and Philip Wesley Comfort, *Tyndale Bible Dictionary* (Wheaton, IL: Tyndale House, 2001), p. 77, date the work to the fifth or sixth centuries.

54. *Passio Bartholomaei,* ed. Bonnet, c. 6–8 (13–21). The same basic plot outline repeats itself throughout the *Apostolic Acts.* See Michéle Brossard-Dandré, "La collection du Pseudo-Abdias: Approche narrative et coherence interne," *Apocrypha* 11 (2000): 198.

55. Levi, "Légende chrétienne de Bartholomée," pp. 200–2, was the first to associate the Christian saint with the Talmudic demon, although, as noted, he based his argument on an expanded, post-Talmudic version of the story. Halevy, "Ben-Thymelion et Bartholomée," pp. 60–65, rejected the parallel between the Christian and Jewish stories, since the atmosphere of the one story is totally unlike that of the other. Levi, "Encore un mot," pp. 68–70, in response to Halevy's critique, concludes that the Talmudic tale derives from an Indian legend, and that it took from the story of Bartholomew only the name of the protagonist and the motif of the breaking of glass upon the exit of the demon from the body of the princess (a motif that is actually only present in post-Talmudic versions of the story). Levi thus accepts Halevy's central point regarding the incompatibility of the Christian and Talmudic stories. In addition, Levi, "Encore un mot," p. 68, accepts the theory of Lipsius, *Apokryphen Apostelgeschichten und Apostellegenden,* vol. 2.2, p. 71, that *Pseudo-Abdias* derived from the Church of the East, which would explain how the Babylonian rabbis were acquainted with it. Lipsius's theory, however, is no longer accepted by scholars. See Rose, *Ritual Memory,* p. 83, n. 15.

Babylonian Talmud's final compilation, although no record in Armenian literature of his activities as an exorcist has as yet been uncovered.[56] Theoretically, the final editor of the Latin collection of the *Apocryphal Acts of the Apostles* could have had access to oral traditions or written documents originally coming from the eastern provinces of the Roman Empire, and these traditions or documents might also have been available to the Babylonian rabbis. The study of *Pseudo-Abdias*'s sources, unfortunately, is one of countless issues that have yet to be explored regarding this almost completely neglected text.

Another possibility could be suggested by the evolution of Bartholomew's character, from apostle, to seeker of secrets, to recipient of esoteric revelations, to demonologist, to exorcist, and, finally, to martyr in the Christian tradition and to demon in the rabbinic tradition. In this case, both the western, Latin story and its eastern Aramaic reinterpretation would possibly stem from an oral tradition or a written by-product of, for example, the Greek *Questions of Bartholomew*. If so, the milieu for such exchanges would probably be late antique Syria-Palestine. From there, one stream of tradition could have reached western Europe, while the other stream could have reached Mesopotamia. The phenomenon of saints or gods being transformed into demons is well documented in the history of religion,[57] and both understandings of the development of the tradition hypothesize that the rabbis transformed the Christian saint into a demon.

We avoid the necessity, however, of positing a Syrian or Palestinian "missing link" between *Pseudo-Abdias* or the *Questions of Bartholomew* on the one hand and the Bavli on the other if we say simply that the Bavli is based directly on the New Testament, which states explicitly that "Jesus gave [the twelve apostles] authority over unclean spirits, to cast them out, and to cure every disease and every sickness."[58] At first glance it is unclear why the Bavli

---

56. See Michael van Esbroeck, "La naissance du culte Barthélémy en Arménie," *Revue des études Arméniennes* 17 (1983): 171–85; and idem, "The Rise of Saint Bartholomew's Cult in Armenia from the Seventh to the Thirteenth Centuries," in *Medieval Armenian Culture*, ed. Thomas Samuelian and Michael Stone (Chico, CA: Scholars Press, 1984), pp. 161–78. According to Eusebius, *Ecclesiastical History* 5.10.2–3, Bartholomew preached in India and left there a copy of the Gospel of Matthew written "in Hebrew letters," although in late antiquity, the term "India" was geographically imprecise.

57. See, for example, Dale B. Martin, "When Did Angels Become Demons?" *Journal of Biblical Literature* 129, no. 4 (2010): 658. In addition, Zoroastrianism transformed many earlier Indo-Iranian gods into demons.

58. Matthew 10:1, 5–8. See also Mark 3:15 and 6:7 and Luke 9:1. Quotations from the New Testament are taken from the NSRV.

focused on Bartholomew, given that the New Testament tells us nothing more than his name, but it is likely that Bartholomew's prominence in Armenia beginning in the fourth century C.E. made an impression on the rabbis and influenced their choice.[59] This theory also has the advantage of positing rabbinic familiarity with a prominent motif in the New Testament, in keeping with the conclusions of several recent studies about Babylonian rabbinic knowledge of important New Testament traditions and themes.[60] The theme of the hero rescuing the emperor's sick or possessed daughter and refusing a reward is a familiar one in world folk literature, and it was perhaps added to the rabbinic compilation as a folk motif rather than incorporated into rabbinic literature from a preexisting Christian Bartholomew tradition.

SUMMARY AND CONCLUSIONS

Why do narratives in the Babylonian Talmud switch from Hebrew to Aramaic and back again? As noted in the introduction, language switching often serves, together with other criteria, as an important indication that the "original" source no longer survives and a new source has intervened. In the narrative compilation under consideration, Babylonian rabbis discarded the original conclusion, which in all likelihood had been in Hebrew like the rest of the compilation, and replaced it with a new conclusion in Aramaic. It is possible that the final scene was composed in Aramaic simply because the storytellers who created it habitually composed their literature in Aramaic, which according to all available evidence gradually replaced Hebrew as the preferred language of rabbinic discourse in the centuries immediately preceding the Muslim conquest in the seventh century C.E.

The analysis of this narrative, we argued, is one of a number of recent studies contributing to the contextualization of the Babylonian Talmud. For

---

59. Between the reign of Theodosius I (379–395 C.E.) and Justinian (527–565 C.E.), "Bartholomew was promoted to the role of palladium or symbol of divine protection for East *limes.*" Theodosiopolis, a city built by Theodosius I in western Armenia (modern Erzurum, Turkey; called Karin before it passed to Rome following the partition of Armenia between Rome and Persia in 387 C.E.), "claimed the favor of the apostle Bartholomew." See van Esbroeck, "Rise of Saint Bartholomew's Cult," p. 167. See also Gérard Garitte, *La Narratio de rebus Armeniae* (Leuven: L. Durbecq, 1952), pp. 65–67.

60. See the literature cited in n. 14 of the introductory chapter.

our purposes it is not necessary to take a stand about the precise channels through which the rabbis acquired knowledge of the New Testament and learned of religious developments in Armenia. There is no necessity, for example, of positing Babylonian rabbinic familiarity with the complete New Testament from the Roman East, with the Syriac *Diatessaron* or the *Peshita*, both of which circulated in Mesopotamia, or even with a single New Testament book. Nor is it necessary to posit direct contact between Babylonian rabbis and Armenian Christians. What is important for our purposes is (1) that the Bavli's particular preoccupation with the figure of Bartholomew illustrates the degree to which Babylonian rabbis were cognizant of religious developments among the Christian population of Armenia, and (2) that part of Bavli Meilah's inspiration was the New Testament's portrayal of the apostles as exorcists.

In light of our conclusion that the rabbis took the Christian exorcist Bartholomew and transformed him into a demon who had to be exorcised, our inability to pin down the precise nature of his character as perceived by the rabbis is frustrating, to say the least, and it stands in the way of our ability to precisely characterize the compilation's attitude toward Christianity. This ambiguity itself, however, appears significant, since it clearly does not seem to be the point of the compilation to vilify the demon and, along with him, Christianity. While we should hesitate before drawing unduly far-reaching conclusions on the basis of a single case, it is significant that for the authors of this compilation, neither Christianity nor Rome had the valence of "the enemy" par excellence. Just as the compilation's editor wants to downplay the wickedness of the Romans, so too he wishes to soft-pedal the malevolence of the demon, apparently in the interests of emphasizing, by contrast, the profound wickedness of the rabbis and their responsibility for the disasters that befall the Jewish people,[61] which paves the way for the sudden reversal at the conclusion of the narrative chain when the rabbis save the day.

Before the rabbis can bring about this salvation, however, the compilation appears to be saying that they must come to terms with the fact that "even the maidservant of my father," Hagar, was privileged to receive an encounter with the divine that was superior to that granted even to the great miracle worker

---

61. See Kalmin, *Jewish Babylonia*, pp. 43–50, for analysis of b. Gittin 55b–56a, another narrative that depicts rabbis as responsible for a disaster that befalls the Jewish people: the Roman destruction of the second Temple and the exile of the Jews from their land. See especially p. 47 there.

R. Shimon bar Yohai. R. Shimon's character development is not rendered with exquisite subtlety, and he is depicted as transforming himself from scene to scene with little or no motivation, but the lesson seems to be clear: R. Shimon must humble himself and agree to work with whatever heaven grants him, even if it means acknowledging his inferiority in the eyes of heaven compared to the most marginal of biblical characters, and all the more so to the greatest biblical heroes. This lesson is particularly clear if we read the Bavli's account of (1) the scriptural source for the impurity of reptile blood and (2) R. Shimon's encounter with Ben Thalamion, together with *Bereshit Rabbah's* complaint about the inordinate amount of space that the Torah devotes to the mundane speech of Abraham's slave versus the particle of a word the Torah made available to the rabbis to derive "the essence of Torah."

The rabbis, particularly the Babylonian rabbis in later generations, had a powerful sense of the superiority of their Torah to the Torah of Moses, criticizing their nonrabbinic contemporaries for being stupid enough to stand before a Torah scroll and not to stand before a rabbinic sage, despite the fact that the rabbi was able to interpret the Torah in a way that made it mean something different than what the text actually said: "Said Rava, 'How stupid are other people, who stand before a Torah scroll but do not stand before a great man. For in the Torah scroll it is written, "Forty lashes," but the rabbis came and reduced it by one.'"[62] Similarly, the well-known story of Moses in the study house of R. Akiba is another expression of rabbinic protest in the face of their consciousness of superiority to the heroes of the biblical past and their simultaneous awareness of their status as "second-class citizens" in the eyes of heaven.[63] In the latter story, God offers no explanation when Moses, giving voice to the rabbinic protest, wonders at the fact that God gave the Torah through him despite the fact that R. Akiba, symbolic of the greatness of the rabbis, far outstrips him in knowledge of Torah. Instead, God commands Moses to "be silent, for such is My decree," the same response He gives when Moses wonders at the unjust fate suffered by the same great R. Akiba, who suffers a gruesome death at the hands of the Romans. The mystery of the rabbis' second-class status, therefore, is as great as that of the suffering of the righteous in the eyes of the author of that story. In Meilah 17a–b as well, no justification is given, but it is seen as a reality the rabbis must come to terms

62. B. Makkot 22b.
63. B. Menahot 29b.

with and submit themselves to, thereby paving the way for redemption for the entire people.

Ultimately the narrative chain before us is not a polemic against Christianity, just as it is not a polemic against the Romans. For the editor of this compilation, the characters of the Romans and the "Christian demon" are a means to an end, to teach the rabbis something important about themselves, about a mode of behavior, an attitude of humility they need to adopt in order to bring about an end to the unfortunate fate of the Jewish people in the present era, subject to foreign power and the victim of persecution, a fate that the rabbis themselves were responsible for.

THREE

The Miracle of the Septuagint in Ancient Rabbinic and Christian Literature

THE PRESENT CHAPTER FOCUSES IN detail on a tradition of nonrabbinic origin deriving from the Roman East during the early centuries of the Common Era, which in rabbinic literature is first attested in the Bavli by the latest Babylonian rabbis. The same tradition is attested at approximately the same time in a Syriac Christian text from Mesopotamia, a parallel that perhaps provides further evidence of a cultural link between late antique rabbinic Babylonia and Christian Mesopotamia. Alternatively, perhaps this tradition independently reached the Bavli and Mesopotamian Christians at approximately the same time, and we are faced with evidence of independent contact between the Roman East on the one hand and Christian and Jewish Mesopotamia on the other. According to both scenarios, we have further support for the central claims of this book: that it is critically important to study the Bavli in light of multiple cultural contexts, and that many parallels between Mesopotamian literature and literature from the Roman East are evidence either of direct contact or of indirect contact mediated by a third source.

A *sugya* in b. Megillah 8a–9a, together with several of its most important Jewish and non-Jewish parallels, will illustrate these claims. The *sugya* opens with a Baraita quoted in contradiction to the Mishnah. According to the Mishnah, Torah scrolls can be written in any language, while according to the Baraita, a Torah scroll must be written in the Hebrew language and in Hebrew script. Several responses to the contradiction follow, but the one of interest to me here was authored either by Rav Ashi (a Babylonian rabbi from the late fourth century or early fifth) or by the anonymous editors postdating Rav Ashi, perhaps by a century or more.[1] According to this response, the

---

1. For discussion of the dating of the statement, see nn. 2–5.

Baraita that requires Hebrew refers to books of the Bible other than the five books of Moses, "and [the Baraita] follows the opinion of R. Yehudah."[2] The statement alluded to by Rav Ashi or the later editors reads as follows: "Said R. Yehudah, 'Even when our rabbis permitted Greek, they only permitted it in the case of a Torah scroll, because of the case involving Ptolemy the king.'"[3] Rav Ashi or the anonymous editors proceed to quote still another Baraita,[4] which tells the story of King Ptolemy, as follows:

> (A) As it is taught [in a Baraita]:[5] It happened that Ptolemy the king gathered seventy-two elders and put them in seventy-two houses but did not reveal to them why he gathered them.
>
> He went to each one of them and said to them, "Write for me the Torah of Moses your rabbi."

2. Ms Göttingen 3 reads "Rabbah" instead of "Rav Ashi," but mss Vatican 134, Oxford Opp. Add. Fol. 233, Columbia X 893 T 141, Munich 95, Munich 140, London-BL Harl. 5508 (400), and Cambridge-T-S F2 (2) 73 all read "Rav Ashi." In the case before us, the name "Rabbah" most likely refers to the mid-fourth-century Mahozan, because his comment is placed after that of the late-third- or early-fourth-century Pumbeditan teacher of Abaye (see b. Megillah 8b–9a), to whom Abaye responds with an objection. Even according to the reading of ms Göttingen 3, therefore, the chronological picture does not change significantly.

3. Before the statement by R. Yehudah, Tannaitic material that provides the context for his statement is quoted and is interrupted several times by anonymous editorial objections and responses. The substance of the opinion of R. Yehudah, however, is not affected by this anonymous give-and-take. It is conceivable that the words concluding Rav Ashi's statement, "and [the Baraita] follows the opinion of R. Yehudah," are an interpolation by anonymous editors who postdate Rav Ashi, but since in either case the eastern provincial Roman material in question is attested later than the fourth century, and is as late as the sixth or seventh century, this possibility has no affect on my argument. For discussion of the issue of the relatively late dating of anonymous editorial statements in the Talmud, see the introduction.

4. Once again, it makes no difference to my argument whether Rav Ashi or the anonymous editors quote the Baraita.

5. *De-Tanya* in Aramaic. Mss Oxford and BL Harl. 5508 (400) preface this word with the question, "What is it?" If this reading is correct, then the anonymous editors are apparently quoting the tradition alluded to by Rav Ashi. Ms Munich 140 reads in the margin, "The case of Ptolemy, what is it?" The body of the text then reads, "It is taught [in a Baraita]" *(Tanya)* instead of "As it is taught [in a Baraita]" *(De-Tanya)*, which is found in most versions. According to the reading of ms Munich 140 as well, Rav Ashi alludes to but does not quote the Baraita that tells the story of King Ptolemy. Ms Vatican 134, however, does not read, "As it is taught [in a Baraita]," but instead reads, "because of the case involving Ptolemy the king, who gathered seventy-two, . . . " according to which there is a smooth transition between R. Yehudah's statement and the story of King Ptolemy. According to the reading of ms Vatican 134, there is no need to posit a change of speaker, and there is a greater likelihood that Rav Ashi (rather than the anonymous editors) cites the story. See the discussion below. Ms Vatican 134, however, may reflect a later editorial attempt to smooth over the rough spots in the text.

God put counsel into the mind of each of them and all of them agreed.

(B) And they wrote to him, "God created in the beginning" (see Gen 1:1); "I will make a man in the image and in the likeness" (see Gen 1:26); "And He ceased on the sixth day and rested on the seventh day" (see Gen 2:2); "Male and female He created him," but they did not write, "He created *them*" (see Gen 5:2); "I will go down and mix up their languages" (see Gen 11:7); "And Sarah laughed to those close to her" (see Gen 18:12); "For when angry they slay an ox, and when pleased they uproot a crib" (see Gen 49:6); "And Moses took his wife and his sons and rode them on an animal that carries people" (see Ex 4:20); "And the people Israel dwelled in Egypt and in other lands for 430 years"[6] (see Ex 12:40); "And he sent the chosen ones[7] of the Israelites" (see Ex 24:5); "And He did not send forth His hand on the chosen ones[8] of the Israelites" (see Ex 24:11); "I did not take a beloved object of any one of you" (see Num 16:15); "That the Lord your God apportioned to give light to all of the nations" (see Deut 4:19); "And go and worship other gods that I did not command to worship" (see Deut 17:3); and they wrote to him, "And hairy legs,"[9] and they did not write to him, "And the *arnevet*" (see Lev 11:6 and Deut 14:7), since Ptolemy's wife's name was *Arnevet*, so that he would not say, "The Jews are mocking me by placing the name of my wife in the Torah."[10]

---

6. The printed edition reads, "400 years." Mss BL Harl. 5508 (400), Munich 140, Munich 95, Oxford, Vatican 134, and Cambridge-T-S F2 (2) 73 all read "430 years."

7. Or "the little ones." For these possible translations of *za'atutei*, see Emanuel Tov, "The Rabbinic Tradition concerning the 'Alterations' Inserted into the Greek Pentateuch and Their Relation to the Original Text of the LXX," *Journal for the Study of Judaism* 15 (1984): 13–14 and 19–20.

8. See ibid.

9. See ibid., p. 7.

10. For earlier scholarly analysis of the rabbinic traditions about the Septuagint, see, for example, Avigdor Aptowitzer, "Die rabbinischen Berichte über die Entstehung der Septuaginta," *Ha-Kedem* 2 (1908): 11–27 and 102–22; and 3 (1909): 4–17; Karlheinz Müller, "Die rabbinischen Nachrichten über die Entstehung der LXX," in *Wort, Lied und Gottespruch: Beiträge zur Septuaginta, Festschrift Josef Ziegler*, ed. Josef Schreiner (Würzburg, 1972), vol. 1, pp. 527–36; Tov, "The Rabbinic Tradition," pp. 65–89 (a revised version appeared in idem, *The Greek and Hebrew Bible: Collected Essays on the Septuagint* [Leiden: Brill, 1999], pp. 1–20); idem, "Review of G. Veltri, *Eine Tora für den König Talmai*," *Scripta Classica Israelica* 14 (1995): 178–83; Itamar Gruenwald, "Ha-Polmos be-Inyan Targum ha-Torah le-Yevanit," in *Te'udah*, vol. 4, *Mehkarim le-Mada'ei ha-Yahadut*, ed. Mordechai Friedman and Moshe Gil (Tel Aviv: University of Tel Aviv, 1986), pp. 65–78; Abraham Wasserstein, "On Donkeys, Wine and the Uses of Textual Criticism: Septuagintal Variants in Jewish Palestine," in *Ha-Yehudim ba-Olam ha-Hellenisti ve-ha-Romi: Mehkarim le-Zikhro shel Menahem Stern*, ed. Aharon Oppenheimer, Yeshayahu M. Gafni, and Daniel Schwartz (Jerusalem: Zalman Shazar Center for Jewish History, 1996), pp. 119–41; Giuseppe Veltri, *Eine Tora für den König Talmai: Untersuchungen zum Übersetzungsverständnis in der jüdisch-hellenistischen und*

I have divided the Ptolemy Baraita into two parts (A and B), since only part A is without parallel in Palestinian rabbinic compilations but has close parallels in Christian and Hellenistic Jewish sources.[11] It is likely, therefore, that this Tannaitic statement is a combination of originally independent traditions, one of which (part B) was a list of passages purportedly sent to Ptolemy that depart from the Hebrew text of the Pentateuch. The Jewish "elders" sent these passages to Ptolemy to prevent the king from taking offense at or forming mistaken impressions about the beliefs of the Jews.[12] The second originally independent tradition constituting the Baraita (part A) was apparently a story depicting the translation of the Torah of Moses into Greek as having been aided by divine inspiration (but see below).

As noted, the Ptolemy Baraita is attested in nonrabbinic traditions from the eastern Roman provinces. In rabbinic literature, this Baraita is only attested in the Bavli, introduced into the discussion as part of the later layers of Talmudic discourse. Two possibilities present themselves: either (1) the Bavli and Christian literature drew the tradition from a common source deriving from the eastern Roman provinces, or (2) Christian literature is the source of the Bavli's tradition.[13] The fact that the Bavli's account consists entirely of striking

---

rabbinischen Literatur (Tübingen: Mohr/Siebeck, 1994); idem, *Libraries, Translations, and "Canonic" Texts: The Septuagint, Aquila and Ben Sira in the Jewish and Christian Tradition* (Leiden: Brill, 2006); and Abraham Wasserstein and David J. Wasserstein, *The Legend of the Septuagint: From Classical Antiquity to Today* (Cambridge: Cambridge University Press, 2006), pp. 51–94.

11. For parallels to Part B in Palestinian rabbinic compilations, see *Mekhilta Bo, Pisha, Parashah* 14, ed. Jacob Z. Lauterbach (1933–35; Philadelphia: Jewish Publication Society, 1976), pp. 111 12; *Mekhilta Bo, Pisha, Parashah* 14, ed. Haim Shaul Horowitz and Yisrael Avraham Rabin (1931; Jerusalem: Wahrmann Books, 1960), pp. 50–51; and y. Megillah 1:8 (71d). Not surprisingly, the parallel versions of part B in the *Mekhilta*, the Yerushalmi, and Bavli are not identical, but they are easily recognizable as different versions of the same tradition. For an account of the differences, see Veltri, *Eine Tora*, pp. 22–112. Veltri greatly exaggerates the extent to which manuscript variants destabilize the tradition. He clouds the waters by including within his discussion versions and variants of the traditions found in post-Talmudic compilations such as *Tanhuma, Midrash ha-Gadol,* and the like. If we restrict ourselves to ancient versions of the tradition, that is, to the *Mekhilta*, the Yerushalmi, and the Bavli, the chaos documented by Veltri is substantially reduced, and the variants reduce themselves to matters of detail.

12. As documented by Veltri, *Eine Tora,* part B itself is probably an amalgam of originally independent traditions, but since my interest in this discussion is in part A, a source-critical analysis of part B is outside the purview of this study.

13. Compare ibid., pp. 157–62, which distinguishes sharply between the Christian and the rabbinic traditions. Certainly there are differences, but, pace Veltri, it is possible that one tradition borrowed certain elements from the other and did not incorporate other

motifs found in texts composed in the eastern Roman provinces as early as the third century C.E. makes it likely that the account reached Mesopotamia from the Roman Empire,[14] and a parallel in a Mesopotamian Christian compilation roughly contemporaneous to the Bavli raises the possibility that the tradition reached rabbinic Babylonia from the Roman East via Mesopotamian Christian literature composed in Syriac. It is unlikely that this tradition reached Mesopotamian Christians via the Babylonian rabbis since the Mesopotamian Christian tradition is almost identical to the version of *Cohortatio ad Graecos*, a third-century source from the Roman East (see below). It is also extremely unlikely that the Christian sources from the Roman East derived the tradition from the Bavli, because of the Bavli's later composition compared to the earliest attestation of the story in Christian traditions.

What are the antecedents of part A preserved in texts deriving from the Roman East?[15] The tradition has a close parallel in Philo, who wrote in Alexandria in the first half of the first century C.E. The rabbis of the Bavli might have known the tradition from any one of a number of sources dependent on Philo, two of which will be examined in detail in the ensuing discussion.[16] Philo's account is as follows:

---

elements. In a later publication, *Libraries, Translations, and "Canonic" Texts*, pp. 135–39, Veltri expresses certainty that Babylonian rabbis read Christian sources, from whom they took the peculiar element of "cells." In this later book, Veltri has no doubt that the Baraita in the Bavli is of Babylonian origin, since no Palestinian rabbinic source prior to the Bavli tells the Septuagint legend. Veltri claims further (*Libraries, Translations, and "Canonic" Texts*, pp. 138–39) that "Babylonian teachers read the legend of the Septuagint in the edition of Epiphanius of Salamis, the only Patristic source which collected all the elements the Rabbis needed with the notable exception of the number, because Epiphanius speaks of 36 and not of 72 'cells.'" Compare the discussion below. In contrast, Wasserstein and Wasserstein, *Legend of the Septuagint*, pp. xxii, 54, are inappropriately certain that the miracle story is a rabbinic invention and that the Christians borrowed the story from the rabbis.

14. Compare Wasserstein and Wasserstein, *Legend of the Septuagint*, pp. 89–94.

15. See Veltri, *Libraries, Translations, and "Canonic" Texts*, p. 31, n. 12, for references to collections of ancient accounts of the Septuagint legend. See also ibid., pp. 32–77 and 100–46. Wasserstein and Wasserstein, *Legend of the Septuagint*, pp. 63–65, believe that the Bavli's account derives from *Aristeas*, but their arguments are unconvincing.

16. *The Letter of Aristeas*, apparently composed by an Alexandrian Jew in the second century B.C.E., is the earliest extant account of the translation of the Pentateuch into Greek. See also Aristobulus, quoted in Eusebius, *Praep. Ev.* 12.12.2. For bibliographical references on the *Letter of Aristeas*, see Müller, *The First Bible of the Church*, p. 47, and the references cited in n. 4; Schürer, *History of the Jewish People in the Age of Jesus Christ*, vol. 3, pt. 1, pp. 677–87; Elias J. Bickerman, "Zur Datierung des Pseudo-Aristeas," *Zeitschrift für die neutestamentliche Wissenschaft* 20 (1930): 280–98 (reprinted, in revised form, in idem, *Studies in Jewish and Christian History* [Leiden: Brill, 1976], vol. 1, pp. 109–36); Moses Hadas, ed.

Judging [the island of Pharos] to be the most suitable place in the district, where they might find peace and tranquility and the soul could commune with the laws with none to disturb its privacy, they fixed their abode there; and, taking the sacred books, stretched them out toward heaven with the hands that held them, asking of God that they might not fail in their purpose. And He assented to their prayers.... Sitting here in seclusion, with none present save the elements of nature—earth, water, air, heaven—of whose genesis they were about to give the first sacred exposition—for the laws begin with the story of the world's creation—[and] as if divinely possessed, they proclaimed [literally "prophesied"],[17] not some one thing and some another, but all of them identical words and phrases, as though a prompter was calling out to each one individually without being seen.... If Chaldeans [that is, Hebrew speakers] have learned Greek, or Greeks Chaldean, and read both versions, the Chaldean and the translation, they regard them with awe and reverence as sisters, or rather one and the same, both in matter and words, and speak of the authors not as translators but as prophets and priests of the mysteries, whose sincerity and singleness of thought have enabled them to go hand in hand with the purest of spirits, the spirit of Moses.[18]

While the wording of the Bavli's account is unmistakably different from that of Philo, the ideas are clearly similar. Like Philo, the Bavli unambiguously speaks of the divinely inspired agreement between the translators.[19] The

---

and trans., *Aristeas to Philocrates: Letter of Aristeas* (New York: Harper, 1951), pp. 3–59; Emanuel Tov, "The Septuagint," in *Mikra: Text, Translation, Reading and Interpretation of the Hebrew Bible in Ancient Judaism and Early Christianity*. Compendia Rerum Iudaicarum ad Novum Testamentum, vol. 1, sec. 2, ed. Martin J. Mulder (Assen: Van Gorcum, 1990), p. 164; and Wasserstein and Wasserstein, *Legend of the Septuagint*, pp. 19–26. Compare Erich Gruen, *Heritage and Hellenism: The Reinvention of Jewish Tradition* (Berkeley: University of California Press, 1998), pp. 210–11. For the relationship between the accounts in Philo and *Aristeas*, see, for example, Sidney Jellicoe, *The Septuagint and Modern Study* (Oxford: Oxford University Press, 1968), pp. 39–41; Müller, *The First Bible of the Church*, p. 61; Hadas, *Aristeas to Philocrates*, pp. 21–26; and Robert Hanhart, "Fragen um die Entstehung der LXX," *Vetus Testamentum* 12 (1962): 145–47.

17. Dines, *The Septuagint*, p. 67.
18. See Philo, *De Vita Mosis* 2.36–40, translation adapted from Colson by Jennifer M. Dines, *The Septuagint* (London: T & T Clark, 2004), p. 67. See also pp. 67–69 for commentary; and Mögens Müller, *The First Bible of the Church: A Plea for the Septuagint* (Sheffield: Sheffield Academic Press, 1996), pp. 61–64; Hadas, *Aristeas to Philocrates*, p. 73; Veltri, *Libraries, Translations, and "Canonic" Texts*, pp. 37–40; and Wasserstein and Wasserstein, *Legend of the Septuagint*, pp. 35–45.
19. Wasserstein and Wasserstein, *Legend of the Septuagint*, p. 44. However, note that Philo does not explicitly say that the elders produced identical translations of the same material. Rather, he may be saying that they rendered the same Hebrew words and phrases with the identical Greek equivalents. Nevertheless, already in Philo the translation partakes of the

Bavli briefly but unambiguously describes God's direct intervention, and Philo clearly implies the same.

Philo, unlike the Bavli, does not specify the number of translators, but other western versions claim, like the Bavli, that the translation was carried out by either seventy or seventy-two men. Josephus's account, for example, vacillates between seventy and seventy-two translators. This inconsistency may not be significant, however, since the numbers in Josephus are probably modeled on the biblical account of the seventy elders who, together with Moses and Aaron, ascended Mount Sinai and beheld a vision of God just prior to the revelation of the Torah, on which several versions of the Septuagint story appear to be modeled.[20] For the same reason, the fact that some versions of the tradition specify seventy translators and others specify seventy-two likewise might not be significant.

Significantly, however, the earliest Jewish witnesses to the tradition—Aristeas, Philo, and Josephus—mention the role of the king in initiating the translation,[21] but they omit the detail of the enforced separation of the translators. On the one hand, Philo's emphasis on the translators independently arriving at the exact same words by means of divine inspiration could have led to the motif of forced separation in different houses or rooms found in the Bavli and in Christian literature from the Roman Empire beginning in the third century; on the other hand, the motif is so odd that it is unlikely to have arisen independently in more than one account.[22]

Irenaeus, bishop of Lyons in Gaul and apparently a native of Asia Minor,[23] who flourished in the third quarter of the second century, is an early Christian author who preserves most of the elements found in the Bavli's

---

miraculous and is in part the product of divine intervention. *The Letter of Aristeas* describes the elders conferring with one another to reach agreement, although *Aristeas* 307 hints that God may have played a role in the translation: "The outcome was such that in seventy-two days the business of translation was completed, just as if such a result was achieved by some deliberate design."

20. See Exodus 24:1–17 and Numbers 11:16–17; Hadas, *Aristeas to Philocrates*, pp. 71–72; Harry Orlinsky, "The Septuagint and Its Hebrew Text," in *The Cambridge History of Judaism*, vol. 3, *The Early Roman Period*, ed. W. D. Davies and Louis Finkelstein (Cambridge: Cambridge University Press, 1989), pp. 539 and 544–45; and Veltri, *Libraries, Translations, and "Canonic" Texts*, pp. 134–35.

21. Tov, "The Septuagint," p. 163; and Veltri, *Eine Tora*, p. 157.

22. Hadas, *Aristeas to Philocrates*, p. 79. Our conclusions in this chapter, however, do not depend on acceptance of this point.

23. Jellicoe, *The Septuagint and Modern Study*, p. 43; and Wasserstein and Wasserstein, *Legend of the Septuagint*, p. 101.

account. According to Irenaeus, Ptolemy separated the seventy translators to prevent collusion between them; like Philo, however, Irenaeus makes no mention of the king providing private dwellings for the translators. Irenaeus puts these motifs to Christian use, arguing for the Septuagint's superiority over competing Greek translations composed by Jews. His account is as follows:[24]

> Before the Romans established their dominion and the Macedonians still ruled Asia, Ptolemy, the son of Lagus, ... eager to supply the library in Alexandria with the most important writings of all humanity, communicated to Jerusalemites his wish to possess their writings in the Greek language. They ... sent Ptolemy seventy elders, especially learned among them in scriptural exegesis and in both languages, so that they might fulfill his wish. Since Ptolemy, fearing that they could obscure the true content of the writings by agreement, wanted to test each one, however, he separated them from one another and commanded that all should translate the same work; he did this for all the books. But when they assembled before Ptolemy, and compared their translation to one another, glory be to God, the writings were proven to be truly divine. For all had rendered the same texts with the same words and the same meanings ... so that even the pagans present acknowledged that the books had been translated by divine inspiration.[25]

Another Christian work, the *Cohortatio ad Graecos,* probably of third century provenance, features the same motifs, and is the first Christian text to mention the seventy translators' confinement in separate rooms.[26] It is thus closer still to the Bavli's version of the story:

> Ptolemy charged the attendant ministers to see that they wanted for nothing, but to keep them from communicating with each other, in order that their agreement might afford a further proof of the accuracy of the translation. When he found that the seventy men had not merely expressed the same ideas but had employed the very same phraseology, and had not so much as in a single word failed to agree with each other, ... he held the books to be divine

---

24. Irenaeus, *Against Heresies* 3.21.2–3, quoted in Eusebius, *Ecclesiastical History* 5.8.11–15. See Müller, *The First Bible of the Church,* pp. 72–73.

25. The translation is by Martin Hengel, *The Septuagint as Christian Scripture: Its Prehistory and the Problem of Its Canon* (Edinburgh: T & T Clark, 2002), pp. 38–39.

26. Jellicoe, *The Septuagint and Modern Study,* p. 44. See also Müller, *The First Bible of the Church,* p. 72; Veltri, *Libraries, Translations, and "Canonic" Texts,* pp. 44–47; Hengel, *The Septuagint as Christian Scripture,* pp. 37–38; Wasserstein and Wasserstein, *Legend of the Septuagint,* pp. 100 and 106–8. Pseudo-Justin, *Cohortatio ad Graecos,* ed. M. Marcovich, PTS 32 (Berlin: Walter de Gruyter, 1990), pp. 4–6 (= Cohor. 14 [*Opera Iustini,* 56]).

and laid them up in his library. . . . We ourselves have been in Alexandria and have seen the traces, still preserved, of the cells in the island of Pharos, and have heard the story which we tell you from the inhabitants, who have had it handed down as a tradition of their country. You may learn it from others also, and chiefly from those wise and distinguished men who have written of it, Philo and Josephus, but there are many others besides.[27]

After this time, the motif of enforced separation in different rooms or houses becomes a commonplace in works of Christian authorship.[28]

The earliest attestation of the legend of the Septuagint in Syriac Christian sources apparently dates from the latter half of the sixth century C.E. It is found in an ecclesiastical history attributed to Zacharias of Mitylene, but an anonymous monk of Amida, in Mesopotamia, composed most of the work. He completed it in 569 C.E. and also drew from other sources.[29] This account, composed in geographical proximity to the Babylonian rabbis, informs us that King Ptolemy Philadelphus assembled seventy men to translate the Holy Scriptures from Hebrew to Greek. It contains none of the miraculous elements found in the rabbinic account, however, stating only that Ptolemy was "moved by God."

The earliest version of the miracle story preserved from this part of the world is the Georgian translation of Epiphanius's *On Weights and Measures,* which may date from the seventh century and which perhaps has an even earlier background.[30] Epiphanius's version of the story also survives in an Armenian translation, although the Georgian translation appears to be ear-

---

27. The translation is by Hadas, *Aristeas to Philocrates,* p. 75. See also Müller, *The First Bible of the Church,* p. 72; and Wasserstein and Wasserstein, *Legend of the Septuagint,* pp. 106–7.

28. See Paul Wendland, ed., *Aristeae ad Philocratem epistula cum ceteris de origine versionis LXX interpretum testimoniis* (Leipzig, 1900), pp. 87–166 and 228–29; Hadas, *Aristeas to Philocrates;* Jellicoe, *The Septuagint and Modern Study,* pp. 43–47; Hanhart, "Fragen um die Entstehung der LXX," pp. 148–50; Orlinsky, "The Septuagint and Its Hebrew Text," pp. 553–54; Müller, *The First Bible of the Church,* pp. 68–94, especially the survey of literature on pp. 68–69, n. 1; and Wasserstein and Wasserstein, *Legend of the Septuagint,* pp. 95–137. The ancient Christian author cited most often is Jerome, *Prologus in Pentateucho* 1.3.29–30.

29. See F. J. Hamilton and E. W. Brooks, trans., *The Syrian Chronicle Known as That of Zachariah of Mitylene* (London: Methuen, 1899), p. 325. See also Pauline Allen, "Zachariah Scholasticus and the Historia Ecclesiastica of Evagrius Scholasticus," *Journal of Theological Studies* 31 (1980): 472; and Wasserstein and Wasserstein, *Legend of the Septuagint,* pp. 132–34.

30. *Les versions géorgiennes d'Épiphane de Chypre, traité des poids et des mesures,* ed. and trans. Michel-Jean van Esbroeck (Leuven: Peeters, 1984), vol. 2, pp. 6–7; and Wasserstein and Wasserstein, *Legend of the Septuagint,* p. 134–35.

lier.³¹ Since the Bavli was finally redacted in the sixth or seventh century (although without a doubt the Bavli contains much earlier material),³² the Georgian translation of *On Weights and Measures* might be contemporaneous with the Bavli's tradition. Epiphanius's account is close to that of the Bavli in that it describes the translators working in separate cells and inspired by God to miraculously produce identical translations (but see below). Veltri, however, goes beyond the evidence when he claims that the rabbis based their account on that of Epiphanius,³³ since the Bavli did not receive anything else we know of from Georgian sources. Also arguing against the Bavli's dependence on Epiphanius is the fact that Epiphanius refers to thirty-six pairs of translators in thirty-six cells rather than the Bavli's seventy-two houses for seventy-two translators.³⁴

Proof that the Bavli derived part A from Christian Mesopotamia may be provided by a Syriac text composed by Shahdost of Tirhan in the eighth century,³⁵ although, as noted, it is possible that the tradition independently reached Christian and Jewish sources in Mesopotamia from the Roman East at approximately the same time. Shahdost, otherwise known as Eustathius of Tarihan,³⁶ knows the version of the story from *Cohortatio ad Graecos,* since the two versions are virtually identical. Shahdost's attestation of the tradition should not be regarded as certain proof of the *earliest possible* arrival of the text to Mesopotamian Christians, but rather as attestation of the *approximate* date of its first arrival, since much material composed or transmitted during late antiquity has perished through neglect or has not yet reached the attention of scholars. It is therefore conceivable that Babylonian rabbis received the tradition from Mesopotamian Christians rather than directly from the Roman East. The fact that the account of the miracle of the Septuagint is encountered in Armenian and Georgian Christian translations

---

31. Van Esbroeck, *Les versions géorgiennes d'Épiphane de Chypre,* vol. 2, pp. 9–14; and Wasserstein and Wasserstein, *Legend of the Septuagint,* pp. 134–35.

32. See the introduction.

33. Veltri, *Libraries, Translation, and "Canonic" Texts,* pp. 138–39.

34. Ultimately, Veltri's theory of the Bavli's dependence on Epiphanius relies on too many unproven assumptions to inspire much confidence.

35. See L. Abramowski and A. E. Goodman, ed. and trans., *A Nestorian Collection of Christological Texts,* Cambridge University Library MS. Oriental 1319, 2 vols. (Cambridge: Cambridge Oriental Publications, 1972), vol. 2, p. xviii. See also Wasserstein and Wasserstein, *Legend of the Septuagint,* pp. 139–40.

36. Abramowski and Goodman, *A Nestorian Collection of Christological Texts,* vol. 2 (translation volume), p. xv, n. 2.

in this part of the world in earlier centuries is some support for the theory that Babylonian rabbis may have received it from earlier Mesopotamian Syriac Christian sources, since the tradition was clearly "in circulation" in Christian circles in this part of the world at this time.

Shahdost's version of the story is as follows:

> ... the seventy elders whom Ptolemy, the king of Egypt sent for, summoning them from Jerusalem, in order that they might translate for him the books of the prophets from Hebrew into Greek. In order that these might be free from all disturbance, and translate rapidly, he commanded that there should be built for them small lodgings corresponding to the number of them, not in Alexandria, but at (a distance of) seventy stadia, so that each one of them should complete his translation by himself alone. And it was commanded the attendants who were stationed with them that they should meet every need. They should prevent them from talking with one another—so that it should be possible that the accuracy of their translations would be manifestly known, through the conformity of their words. Now because he knew that these seventy men employed not only the (same) sense but also the (same) words, and had not deviated among themselves in a single word from the conformity of words, but had written there the same (words), and about the same matters, then he believed that the translation had been made by the power of God. And he knew that they were worthy of all honors, as men who love God. He gave instructions that they should return to their land with many gifts.[37]

The conformity between Shahdost's account and that of *Cohortatio ad Graecos* is obvious, down to incidental details. Shahdost's reference to seventy rather than thirty-five (or thirty-six) translators, furthermore, points to the *Cohortatio* rather than Epiphanius as his inspiration. He specifies the distance from Alexandria as seventy stadia rather than the seven of the *Cohortatio*, but this might be a scribal error or attestation of a different version. Finally, Shahdost mentions the translation of the books of the prophets, as opposed to the *Cohortatio*'s "certain ancient histories written in Hebrew characters," but it is obvious that Shahdost's version is an improvement on the version of the *Cohortatio* from a late antique or early medieval Christian perspective.

In analyzing the relationship between the Talmudic and the Christian traditions, it is important to note that the Bavli presents the tradition as a Baraita, that is, as a source that derives from Palestine and dates to the early

---

37. Ibid., vol. 1 (text volume), pp. 56–57; vol. 2 (translation volume), pp. 35–36.

third century or earlier. If we take seriously the tradition's status as a Baraita, then as a Palestinian rabbinic tradition it might have given rise to the Christian traditions, taking on a polemical Christian slant, and it also might have traveled from the rabbis of Palestine to the rabbis of Babylonia. On the other hand, this purported Baraita is preserved in no Palestinian rabbinic compilations but only in the Bavli, which argues against the Bavli having received this tradition from Palestinian rabbis.[38] One could argue that Palestinian rabbis were familiar with the tradition but suppressed it from their official compilations due to its importance in Christian propaganda.[39] We know that Jews produced other Greek translations of the Bible in antiquity, perhaps in part to counteract Christian claims based on the Septuagint, and these translations are attested in Palestine.[40]

In Babylonia, however, the argument might run, where there was less pressure from Christian groups, the Septuagint tradition lacked polemical bite, and Babylonian rabbis therefore had no compunction about quoting from it. On the other hand, as noted in the introduction, recent scholars have forced us to rethink the earlier scholarly tendency to characterize rabbinic Babylonia as relatively "Christian-free," making the above conjecture therefore lose much of its explanatory power.[41] In addition, the fact remains that the story is absent from Palestinian rabbinic compilations, and the burden of proof, here and throughout this book, rests on those who wish to claim that Palestinian rabbis knew it but suppressed it.

The motif of the translators' working in enforced isolation but nevertheless producing identical translations due to divine inspiration is central to Christian claims that the Septuagint is divinely inspired and therefore on a par with or superior to the Hebrew Bible. Some Christian authors explained the Septuagint's many departures from the Hebrew text as the result of Jewish tampering with the Hebrew text, resulting in the removal of prophetic references to the Christian messiah.[42] It is ironic that the Bavli preserved intact the motif of enforced separation as proof of divine inspiration,

---

38. This argument is not foolproof, however, since it is likely that *some* Baraitot only preserved in the Bavli derive from Palestinian rabbis.

39. Schürer, *History of the Jewish People*, vol. 3, pt. 1, p. 480; Wasserstein and Wasserstein, *Legend of the Septuagint*, pp. 66–67.

40. See, for example, Dines, *The Septuagint*, pp. 81–93, and the bibliography cited on pp. 106–7; Tov, "Review of Veltri," pp. 76–77; Schürer, *History of the Jewish People*, vol. 3, pt. 1, pp. 493–96.

41. See the introduction.

42. Hanhart, "Fragen um die Entstehung der LXX," pp. 149–51.

given its importance in Christian propaganda. Perhaps the Bavli did so not because of the relative lack of Christian pressure in Mesopotamia, but because this pressure had nothing to do with the Greek language. A Greek translation of the Bible played no role in the self-definition of Mesopotamian Christian communities, and therefore a tradition about the divine role in its production could be transmitted by Babylonian rabbis without fear that they were playing into the hands of their Christian adversaries.

It is also possible that the Bavli preserves the tradition because it uses its portrayal of divine inspiration in a strikingly original way. In the Bavli, where the miracle story in part A is combined with the account of the passages changed by the elders in part B, Ptolemy is perhaps not the benevolent, knowledge-seeking king he is for Philo and the *Letter of Aristeas*. Rather, for the Bavli the king's act of placing the elders in separate dwellings without explanation may have been the act of a tyrant taking prisoners, given the account of what transpires in part B. Ptolemy's request to them to "write the Torah of Moses your rabbi" is perhaps an attempt to discover if there is anything offensive, self-contradictory, or embarrassing to rabbinic belief in the Pentateuch. The text according to the Babylonian rabbis does not say that they translated the entire Pentateuch the same way,[43] but only that they translated potentially problematic verses the same way, several verses that appear to support beliefs that the rabbis found obnoxious,[44] and one verse that if translated literally would have personally insulted the king.[45] Perhaps in the Bavli we have an echo of a slant on the story found already in Irenaeus, according to whom Ptolemy separated the translators because he suspected that they might try to hide the truth contained in Scripture. In Irenaeus's account as well, therefore, we may find a precedent for the Bavli's depiction of a hostile king.

There is no unambiguous evidence, therefore, pace Veltri, that the ancient rabbis approved of the Septuagint. On the contrary, perhaps the Bavli's version of the tradition is evidence that the rabbis were not happy with it.[46] It

43. Although Ptolemy in part A does command them to "write for me the Torah of Moses your rabbi."
44. Veltri, *Libraries, Translations, and "Canonic" Texts*, pp. 138–39.
45. Hanhart, "Fragen um die Entstehung der LXX," p. 152.
46. Veltri restates his claim regarding the lack of evidence for ancient rabbinic disapproval of the Septuagint in *Libraries, Translations, and "Canonic" Texts*, p. ix. On pp. 6–7, he writes that rabbinic rejection of the Septuagint was not a reaction to its acceptance by Christianity. Rather, it was the result of the loss of the Greek language among the Jews and the disappearance of the Jewish community of Alexandria. Wasserstein, "On Donkeys,

was necessary to produce it, the Baraita might be saying, but it was not the product of divine inspiration, beyond the few texts the elders changed with the help of God to escape the wrath of the king.

I am not claiming that it is impossible to read the Bavli as glorifying the Septuagint as the product of divine inspiration.[47] In fact, it may have appealed to the Babylonian rabbis simply as a miracle story, depicting God's intervention in the affairs of His people in the distant past and in a foreign land. Rather, I am claiming that an alternative understanding is equally plausible, according to which only the specific verses changed for Ptolemy's benefit were inspired by God. The divine inspiration, according to this understanding, enabled the translators, or even the entire Jewish people, to escape harm and embarrassment at the hands of the pagan king. This interpretation makes it easy to understand why the story found a home in the Bavli, since the theme of God's rescue of the Jewish people from a would-be pagan oppressor is one that clearly would have resonated in any one of a variety of late antique settings.[48]

Avraham ibn Daud, the twelfth-century author of *Divrei Malkhei Yisrael*, interpreted the king's motives negatively, although, ultimately, God's intervention produced a happy ending:

Wine, and the Uses of Textual Criticism," pp. 122 and 125, also assumes that the Bavli account is favorable to the Septuagint. See also Wasserstein and Wasserstein, *Tradition of the Septuagint*, p. 59.

47. Apparently, the anonymous editors of this discussion in the Bavli interpret the Baraita in this fashion, but this does not obligate us to interpret it the same way. See Müller, "Die rabbinischen Nachrichten," p. 73, who explains that the Bavli's tradition describes the identical translation of ten passages, rather than of the entire Torah. The "miracle" was that they and the Jewish people were spared Ptolemy's wrath and ridicule, since they did not render literally the offensive and embarrassing passages; it was not that they produced a divinely inspired translation. Müller, "Die rabbinischen Nachrichten," p. 91, says explicitly that the Bavli's account of the divinely given agreement can be interpreted not only in the sense of the inspiration of the translation, but also as God intervening to save the seventy-two translators from Ptolemy's prison. Only in the Bavli is it said explicitly that Leviticus 11:6 was altered "so that [the king] could not say that the Jews put the name of his wife in the Torah in order to mock him." This appears to be the implication in the Yerushalmi's account, but it is not stated explicitly. See also Veltri, *Eine Tora*, pp. 16–17, who cites other scholars who interpret the tradition the same way. Veltri claims, incorrectly in my view, that these scholars interpret the Bavli's tradition through the lens of later rabbinic versions of the legend. See Veltri, *Eine Tora*, p. 160, for references to other scholars, medieval and modern, who interpreted Ptolemy's intentions as malevolent and viewed the divine inspiration as enabling the translators to free themselves from Ptolemy's compulsion.

48. Compare Wasserstein and Wasserstein, *Legend of the Septuagint*, p. 60.

The Torah was written [for Ptolemy] in Greek. His malice impelled him and he sought a quarrel with Israel. He sought a pretext in Israel's teaching to exile them from society, for "since my youth they have often distressed me, let Israel now declare" (Ps 129:1). Seventy elders wrote it down. King Ptolemy separated them from one another and lodged each one in his own house.... Come and see how He guarded them from Greece's sentence. "They have never overcome me" (Ps 129:2). King Ptolemy honored the seventy elders with great and royal gifts. He let them return, joyous and happy, and he himself rejoiced at their wisdom.[49]

Similarly, Yaaqov Emden, an eighteenth-century Dutch Talmudic commentator, also understood the king in the Bavli's story to be wicked. This understanding forces Emden to conclude that the Bavli's story differs from that of the book of *Aristeas,* which Emden knows involves a *virtuous* king:[50]

> This [story] is not dealing with Talmios Philadelpho [that is, Ptolemy Philadelphus], for it is known that he was a lover of Israel, and that he requested the well-known translation from the high priest with humility and by plying them with silver and great gifts for the holy Temple, the high priests, and for the elders [who] translated the Torah, as is well known [from] the book of *Aristeas.*

Emden thus contrasts the Ptolemy of the book of *Aristeas* with the malevolent king portrayed in the Bavli.

To conclude, this chapter has perhaps contributed to the growing body of evidence pointing to the fourth century and later as a period of the eastern provincial Romanization of Babylonia, Mesopotamia, western Persia, and eastern Syria. Alternatively, this chapter has perhaps provided additional evidence for the existence of a cultural connection between the Jewish and Christian communities of late antique Mesopotamia. Ultimately, we cannot tell (1) whether the source of the Bavli's legend is a Syriac translation of *Cohortatio ad Graecos,* or some similar work, that arrived simultaneously or virtually simultaneously in rabbinic Babylonia and Christian Mesopotamia, or (2) whether a Syriac translation of the story first reached Christian Mesopotamia and only subsequently traveled to rabbinic Babylonia.

---

49. Veltri, *Eine Tora,* pp. 246–47 (English translation of the German is mine).
50. *Hagahot ve-Hidushim al Massekhet Megillah,* found in the back of the standard printed Talmuds.

FOUR

The Demons in Solomon's Temple

THIS CHAPTER EXAMINES A TALMUDIC narrative about King Solomon and Ashmedai, king of the demons, in its eastern provincial Roman and Persian cultural context. The chapter further exemplifies our claim about the importance of Christian traditions from the Roman East as a source of the literary motifs and traditions composing the Bavli.

This study documents several substantive parallels between the *Testament of Solomon*[1] (henceforth, *TSol*) and b. Gittin 68a–b. We will argue that these parallels support our claim that traditions made their way from the eastern Roman provinces to Mesopotamia during late antiquity. In light of Sarah Schwarz's convincing claim that *TSol* qua compilation is of medieval provenance, constructed, however, out of numerous smaller, much older elements,[2] it is unlikely that the numerous parallels between *TSol* and b. Gittin 68a–b are the result of the Bavli's direct acquaintance with *TSol*.[3] It

---

1. And other significant traditions from the Roman East. For ease of expression, we begin the discussion by referring specifically to *TSol*'s relationship to Bavli Gittin, waiting until the body of the chapter to complicate matters by mentioning the other relevant literary compilations. All of the quotations from this work are from *Testament of Solomon*, trans. D. C. Duling, in *The Old Testament Pseudepigrapha*, vol. 1, *Apocalyptic Literature and Testaments*, ed. James H. Charlesworth (Garden City, NY: Doubleday, 1983), pp. 960–87. Duling translated *The Testament of Solomon*, ed. C. C. McCown (Leipzig, 1922), an eclectic text. We have made note of significant manuscript variants, where relevant, in the notes. See also the important corrections and comments on Duling's translation by H. M. Jackson, "Notes on the Testament of Solomon," *Journal for the Study of Judaism* 19 (1988): 19–60.

2. At present it is impossible to say precisely how early, but see appendix 1 at the end of the chapter.

3. Sarah Schwarz, "Building a Book of Spells: The So-Called *Testament of Solomon* Reconsidered," PhD diss., University of Pennsylvania, 2005, pp. 6–7.

is more likely that these parallels were independently incorporated into the Bavli and *TSol* from preexisting but no longer extant Jewish or Christian sources. This conclusion regarding the importance of parallels between *TSol* and Bavli Gittin does not, of course, diminish the importance of the Palestinian rabbinic traditions that undoubtedly played a significant role in the composition of the Solomon/Ashmedai tale.[4]

It is possible that not all of the parallels are evidence of a common source, since in some cases we may be dealing with common folk motifs incorporated into the two compilations independently or with the coincidental creation of the same or similar motifs by two authors working independently. For this reason, the ensuing discussion concentrates only on traditions that exhibit clusters of shared motifs that are difficult to dismiss as sheer coincidence. Parallels involving individual shared motifs, more likely the result of coincidence, are cited only in notes.

The shared motifs and traditions were not simply incorporated into the Bavli unchanged, and this chapter also examines the new composition created by the rabbis when they appropriated this material. What cultural work does this extraordinary composition perform in its new setting? It is important to emphasize that our answer to this question is independent of the issue of the points of origin of the specific traditions that compose the story. In answering this question, therefore, we will be arguing that the origin of these specific traditions in the Roman East is not the only important fact about them, since ultimately the Babylonian rabbis make use of the traditions to respond to their own situation. The literary analysis of this chapter yields precious information about Babylonian Jewish society, enabling us to make the leap from the printed page to social reality, with the help of the rich archaeological record of Babylonian magic bowls from approximately the same time and place as the Talmudic rabbis. The aspirations of Babylonian rabbis to dominate the local Jewish community motivated them to appropriate and transform literature from the Roman East (1) by portraying

---

4. See, for example, the texts cited in nn. 28 and 30. See also t. Sotah 15:1; *Pesikta de-Rav Kahana,* ed. Mandelbaum, p. 84 (= *Shir ha-Shirim Rabbah* 3:6); y. Kilayim 9:3 (= y. Ketubot 12:3 and *Kohelet Rabbah* 3:3 [see Menahem Hirshman, "Midrash Kohelet Rabbah," PhD diss., Jewish Theological Seminary, 1982, vol. 2, p. 233]); y. Sanhedrin 2:6 (20c); *Kohelet Rabbah* 2:1:5; and *Shir ha-Shirim Rabbah* 1:10:1. See also *Vayikra Rabbah* 22:4, ed. Margaliot, pp. 506–8 (= *Kohelet Rabbah* 5:8), for a close parallel to the motif of the *Shamir.* Basically the same story is told by Aelian, *On the Characteristics of Animals* I, III, 26.

Solomon as a magician who fails because he is deficient in rabbinic learning,[5] and (2) by portraying Ashmedai, king of the demons, as a rabbinized holy man. The Babylonian rabbinic authors of the story, competing with holy men and magicians for dominance in Jewish society, make no mention of Solomon's most important sins according to the Bible because of the particular messages they wish to convey. They use the figure of Solomon to teach their rabbinic audience that only rabbis, through their understanding of Scripture and rabbinic traditions and their appreciation of the limits of human authority and the appropriate boundaries between the human and the spirit worlds, are able to rid the king's palace and the human body of demonic possession,[6] and to enable human beings to live their lives free of the crippling fear of demons. The story is critical of Solomon for being a magician, for being ignorant of Torah and knowledgeable only about the behavior of demons, and for lusting for power over the spirit world and not being content to rule the earth. The narrative wants to convince its audience of rabbis and rabbis-in-training that the tools at their disposal are more powerful than those at the disposal of Solomon the magician and his latter-day disciples.

In addition, the story depicts Ashmedai as a rabbinized Jewish holy man,[7] depicting him as a Torah scholar and as conforming to the highest standards of rabbinically approved conduct. Part of the story's raison d'être is to teach its audience of rabbis and would-be rabbis, particularly those who might be drawn to the lifestyle of the solitary ascetic, of the importance of Torah study and rabbinically approved virtues. In addition, the story rabbinizes the holy man to domesticate him, to reassure its rabbinic audience of the manageable nature of the threat the holy man might pose to the rabbis in their attempt to dominate Jewish society, as long as people stay away from him to the extent possible and he is allowed to remain undisturbed on his mountaintop.

5. At times I state below that Solomon knows no Torah or is deficient in Torah learning. Such descriptions are a shorthand way of saying that Solomon knows no *rabbinic* Torah learning and is deficient as a *rabbinic* sage. Knowledge of the written Torah alone does not make Solomon a sage worthy of respect in the eyes of the rabbis, and on the contrary is one of the major reasons the rabbis deem him deserving of criticism.

6. The role of demons in causing illnesses in no way precludes the importance of physical causes in the thought world of the rabbis.

7. For further discussion of the Jewish holy man in ancient rabbinic literature, see Kalmin, "Holy Men, Rabbis, and Demonic Sages," pp. 213–49.

B. GITTIN 68A–B: THE SOLOMON/ASHMEDAI STORY

The tradition in the Bavli that forms the basis of our inquiry is a lengthy narrative about King Solomon and Ashmedai, king of the demons.[8] The story reads as follows:[9]

(I) Introduction: The Exegetical Conundrum: How Can Solomon Build the Temple without Using Iron Tools?

> (1) "I got myself male and female singers, as well as the luxuries of commoners, *shiddah ve-shiddot*"[10] (Eccl 2:8).... "*Shiddah ve-shiddot.*" Here [in Babylonia] they explain, "A male and female demon." In the west [that is, Palestine] they say, "A box." ...[11]
>
> (2) The Master said, "Here [in Babylonia] they explain, 'A male and female demon.'" What are [these demons] needed for?
>
> (3) As it is written, "When the Temple was built, only finished stones cut at the quarry were used, [so that no hammer or ax or any iron tool was heard in the Temple while it was being built]" (1 Kgs 6:7).

(II) The Rabbis Advise Solomon: He Needs to Obtain the *Shemira*.

> (4) [Solomon] said to the rabbis, "How will I do this?"
>
> (5) They said to [Solomon], "There is the *Shemira* that Moses used [to carve] the stones of the [high priest's] vest."

---

8. For earlier discussions of b. Gittin 68a–b, see, for example, Gilad Sasson, "Melekh ve-Hedyot—Yahasam shel Hazal le-Shlomo ha-Melekh," PhD diss., Bar Ilan University, 1995, pp. 225–48 (and the literature cited in n. 60, pp. 225–26); idem, "Be-Ikvot ha-Masoret al Shlomo ha-Magikan be-Sifrut Hazal," *Jewish Studies Internet Journal* 6 (2007): 37–53; Eli Yasif, *Sipur ha-Am ha-Ivri: Toldotav, Sugav u-Mashma'uto* (Jerusalem: Mosad Bialik, 1994), pp. 102–3. For an attempt to explain the link between the magical/medical cures in b. Gittin 67b–70a and the Shlomo/Ashmedai story, see Dan Levene, "'A Happy Thought of the Magicians,' the Magical *Get*," in *Shlomo: Studies in Epigraphy, Iconography, History and Archaeology in Honor of Shlomo Moussaieff*, ed. Robert Deutsch (Tel Aviv: Archaeological Center Publication, 2003), pp. 175–83.

9. I translate the text according to the printed edition, with variant readings from manuscripts indicated in the notes. The section headings, introduced by Roman numerals, are not part of the story but are my division of the story to make it easier to follow.

10. JPS translates "coffers and coffers of them." See below for the midrashic understanding of the verse.

11. See Sokoloff, *Dictionary of Jewish Babylonian Aramaic*, pp. 1132–33.

(6) [Solomon] said to [the rabbis], "Where can it be found?"[12]

(7) [The rabbis] said to [Solomon], "Bring a male and female demon and subdue them. Perhaps they know and will reveal it to you."

(III) Solomon Subdues the Demons and They Advise Him to Consult Ashmedai.

(8) [Solomon] brought a male and female demon and subdued them.

(9) [The demons] said, "We don't know. Perhaps Ashmedai king of the demons knows."

(10) [Solomon] said to [the demons], "Where is he?"

(11) They said to [Solomon], "He is on a certain mountain. He has dug a well and filled it with water and covered it with a stone and sealed it with his seal. Every day he ascends to heaven and learns the heavenly Torah lesson and descends to earth and learns the earthly Torah lesson and inspects his seal and uncovers it and drinks and covers it and seals it and leaves."

(IV) Solomon Sends Benaiah ben Jehoiada to Capture Ashmedai.

(12) [Solomon] sent Benaiah ben Jehoiada, giving him a chain on which the [divine] name was engraved, and a ring on which the [divine] name was engraved, balls of wool, and skins of wine. [Benaiah] went and dug a well underneath [the well of Ashmedai] and poured out the water and stopped it up with the balls of wool. And he dug a well above it and poured in the wine and covered it. He went up and sat in a tree. When [Ashmedai] came, he inspected his seal, uncovered it, and found it [to be] wine.

(13) [Ashmedai] said, "It is written, 'Wine is a scoffer, strong drink a blusterer; he who is muddled by them will not grow wise' (Prov 20:1); and it is written, 'Lechery, wine, and new wine destroy the mind' (Hos 4:11). I will not drink."

(14) When he became thirsty it became impossible for him [to restrain himself]. [He said, "It is written, 'Wine gladdens the heart of man' (Ps 104:15).][13] I will drink."

(15) [Ashmedai] got drunk and fell asleep. [Benaiah] came down [from the tree in which he was hiding], threw the chain over [Ashmedai], and shackled him.[14]

---

12. This line is missing in mss Munich 95, Vatican 130, and Vatican 140.
13. This line is found in *Hagadot ha-Talmud* and mss Arras and Vatican 130. See *Dikdukei Soferim:* Gittin, notes on line 49.
14. See Sokoloff, *Dictionary of Jewish Babylonian Aramaic,* p. 1160.

(16) When [Ashmedai] awoke, he struggled with the chain.

(17) [Benaiah] said to him, "The name of your Master is upon you, the name of your Master is upon you!"

(V) Ashmedai the Riddler.

(18) As [Benaiah] was bringing him along, [Ashmedai] came to a palm tree, rubbed against it, and it came down. He came to a house and knocked it down. He came to the hut of a widow; she came out and pleaded with him [to spare her hut]. He bent his body away from it and broke a bone.

(19) [Ashmedai] said, "This is as it is written, 'A gentle tongue can break a bone'" (Prov 25:15).

(20) [Ashmedai] saw a blind man lost on the road and lifted him onto the proper path. He saw a drunken man lost on the road and lifted him onto the proper path. He saw a wedding party rejoicing and he cried. He heard a man say to a shoemaker, "Make me shoes that will last for seven years," and he laughed. He saw a diviner divining and he laughed.

(VI) Ashmedai is Imprisoned in Solomon's Palace.

(21) When [Ashmedai] reached [the palace], they did not bring him in to Solomon until three days [had passed].

(22) The first day, [Ashmedai] said to them, "Why doesn't the king summon me to him?"

(23) They said to him, "[The king] has had too much to drink."

(24) [Ashmedai] took a brick and placed it on another. They went and told this to Solomon.

(25) [Solomon] said to them, "This is what [Ashmedai] said to you: 'Give [Solomon] more to drink.'"

(26) The next day, [Ashmedai] said to them, "And why doesn't the king summon me to him?"

(27) They said to [Ashmedai], "[King Solomon] has had too much to eat."

(28) [Ashmedai] took a brick off of another and placed it on the ground. They went and told this to Solomon.

(29) [Solomon] said to them, "This is what [Ashmedai] said to you: 'Withhold food from [King Solomon].'"

(VII) Ashmedai and Solomon Confront One Another.

(30) [In][15] three days, [Solomon] brought [Ashmedai] before him. [Ashmedai] took a reed and measured out four cubits and threw it in front of [Solomon].

(31) [Ashmedai] said to [Solomon], "When [you][16] die, [you][17] will have only four cubits in this world. Now you have subdued the entire world and you are not satisfied until you also subdue me?"

(32) [Solomon] said to [Ashmedai], "I don't want anything from you. I want to build the Temple and I need the *Shemira*."

(33) [Ashmedai] said to [Solomon], "I don't have it. The Prince of the sea has it, and he gives it only to the woodcock whose oath he trusts."

(34) "And what does [the woodcock] do with it?"

(35) "He brings it to a mountain where there is no cultivation and places it on the edge of the rock[18] and the mountain splits. [The woodcock] brings seeds from trees and throws them there and things grow there."

(36) (This is [the meaning of] what we translate: *nagar tura*—the carpenter of the mountain.)[19]

(VIII) Benaiah Tricks the Woodcock and Obtains the *Shemira*.

(37) They checked the nest of the woodcock [and found] its young, and they covered its nest with clear glass. When [the bird] came it wanted to enter [to reach its young] but could not. [The bird] fetched the *Shemira* and placed it upon [the glass]. [Benaiah] shouted and [the bird] dropped [the *Shemira*].

(38) [Benaiah] took it and [the bird] hanged himself, [remorseful at having failed to keep] its oath.

---

15. Ms Vatican 140 reads, "At the end of three days." Mss Munich 95, Vatican 130, Arras, Archivio Storico Communale Fr. Ebr. 21, and Haggadot ms Paris read "At the beginning of three days." The printed text reads "At the end of" in brackets. I have translated "In three days," since the phrases "At the end of" and "At the beginning of" are probably explanatory additions.

16. Literally, "that man," indirect speech employed as a euphemism.

17. See the previous note.

18. Ms Munich 95 inserts the sentence in parentheses (see immediately below) here. It is obviously out of place here, but the fact that it is found in different places in different manuscripts suggests that it is a later addition to the text. See Friedman, "Al Derekh Heker ha-Sugya," pp. 29–30. See also the following note.

19. See Lev 11:19. *Nagar tura* is an Aramaic translation of the obscure Hebrew word *dukhipat*, which JPS translates as "hoopoe." See also *Vayikra Rabbah* 22:4, ed. Margaliot, pp. 506–8 (= *Kohelet Rabbah* 5:8). The line in parentheses is present in mss T-S F1 (1)31 and Vatican 130. See also the previous note. Ms 140 reads just, "And this is what we translate," which is obviously truncated.

(IX) Ashmedai Explains His Riddles.

(39) Benaiah said to [Ashmedai], "Why, when you saw that blind man lost in the road, did you lift him onto the proper path?"

(40) [Ashmedai] said to [Benaiah], "They announced about him in heaven that he is completely righteous, and whoever does him a favor merits the world to come."

(41) [Benaiah said to Ashmedai], "And why, when you saw the drunken man lost on the road, did you lift him onto the proper path?"

(42) [Ashmedai] said to [Benaiah], "They announced about him in heaven that he is completely wicked. I did him a favor so that he would receive [the reward due to him in this] world [and thus have no merit left over in the world to come]."

(43) [Benaiah said to Ashmedai], "Why, when you saw the wedding party, did you cry?"

(44) [Ashmedai] said to [Benaiah], "The man must die within thirty days, and she must wait thirteen years for a young levir [to reach maturity, at which time he can marry her or release her from the levirate bond]."

(45) [Benaiah said to Ashmedai], "Why, when you heard the man say to the shoemaker, 'Make me shoes [that will last] seven years,' did you laugh?"

(46) [Ashmedai] said to [Benaiah], "He doesn't even have seven days [to live] and he wants shoes for seven years?"

(47) [Benaiah said to Ashmedai], "Why, when you saw the diviner divining, did you laugh?"

(48) [Ashmedai] said to [Benaiah], "Because he was sitting on the king's treasury. Let him divine what's underneath him."

(X) Ashmedai Tricks Solomon and Deposes Him.

(49) [Solomon] detained [Ashmedai] until he built the Temple.[20] One day he was standing alone.

(50) [Solomon] said to [Ashmedai], "It is written, '[God . . . is] like the *to'afot re'em*' (Num 24:8), and we explained,[21] '"Like the *to'afot*," these are the min-

---

20. Mss Vatican 130, Vatican 140, and Arras add here "at the end of the kingship of Solomon."

21. It is not entirely clear who Solomon quotes. An obvious possibility is the rabbis, but nowhere else in the story does Solomon behave like a rabbi. It is unclear, therefore, why he would include himself as one of them by using the first-person plural. Perhaps he refers to

istering angels; *"re'em,"* these are the demons.' How are you greater than us [humans]?"

(51) [Ashmedai] said to [Solomon], "Remove the chain from me and give me your ring and I will show you my greatness."

(52) [Solomon] removed the chain from him and gave him his ring.

(53) [Ashmedai] swallowed it, placed one wing in the heavens and the other wing on earth and hurled [Solomon] a distance of four hundred miles.

(54) Regarding that time Solomon said, "What good is all of the toil a man toils under the sun?" (Koh 1:3)....[22]

(55) [Solomon] went around to people's doorways. Everywhere he went he said, "I, Kohelet, was king over Israel in Jerusalem" (Koh 1:12).

(XI) The Rabbis Restore Solomon to the Throne.

(56) When [Solomon] came to the Sanhedrin, the rabbis said, "Wait a minute. A madman doesn't say only one thing. What's going on here?"

(57) [The rabbis] said to Benaiah, "Has the king summoned you to him?"

(58) [Benaiah] said, "No."

(59) [The rabbis] sent to the queens, "Has the king come to you?"

(60) [The queens] sent to [the rabbis], "Yes, he has come."

(61) [The rabbis] sent to [the queens], "Have you checked his legs?"

(62) [The queens] sent to [the rabbis], "He comes wearing socks and demands [to have sex with] [us][23] when [we][24] are [impure by reason of] menstruation, and he also demands [to have sex with] Bathsheba his mother."

(63) [The rabbis] brought Solomon and gave him a ring and a chain on which was engraved the [divine] name. When [Ashmedai] entered, he saw [Solomon] and flew away.

---

himself and his fellow magicians, who are aware that the text refers to demons and angels but need help understanding the text.

22. For commonalities, in my opinion not particularly strong, between Ashmedai's usurpation of Solomon's throne and the Assyrian "substitute king ritual," see Alexander H. Krappe, "Solomon and Ashmodai," *American Journal of Philology* 54, no. 3 (1933): 260–68; and Levene, "The Magical *Get*," p. 181, n. 27. See also Simo Parpola, "Excursus: The Substitute King Ritual," in *Letters from Assyrian Scholars to the Kings Esarhaddon and Assurbanipal* (Kevelaer: Butzon & Bercker, 1970–83), pp. xxii–xxxiv.

23. Literally, "them." See above.

24. Literally, "they."

(XII) Solomon Never Fully Recovers.

(64) And even so, [Solomon] was frightened of him. And this [is the meaning of] what is written, "There is Solomon's couch encircled by sixty warriors of the warriors of Israel, all of them trained in warfare, skilled in battle, each with sword on thigh because of terror by night" (Song of Songs 3:7–8).

(65) Rav and Shmuel; one said, "[Solomon was first] a king and [then] a commoner," and the other said, "[First] a king and [then] a commoner and [finally] a king [again]."

THE SOLOMON/ASHMEDAI STORY IN ITS PROVINCIAL ROMAN, BABYLONIAN JEWISH, AND PERSIAN CULTURAL CONTEXT

The primary goal of this section of the chapter is to show the substantial links between the Solomon/Ashmedai story in the Bavli and literature deriving from the eastern Roman provinces. We open, however, with a brief discussion of the possible relevance of Persian culture, although final conclusions must await examination of more evidence.[25]

It has been hypothesized that the form of the demon's name—Ashmedai—is of Persian origin.[26] In addition, the words for "seal" *(gushpanka)* and "socks" *(mokei)* are Persian in origin.[27]

Continuing the discussion of Persia, Rella Kushelevsky suggests that the transition from an angel in a Palestinian rabbinic version of the story[28] to a demon in Bavli Gittin is due to the fact that the Bavli wishes to teach that the

---

25. In the meantime, see the outdated discussion in McCown, *Testament of Solomon*, pp. 55–56. See also appendix 3 below for a preliminary discussion of the Mesopotamian context.

26. See Shlomo Pines, "Wrath and Creatures of Wrath in Pahlavi, Jewish and New Testament Sources," in *Irano-Judaica: Studies Relating to Jewish Contacts with Persian Culture throughout the Ages*, ed. Shaul Shaked and Amnon Netzer (Jerusalem: Ben-Zvi Institute, 1982), pp. 76–79; Shaul Shaked, "The Zoroastrian Demon of Wrath," in *Tradition and Translation: Zum Problem der interkulturellen übersetzbarkeit religiöser Phänomene*, ed. Christoph Elsas and Carsten Colpe (Berlin: Walter de Gruyter, 1994), pp. 285–89; and James R. Russell, "God Is Good: On Tobit and Iran," *Iran and the Caucasus* 5 (2001); reprinted in idem, *Armenian and Iranian Studies* (Cambridge, MA: Harvard University Department of Near Eastern Languages and Literatures, 2004), pp. 1131–33.

27. *Arukh ha-Shalem*, ed. Kohut, vol. 2, p. 383; and vol. 5, pp. 222–23.

28. See *Pesikta de-Rav Kahana*, ed. Mandelbaum, pp. 385–86.

demon is subordinate to God, in response to Persian dualism.²⁹ This intriguing theory lacks supporting evidence, however, and the well-attested motif of demons contributing to the construction of the Temple in *TSol*, the *Testimony of Truth*, and Palestinian rabbinic sources,³⁰ all texts deriving from the Roman East, removes the need to speak of the "transition" to a demon in the Bavli.

Persian literature may be the source for the Bavli's motifs of (1) the pretender to the throne taking the place of the legitimate king, and (2) the king's wives playing a critical role in the discovery of the masquerade (see below). Just as plausibly, however, these parallels might be the stuff of folklore rather than an indication of cultural borrowing.

The Persian text in question is the Behistun inscription of Darius the Great (521–486 B.C.E.), which tells the story of a magian named Gaumata who usurps the throne of Iran. Cambyses (559–529 B.C.E.) has a brother, Bardiya, whom he secretly kills. Gaumata finds out about the killing, passes himself off as Bardiya, and takes the throne while Cambyses is at war in Egypt. The imposter fools everyone, even the royal family, but the queen eventually identifies Gaumata by the fact that he has no ears. She informs on him to Darius, who kills the usurper and takes over the Iranian throne.³¹

Both the Persian and the Talmudic traditions, therefore, feature a pretender to the throne who has a bodily defect that distinguishes him from the true king. The traditions differ, however, since according to the Ashmedai story the bodily defect is hidden by socks and according to the Persian story it enables the queen to discover the ruse.³² In the Ashmedai story Solomon's wives do not unmask the imposter, but the information they provide helps the rabbis solve the mystery.³³ This difference between the Persian and the

---

29. Rella Kushelevsky, "Pe'arim bein Girsa'ot ke-Mekhonenei Teima," in *Ma'aseh Sipur: Mehkarim be-Siporet ha-Yehudit Mugashim le-Yoav Elstein* (Ramat Gan: Bar Ilan University Press, 2006), p. 225.

30. See *Shir ha-Shirim Rabbah* 1:5, p. 8; and *Pesikta Rabbati* 6:7.

31. R. G. Kent, *Old Persian: Grammar, Texts, Lexicon* (New Haven: American Oriental Society, 1953). See the discussion of this passage by M. Omidsala, "Of the Usurper's Ears, the Demon's Toes, and the Ayatollah's Fingers," *Psychoanalytic Study of Society* 18 (1993): 107. Krappe, "Solomon and Ashmodai," pp. 261–68, and Russell, "God Is Good," p. 1132, think the Talmud's Ashmedai story is based upon Herodotus's version of the Gaumata story (*The History* III.68–69), although their arguments fail to convince.

32. In the Ashmedai story, it is not stated explicitly that Ashmedai assumes the form of Solomon, although that is certainly implied.

33. Compare Krappe, "Solomon and Ashmodai," p. 265; and Omidsala, "Of the Usurper's Ears," p. 110.

Talmudic accounts might reflect an editorial decision on the part of the Bavli's storytellers, in line with the Babylonian rabbis' well-documented penchant for emphasizing the importance of rabbis.³⁴

The commonalities between the Persian and the Talmudic stories are suggestive, but they are not necessarily indicative of a cultural connection between the Bavli and Persian literature, since they might be general enough to be explicable as diverse workings out of a small collection of folk motifs.³⁵ A Persian cultural connection with the Babylonian Talmudic story should not be excluded in this context, therefore, but neither should it be considered proven.

The motif of the demons controlled by the king and put to work by him on building projects is paralleled in Persian literature in the *Shahname*, which describes vanquished demons that perform tasks for King Jamshed, who after the conversion of Iran to Islam was identified with Solomon.³⁶ The *Shahname* portrays demons making bricks and constructing King Jamshed's throne as well as buildings such as palaces, bathhouses, and temples, but not the Temple of Jerusalem.³⁷ We would not expect the *Shahname* to focus on the Jerusalem Temple, however, given the work's focus on Zoroastrianism.

As noted, the *Shahname* was composed well after the final redaction of the Bavli, although it contains much material from earlier centuries. It is likely, however, that the *Shahname* has no bearing on our discussion of the origin of the Ashmedai traditions in the Bavli, given the well-attested nature of these motifs in early traditions from the Roman East (see below), which lessens the likelihood that Persia was their place of origin.

---

34. See Kalmin, *Jewish Babylonia*, pp. 37–60.

35. See Stith Thompson, *Motif-Index of Folk Literature* (Bloomington: Indiana University Press, 1966), vol. 4, Folk motif K1934.1—"Imposter [magician, demon] takes the place of the king"; vol. 5, Folk motif L411—"Proud king displaced by angel"; Yasif, *Sipur ha-Am ha-Ivri*, pp. 102–3. See also Kushelevsky, "Pe'arim," pp. 223–24.

36. Omidsala, "Of the Usurper's Ears," p. 109, n. 1.

37. For a detailed discussion of the accounts in the *Shahname*, see M. Omidsala, "Jamsid," in *Encyclopedia Iranica*, section 2, Jamsid, www.iranicaonline.org/articles/jamsid-ii; and Prods O. Skjaervo, "Jamsid-i," in *Encyclopedia Iranica*, www.iranicaonline.org/articles/jamsid-i; and "DIV," in *Encyclopedia Iranica*, www.iranicaonline.org/articles/div. See also *Qoran*, Surah 34:12–13; and *The History of al-Tabari*, vol. 3, *The Children of Israel*, trans. William M. Brinner (Albany: SUNY Press, 1991), pp. 162, 164–65, 167, 172–74, who quotes (p. 172) Abu Jafar.

THE SOLOMON/ASHMEDAI STORY IN ITS EASTERN PROVINCIAL ROMAN CULTURAL CONTEXT: *TSOL* AND THE BAVLI

Several striking clusters of parallels between *TSol* and b. Gittin 68a–b, however, support our claim that the Roman East was an indispensible part of the cultural matrix that gave rise to the Bavli.

A critically important motif that Bavli Gittin and *TSol* share in common is King Solomon's compulsion of the demons (1) to contribute to the construction of the Temple, and (2) to reveal knowledge about other demons and supernatural creatures.[38] Palestinian rabbinic traditions attest the motif of demons building the Temple,[39] but in contrast to Bavli Gittin and *TSol*, without exception they are depicted as doing so willingly. In Bavli Gittin Solomon compels demons to reveal the location of Ashmedai (see parts 8–11 above) and the *Shemira* (parts 32–35 above), and he forces Ashmedai to cooperate by means of a chain and a ring inscribed with the name of God (parts 15–17). *TSol* abounds with similar descriptions of demons brought to Solomon against their will, and of their being forced by Solomon's ring to contribute to the construction of the Temple, to reveal the diseases or sorrows they cause, the angel that neutralizes them, and the whereabouts of other demons.[40] These descriptions, in fact, constitute the bulk of *TSol*'s twenty-six chapters, which means that *TSol* and Bavli Gittin share a great deal in common despite the many respects in which the two texts go their own way.

Sarah Iles Johnston argues that a possible antecedent of *TSol*'s conception of Solomon's use of demons to build the Temple might be the conception of magicians using magical assistants to do things that benefit the magician who controls them, such as making a woman fall in love with the magician or fetching things that the magician needs. Johnston finds examples in the Greek and Demotic magical papyri of the first few centuries C.E., from Greece and its colonies as early as the sixth century B.C.E., and from Mesopotamia as early as the start of the first millennium B.C.E.[41] Nevertheless, the specific

---

38. See Sasson, "Melekh ve-Hedyot," pp. 240–41.

39. See the references cited in n. 30. Ibid., p. 214, n. 19, claims with insufficient justification that this fact implies that the Bavli knew *TSol* qua compilation.

40. See ibid., p. 240.

41. Sarah Iles Johnston, "The Testament of Solomon from Late Antiquity to the Renaissance," in *The Metamorphosis of Magic from Late Antiquity to the Early Modern Period,* ed. Jan N. Bremmer and Jan R. Veenstra (Leuven: Peeters, 2002), p. 42. See *Apoc. Ad.*

working out of this theme in the case of Solomon's construction of the Temple with the help of demons, clearly present in *TSol* and in Bavli Gittin, is too close an affinity to be fully explicable in terms of the Mesopotamian, Greek, and Egyptian precedents. We are probably faced with evidence, therefore, that sources in *TSol* and the Bavli share a common ancestry.

Examination of the two compilations reveals additional parallels. *TSol* 20:1–17, for example, reads as follows:[42]

> Now it happened that one of the artisans, an old man, threw himself down before me, saying, "King Solomon, Son of David, have mercy on me, an elderly man."
>
> I said to him, "Tell me, old man, what you want."
>
> He replied, "I beg you, King. I have a son, my only son, and every day he does terribly violent things to me, striking me in the face and head and threatening to send me to a terrible death. Because he did this, I came forward (to request) a favor—that you will avenge me."
>
> When I heard these things I commanded his son to be brought before me.
>
> When he came I said to him, "Do you admit to this?"
>
> He replied, "I did not become so filled with rage, King, that I struck my father with my hand. Be kind, O King, for it is not right to pay attention to such a story and (to his) distress."
>
> Therefore when I, Solomon, heard the young man, I summoned the elderly man to come and reconsider. But he did not want (to come) and said, "Let him be put to death."
>
> Then, noticing that the demon Ornias was laughing, I became very angry that he would laugh in my presence. Dismissing the young man, I ordered Ornias to come out and I said to him, "Cursed one, did you laugh at me?"
>
> He replied, "I beg you, King; I did not laugh because of you but because of the wretched old man and the miserable young man, his son, because after three days he will die. See, the old man has the intent of doing away with him in an evil manner."
>
> I said, "Does he really have such an intent?"

7:13–16 for a description of Solomon's use of demons for much the same purpose as any other Mediterranean magician would have used them: to obtain the object of his personal desires.

42. See appendix 2 at the end of the chapter, for discussion of *Obsequies of the Holy Virgin,* a Syriac text that supports an early dating for the tradition preserved in *TSol* 20:1–17.

The demon said, "Yes, king."

....

Then I ordered Ornias to be brought to me again and I said to him, "Tell me how you know that the young man will die in three days."

He responded, "We demons go up to the firmament of heaven, fly around the stars, and hear the decisions which issue from God concerning the lives of men."[43]

....

When I, Solomon, heard these things, I commanded the demon to be kept under guard for five days. After five days I summoned the old man but he did not want to come. Then when he did come, I saw that he was depressed and mourning. I said to him, "Where is your son, old man?"

He replied, "I have become childless, O King, and without hope I keep watch at the grave of my son."

Upon hearing these things and knowing that the things which were spoken to me by the demon were true, I glorified the God of heaven and earth.[44]

This section parallels a scene in Bavli Gittin, examined preliminarily above (parts 18–20):

> As [Benaiah] was bringing him along, [Ashmedai] ... saw a blind man lost on the road and lifted him onto the proper path. He saw a drunken man lost on the road and lifted him onto the proper path. He saw a wedding party being entertained and he cried. He heard a man say to a shoemaker, "Make me shoes that will last for seven years," and he laughed. He saw a diviner divining and he laughed.

After a hiatus, this scene is resumed later on in the story (parts 39–48):

> Benaiah said to [Ashmedai], "Why, when you saw that blind man lost in the road, did you lift him onto the proper path?"
>
> [Ashmedai] said to [Benaiah], "They announced about him in heaven that he is completely righteous, and whoever does him a favor merits the world to come."
>
> [Benaiah said to Ashmedai], "And why, when you saw the drunken man lost on the road, did you lift him onto the proper path?"

43. See Duling, *Testament*, p. 982.
44. Ibid., p. 983.

[Ashmedai] said to [Benaiah], "They announced about him in heaven that he is completely wicked. I did him a favor so that he would receive [the reward due him in this] world [and thus have no merit left over in the world to come]."

[Benaiah said to Ashmedai], "Why, when you saw the wedding party, did you cry?"

[Ashmedai] said to [Benaiah], "The man must die within thirty days, and she must wait thirteen years for a young levir [to reach maturity, at which time he can marry her or release her from the levirate bond]."

[Benaiah said to Ashmedai], "Why, when you heard the man say to the shoemaker, 'Make me shoes [that will last] seven years,' did you laugh?"

[Ashmedai] said to [Benaiah], "He doesn't even have seven days [to live], and he wants shoes for seven years?"

[Benaiah said to Ashmedai], "Why, when you saw the diviner divining, did you laugh?"

[Ashmedai] said to [Benaiah], "Because he was sitting on the king's treasury. Let him divine what's underneath him."[45]

The fact that both in Bavli Gittin and in *TSol* the protagonist performs seemingly inexplicable actions that turn out to make perfect sense or to be perfectly just is only one of several respects in which the texts are parallel.[46] Both in the Talmud and in *TSol*, a demon laughs because he possesses foreknowledge about the fate of one of the characters in the story, and in both compilations the demon possesses this knowledge because of an announcement he heard in heaven. The Gittin story, furthermore, elsewhere specifies that Ashmedai learns the heavenly Torah lesson every day, reinforcing the idea that he has knowledge that derives from heaven and partially paralleling *TSol*'s claim that the demons "go up to the firmament of heaven, fly around among the stars, and hear the decisions which issue from God concerning the lives of men."

---

45. See also Sasson, "Melekh ve-Hedyot," pp. 241–42.

46. This shared motif alone would not be particularly worthy of comment, since it is common in world literature. See, for example, J. M. Foley, "Word-Power, Performance and Tradition," *Journal of American Folklore* 105 (1992): 275–301. See also Susan Niditch, *Underdogs and Tricksters: A Prelude to Biblical Folklore* (San Francisco: Harper & Row, 1987), pp. xiii–xiv, 4, 15, 25, and 60. The fact that several other striking parallels accompany this shared feature, however, increases the likelihood that it should not be viewed as mere coincidence.

We find another fascinating parallel between Gittin and *TSol* 5:1–5, where Solomon speaks with the bound demon Asmodeus.[47] *TSol* 5:1–5 reads as follows:

> I commanded another demon be brought to me; and he (Beelzeboul) brought me the evil demon Asmodeus, bound.
>
> I asked him, "Who are you?"
>
> He scowled at me and said, "And who are you?"
>
> I said to him, "You (dare to) answer (so arrogantly) when you have been punished like this?"
>
> He continued to give forth the same look and said to me, "How should I answer you? You are the son of a man, but although I was born of a human mother, I (am the son) of an angel; it is impossible for one of heavenly origin (to speak) an arrogant word to one of earthly origin.... So do not ask me so many things, Solomon, for eventually your kingdom will be divided. This glory of yours is temporary. You have us to torture for a little while; then we shall disperse among human beings again with the result that we shall be worshiped as gods because men do not know the names of the angels who rule over us.[48]

Along the same lines, in *TSol* 15:7–12 we find a similar portrayal of Solomon's interaction with a demon:

> Accordingly, when I, Solomon, had prayed to my God and invoked the angel Rathanael about whom he spoke, I made use of the seal and sealed her down with a triple-link chain, and as I bound her down, I made use of the seal of God. Then the (evil) spirit prophesied to me, saying, "You are doing these things to us now, King Solomon, but after a period of time your kingdom shall be divided. At still a later time this Temple shall be destroyed and all Jerusalem shall be demolished by the kings of the Persians and Medes and Chaldeans. Also, the implements of the Temple which you are making shall serve other gods. Along with these (events) also all the vessels in which you have entrapped us shall be broken in pieces by the hands of men. Then we shall come forth with much power and we shall be scattered here and there throughout the world. We will lead astray all the inhabited world for a long time.... Because of this, King Solomon, your time is evil, your years are short, and your kingdom shall be given to your servant.[49]

---

47. See Sasson, "Melekh ve-Hedyot," p. 242. This is not to say, of course, that the accounts in the two corpora are identical. These differences, however, do not negate their noteworthy similarities.

48. Duling, *Testament,* pp. 965–66.

49. Ibid., p. 975.

Once again there is a striking parallel in Bavli Gittin (parts 12, 15–16, and 30–31). The account in the Talmud is much briefer, but the parallels are no less striking:

> [Solomon] sent Benaiah ben Jehoiada, giving him a chain on which the [divine] name was engraved, and a ring on which the [divine] name was engraved....
>
> [Benaiah] came down, threw the chain over [Ashmedai], and shackled him. When [Ashmedai] awoke, he struggled with the chain.
>
> [Benaiah] said to him, "The name of your Master is upon you, the name of your Master is upon you!"...
>
> [In] three days [Solomon] brought [Ashmedai] before him. [Ashmedai] took a reed and measured out four cubits and threw it in front of [Solomon].
>
> [Ashmedai] said to [Solomon], "When [you] die, [you] will have only four cubits in this world. Now you have subdued the entire world and you are not satisfied until you also subdue me?"

Both compilations depict Ashmedai (Asmodeus) brought before King Solomon, immobilized by the magic power of Solomon's ring, which bears the power of God. In both texts Ashmedai complains about the treatment he is receiving from the king, angrily pointing out the transitory nature of the king's lofty position in the world and that eventually the king will be left with nothing. The anger of Asmodeus, impossible to miss in *TSol*, is more subtle, but is nonetheless palpable, in the Talmud's portrayal of Ashmedai. Each of these elements by themselves could be dismissed as mere coincidence; their coexistence together in a single passage is much more difficult to dismiss.

TSol 10:4–7 may be the source of another significant parallel.[50] This scene describes Solomon sending his servant to the mountains in the company of a demon, bound by a ring bearing God's seal, to bring back a stone for use in the Temple. *TSol*'s narrative parallels Gittin 68a–b's depiction of Solomon sending Benaiah to the mountains to capture Ashmedai by binding him with his ring and chain in order to find the *Shemira*, which Solomon needs to build the Temple (parts 4–17 above).[51] Interestingly, in Jeremiah 17:1, Ezekiel 3:9, and Zechariah 7:11–12, the word *Shamir* (the Hebrew equivalent of the Aramaic *Shemira*) refers to something with an extremely

---

50. See ibid., p. 972.
51. See Davies-Browne, *Significance of Parallels*, p. 273–78; and Sasson, "Melekh ve-Hedyot," p. 241.

hard surface,[52] although in the present story and throughout rabbinic literature the precise nature of the *Shamir* (or the *Shemira*) is not clear.[53]

NAG HAMMADI TEXTS AND THE BAVLI

The *Testimony of Truth* 9:3, a Christian tractate discovered at Nag Hammadi, Egypt, and composed in the late second century or early third C.E., also contains striking parallels to the Solomon/Ashmedai story in Bavli Gittin and thus further supports my claim regarding the powerful cultural currents flowing from the Roman East to Jewish Babylonia. The relevant passage is as follows:[54]

> They [that is, the narrator's non-encratite Christian opponents] are wicked in their behavior. Some of them fall away [to the worship of] idols. [Others] have [demons] dwelling with them [as did] David the king. He is the one who laid the foundation of Jerusalem; and his son Solomon, whom he begat in [adultery], is the one who built Jerusalem by means of the demons, because he received [power]. When he [had finished building, he imprisoned] the demons [in the temple]. He [placed them] into seven [waterpots]. They remained a long [time in] the [waterpots], abandoned [there]. When the Romans [went] up to [Jerusalem] they discovered [the] waterpots, [and immediately] the [demons] ran out of the waterpots as those who escape from prison. And the waterpots [remained] pure (thereafter). [And] since those days, [they dwell] with men who are [in] ignorance, and [they have remained upon] the earth.[55]

---

52. See n. 4 above, for parallel texts that conceive of the *Shamir*'s equivalent as a kind of flora. Traditional commentators describe it as a worm.

53. See the texts cited in Jastrow, *Dictionary,* p. 1596. Once again the parallels are not exact, since in contrast to the emerald stone in *TSol,* the *Shamir*'s purpose in the Talmud is not to decorate or provide light.

54. B. A. Pearson, "The Testimony of Truth (IX,3)," in *The Nag Hammadi Library in English,* ed. James M. Robinson, rev. ed. (Leiden: Brill, 1988), p. 449; and Hans-Gebhard Bethge, Bentley Layton, and Societasa Coptica Hierosolymitana, "On the Origin of the World," *Nag Hammadi Library,* rev. ed. Robinson, p. 177. The Nag Hammadi codices themselves have been dated paleographically to the fourth century C.E., but obviously this date does not preclude an earlier dating of the composition and final editing of some of the individual textual corpora.

55. S. Giversen and B. A. Pearson, trans., "The Testimony of Truth (IX,3)," in Robinson, *The Nag Hammadi Library in English,* p. 415. See also Scott T. Carroll, "The *Apocalypse of Adam* and Pre-Christian Gnosticism," *Vigiliae Christianae* 44 (1990): 270.

We find several commonalities between this Nag Hammadi text and traditions in the Bavli. It is likely, for example, that the *Testimony*'s reference to the demons helping Solomon build "Jerusalem" alludes to their construction of the Temple.[56] The Nag Hammadi text, furthermore, depicts Solomon imprisoning the demons in the Temple even after its construction, just as Bavli Gittin depicts Solomon continuing to detain Ashmedai (parts 49–54). Since the Nag Hammadi text dates from the second or third centuries, we have unambiguous proof that early traditions made their way from the Roman East to rabbinic Mesopotamia.

This conclusion regarding the motif of the confinement of demons in jars is confirmed, despite the corrupt nature of the text, by a passage from the Syriac translation of the twelfth book of Zosimus of Panoplis, who wrote in Egypt at the beginning of the fourth century:[57]

> Among the Egyptians, there is a book called The Seven Heavens, attributed to Solomon, against the demons, but it is not correct (to say) that it is by Solomon, since these bottles had been brought at another time to our priests; that is what the language employed to denote them makes one suppose, because the expression "bottle of Solomon" is a Hebrew expression. At any moment, the great priest of Jerusalem gets them, according to the plain sense, from the lower abyss of Jerusalem. After these writings were spread everywhere, still unfinished, they were corrupted. It is he [that is, Solomon] who composed them,[58] as I have said above. But Solomon only wrote a single book about the seven bottles, while some person invented and composed commentaries at different epochs to explain what this work contained; but in these commentaries there is some deception. All or almost all agree concerning the function of the bottles directed against the demons. The bottles acted like the prayer and the nine letters written by Solomon: the demons cannot withstand them.

---

56. For further discussion of linkages between this text and Jewish traditions, see B. A. Pearson, "Jewish Haggadic Traditions in *The Testimony of Truth* from Nag Hammadi (CG IX,3)," in *Ex Orbe Religionum: Studia Geo Widengren oblata*, ed. J. Bergmann, K. Drynjeff, and M. Ringgren (Leiden: Brill, 1972), p. 459; and S. Giversen, "Solomon und die Dämonen," in *Essays on the Nag Hammadi Texts in Honour of Alexander Böhlig*, ed. M. Krause (Leiden: Brill, 1972), pp. 16–21.

57. Zosimus, "Mystery of the Nine Letters of Solomon," in *Histoire des sciences: La chimie au moyen age*, ed. M. Berthelot (Paris: Imprimerie Nationale, 1893), vol. 2, pp. 264–65; and ms Parisinus Graecus 2316, in R. Reitzenstein, ed., *Poimandres: Studien zur griechisch-ägyptischen und frühchristlichen Literatur* (1904; Darmstadt: Wissenschaftliche Buchgesellschaft, 1966), pp. 295–96.

58. Or "invented them," that is, the talismanic bottles. See Duling, *Testament*, p. 950.

According to this text, the bottles of Solomon were "directed against the demons," and the demons "cannot withstand" the bottles.

Also relevant is the following comment by Zosimus:[59]

> The seven bottles in which Solomon shut up the demons were made of electrum. It is necessary to believe, in this respect, the Jewish writings about the demons.... The angel ordered Solomon to make these bottles.... The wise Solomon also knows how to summon the demons; he gives a formula of conjuration and mentions the electrum.[60]

THE SIGNIFICANCE OF THE STORY

The Bavli, however, is not simply the passive receptor of these traditions, and in the ensuing analysis we will see that the local Jewish cultural context was at least as significant as the source of the traditions in shaping the story before us. We begin with an attempt to characterize Bavli Gittin's attitudes toward the Temple, move from there to the story's attitudes toward Ashmedai, and conclude with a discussion of King Solomon.

It is difficult to pin down Bavli Gittin's precise attitude toward the Temple. On the one hand, the demons, including Ashmedai, undoubtedly contribute to the construction of the Temple by helping Solomon find the *Shemira*. On the other hand, in contrast to several ancient texts,[61] Bavli Gittin apparently removes the demons from direct participation in the Temple's construction since they only help locate the *Shemira* and there is no reason to believe that the *Shemira* is demonic. Further complicating matters is the fact that none of the demons in the Bavli's story is depicted as sinful,[62] with the possible exception of Ashmedai after he has been provoked by the story's human characters (see below). It is possible that the audience is meant to think more highly of Ashmedai than of Solomon, so the decision to remove the demons from direct participation in the Temple's construction may not be fully expli-

---

59. Pablo A. Torijano, *Solomon the Esoteric King: From King to Magus, Development of a Tradition* (Leiden: Brill, 2002), pp. 182–83.

60. See W. Scott and A.S. Ferguson, *Hermetica IV: Testimonia* (Oxford: Oxford University Press, 1936), pp. 104–5.

61. *TSol*, the *Testimony of Truth,* and two sixth- or seventh-century Palestinian midrashic traditions: *Shir ha-Shirim Rabbah* 1:5, p. 8; and *Pesikta Rabbati* 6:7.

62. See, for example, the detailed discussion of Ashmedai below. The demons in Bavli Gittin are actually rather sympathetic characters, in line with the ancient Greek term *daimon*,

cable as an attempt to preserve the Temple's honor. Still, part of what the *Testimony of Truth* finds objectionable about Solomon is the fact that he built Jerusalem with the help of demons (see above). In the Bavli story as well, therefore, the nature of the Temple and the character of the individual responsible for building it might be linked, with the flawed nature of the latter (that is, Solomon) serving in part to impugn the former. On the other hand, the story makes it clear that Solomon was not guilty of sexual depravity while engaged in the building of the Temple, and it makes no mention at all of his sin of idolatry. What appeared to be Solomon's outrageous behavior later on in his career in no way lessened the sanctity of the Temple, since the Temple was already built before Ashmedai began masquerading as king.

Of more obvious importance to Bavli Gittin, however, are the characters and their interactions with one another, their societal roles, and the sources of their expertise, power, and authority. We have Ashmedai, holy man and rabbi, who draws his power from his piety and knowledge of Torah. We have Solomon, who knows about demons but knows no Torah. And we have the rabbis, experts in Torah and, ultimately, in the behavior of demons, who enable the Temple to be built and the rightful king to be restored to the throne. The ensuing discussion analyzes each of these characters in turn and examines their role in the story.

ASHMEDAI AS A RABBINIZED JEWISH HOLY MAN

As noted, Ashmedai fits the profile of a late antique Jewish holy man. Both Jewish and Christian holy men were often portrayed as unlearned but wise and virtuous, the former generally unschooled in Torah and the latter lacking a classical education. Since the text under discussion appears in the Bavli, however, which depicts virtually everyone as a rabbi,[63] the Jewish holy man is also a rabbi, able to quote appropriate biblical verses and explicate them, whose study of the earthly and the heavenly Torah lesson is described by the term *gamar metivta*, which in the Bavli and in post-Talmudic Babylonian geonic

---

which can possess either a positive or a negative valence, and in line with the depiction of demons in several other rabbinic texts. See the discussion of Ben Thalamion in chapter 2.

63. See, for example, Kalmin, "Christians and Heretics," pp. 156–60; and idem, *Jewish Babylonia*, pp. 43–50.

literature describes the content of what rabbis study.[64] Both Jewish and Christian holy men are portrayed as poor or as leading extremely simple lifestyles, both had uneasy relationships with more established religious or political figures,[65] and both are depicted as being appealed to by more conventional members of society for assistance in times of communal need.[66] Both possess power by virtue of "achieved status" rather than social or institutional rank.[67] Both are portrayed as living on the margins of or beyond the borders of settled civilization, and as not easily accessible to more conventional members of society.[68]

As noted, Ashmedai performs actions that seem to make no sense, or that seem to violate the standards of normal social intercourse (parts 18–20). He is the archetypal riddler, parallels to whose behavior are easy to find as folk motifs throughout world literature.[69] Benaiah, who occupies a more central position in society, poses a series of questions, requests for explanations of each puzzling act. Ashmedai successfully explains his behavior, and even, despite appearances to the contrary, turns out to embody the rabbis' loftiest values (parts 39–48). Eager to merit the world to come, Ashmedai shows kindness to a blind man he knows to be fully righteous. He shows kindness to another man he knows to be fully wicked, so that the man will receive his just deserts in the world to come.[70] He has compassion for a bride and groom on their wedding day for he knows their joy will be short lived. He mocks the

---

64. See E. S. Rosenthal, "La-Milon ha-Talmudi," *Tarbiz* 40 (1971): 193–96; Goodblatt, *Rabbinic Instruction,* pp. 78–79; and idem, "Hitpathuyot Hadashot be-Heker Yeshivot Bavel," *Zion* 43 (1978): 21–22; and Yeshayahu Gafni, "'Yeshiva' u-'Metivta,'" *Zion* 43 (1978): 28; idem, "Ha-Yeshivah ha-Bavlit la-Or B. Q. 111a," *Tarbiz* 49 (1980): 295, 297–301; and idem, *Yehudei Bavel,* pp. 194–95.

65. Peter Brown, "The Rise and Function of the Holy Man in Late Antiquity," included, with important additions, in *Society and the Holy in Late Antiquity* (Berkeley: University of California Press, 1982), pp. 138–41; and idem, "Arbiters of the Holy: The Christian Holy Man in Late Antiquity," in *Authority and the Sacred: Aspects of the Christianization of the Roman World* (Cambridge: Cambridge University Press, 1995), pp. 72–73.

66. Peter Brown, "Town, Village and Holy Man: The Case of Syria," in *Society and the Holy in Late Antiquity,* pp. 157–62.

67. N. Mclynn, "A Self-Made Holy Man: The Case of Gregory Nazianzen," *Journal of Early Christian Studies* 6 (1998): 462–64.

68. Brown, "Rise and Function," pp. 111–12.

69. See the literature cited in n. 45.

70. See, for example, b. Ta'anit 11a, according to which the wicked are rewarded in this world even for the slightest meritorious deed, while the righteous are rewarded in the world to come for the slightest meritorious deed. See also y. Hagigah 2:2, y. Sanhedrin 6:9, and y. Horayot 3:9, where the same idea is expressed.

diviner condemned by Scripture.⁷¹ His laughter at the man who will die within seven days seems callous, but in a world where human life is so fragile, the man who demands shoes that will last him seven years can be condemned as presumptuous. The man, apparently, is more certain about his future than he has any right to be.⁷² In addition, Ashmedai shows concern for a widow, a defenseless member of society whom the Torah repeatedly insists must be protected.⁷³ When he breaks a bone while bending out of the way to avoid damaging the widow's home, Ashmedai does not respond with anger but with an apposite quotation of Scripture.

According to the Talmudic story, when the rabbinized holy man is removed from his normal habitat and brought into sustained contact with civilization, both civilization and the personality of the holy man are destabilized. Ashmedai's contact with mainstream society begins with Benaiah's substitution of the demon's water for wine, which occasions Ashmedai's first undisciplined act: using Scripture to justify his excessive consumption of wine (parts 12–15).

Most of the stories from late antiquity describing the Christian desert fathers portray interactions between anchorites and their colleagues or students.⁷⁴ However, in a minority of cases other figures are involved. One type is of particular interest to us here: stories that feature ecclesiastical or political dignitaries as antagonists of the holy men. These dignitaries are usually presented as intellectually or spiritually inferior to the holy men. In New Testament and Greco-Roman pagan stories as well, the dignitaries are shown to be inferior to Jesus on the one hand and philosophers on the other.⁷⁵ Compilations of stories featuring the wise sayings and deeds of the desert fathers "contain stories about the desert fathers' meetings with emperors or bishops. It is always the emperors or bishops who approach the fathers and ask them a favor. The fathers are presented as trying to avoid all contact with them."⁷⁶

Like stories about the anchorites, the Ashmedai narrative portrays more conventional members of society requiring the holy man's services,

---

71. See, for example, Deuteronomy 18:10 and 2 Kings 17:17.

72. See also Rashi, s.v., *Shiva Yomei Leit Lei.*

73. Mss Vatican 130 and Munich 95 read "old woman" *(savta)* instead of "widow," but even according to this reading Ashmedai's behavior is praiseworthy from a rabbinic point of view, conforming to the biblical command, "You shall show deference to the old" (Lev 19:32).

74. Catherine Hezser, "Die Verwendung der hellenistischen Gattung im frühen Christentum und Judentum," *Journal for the Study of Judaism* 27 (1996): 407–9.

75. Ibid., pp. 406–7 and 410.

76. Ibid., p. 412.

and in the process of fulfilling their needs, Ashmedai demonstrates his superior wisdom and righteousness. In addition, like the stories about the anchorites, the story about Ashmedai depicts antagonism between the holy man and the more conventional characters.[77] Ashmedai complains about being held captive by the king, criticizes Solomon's lust for greater glory and forecasts his inglorious end, tosses him four hundred Persian miles, assumes his place on the throne, and reduces him to begging from door to door.

The Ashmedai narrative acknowledges the holy man's power but minimizes it as a threatening alternative to the rabbinic way of life because to obtain it he must engage in rabbinically approved conduct. The story thus attests to a tendency, found in Palestinian rabbinic compilations and in the later strata of the Bavli, to acknowledge the importance of religious actions other than the uniquely rabbinic value of Torah study.[78] The story also domesticates the king of the demons by depicting him as a danger to no one and a source of no disruption as long as human beings make no attempt to rule over him or confine him to civilization. He possesses esoteric information that it is occasionally important for human beings to acquire, but once that information has been supplied the relationship should end. Trouble ensues when Solomon refuses to allow Ashmedai to return to his mountaintop (parts 49–54).

Even the trouble that ensues, however, may be depicted as relatively mild, since the problem is one of Ashmedai's kingly responsibilities rather than actual mayhem, although clearly royal neglect has serious consequences.[79] Ashmedai does not wreak havoc on the palace or the kingdom, although he has not once consulted his chief adviser, Benaiah (parts 57–58), suggesting that under Ashmedai the kingdom will suffer serious neglect. The same conclusion follows from the other actions of Ashmedai as king, which exclusively involve the satisfaction of his sexual appetites, which appear to be considerable but are not necessarily sinful (parts 59–62).[80] It is not certain that the rabbis viewed

---

77. Ibid., pp. 41–42. See also K. Berger, "Hellenistische Gattungen im neuem Testament," in *Aufstieg und Niedergang der römischen Welt* 2:25/2 (1984): 1106.

78. See also chapter 7; Kalmin, *The Sage in Jewish Society*, pp. 49–50, 75–79, and 140–42; and idem, *Jewish Babylonia*, pp. 184–85 and 253.

79. Compare Pekka Särkiö, "Salomo und die Dämonen," in *Verbum et Calamus: Semitic and Related Studies in Honour of the Sixtieth Birthday of Professor Tapani Harviainen*, ed. Hannu Juusola (Helsinki: Finnish Oriental Society, 2004), p. 318.

80. Compare Levene, "The Magical *Get*," pp. 175–84, who in my opinion overemphasizes Ashmedai's lasciviousness in Bavli Gittin, based on his character in other literature. See especially the references cited in n. 6 on p. 176.

Ashmedai as obliged to observe the laws of menstrual purity, so they are not necessarily depicting him as a transgressor of Jewish law.[81] When he tries to have sex with Solomon's mother, furthermore, it is obvious that he is not transgressing at all, since Bathsheba is Solomon's mother, not his own. It is possible that Ashmedai's sexual behavior would have aroused laughter sooner than it would have aroused disgust or moral condemnation in its Babylonian rabbinic audience, although certainty on this issue is at present beyond our grasp. While Ashmedai is not portrayed as an uncontrollable fiend, therefore, it is clear that the nation will not flourish under his leadership.

SOLOMON'S SINS AND THE CONSTRUCTION OF THE TEMPLE

Turning now to Bavli Gittin's attitude toward King Solomon, we noted above that the story makes no mention of Solomon's major transgressions according to the Bible, but that it hardly portrays him as a heroic figure. The story portrays Solomon as unlearned and unwise, a person who understands the behavior of demons but nothing else. In addition, Solomon fails to deliver on his promise of "not wanting anything from Ashmedai" other than help in building the Temple, and continues to imprison him even after he has the *Shemira* and even after the project is complete (part 49).[82] He is therefore guilty of the very real sin of wishing to control realms he has no business controlling, as shown by the fact that his imprisonment of Ashmedai leads directly to Solomon's downfall (parts 49–54). Solomon also apparently abuses his power when he delays summoning Ashmedai, despite the fact that it means a delay in the construction of the Temple (ostensibly his only reason for capturing him), apparently only to demonstrate to the demon that he, Solomon, is in control of the situation and will decide in his own good time when the two kings should meet (parts 21–31).[83] Solomon also resorts to

---

81. It is also not clear that Ashmedai causes Solomon's wives to sin by having sex while they are in a state of menstrual impurity, since it is not clear that this prohibition would also apply to sex with a demon. My claim, it bears emphasizing, is not that Ashmedai is definitely not depicted as a sinner, but only that it is possible to understand the story as depicting him as not a sinner.

82. This point is particularly clear according to the reading of mss Vatican 130, Vatican 140, and Arras: "at the end of the kingship of Solomon."

83. See Sasson, "Melekh ve-Hedyot," p. 230.

deception to capture Ashmedai and imprisons him in the palace, antagonizing the demonic king and leading to his angry defiance and his seizure of the Israelite throne, despite the fact that nothing that Ashmedai did while alone on his mountain gave the slightest indication that he was at all dangerous or that he would be likely to be uncooperative. On the contrary, all we know about him is that he is a devoted student of Torah, that he drinks water rather than wine and is concerned that no one tamper with his water supply, and that he leads a solitary existence. So the intent of the story is not to whitewash Solomon, but to depict him as possessing precisely these shortcomings and not others.[84]

Where do we see Solomon's lack of learning and wisdom? He needs "the rabbis" to tell him how to fulfill the verse "When the Temple was built, only finished stones cut at the quarry were used" (1 Kgs 6:7), and Solomon is capable only of asking the simple question "how will I do this?" The rabbis teach him about the *Shemira* that Moses used to make the stones of the *ephod*, which demonstrates his ignorance about another crucial biblical passage (parts 4–5). When the rabbis tell him about the *Shemira*, Solomon again responds with the simplest of questions—"Where can it be found?"[85]— which further demonstrates his ignorance (part 6). When the demons suggest that perhaps Ashmedai knows the *Shemira*'s whereabouts, Solomon, true to form, again asks an extremely simple question: "Where is he?"[86] (parts 9–10). When the rabbis advise Solomon to fetch male and female demons and subdue them, however, he does so without needing to ask where to find them and how to subdue them, indicating his expertise in demonic behavior, in sharp contrast to his ignorance of Torah (parts 7–8).[87] Solomon sends Benaiah to capture Ashmedai, equipping him with a chain and a ring on which is engraved the name of God, along with balls of wool (part 12), once again demonstrating his expertise in demonic behavior, which he displays yet again when Ashmedai arrives at the king's palace, since only Solomon is able to decipher Ashmedai's symbolic actions (parts 21–29).[88]

---

84. See also John Bowman, "Solomon and Jesus," *Abr-Nahrain* 23 (1984–85): 3.
85. This question is missing in some manuscripts, however. See n. 12.
86. Clearly there are limits, therefore, to even Solomon's knowledge of the demons, and the demons themselves know even more than he does.
87. Solomon does not possess limitless knowledge about demons, however, since he thinks the demons might know the whereabouts of the *Shemira*.
88. When Benaiah successfully outsmarts the woodcock, it is unclear first whether or not the woodcock is considered by the story to be part of the demonic or angelic realm or instead part of the natural world, and second it is unclear whether Benaiah is acting on his

Solomon asks Ashmedai, "How are you greater than us [humans]?"—indicating his inability to understand a biblical verse about the spirit world *(to'afot re'em)*, which results in his being mistaken for a madman (parts 50–55). So throughout the story Solomon has practical knowledge of the spirit world but inadequate understanding of Scripture, even Scripture that concerns the spirit world. The rabbis once again intervene, recognizing that this "beggar" is not a madman but is, in fact, the king he claims to be. The rabbis equip the deposed Solomon with another ring and chain engraved with the name of God, and the demonic usurper flies away at his approach (parts 56–63). The rabbis, therefore, are expert not only in the interpretation of Scripture and the behavior of human beings, but also, by the time the story concludes, in the behavior of demons. Despite the fact that Solomon regains his throne, he never regains his former glory, since for the rest of his life he is terrified of demonic attack (part 64).

CONCLUSION

The present chapter argued that traditions from the Roman East are a significant part of the source material comprising the Solomon/Ashmedai story in Bavli Gittin. Persian traditions appear to have been much less significant, although firm conclusions are not possible at present. In addition, we must defer systematic discussion of relevant Mesopotamian parallels until study of the Babylonian magic bowls has progressed to a more sophisticated level.[89]

Ultimately, however, we argued that while the Roman East provides the bulk of the story's raw material, the rabbis' own cultural context in Babylonia provides a critically important prism through which to understand the story. Babylonian rabbis competed with other powerful individuals for dominance in Jewish society, and the story shows that the holy man and the magician were two of these powerful individuals. The story domesticates the holy man by depicting him as conforming to rabbinic values, but at the same time it issues a warning regarding him: sometimes it may be necessary to exploit him, but to the extent possible he should be kept away from civilized society,

---

own initiative or is following Solomon's instructions. This scene, therefore, may contribute to the portrayal of Solomon as in control of the spirit world, although firm conclusions are not yet possible.

89. See, however, the discussion below.

since extended contact with him has a negative impact both on the holy man and on civilized society.[90]

Babylonian rabbis also competed with magicians, a conclusion supported by the rich archaeological record of magic bowls in close geographical proximity to the rabbinic settlements of Babylonia.[91] The Solomon/Ashmedai story is an attempt on the rabbis' part to convince themselves and their followers that the weapons at their disposal confer greater power than those that are available to these competitors. The story shows that the rabbis who created the Bavli were acutely aware of the practitioners of the magic inscribed in these bowls, and that we are not faced with a puzzling disconnect between the major archaeological and literary records that survived from late antiquity, a phenomenon so familiar to historians and literary scholars of ancient Judaism.[92]

We saw that the Solomon/Ashmedai story passes in silence over Solomon's most heinous crimes, but that clearly the story is not a sustained attempt to whitewash him. The story credits Solomon with expertise about demons, but depicts him as deficient in Torah and as sinfully desiring to rule over the spirit world. Solomon's excessive thirst for power and his inability to understand Scripture compromise even his earthly power, and he ends his life weakened by terror of demonic attack.

While other cultures, particularly Christian, had much to say about the Temple and about Solomon, there is no proof that ancient Jews and Christians competed over the question of who possessed the superior claim to the title of "Son of David,"[93] or that the rabbis told the Ashmedai story to

---

90. Palestinian rabbinic stories also faced the issue of how to most effectively deal with the competition supplied by the holy man, but they came up with a much different solution. See Kalmin, "Holy Men, Rabbis, and Demonic Sages," pp. 213–34.

91. Regarding the dating of the magic bowls, see Bohak, *Ancient Jewish Magic,* p. 184 and n. 104; and Harari, *Ha-Kishuf ha-Yehudi,* p. 183 and n. 83.

92. As several scholars have noted, however, there is no unambiguous rabbinic reference, in either Babylonian or Palestinian rabbinic literature, to magical incantations inscribed on bowls.

93. Compare C.C. McCown, "The Christian Tradition as to the Magical Wisdom of Solomon," *Journal of the Palestine Oriental Society* 2 (1922): 16; and Torijano, *Solomon the Esoteric King,* pp. 113–14, n. 24, 117–19 and passim. See also E. Lövestam, "Jésus Fils de David chez les Synoptiques," *Studia Theologica* 28 (1974): 97–109. All of the texts quoted in support of this contention are Christian, and we thus have no reliable access to the Jewish side of this so-called debate. It is true that some Jewish texts glorify Solomon or maintain his sinlessness (for example, b. Shabbat 56b), but none do so in comparison with Jesus or even a figure who could serve as a convincing stand-in for Jesus. Some Christians used the comparison between Jesus and Solomon as a rhetorical technique by which to assert the superiority of Christianity to Judaism, but these polemical sources do not

criticize Jesus Christ.⁹⁴ Neither is there any proof that the story responded to Christian claims about the superiority of Christian "Temples" constructed in Jerusalem during and after the reign of Constantine.⁹⁵

Instead, it is likely that the rabbis told the story in part to express their reservations about a biblical character who was portrayed on the one hand as a terrible sinner and on the other hand as the beloved of God and inheritor of the promise to David. More fundamentally, the story portrays Solomon with these particular flaws and not others because of his crucial importance for ancient magicians, which he possessed because of his legendary power over demons.⁹⁶

Gilad Sasson documents the wide diffusion of the portrayal of Solomon as healing via the exorcism of demons, and the striking fact of the absence of this portrayal of Solomon in rabbinic literature. This striking absence prompts Sasson to argue that the editors of Bavli Gittin removed from the Ashmedai story the motif of Solomon's magical/medical cures via the exorcism of demons, due to their desire to avoid portraying Solomon like Jesus, another famous exorcist.⁹⁷ Sasson claims that only by positing the presence of this motif in the Ashmedai story are we able to explain the story's connection to the surrounding discussion, a collection of magical/medical cures.⁹⁸

---

constitute a verifiable record from the Christian side of an actual debate from late antiquity. Solomon's character provided an effective tool by which the Christians could argue for the supremacy of the new covenant to the old, since the biblical son of David, the original inheritor of the promise to David, was clearly a flawed individual and a dead end.

94. Compare Sasson, "Melekh ve-Hedyot," pp. 243–48.

95. See, for example, Jerome, *Epistulae* XLVI (Corpus Scriptorum ecclesiasticorum latinorum 54:334); Zeno, *Tractatus* I,14 (Patrologia Latina 11: 355). See also Theodotus, *Interpretatio in Ezechielem*. XLVIII, 35 (Patrologia Graeca 81:1253); and Joshua Schwartz, "The *Encaenia* of the Church of the Holy Sepulchre, Temple of Solomon and the Jews," *Theologische Zeitschrift* 43, no. 3 (1987): 266–79.

96. See, for example, Josephus, *Antiquities* 8.42–49. See also the exhaustive documentation in Torijano, *Solomon the Esoteric King*, pp. 41–87, 129–41, and 192–224. In addition, however, part of what is operating in Bavli Gittin's failure to mention Solomon's most serious biblical sins is a Babylonian working out of a convention that has a centuries-old pedigree in the Roman East, notably in the account of Solomon's Temple-building in 2 Chronicles. See also *Vayikra Rabbah* 12:5, ed. Margaliot, p. 262; and *Pesikta de-Rav Kahana*, ed. Mandelbaum, pp. 385–86. In *TSol* as well, Solomon is sinless while engaged in the construction of the Temple. His climactic sins figure only in *TSol* 26 (according to mss HNPQ), after the construction of the Temple is complete.

97. For the same reason, argues Sasson, "Shlomo ha-Magikan be-Sifrut Hazal," pp. 51–53, the rabbis never explicitly mention the tradition of Solomon healing via exorcism.

98. Ibid., pp. 50–51; and Sasson, "Melekh ve-Hedyot," pp. 242–43.

Against Sasson's argument, however, it should be noted that the Ashmedai story is linked to its context quite well even without this motif, since the story describes the rabbis' discovery of the need to forcibly remove Ashmedai from Solomon's palace. The story's connection to its surrounding context, therefore, consists of the presence in both of demons that need to be exorcised, together with the assertion in both that only rabbis possess the knowledge and wisdom necessary to perform such exorcisms, and even to know that they need to be performed in the first place.[99]

Solomon is important to the Babylonian rabbis not because he is the Jewish answer to Jesus, but because he is a nonrabbinic cultural hero, a magician who has power over demons and is therefore a competitor to the rabbis for dominance in Babylonian Jewish society, and who therefore might draw rabbis away from the rabbinic way of life. The rabbis ignore Solomon's most serious sins because idolatry and marriage to foreign wives are not the sins of a magician; rather, a magician's sin is the arrogant attempt to rule the spirit world, and a magician is deficient because he possesses expertise in the behavior of demons but none in the interpretation of Scripture. The key to the story is not the Temple, except insofar as the construction of the Temple was Solomon's primary cultural achievement. We can assume that the rabbis were aware of Solomon's importance for contemporaneous Jewish magicians, which was due to Solomon's prominence as an exorcist in the magic bowls, created and utilized in the same place and time as the Babylonian rabbis themselves.[100]

APPENDIX 1: PROBLEMS INVOLVED IN DATING THE *TESTAMENT OF SOLOMON*

Most scholars place the composition of *TSol* somewhere in the Roman East,[101] and date many of its constituent traditions between the first and the fourth

---

99. For another attempt to explain the connection between the story and the surrounding context in Gittin, which also theorizes the common feature of the need to remove demons, see Levene, "The Magical *Get*," pp. 175–84. See especially n. 22 on p. 179 there for examples of illnesses mentioned in the Bavli Gittin passage that are explicitly identified as names of demons on magic bowls. See also n. 23 on pp. 179–80.

100. See also Bohak, *Ancient Jewish Magic*, pp. 357–425; and Harari, *Ha-Kishuf ha-Yehudi*, pp. 68–90, 272–330. For magic bowls that mention individuals with the title "Rav," see James Nathan Ford and Alon Ten-Ami, "Ke'arat Hashba'ah al shem Rav Mesharshia bar Qaqay," *Tarbiz* 80, no. 2 (2012): 219–30 and the literature cited in nn. 1–4 on pp. 220–21 there.

101. See, for example, Todd Klutz, *Rewriting the "Testament of Solomon": Tradition, Conflict and Identity in a Late Antique Pseudepigraphon* (London: T & T Clark, 2005),

centuries C.E.,[102] conclusions we follow in this chapter. Many scholars date *TSol*'s final composition between the third and fifth centuries C.E.,[103] but that position has recently come under attack.[104] Sarah Schwarz, for example, convincingly describes *TSol* as a collection of diverse traditions and clusters of traditions that accumulated gradually until they coalesced finally in the Middle Ages. Even according to Schwarz, however, many of these traditions are ancient and can be compared productively with other ancient texts.[105]

Schwarz claims that the narrative framework of *TSol*—the story of Solomon building the Temple with the help of demons—was added to the compilation at a relatively late date, but that the tradition itself of Solomon's use of demons to help him build the Temple "independently circulated in the early history of this tradition." Schwarz's conclusions render it extremely unlikely that the commonalities between the Bavli and *TSol* derive from the fact that the Bavli had *TSol* before it, but they do not affect our claim that the Bavli's story incorporates many early traditions deriving from the Roman East.[106]

---

pp. 35–37. Certainty, however, is not yet possible. See, for example, C. C. McCown, *The Testament of Solomon* (Leipzig: J. C. Hinrichs, 1922), pp. 109–10; and Duling, *Testament*, pp. 943–44.

102. See, for example, Duling, *Testament*, pp. 942, 944–47, 949–50, and 954–56; idem, "The Eleazar Miracle and Solomon's Magical Wisdom in Flavius Josephus's *Antiquitates Judaicae* 8.42–49," *Harvard Theological Review* 78 (1985): 1–25; and idem, "The Testament of Solomon: Retrospect and Prospect," *Journal for the Study of the Pseudepigrapha* 2 (1988): 87–112; Torijano, *Solomon the Esoteric King*, pp. 41–87, 95–105, 109–19, 129–34, 175–78, 200–208, and 226–30; Sasson, "Melekh ve-Hedyot," p. 211; and B. P. Davies-Browne, "The Significance of Parallels between the Testament of Solomon and Jewish Literature of Late Antiquity (between the Closing Centuries BCE and the Talmudic Era) and the New Testament," PhD diss., St. Andrews, Scotland, 2003, pp. 75–239 and 299–311.

103. See, for example, Karl Preisendanz, "Salomo," in *Paulys Real-Encyclopädien der classischen Altertumswissenschaft*, Suppl. 8 (1956), col. 689; Duling, *Testament*, pp. 940–43; idem, "Retrospect and Prospect," pp. 88–91; Torijano, *Solomon the Esoteric King*, pp. 54–55; Johnston, "Testament of Solomon," pp. 37–39; Klutz, *Rewriting the "Testament of Solomon,"* pp. 34–35, 74–110. See also the fifth- or sixth-century fragments corresponding to *TSol* 18:27–28 and 33–40 edited by Karl Preisendanz, "Ein Wiener Papyrusfragment zum Testamentum Salomonis," *Eos* 48 (1956): 161–67; and R. Daniel, "The Testament of Solomon xviii 27–28, 33–40," in *Festschrift zum 100-jährigen Bestehen e34 Papyrussammlung der österreichlische Nationalbibliothek: Papyrus Erzherzog Rainer* (Vienna: Brüder Hollinek, 1983), vol. 1, pp. 294–304.

104. See James Harding and Loveday Alexander, "Dating the Testament of Solomon," 1999, www.st-andrews.ac.uk/divinity/rt/otp/guestlectures/harding; Sarah Schwarz, "Reconsidering the *Testament of Solomon*," *Journal for the Study of the Pseudepigrapha* 16, no. 3 (2007): 203–37, and the literature cited in nn. 7–8 on p. 209; and eadem, *Building a Book of Spells*.

105. Schwarz, *Building a Book of Spells*, pp. 6–7.

106. See ibid., pp. vi, 6–7, 111–12.

APPENDIX 2

A partially preserved version of the story of the quarreling father and son in the *Obsequies of the Holy Virgin* supports an early dating of *TSol* 20:1–17, one of the texts examined above with striking parallels in the Solomon/Ashmedai story in Bavli Gittin. The relevant portion of the text of the *Obsequies* is as follows:[107]

> And he gave a sign to his father that he might know God. And the son answered and said to his father: "I beg of you, my father, if I have found grace in your eyes, bring a little of our earnings, and give it to this one who is afflicting my soul, that perchance he may leave me and I may not die." Then his father brought the half of his property, and placed it before his beloved son, and answered and said with a loud voice: "I beg of him who is afflicting the soul of my son, take these goods, and grant me the life of my son." And after these things the boy was greatly afflicted; and again he answered and said to his father: "My father, he who is afflicting my soul does not cease from me; perhaps what you have brought to him is altogether too little for him; and because he has seen that it is too little for him, he afflicts me exceedingly." And his father arose, and brought all that he possessed, and along with it he borrowed other (property) and brought it, and placed it before his beloved son, and said with a loud voice: "I beg of him who is afflicting the soul of my son, take all that I have, and leave me only my son." But the boy was greatly afflicted; and when he was near death, he turned to his father and said to him: "My father, you see that neither gold nor silver nor anything else can be given for life, save a heart that is sincere towards God. Rise, therefore, my father, and take these goods, and build with them places for strangers, that they may enter and dwell and rest in them; and give also of them to the poor and orphans, and we shall find peace for our souls." These things the son said to his father, and his life ended; and his father did all that his son had said to him. And when eight days were past, and they did not come to king Solomon, according to the covenant they had made before him, that after seven days they would go to him—and the eighth (day) passed, and the ninth, and they did not go to king Solomon—the king sent after them, saying: "Why have you not come, that I might settle (matters) between you, as I said to you?" And the father of the boy answered and said: "My lord, it is eight days since my son departed out of the world. Had I known he was dying, I would have given all I had to my son not to distress him; but all that he said to me, I have done." And when Solomon heard this from the man he said: "The evil spirits

---

107. This text parallels the story of the old man, the young boy, and Solomon, included in *TSol* in mss DEFHPNQ. In ms D, the dispute of the father and son and Ornias's prophecy appears in *TSol* 4:1–18. It is also included in the manuscript published by A. Delatte, "Testament de Salomon," *Anecdota Atheniensia* 36 (1927): 211–27.

know what is going to happen. Because of this, men say, 'It is not they who mock at us,' because they do not know the things which are said by them."[108]

This text is preserved in a manuscript dated paleographically to the later fifth century C.E., making it likely that the story is even earlier, although it is impossible to say precisely how early.[109] Both in the *Obsequies* and in *TSol* 20 we find a son and a father who appear before Solomon. The son is afflicted by a demon and eventually dies, although in the former text the father attempts to save his son, while in *TSol* 20 the father kills him. Both in the *Obsequies* and in *TSol* Solomon and a demon are involved, Solomon summons the old man before him[110] but he does not want to come, and the issue of demons knowing the future is significant. In keeping with *TSol*'s keen interest in demons, the demon Ornias's character is much more developed, and we are told in detail how demons know the future, whereas in the *Obsequies* demons are mentioned only in a single line toward the very end of the story.

W. Wright, the editor of the *Obsequies*, describes the manuscript as in poor condition, and the text before us bears this out. The first two pages present the story of Solomon, the old man, and his son, after which the text abruptly switches to a dialogue between Paul and the Apostles, and Solomon and the demons are never mentioned again. Even in its disjointed state, however, the text provides evidence that the story circulated in late antiquity in widely separated geographical contexts. Clearly the *Obsequies* presents this story independently of the full *TSol* context and further confirms the conclusion that *TSol* comprises early traditions despite the fact that its final form cannot be confirmed prior to the later Middle Ages.[111]

APPENDIX 3

It would be premature to draw conclusions about the applicability of Mesopotamian culture to the analysis of the Solomon/Ashmedai story prior to systematic analysis of the magical discourse of Mesopotamia, in particular

---

108. W. Wright, *Contributions to the Apocryphal Literature of the New Testament* (Oxford: Clarendon Press, 1865), pp. 42–43.

109. Schwarz, *Building a Book of Spells*, p. 115. The relevance of this text for study of *TSol* was first noted by M. R. James, "The Testament of Solomon," *Journal of Theological Studies* 24 (1922): 467–68, which is a review of McCown, *Testament*.

110. In the *Obsequies*, Solomon summons the boy before him as well.

111. Schwarz, *Building a Book of Spells*, pp. 114–20.

the Babylonian magic bowls. In the meantime, I note preliminarily that Levene, "The Magical *Get*," pp. 181–83, has shown several ways in which the vocabulary of the Ashmedai story and the magical/medical texts in Bavli Gittin, which together composes an extended discussion covering several folio pages of the Talmud (67b–70b), parallels that of the Babylonian magic bowls. See also Torijano, *Solomon the Esoteric King*, pp. 119–22. Levene, "The Magical *Get*," p. 182, also makes the important observation that Ashmedai is referred to both in the Bavli and in the magic bowls as the king of the demons, in contrast to *TSol* 2:9—3:1 (see Duling, *Testament*, p. 964), according to which the king of the demons is Beelzeboul rather than Ashmedai. See also M. J. Geller, "Two Incantation Bowls Inscribed in Syriac and Aramaic," *Bulletin of the School of Oriental and African Studies* 39 (1976): 426. To my knowledge, no late antique text from the Roman East refers to Ashmedai/Asmodeus as king of the demons.[112] Also, Alon Ten-Ami informs me that Song of Songs 3:7–8, cited at the conclusion of the Solomon/Ashmedai story, is one of the verses cited in the magic bowls in order to "divorce" demons from people afflicted by them. While we will see below that the Ashmedai story has much in common with *TSol*, in this significant respect as well the Talmudic story reveals itself to be a product of Mesopotamian Jewish culture.[113]

112. Ashmedai is mentioned relatively infrequently in the magic bowls, however, and other demons are referred to in the bowls as "king of the demons." Alon Ten-Ami informs me, furthermore, that "Bagdana" is referred to most frequently as king of the demons in the bowls.

113. The Babylonian magic bowls might likewise be a source of parallels to *TSol* that attest to the movement of traditions from the Roman East to late antique Mesopotamia. See, preliminarily, McCown, *Testament*, pp. 65–66; and Davies-Browne, *Significance of Parallels*, pp. 287–98. Montgomery Bowl 42, for example (see James A. Montgomery, *Aramaic Incantation Texts from Nippur* [Philadelphia: University Museum, 1913], pp. 258–64; and Schwarz, *Building a Book of Spells*, pp. 127–28), describes Elijah the Prophet encountering Lillith on her way to kill a baby. Elijah binds Lillith by placing a ban upon her, and she responds by revealing, "Every time that they repeat or I see my names written, it will not be in the power of me or of all my band to do evil or harm. And these are my names" (see Montgomery, *Aramaic Incantation Texts*, p. 260). As Schwarz observes, "The element of the bound demon providing the requisite information for future practitioners to use in their efforts is unusual and strikingly similar to the traditions in the *TSol*." See Schwarz, *Building a Book of Spells*, p. 128.

FIVE

Zechariah and the Bubbling Blood

AN ANCIENT TRADITION IN JEWISH, CHRISTIAN,
AND MUSLIM LITERATURE

THIS CHAPTER EXAMINES JEWISH, CHRISTIAN, and Muslim traditions about a murder in the Temple of Jerusalem and the fate of the victim's blood after death. The accounts examined here range chronologically and geographically from the first century C.E. in Syria to the thirteenth century in what is modern-day Iraq. We will argue that the story's meaning changed over time, and that the "original" story[1] was a nonrabbinic, probably Christian Hebrew tale that reflected the view that God had rejected the Israelites and had compassion for a prophet they had murdered, and that the rabbis incorporated this story into their literature, adding an Aramaic phrase that transformed it into a story about God's enduring *compassion* for the Israelites and a meditation on the problems involved in the effectuation of that compassion in a world without prophets. In addition, we will attempt to contribute to the ongoing scholarly analysis of the relationship between rabbinic literature on the one hand and Syriac, Arabic, and Ethiopic literature on the other.[2] In the process, we will reevaluate the relationship between ancient and early medieval Christianity, Islam, and Judaism. We will find surprising parallels between late antique rabbinic literature and Ethiopian Christian commentaries on the New Testament, and commonalities between

---

1. When we use the term "original" throughout this book, we refer to the most original version of a story we are presently capable of reconstructing.
2. For a discussion of the tradition in Ethiopian Christian literature, see Roger W. Cowley, "The 'Blood of Zechariah' (Mt. 23:35) in Ethiopian Exegetical Tradition," in *Studia Patristica* 18, vol. 1, *Papers of the Ninth International Conference of Patristic Studies, Oxford, 1983*, ed. Elizabeth A. Livingstone (Kalamazoo, MI: Cistercian Publications, 1985), p. 296; and idem, *Ethiopian Biblical Interpretation: A Study in Exegetical Tradition and Hermeneutics* (Cambridge: Cambridge University Press, 1988), pp. 65–70.

rabbinic literature, particularly the Bavli, and Syriac and Arabic literature composed in Persia, Mesopotamia, and Syria in the seventh to thirteenth centuries C.E., which served as a crucial link between Ethiopian Christian literature and the literature of the ancient world.

We will argue that the story, consisting of a Hebrew core to which several Aramaic phrases were added, was originally a nonrabbinic story incorporated into Palestinian rabbinic compilations,[3] and from there into the Bavli. The nonrabbinic character of the Hebrew core will be shown by its anomalous character within rabbinic literature and confirmed by parallels in Christian sources. As noted, rabbinic receptivity to nonrabbinic materials has been observed before, but the Bavli has been particularly prominent in these discussions,[4] and it is significant that we find such receptivity in Palestinian rabbinic corpora.

Examination of the numerous versions of this tradition reveals that it traveled from the Roman East to Mesopotamia in late antiquity and the early Middle Ages, like all of the other traditions examined in this study, since the earliest versions of the Zechariah tradition derived from the eastern Roman provinces and traveled from there to Mesopotamia and to Muslim Baghdad. We do not encounter the by now familiar phenomenon of traditions reaching the Bavli from nonrabbinic sources in the Roman East, however, since the Bavli clearly drew the tradition from Palestinian rabbinic literature.

The version of the tradition that most concerns us in the present study depicts the murder in the Temple of a priest named Zechariah. Several scholars speak of the Christian appropriation of the Jewish story of the murder of Zechariah ben Jehoida and its transformation into a story of the murder of Zechariah, the father of John the Baptist.[5] Others speak of the "mistaken

---

3. For purposes of clarity, we confine the discussion to the earliest versions of the story in rabbinic literature, in the Yerushalmi and the *Pesikta de-Rav Kahana,* and to the parallel in the Babylonian Talmud. See also the references to the version in t. Yoma 1:12 and parallels, cited in n. 10. In many contexts in Palestinian midrashic compilations, however, the story of Zechariah is a later addition, copied from the Bavli. See Pinhas Mandel, "Ha-Sipur be-Midrash Eikhah: Nusah ve-Signon," MA thesis, Hebrew University, 1983, pp. 166–70. For a discussion of the versions in *Kohelet Rabbah* and *Eikhah Rabbah,* see Richard Kalmin, "Zechariah and the Bubbling Blood: An Ancient Tradition in Jewish, Christian, and Muslim Literature," in *Jews and Christians in Sasanian Babylonia,* ed. Geoffrey Herman (Piscataway, NJ: Gorgias Press, forthcoming).

4. See the introduction.

5. See, for example, Jean-Daniel Dubois, "La mort de Zacharie: Mémoire juive et mémoire chrétienne," *Revue des Études Augustiniennes* 40 (1994): 36; and Schwemer, *Studien zu den frühjüdischen Propheten-legenden,* Vitae Prophetarum, vol. 2, p. 294.

combination" of the Chronicler's account of Zechariah who was killed in the Temple with the story about Zechariah, the father of John the Baptist.[6] It is unlikely, however, that so many ancient authors are guilty of the amateurish mistakes attributed to them by modern scholars, and in the present instance we will find compelling reason to conclude that the story originated in Christian circles and was subsequently incorporated into Jewish sources after the removal of its anti-Jewish sting. Despite the "original" story's polemical nature and the rabbis' adoption of the story as a response to the polemic, this study supports and adds detail to the recent scholarly characterization of the relatively fluid boundaries between Judaism and Christianity in the early centuries of the Common Era, since this polemical story passes from one religious tradition to another.

EARLY PALESTINIAN VERSIONS OF THE ZECHARIAH NARRATIVE

Modern scholars, particularly in the past several decades, have provided much insight into the rabbinic story of the Israelites' murder of Zechariah in the Jerusalem Temple, and the bubbling blood that refuses to rest until the avenging of Zechariah's murder.[7] Pinhas Mandel greatly advanced our ability to understand the story by refining Joseph Heinemann's insight that it survived in two primary versions. Mandel argues that one of the versions is Palestinian, in Hebrew, and the second is Babylonian, in Aramaic, although we will see that his insight is also in need of refinement. The earliest Palestinian versions, which differ only in minor details, survived in the

---

6. See, for example, Isaac Kalimi, "The Story about the Murder of the Prophet Zechariah in the Gospels and its Relation to Chronicles," *Revue Biblique* 116, no. 2 (2009): 253–54.

7. See, for example, Sheldon H. Blank, "The Death of Zechariah in Rabbinic Literature," *Hebrew Union College Annual* 12–13 (1937–38): 327–46; Yosef Heinemann, *Aggadot ve-Toldoteinhen* (Jerusalem: Keter, 1974), pp. 31–39; Betsy Amaru, "The Killing of the Prophets: Unraveling a Midrash," *Hebrew Union College Annual* 54 (1983): 166–70 and 178–80; Mandel, "Ha-Sipur be-Midrash Eikhah: Nusah ve-Signon," pp. 33*–34*, 165–73, and 96*–98*; Michael D. Swartz, "Bubbling Blood and Rolling Bones: Agency and Teleology in Rabbinic Myth," in *Antike Mythen: Medien Transformationen und Konstruktionen,* ed. Ueli Dill and Christine Walde (Berlin: Walter de Gruyter, 2009), pp. 224–31, 238–41; idem, *The Signifying Creator: Non-Textual Sources of Meaning in Ancient Judaism* (New York: New York University Press, 2012); and Isaac Kalimi, *The Retelling of Chronicles in Jewish Tradition and Literature* (Winona Lake, IN: Eisenbrauns, 2009), pp. 261–68.

Yerushalmi and the *Pesikta de-Rav Kahana*.[8] Other Palestinian midrashic corpora also preserve the story; but in these other contexts, scribes working long after the classical rabbinic period incorporated features of the Babylonian Talmudic version to varying degrees.[9]

The earliest rabbinic compilation to record the general outlines of the story is the *Tosefta*, redacted during the third century C.E.[10] This version of the story blames Temple priests for the murder of an unnamed priest on the ramp leading to the altar in the Temple. It illustrates the moral bankruptcy of the Temple priesthood, one of the rabbis' favorite themes, but it does not explicitly link the priests' debased moral state to the destruction of Jerusalem and the Temple.

Versions of the story in fourth- and fifth-century rabbinic compilations, the Yerushalmi and the *Pesikta de-Rav Kahana*,[11] refer to the victim as Zechariah and implicate the entire Israelite people in his murder. Several statements about the wickedness of the people of Jerusalem introduce this version of the story (parts 1–4 below), and it is evident that the Jerusalemites are a pars pro toto representing the Israelite people as a whole. The version of the Yerushalmi[12] is as follows:

(1) [Hebrew:] Said R. Yohanan, "Eighty thousand young priests were killed over the blood of Zechariah."

(2) R. Yudan asked R. Aha, "Where did they kill Zechariah? In the women's courtyard or in the Israelite courtyard?"

[R. Aha] said to him, "Not in the Israelite courtyard and not in the women's courtyard, but in the priests' courtyard."

(3) And they did not treat his blood like the blood of the ram or like the blood of the deer. In those cases it is written, "[And if any Israelite or any stranger who resides among them hunts down an animal or a bird that may be eaten], he shall pour out its blood and cover it with earth" (Lev 17:13). But here [in the case of

---

8. Mandel, "Ha-Sipur be-Midrash Eikhah: Nusah ve-Signon"; and idem, "Midrash Eikhah Rabati: Mavo u-Mahadurah Bikortit la-Parashah ha-Shelishit," PhD diss., Hebrew University, 1997, vol. 1, p. 195.

9. See Kalmin, "Zechariah and the Bubbling Blood" (forthcoming).

10. See t. Yoma 1:12 (unnamed priest) (= t. Shevu'ot 1:4). See also the parallel versions in *Sifrei Bemidbar*, ed. Horowitz, p. 222 (unnamed priest); y. Yoma 2:2 (39d) (unnamed priest); and b. Yoma 23a (unnamed priest).

11. Y. Ta'anit 4:7 (69a–b); and *Pesikta de-Rav Kahana*, ed. Mandelbaum, pp. 257–58.

12. For a discussion of the version in the *Pesikta de-Rav Kahana*, which differs from the version of the Yerushalmi in only minor details, see Kalmin, "Zechariah and the Bubbling Blood."

Zechariah, it is written], "For the blood she shed is still in her. She set it upon a bare rock. [She did not pour it out on the ground to cover it with earth]" (Ezek 24:7). Why all this? "So that it may stir up [My] fury to take vengeance [did] I set her blood upon the bare rock so that it was not covered" (Ezek 24:8).

(4) Israel committed seven sins that day. They murdered a priest and a prophet and a judge, and they shed innocent blood, and they defiled the [Temple] courtyard, and it was the Day of Atonement[13] that fell on the Sabbath.

(5a) [The story begins, still in Hebrew:] And when Nebuzaradan[14] ascended [to Jerusalem], he saw the blood boiling.

(5b) [Nebuzaradan] said to them, "What kind of blood is this?"

(5c) They said to him, "It is the blood of bulls and sheep and rams that we used to offer on the altar."

(5d) Immediately he sent and they brought bulls and rams and sheep and slaughtered them before [the blood] but the blood still boiled. And when [the Israelites] did not confess to him, he took them and suspended them on the scaffold.[15]

(5e) [The Israelites] said, "Since the Holy One blessed be He wants to claim this blood from us [we will reveal it to him]. They said to him, "It is the blood of a priest and a prophet and a judge who prophesied about us all of the things that you are doing to us. We stood over him and killed him."

(5f) Immediately he brought eighty thousand young priests and killed them upon [the blood]. But still the blood boiled.

(6) [Aramaic:] At that moment [Nebuzaradan] rebuked [Zechariah]. He said to him, "Do you want me to destroy[16] your entire nation on your account?"

---

13. See Epiphanius, *Panarion* 26. 12. 1–4 (Griechischen christlichen Schriftsteller, Series Graeca 25), pp. 290–92. According to Epiphanius, who flourished in fourth-century Palestine, roughly at the same time and place as the redaction of the Yerushalmi and the *Pesikta de-Rav Kahana*, *Genna Marias*, a text he characterizes as Gnostic, relates the murder of the prophet and High Priest Zechariah in the Temple on the Day of Atonement. Epiphanius, therefore, knows a Christian tradition that combines the story of the murder of Zechariah with one of the traditions that introduce the Palestinian rabbinic version of the story.

14. Nebuzaradan is Nebuchadnezzar's general.

15. He tortures them to induce them to confess. See Saul Lieberman, "Roman Legal Institutions in Early Rabbinics and in the *Acta Martyrum*," in *Texts and Studies* (New York: Ktav, 1944), pp. 13–15.

16. The word *novad* is not first-person plural, but first-person singular, a form commonly found in Aramaic. See E. Y. Kutscher, "Aramaic," in *Encyclopaedia Judaica*, vol. 3 (1971), col. 272. See also Michael Sokoloff, *A Dictionary of Jewish Palestinian Aramaic of the Byzantine Period* (Ramat-Gan, Israel: Bar Ilan University Press, 1992), p. 32. See Jeremiah 40:2–4 for a biblical source for this text's partly sympathetic portrayal of Nebuzaradan.

(5g) [Hebrew:] At that moment the Holy One blessed be He was filled with compassion and said, "If this one [that is, Nebuzaradan], who is flesh and blood and cruel, is filled with compassion for my children, I, about whom it is written, 'For the Lord your God is a compassionate God; He will not fail you nor will He destroy you. He will not forget the covenant with your fathers' (Deut 4:31), how much the more so [should I have compassion for My children]?"

(5h) At that moment He motioned to the blood and it was swallowed in its place.

Several scholars claim that the Zechariah referred to in this passage is Zechariah ben Jehoiada,[17] killed by order of King Joash according to 2 Chronicles 24:17–22:

> But after the death of Jehoiada, the officers of Judah came, bowing low to the king; and the king listened to them. They forsook the House of the Lord God of their fathers to serve the sacred posts and idols; and there was wrath upon Judah and Jerusalem because of this guilt of theirs. The Lord sent prophets among them to bring them back to Him; they admonished them but they would not pay heed. Then the spirit of God enveloped Zechariah son of Jehoiada the priest; he stood above the people and said to them, "Thus God said: 'Why do you transgress the commandments of the Lord when you cannot succeed? Since you have forsaken the Lord, He has forsaken you.'" They conspired against him and pelted him with stones in the court of the House of the Lord, by order of the king. King Joash disregarded the loyalty that his father Jehoiada had shown to him, and killed his son. As he was dying, he said, "May the Lord see and requite it."

While the biblical account above describes the murder of Zechariah by stoning, the continuation (see below) refers to "the blood of the son of Jehoiada the priest,"[18] which may have formed the basis for the rabbinic narrative's emphasis on blood.

It is far from unambiguous, however, that the rabbinic story's Zechariah should be understood as the Chronicler's Zechariah ben Jehoiada. Scholars

---

17. Heinemann, *Aggadot ve-Toldoteihen*, pp. 31–38; Scholter, "Israel Murdered Its Prophets," p. 76; Amaru, "Killing of the Prophets," pp. 160–70; and Hans-Jürgen Becker, "Die Zerstörung Jerusalems bei Matthäus und den Rabbinen," *New Testament Studies* 44, no. 1 (1998): 63.

18. The Masoretic text refers to "the blood of the *sons* of Jehoida," but Kalimi, *Retelling of Chronicles*, p. 37, argues that the reading of the Septuagint and the Vulgate ("the blood of the *son*") is preferable since the Bible describes the murder of only one son.

have noted, for example, that the rabbinic story ignores the Chronicler's explicit description of the divine punishment that Joash suffered as a result of his murder of Zechariah.[19] Immediately after the account of Zechariah's murder, 2 Chronicles 24:23–25 describes Joash's punishment as follows:

> At the turn of the year, the army of Aram marched against [Joash]; they invaded Judah and Jerusalem, and wiped out all the officers of the people from among the people, and sent all the booty they took to the king of Damascus. The invading army of Aram had come with but a few men, but the Lord delivered a very large army into their hands, because they had forsaken the Lord God of their fathers. They inflicted punishments on Joash. When they withdrew, having left him with many wounds, his courtiers plotted against him because of the blood of the son[20] of Jehoiada the priest, and they killed him in bed.

Scholars have suggested several explanations for what might have motivated the rabbis to ignore the Chronicler's explicit description of the punishment of Joash, and to blame instead the entire Israelite people and seek out a new punishment: the destruction of the first Temple and the slaughter of eighty thousand young priests.[21] It is possible, however, that the rabbinic story (parts 5a–h and 6) is one of a large number of legends that circulated in ancient Palestine about the murder in the Temple of a variety of different figures named Zechariah (see above).[22] Perhaps the significance of the name Zechariah—"God Remembers" or "Remember God"—provides a key to the significance of the name in these diverse contexts,[23] or perhaps "Zechariah" was chosen simply because Zechariah was a standard name for priests in ancient Jewish literature.[24] It may be a mistake, therefore, to insist on iden-

---

19. See, for example, Heinemann, *Aggadot ve-Toldoteihen*, p. 32.

20. See n. 18 above.

21. See, for example, Amaru, "Killing of the Prophets," pp. 178–80. See also Schwemer, *Studien zu den frühjüdischen Propheten-legenden*, vol. 2, pp. 297 and 300.

22. Similar stories were also told about priests with names other than Zechariah. See, for example, Josephus, *Antiquities* 11.297–301, for his account of the murder of the priest Jeshua in the Temple, an outrage that Josephus claims led to the defilement of the Temple and to the Israelites' enslavement by the Persians. See also Eusebius, *Ecclesiastical History* 2.23.11–18, ed. and trans. Kirsopp Lake (1926; Cambridge, MA: Harvard University Press, 1998), who relates the account of Hegesippus (second half of the second century) of the stoning in the Temple of James, brother of Jesus.

23. See also Dubois, "La mort de Zacharie," pp. 36–38; and Galit Hasan-Rokem, *Web of Life: Folklore and Midrash in Rabbinic Literature* (Stanford: Stanford University Press, 2000), p. 170.

24. See Daniel Schwartz, "Ha-Im Hayah Rabban Yohanan ben Zakkai Kohen?" *Sinai* 88, nos. 1–2 (1981): 37–39.

tifying this character as a specific Zechariah in the absence of compelling proof. It is important to note, furthermore, that it is not until the Byzantine period, in the fourth or fifth century, that we find *in any text* explicit identification of the murdered priest, Zechariah, as Zechariah ben Jehoiada.

ANALYSIS OF THE EARLY PALESTINIAN RABBINIC VERSIONS

The story in the Yerushalmi is almost entirely in Hebrew, with the notable exception of part 6, which is in Aramaic: "At that moment [Nebuzaradan] rebuked [Zechariah]. He said to him, 'What do you think? Do you want us to kill your entire nation on your account?'" It is likely that the change in language serves a narrative function, since Nebuzaradan's Aramaic interjection (part 6) is a pivotal point in the story, resulting in God's intervention and a sudden end to the slaughter. This conclusion, however, does not preclude other explanations, for example, that language switching from Hebrew to Aramaic and back again indicates that the Aramaic section may be a later addition to the text.[25]

Strengthening this second explanation is the fact that removal of part 6 solves a problem in the text. To appreciate this fact, it is necessary to examine in detail the passage, which at first glance appears to be rendered incoherent by removal of the Aramaic section. Without the Aramaic, Nebuzaradan kills the young priests, the narrator informs us that the blood continued to boil, and immediately thereafter God reasons a fortiori (part 5g) that if the cruel Babylonian general had compassion, how much the more so should God Himself. It will be helpful to reproduce this portion of the story, minus the Aramaic:

> (5f) Immediately [Nebuzaradan] took eighty thousand young priests and killed them upon [the blood] until the blood reached the grave of Zechariah. But still the blood boiled.
>
> (5g) At that moment the Holy One blessed be He was filled with compassion and said, "If this one, who is flesh and blood and cruel, here today and gone tomorrow, is filled with compassion for my children, I, about whom it is written, 'For the Lord your God is a compassionate God; He will not fail you nor will He destroy you' (Deut 4:31), how much the more so [should I have compassion for my children]?"

25. See also the examples discussed in detail in the introduction, and in chapter 2.

Does removal of the Aramaic phrase yield a more coherent narrative? In one significant sense the answer is "yes," since the Aramaic creates some tension in the story. In part 5e the Israelites inform Nebuzaradan that the blood is boiling because *God* wants to punish the Israelites, while in part 6 Nebuzaradan addresses Zechariah as if *he* is responsible for the blood continuing to boil ("[Aramaic:] At that moment [Nebuzaradan] rebuked [Zechariah]. He said to him, 'Do you want us to kill your entire nation on your account?'"). The Aramaic addition, therefore, creates a rough spot in the narrative that makes it difficult to fully comprehend.[26]

According to the Hebrew text minus the Aramaic, however, God describes Nebuzaradan as having compassion for the Israelites (part 5g) right after the Babylonian general killed eighty thousand young priests, and it is difficult to understand how this can be viewed as "compassion." If we understand God in part 5g as referring to *Zechariah* rather than to the *Israelites,* however, then our problem is solved. According to this interpretation, God says: "If this one, who is flesh and blood and cruel, is filled with compassion for my son [that is, Zechariah], I, about whom it is written, 'For the Lord your God is a compassionate God; He will not fail you nor will He destroy you. He will not forget the covenant with your fathers' (Deut 4:31), how much the more so [should I have compassion for my son]?" God refers to Nebuzaradan's persistent attempts to make the blood stop boiling, characterizing his actions as "compassion" for the murdered Zechariah, since the Babylonian general wants the blood to be absorbed in the ground, thereby achieving peace and reconciliation rather than continuing forever in its unsettled state. Seen in this light, it makes perfect sense that God's very next move is to "signal to the blood" to be absorbed into the ground, ending Zechariah's torment. Supporting this interpretation is the fact that part 3, one of the statements introducing the story in the Yerushalmi, states explicitly that the Israelites' failure to "bury" the blood of Zechariah contributed greatly to the heinousness of their crime, infuriating God and inciting Him to take vengeance against His sinful people.

This interpretation requires a tiny emendation of the text, removing one *yud* from the word "My children" *(bet, nun, yud, yud)* so that it can be read in the singular: "My child" or "My son" *(bet, nun, yud)*. This is a particularly slight emendation because the word I wish to translate as "My child" *(bet,*

---

26. It is possible, of course, that the story depicts the Babylonian general as unable to grasp the fact that God is completely in control.

nun, yud) can mean both "My child" (in which case it would be pronounced *beni*) and "My children" (in which case it would be pronounced *banay*), since the difference between "My child" and "My children" in Hebrew can be impossible to distinguish orthographically, with the consonants identical and only the vowels distinguishable, and neither the *Pesikta de-Rav Kahana* nor the Yerushalmi were written with vowels.[27] Once Nebuzaradan's Aramaic rebuke of Zechariah was added to the text, requiring the interpretation that God and Nebuzaradan were being compassionate toward the *Israelites* ("My children"), the extra *yud* was added to clarify the text, since the word *banay* must refer to the plural ("My children") rather than the singular ("My son").

The (hypothesized) original, completely Hebrew version of the story,[28] therefore, ended with God stopping the slaughter not because He decided to be compassionate toward the Israelites, but because He decided to be compassionate toward Zechariah. The lesson according to this version is that Israel's sins were too terrible to be forgiven, or that Israel, by killing her prophets, had removed the mechanism by which she traditionally achieved forgiveness. The prophets of old interceded with God on Israel's behalf, enabling her relationship with God to end in something other than total disaster, but with the traditional prophets gone, that arrangement was no longer in effect. The "original" Hebrew story, therefore, did not depict a "bloodthirsty" Zechariah, who refuses to be placated by the slaughter of thousands of Israelites, but a tragic Zechariah, who is powerless to act on his own behalf.

If we object that it is unlikely that a rabbinic text would deliver such a message, we must counter that rabbis only transmitted the story with the Aramaic passage, which changes the story's message radically. It is impossible to say with certainty what kind of storyteller created the hypothesized Hebrew story, since it is undeniable that the perspectives and creative efforts of many ancient groups and individuals perished through neglect. While Christians did not necessarily have a hand in the creation of the Hebrew story (but see below), they certainly constitute a conspicuous example of a group (or, more precisely, groups) that at some point in their history undoubtedly composed texts in Hebrew[29] and had a view of the relationship between

---

27. The same is true of nearly all classical rabbinic texts.
28. Or the most original version of the story that we can presently reconstruct.
29. It is uncertain, however, whether we can trust the specific attestations of such Hebrew texts by patristic authors. See, for example, Eusebius, *Ecclesiastical History* 5.10.2–3; and Epiphanius, *Panarion* II.30.3.7; Frank Williams, *The Panarion of Epiphanius of Salamis* (Leiden: Brill, 1994), p. 122.

Israel and its God that differed radically from standard rabbinic views and that closely approximated the view described here.

The addition of the Aramaic phrase in part 6, in which Nebuzaradan directly addresses Zechariah's blood, appears to be motivated in part by exegetical considerations, to explain how God could describe the Babylonian general as compassionate right after he tortures and murders thousands of Israelites. In addition, the Aramaic was probably added to change the story from one in which God refuses to have mercy upon the Israelites to a story in which God *does* ultimately have compassion for them. Perhaps the Aramaic was also added to increase the drama of the narrative, by creating a direct confrontation between Nebuzaradan and Zechariah and by enabling Zechariah to display a certain amount of independent motivation, and to signal the arrival of the narrative's turning point, since Nebuzaradan's Aramaic outburst induces God to intervene and finally bring a stop to the slaughter.

Addition of the Aramaic phrase also appears to be motivated by the desire to distance God from full responsibility for the deaths of thousands of Israelites. As noted, Nebuzaradan's Aramaic statement to Zechariah contradicts the Hebrew story's clear message that from beginning to end God alone determines the actions of the blood and therefore the fate of the Israelites. With the Aramaic addition, God's reaction to Nebuzaradan's rebuke appears to be a powerful endorsement of the general's belief that Zechariah is partly responsible for the behavior of his blood and therefore for the harshness of the Israelites' punishment. God desires to punish the Israelites for shedding innocent blood, but with the Aramaic addition, it is Zechariah who determines the severity of the punishment. At the same time, however, the Aramaic addition depicts a God who needs a murderous Gentile intercessor to convince Him to stop the slaughter of His people, so whoever added the Aramaic rebuke appears to have powerfully conflicted feelings about the role of God in the world and the character of God's relationship to the Israelites. With the addition of the Aramaic, the story still delivers a stunning message: that in this day and age, God rarely intervenes to stop devastation because the Israelites killed their prophets, whose job it had been to check the force of God's righteous anger against His sinful people. Instead of the great prophets of old, who could be counted on to argue with God on Israel's behalf, the Israelites now depended on strangers, whose "mercy," if it could be counted on at all, might be won at the price of massive slaughter, making the effectuation of God's compassion in the world far more difficult than it had ever been. Still, even in this hostile, uncertain world, it is words and a change of mind and heart rather than bloodshed that succeed in arousing God's compassion.[30]

If we are correct in our reconstruction of the "original" Hebrew story, we may have another reason to believe that the Zechariah mentioned in 2 Chronicles is not the original protagonist, for one of the most prominent features of the Chronicler's Zechariah is his call for vengeance at the story's climax: "May the Lord see and requite it." Perhaps part 6 was added, in fact, by transmitters of the story who *were* convinced that Zechariah was Zechariah ben Jehoiada. Perhaps with this identification came the need to make Zechariah's desire for vengeance a significant part of the plot, as it unmistakably was in Chronicles. We should not press this point too far, however, since the storyteller(s) did not feel bound to incorporate other prominent features of the biblical narrative, and it is not at all clear why they included certain features and ignored or contradicted others.

Several rabbinic versions of the story, both Palestinian and Babylonian, postdating the versions of the Yerushalmi and the *Pesikta* but nevertheless still deriving from late antiquity depict God or Nebuzaradan addressing Zechariah's blood and expressing concern that it receive its due.[31] It is, in fact, a common idea in biblical, second-Temple, and classical rabbinic sources that innocent blood shed by man is offensive to God, who will surely avenge it, and we find other cases in which innocent blood cries out until it is avenged.[32] Job 16:18, for example, quotes Job's anguished plea: "Earth, do not cover my blood; let there be no resting place for my outcry."[33] These facts further support my claim that a late antique rabbinic author could tell a story in which the protagonist's concern for a dead man is expressed through

---

30. For the latter point about discourse versus blood, see Matthew Kraus, "Zechariah's Blood and the Destruction of the Temple: An Anthropological Reading of Lamentations Rabbah 23," paper delivered at the Society of Biblical Literature Conference in San Diego, 2007.

31. See below for the discussion of the Bavli's version, and see Kalmin, "Zechariah and the Bubbling Blood," for discussion of the versions in *Eikhah Rabbah* and *Kohelet Rabbah*.

32. For a parallel in classical Greek sources, see Aeschylus, *Choephori*, ed. A. F. Garvie (Oxford: Oxford University Press, 1986), lines 66–74 and 152–56. See there, p. 64: "Because of blood drunk up by the nurturing earth the avenging gore lies solid and does not flow away." See also p. 65: "Just as there is no remedy for the violation of virginity . . . so it is impossible to purify or wash away the stain of murder." See also pp. 82–85 there.

33. See also Genesis 4:10; Isaiah 26:21; Ezekiel 24:7–8; Job 16:18; *Assumption of Moses* 9:6–7; 1 Enoch 47:1–4; Matthew 25:35; m. Sanhedrin 6:5; and *Bereshit Rabbah*, ed. Theodor and Albeck, pp. 215–16. See also the discussion below.

solicitude for the fate of his blood and concern that it receive a "decent burial." Surprisingly, an Amharic commentary on Matthew 23:35 further supports this claim.

Matthew 23:35 reads as follows:

> Therefore I am sending you prophets and wise men and teachers. Some of them you will kill and crucify, others you will flog in your synagogues and pursue from town to town. And so upon you will come all the righteous blood that has been shed on earth, from the blood of righteous Abel to the blood of Zechariah son of Berekhiah,[34] whom you murdered between the Temple and the altar.

The Amharic commentary reads as follows:

> (1) Another says, "He was comparing the accusation of the blood of the one with the other, for the blood of Abel said, 'Cain my brother killed me,' and the blood of Zechariah remained bubbling for seventy years."

> (2) Another says, "When the angel took Enoch to show him the place of souls, he [Enoch], having seen among many souls one soul separated by itself, crying out and making accusations, asked him [the angel], saying, 'Whose soul is this?' He replied, 'The soul of Abel, whom Cain killed, will accuse him until the time when his seed will perish from the face of the earth in the water of the flood' (1 Enoch 22:6–7). Similarly, the blood of Zechariah remained bubbling throughout seventy years. The king was called Titus; seeing it, he asked what it was. People said to him, 'There was a good priest, and they put him to death unjustly.' [He asked], 'What can be done for it, so that it cease its bubbling?' They said to him, '[It will cease] if they put to death relatives of those who put him to death.' When he [Titus] had about seven of Herod's relatives brought and put to death for it, it ceased bubbling."[35]

Clearly there are striking similarities between the rabbinic story and the Amharic commentary. Most notably, the rabbinic and Ethiopian traditions share in common the motif of the blood that bubbles until the arrival of a foreign leader. And significantly for our purposes, the Ethiopian story implies that Titus is motivated by compassion for Zechariah but not for the Israelites when he puts to death the seven relatives, as is shown by his question—"What can be done for it, so that it cease its bubbling?"—which cor-

---

34. For variants of this name, see Kalimi, *Retelling of Chronicles*, pp. 49–53.

35. *Wängel Qəddus* (Addis Ababa, 1916), p. 163. See Cowley, "The 'Blood of Zechariah,'" p. 293, who translates the text from a manuscript in his possession.

responds to our understanding of Nebuzaradan's actions in the "original" rabbinic story. In addition, the soul of Abel, "separated by itself and crying out," appears to be suffering and will continue to suffer until the murder has been avenged, and the text explicitly states that Zechariah's blood is similar to Abel's soul.

Roger Cowley contends that it is unlikely that there is a direct connection between the rabbinic and the Ethiopian commentaries,[36] but it is possible that the similarities noted above indicate that rabbinic sources on the one hand and the Syriac and Arabic commentaries upon which the Ethiopian sources are based on the other drew upon a common storehouse of themes and motifs.[37]

Supporting this conclusion is the work of Abū al Faraj 'Abd Allāh ibn al-Tayyib, a Christian who wrote in Arabic and flourished in Baghdad during the first half of the eleventh century, and whose commentary was an important source used by the Ethiopian Christians.[38] According to Sebastian Brock, through Ibn al-Tayyib's Arabic commentaries "the East-Syrian exegetical tradition reaches the later Coptic and Ethiopian traditions,"[39] and Cowley describes Ibn al-Tayyib's influence on Ethiopian exegetical tradition as "very pervasive."[40] Ibn al-Tayyib writes that Herod killed Zechariah, and his blood cried out and bubbled for fifty-eight years until Titus avenged it.[41] Ibn al-Tayyib's version of the story, therefore, like the Ethiopian commentary and our hypothesized rabbinic story, depicts Zechariah's suffering blood avenged by a sympathetic Gentile king. Ibn Mas'ud (d. 652), Ibn al-'Abbās (d. 686), and al-Suddi (d. 745), seventh- and eighth-century authors of histories and commentaries on the Qoran, similarly depict Nebuchadnezzar killing tens of thousands of Israelites to induce God to stop the bubbling blood of John the Baptist, murdered according to legend by an Israelite king. They

---

36. Cowley, "The 'Blood of Zechariah,'" p. 296; and idem, *Ethiopian Biblical Interpretation*, pp. 87 and 92–93.

37. See also the discussion below.

38. See Cowley, "The 'Blood of Zechariah,'" pp. 295 and 299; and idem, *Ethiopian Biblical Interpretation*, pp. 87 and 92–93.

39. Sebastian P. Brock, *A Brief Outline of Syriac Literature* (Kottayam: St. Ephrem Ecumenical Research Institute, 1997), p. 94.

40. Cowley, *Ethiopian Biblical Interpretation*, p. 387. See also Julian Faultless, "The Two Recensions of the Prologue to John in ibn al-Tayyib's Commentary on the Gospels," in *Christians at the Heart of Islamic Rule: Church Life and Scholarship in 'Abbasid Iraq*, ed. David Richard Thomas (Leiden: Brill, 2003), p. 178.

41. See Cowley, "The 'Blood of Zechariah,'" pp. 294–96, 298.

make no mention of the Gentile king's compassion for the Israelites as a motive for stopping the blood from boiling, only of the need to avenge the murder of John the Baptist.[42]

Just as clearly, however, there are striking differences between the rabbinic story and the Amharic commentary. The major differences are the explicit identification of Zechariah's murderer in the Ethiopian account, the number of years that the blood boiled, and the specification of seven relatives killed by Titus to avenge Zechariah's murder. In the Palestinian version of the rabbinic story, furthermore, the blood continues to boil even after Nebuzaradan slaughters the priests, prompting God to intervene and put a stop to the slaughter. In the Ethiopian story, in contrast, the blood stops boiling immediately after Titus kills the seven relatives, with no explicit intervention by God. These distinctions serve as a warning against overly facile use of the Christian story as a hermeneutical key for understanding the rabbinic story.[43]

Significantly, however, the absence of God from the Ethiopian commentary and from Ibn al-Tayyib has an exact parallel in all but one manuscript of the Babylonian rabbinic version of the story.[44] An eleventh-century Arabic work by 'Abū-Raihūn Muḥammad ibn 'Aḥmad al-bīrūnī (d. 1048) also makes no mention of God:

> *Alma'mūn b. 'Aḥmad Absalamī al-Harawī* saw in Jerusalem some heaps of stones at a gate, called the Gate of the Column; they had been gathered so as to form something like hills and mountains. Now people said that those were thrown over the blood of John the son of Zacharias, but that the blood rose

---

42. See Heinrich Schützinger, "Die arabische Legende von Nebukadnezar und Johannes dem Täufer," *Der Islam* 40 (1965): 113–41, esp. pp. 114–17, 128, and 132–34; and Brannon N. Wheeler, *Prophets in the Quran: An Introduction to the Quran and Muslim Exegesis* (New York: Continuum, 2002), pp. 294–96. See also *The History of al-Tabari*, vol. 4, *The Ancient Kingdoms*, trans. Moshe Perlmann (Albany: SUNY Press, 1987), pp. 103–6.

43. Also distinguishing the Ethiopian and the rabbinic traditions: (1) In the rabbinic story, the Israelites give evasive answers until Nebuzaradan slaughters thousands of priests, prompting them to admit that it is the blood of "a priest and a prophet and a judge" who they unjustly killed; in the Ethiopian story, in contrast, unnamed "others" immediately inform Titus that the Israelites unjustly killed a good priest. (2) In the rabbinic story, Nebuzaradan kills the priests on his own initiative; in the Ethiopian story, Titus acts only after receiving advice from the unnamed "others." (3) In the rabbinic story, Nebuzaradan randomly kills a huge number of priests; in the Ethiopian story, Titus kills seven relatives of Zechariah's murderers. See also the discussion below.

44. See below, and see Heinemann, *Aggadot ve-Toldoteihen*, p. 38.

over them, boiling and bubbling. This went on until Nebukadnezar killed the people and made their blood flow over it, then it was quiet.[45]

We should not overestimate the importance of the absence of God from these versions in distinguishing them from the rabbinic versions, however, since many rabbinic traditions presuppose the activity of God behind the scenes. It would not be surprising if the same is true of the Arabic,[46] Syriac,[47] and Ethiopian versions of this narrative, and we will see below that the Bavli's version of the narrative, according to all but one manuscript, likewise makes no explicit mention of God. Given all we are learning about the frequency with which the Bavli and nonrabbinic corpora made use of common sources and literary motifs, however, we should not ignore this significant parallel between the Arabic, Syriac, Ethiopian, and Babylonian rabbinic versions of the story, a parallel absent from the Palestinian rabbinic versions of the narrative.

Significantly, the conclusion of the Ethiopian story is modeled after the biblical story of David, Saul, and the Gibeonites in 2 Samuel 21:1–14. In the biblical story, God informs King David that a lengthy famine afflicted Israel because King Saul had "put some Gibeonites to death" (2 Sam 21:1). David asks the Gibeonites how he can "make expiation, so that you may bless the Lord's own people" (2 Sam 21:3), and the Gibeonites demand that seven of Saul's male relatives be handed over to them, "and we will impale them before the Lord in Gibeah of Saul" (2 Sam 21:6). David complies, the Gibeonites kill Saul's relatives, and God ends the famine.

The Ethiopian story, therefore, uses the biblical story of the Gibeonites as a model for the vengeance that will calm Zechariah's restless blood. Interestingly, the Yerushalmi as well, in another context, develops the bibli-

---

45. C. Eduard Sachau, ed. and trans., *The Chronology of Ancient Nations* (1879; Whitefish, MT: Kessinger, 2006), p. 297. See also Ronald Herbert Sack, *Images of Nebuchadnezzar: The Emergence of a Legend* (Selinsgrove, PA: Susquehanna University Press, 2004), pp. 44–45.

46. See also the discussion of the account in Tabarī below.

47. *Solomon Akhlat,* writing in Syriac in the early thirteenth century in what is modern-day Iraq, also tells the story with no explicit mention of God. See *The Book of the Bee,* ed. and trans., E. A. Wallis Budge (Oxford: Clarendon Press, 1886), p. 86. See also A. A. Barb, "St. Zacharias the Prophet and Martyr: A Study in Charms and Incantations," *Journal of the Warburg and Courtland Institutes* 11 (1948): 50–52; and the Coptic translation of Cyril of Jerusalem's fourth-century *Discourse on the Cross,* in *Miscellanious Coptic Texts in the Dialect of Upper Egypt,* ed. and trans. E. A. Wallis Budge (1915; New York: AMS Press, 1977), pp. cvi, 778, and 785.

cal account of David, Saul, and the Gibeonites in a manner strikingly similar to the rabbinic accounts, both Palestinian and Babylonian, of the blood of Zechariah.[48] We will expand below on the significance of this additional commonality between Ethiopian Christian and late antique rabbinic literature.

Further complicating our efforts to understand the relationship between the rabbinic and Ethiopian accounts is the uncertain chronology of the Ethiopian commentaries. Roger Cowley contends that while they were compiled in relatively recent centuries, they undoubtedly contain much older traditions, and their importance for shedding light on ancient traditions from other cultures should not be underestimated.[49] To quote Cowley: "I see [the Ethiopian commentaries] as inheritors of much non-Ethiopian exegetical activity of the second to thirteenth centuries A.D., and (while distinctly Ethiopian in their present forms) as parallel to medieval exegesis in other countries."[50] If Cowley is correct, then just as the testimony of a medieval rabbinic commentator, or the version of an ancient tradition preserved in a medieval rabbinic anthology, is valuable[51] testimony regarding the text and the interpretation of the ancient tradition, so too should we not dismiss the importance of the Ethiopian commentaries, especially given the fact that they drew so heavily on Syriac and Arabic commentaries from the seventh to thirteenth centuries, which in turn drew heavily on late antique commentators such as Theodore of Mopsuestia and John Chrysostom, and also given the convergence of what would appear to be independent parallels that they share with the rabbinic Zechariah and Gibeonite accounts.

THE NARRATIVE IN THE BAVLI

Detailed examination of the Zechariah story in the Bavli sheds further light on the relationship between Nebuzaradan's rebuke and the remainder of

---

48. See, however, the important discussion of Cowley, *Ethiopian Biblical Interpretation*, pp. 11–24 and 65–93, especially his cautious formulation on pp. 66 and 92–97.

49. See Roger W. Cowley, *The Traditional Interpretation of the Apocalypse of St. John in the Ethiopian Orthodox Church* (Cambridge: Cambridge University Press, 1983), p. 23; and idem, "The 'Blood of Zechariah,'" p. 297.

50. Cowley, *Ethiopian Biblical Interpretation*, p. viii. See also pp. 11–62, where Cowley discusses the relationship between the Ethiopian commentaries and earlier Christian and Muslim sources, many of them late antique.

51. Although hardly unimpeachable.

the story. The "rough spot" we discerned in the Palestinian versions, attributable, we argued, to the later addition of Nebuzaradan's Aramaic rebuke, is missing from the Bavli's version, since in the Bavli there is no tension between conflicting explanations of the slaughter of the Israelites. It is likely that Babylonian storytellers and editors inherited the story from Palestinian rabbis and edited out this rough spot, in keeping with the relationship we often find between traditions in Palestinian and Babylonian corpora.

The Bavli's version of the tradition exhibits another sign of development vis-à-vis the Palestinian versions, further proof that the tradition moved from the Roman East to Mesopotamia during late antiquity. It will be recalled that according to the version of the Yerushalmi, Nebuzaradan apparently sacrifices the animals to induce the blood to stop boiling, although his precise motivation is less than fully transparent. This point will be clearer if we reproduce the relevant part of the narrative in the present context:

> (5a) And when Nebuzaradan ascended [to Jerusalem], he saw the blood boiling.
>
> (5b) [Nebuzaradan] said to them, "What kind of blood is this?"
>
> (5c) They said to him, "It is the blood of bulls and sheep and rams that we used to offer on the altar."
>
> (5d) Immediately he sent and they brought bulls and rams and sheep and slaughtered them before [the blood] but the blood still boiled. And when [the Israelites] did not confess to him, he took them and suspended them on the scaffold.

Perhaps Nebuzaradan reasons that the blood boils because he destroyed the Temple and the Israelites therefore can no longer offer sacrifices. Perhaps he reasons that the old sacrificial blood boils in protest at the fact that Israel can no longer maintain its cultic relationship with God. Perhaps the blood boils because it is the blood of an individual who has been the victim of a horrible crime that needs to be atoned for. When new sacrifices fail to stop the blood from boiling, Nebuzaradan knows that the Israelites are lying. The Bavli (see below) apparently rewrites this part of the story to make Nebuzaradan's motivations more easily comprehensible.

Of crucial importance for our attempt to analyze the Bavli's version of the tradition, language change confronts us in the Bavli as well, and supports the claim that Nebuzaradan's rebuke is a later addition. Several versions of the Bavli formulate the rebuke entirely in Hebrew, such that in the Bavli as well this passage stands out in what is for the most part a Babylonian Aramaic story.[52]

One of these versions is ms Yad Harav Herzog 1 of Bavli Sanhedrin 96b, considered to be the "best" manuscript of Bavli Sanhedrin.[53] Significantly, this manuscript exhibits several features of the Palestinian versions of the story, and its version of the story is confirmed by an important genizah fragment.[54] We read there:

(1) [Aramaic:] [Nebuzaradan] saw the blood of Zechariah that it was boiling and rising.

(2) [Nebuzaradan] said to [the Israelites], "What is this?"

(3) They said to him, "It is the blood of sacrifices that we offered before the Holy One, blessed be He."

(4) He brought the blood of bulls and deer. He compared it but it was not the same. He brought all kinds of blood. He compared it but it was not the same.

(5) He said to them, "If you tell me, it is well, but if not, I will comb your flesh with combs of iron."

(6) They said to him, "Since you spoke to us thus, how can we hide it from you? We had a prophet [and] a priest who rebuked us for the sake of heaven. We did not accept what he said; rather we rose against him and killed him [Hebrew:] on a Day of Atonement that fell on the Sabbath."[55]

(7) [Aramaic:] He said to them, "I will appease him."

(8) He brought the Great Sanhedrin, slaughtered [them] over [the blood] but it did not rest. [He brought] the Lesser Sanhedrin, slaughtered [them] over [the blood] but it did not rest. [He brought] eighty thousand young priests, slaughtered [them] over [the blood] but it did not rest. He brought children

---

52. Many versions of the Bavli, however, formulate the rebuke partly in Hebrew and partly in Aramaic. See the discussion below.

53. See Mordechai Sabato, *Ketav-Yad Temani le-Massekhet Sanhedrin (Bavli) u-Mekomo bi-Mesoret ha-Nusah* (Jerusalem: Yad Yizhak Ben-Zvi, 1998), pp. 3, 333–43, and passim. In translating this manuscript's version of the story, I make note of manuscript variants only when they bear materially on our discussion.

54. Ibid., pp. 17 and 304–5, notes that this genizah fragment, *T-S Misc. 26.55*, resembles ms Yad ha-Rav Herzog 1 in most respects. I thank Professor Sabato for providing me with a photograph of the genizah fragment, which confirmed his published remarks.

55. This Hebrew phrase is missing from all other versions of the Bavli, both in Gittin and Sanhedrin. The photograph of the genizah fragment, *T-S Misc. 26.55*, is illegible in this spot.

from the schoolhouse, slaughtered [them] over [the blood] but it did not rest. He brought young boys and elders,[56] slaughtered them over it but it did not rest. He brought young men and virgins, slaughtered them over it but it did not rest.[57]

(9) [Hebrew:] [Nebuzaradan] said to him, "Zechariah, Zechariah, the good ones among your people I have destroyed. Is it your desire to destroy them all?"[58]

(10) Immediately the Holy One blessed be He signaled to [the blood] and it was swallowed.[59]

(11) He thought to repent and applied an a fortiori argument to himself, saying, "If Israel, who violated the law by killing one person [was punished severely], I,[60] who destroyed so many Jews, how much the more so [will I be punished severely]?"

(12) [Aramaic:][61] [Nebuzaradan] said, "If the Holy One blessed be He wants to destroy His House and put the blame on me,[62] how much the more so [will I be punished severely]?

(13) He fled, caused a rift in his family,[63] and converted.

As noted, this story is rendered in Babylonian Aramaic, with the exception of a notable section in Hebrew. In part 6, the phrase "on a Day of Atonement that fell on the Sabbath" is in Hebrew, and the same idea in almost the identical phraseology is recorded in one of the passages introducing the Zechariah story in the Palestinian versions, but it is attested in no other version or manuscript of the story itself, either Babylonian or Palestinian. The fact that it was

56. Or "old men."
57. Kalimi, *Retelling of Chronicles,* p. 263 observes the echoes of 2 Chronicles 36:17 in this context: "Therefore he brought up against them the king of the Chaldeans, who slew their young men with the sword in the house of their sanctuary, and had no compassion on youth, maiden, elder, or greybeard, but delivered them all into his hand." For manuscript versions of this passage in Sanhedrin and Gittin, see n. 93.
58. The reading of part 9 in T-S Misc. 26.55 is "[Hebrew:] Zechariah, the good ... I have destroyed. Is it your will that I destroy all of them?" That is, Nebuzaradan's rebuke is entirely in Hebrew, and the parts that are legible match ms Yad ha-Rav Herzog 1 completely.
59. Mention of God signaling to Zechariah is missing from all other versions of the Bavli (including T-S Misc. 26.55), both in Gittin and Sanhedrin. The reading in all other versions is "Immediately [the blood] rested," or some slight variant thereof. See the discussion below, where we argue that here as well, the scribe of ms Yad ha-Rav Herzog 1 copied directly from the Yerushalmi.
60. Literally, "that man."
61. T-S Misc. 26.55 also reverts to Aramaic here.
62. Literally, "wipe His hand on that man."
63. See Sokoloff, *A Dictionary of Jewish Babylonian Aramaic,* p. 932.

apparently added based on a tradition originating in Palestinian corpora, and that it is only in one manuscript of the Bavli,[64] suggests that it was added to the Bavli's text of the story at a relatively late date, probably post-redactionally.[65] Interestingly, the addition was made to the Bavli on the basis of a tradition in Palestinian compilations, a phenomenon that scholars have likewise noticed before, albeit with relative infrequency.

Part 10 is also in Hebrew, and it also preserves a feature of the Palestinian versions of the story found in no other Babylonian version: "Immediately the Holy One, blessed be He signaled to [the blood] and it was swallowed." As noted, in all other manuscript versions of the story in the Bavli there is no explicit mention of God (see above),[66] although we argued that the Babylonian versions of the story probably understood God as active "behind the scenes." In other manuscript versions of the Bavli the story reads here simply, "Immediately [the blood] rested," or a slight variation thereof. According to ms Yad ha-Rav Herzog 1, even the Babylonian version explicitly mentions God, although we are probably confronted here with a second addition to the manuscript based on the Palestinian version of the story that expresses the same idea in exactly the same words.[67]

The most important Hebrew passage in this manuscript and in the genizah fragment, however, is part 9: "[Nebuzaradan] said to him, 'Zechariah, Zechariah, the good ones among your people I have destroyed. Is it your desire to destroy them all?'" We concluded above that the later provenance of Nebuzaradan's rebuke in the Yerushalmi and the *Pesikta de-Rav Kahana* is indicated in part by the change of language from Hebrew to Aramaic. The later provenance of Nebuzaradan's rebuke in the Bavli is apparently also indicated

---

64. Along with ms JTS ENA 2089.6, which records a Hebrew abridgement of the story.

65. See also Friedman, "Al Derekh Heker ha-Sugya," p. 30. For another example of a Hebrew post-redactional addition to an originally Aramaic narrative, see the story involving Rav Hiyya bar Ashi in b. Kiddushin 81b ("All the days of that righteous man he fasted until he died of that death") and Yonah Fraenkel, "Kavim Boltim be-Toldot Masoret ha-Text shel Sippurei ha-Aggadah," *Divrei ha-Kongress ha-Olami ha-Shevi'it le-Mada'ei ha-Yahadut. Studies in Talmud, Halachah, and Midrash* (Jerusalem: Ha-Igud ha-Olami le-Mada'ei ha-Yahadut, 1981), pp. 59–60.

66. See also n. 64.

67. Part 11 is also in Hebrew, both in ms Yad ha-Rav Herzog I and in T-*S* Misc. 26.55, and while it is unquestionably different from the Palestinian versions of the story, it utilizes, like the Palestinian versions, an a fortiori argument. Part 11 thus appears to be modeled on the Palestinian versions, but in its context in the Bavli it serves to prepare the audience for part 13's Babylonian motif (rendered in Babylonian Aramaic) of the conversion to Judaism of the cruel foreign leader who had come to destroy the Israelites. Part 11's character as a later formulation may be indicated by the fact that it is preserved very differently in a parallel version.

by a change of language, but in this case the change is from Aramaic to Hebrew.[68]

There are other notable features of the Bavli's version of the story that distinguish it from the Palestinian versions. For example, we observe in the Bavli the Babylonian characteristic of emphasizing the importance of rabbis,[69] since according to all versions Nebuzaradan begins by killing either "our rabbis" or the Great Sanhedrin and the Lesser Sanhedrin,[70] which the rabbis conceive of as having been dominated by rabbis. Children of the schoolhouse are also slaughtered en masse according to most versions,[71] and we know from other contexts that it was the task of these children to study Scripture, the most basic building block of the rabbinic curriculum of study.[72]

As noted, some scholars make much of the fact that God is not mentioned explicitly in the Babylonian version of the story.[73] Nebuzaradan's conversion at the conclusion of the Babylonian version, however, makes sense only if we understand him to have been impressed by the power of the Jewish God, and we should be careful not to read too much into God's ostensible "absence" from the story. If God played no role, then Nebuzaradan's conversion is only evidence of his mistaken belief in the power displayed by God in punishing the Israelites. If Nebuzaradan is mistaken, then the motif of the murderous enemy of the Jews converting to Judaism no longer serves to demonstrate the superiority of the Jewish God to the human power of the enemy, one of the rabbis' favorite themes.[74] God's "absence" from the Bavli's version of the story, I would argue, is nothing other than a common Babylonian Jewish storytelling device, which we encounter, likewise, in the biblical book of

---

68. For another example of this same phenomenon, see the appendix to the introduction, and Richard Kalmin, "Hillel and the Soldiers of Herod: Sage and Sovereign in Ancient Jewish Society," in *Jewish Religious Leadership: Image and Reality*, vol. 1, ed. Jack Wertheimer (New York: JTS Press, 2004), pp. 112–17; and idem, *Jewish Babylonia*, pp. 43–50.

69. See, for example, Kalmin, *Jewish Babylonia*, pp. 34–35 and passim.

70. See n. 93.

71. See n. 93.

72. See Goodblatt, *Rabbinic Instruction in Sasanian Babylonia*, pp. 108–9; and Catherine Hezser, *Jewish Literacy in Roman Palestine* (Tübingen: Mohr/Siebeck, 2001), pp. 68–72 and 75–84.

73. These scholars do not note the exceptional nature of ms Yad ha-Rav Herzog I.

74. Regarding part 12 of b. Sanhedrin 96b, see Sabato, *Ketav-Yad Temani le-Massekhet Sanhedrin*, p. 149. This statement is problematic in its present context, however, since it implies that Nebuzaradan converts to avoid committing the horrible sin of destroying God's Temple. However, the text in Sanhedrin 96b prior to the Zechariah story already described in detail his destruction of the Temple.

Esther as well as in numerous Babylonian rabbinic stories. Much has been made about God's absence from the book of Esther, but here as well, I would argue, the absence is a storytelling device, perhaps indicating that God's presence in the story, just like His presence in daily life, is not explicit, but rather needs to be inferred. While final conclusions cannot yet be drawn, future studies will perhaps reveal the extent to which this is a Babylonian rabbinic, and perhaps a Persian or Mesopotamian, storytelling device, which distinguishes Babylonian from Palestinian rabbinic culture, and Persia and Mesopotamia from the Greek and Roman world.

THE MURDER OF ZECHARIAH IN NONRABBINIC TRADITIONS: WHICH ZECHARIAH IS IT?

Turning to nonrabbinic accounts, we find a variety of different traditions regarding the identity of the Zechariah murdered in the Temple.[75] Matthew 23:35, for example, identifies him as Zechariah ben Berechiah, the last minor prophet.[76] For reasons noted above, it is unlikely that we can determine at present which Zechariah was the original subject of the story. All we can say for certain is that a legend circulated in antiquity about the murder of a priest in the Temple. According to some traditions the priest was unnamed, and according to others he was named Zechariah. A variety of ancient traditions,

---

75. In addition to the texts cited below, see the *Martyrium Lugdunum* (ca. 177 C.E.), recounted by Eusebius, *Ecclesiastical History* 5.1.3–10, ed. and trans. Lake, pp. 406–11. See also H. F. Campenhausen, "Das Martyrium des Zacharias, seine früheste Bezeugung in zweiten Jahrhundert," *Historisches Jahrbuch* 77 (1958): 383–86; Schwemer, *Studien zu frühjüdischen Propheten-legenden*, vol. 2, pp. 294–321; W. D. Davies and D. C. Allison, *A Critical and Exegetical Commentary on the Gospel According to Saint Matthew*, vol. 3, *Commentary on Matthew XIX–XXVIII* (Edinburgh: T & T Clark, 1997), pp. 318–19; and Kalimi, *Retelling of Chronicles*, pp. 43–54, 57–59, 68–71.

76. See also Becker, "Die Zerstörung Jerusalems," pp. 59–72. It bears emphasizing that while the Masoretic text renders the name as "Zechariah son of Jehoiada the priest" in 2 Chr 24:20, the Septuagint renders the name as "Azariah son of Jehoiada." See Charlene McAfee Moss, *The Zechariah Tradition and the Gospel of Matthew* (Berlin: Walter de Gruyter, 2008), p. 115. Perhaps the Christian sources relied on the Septuagint's version of the name, and therefore could not identify the Zechariah murdered in the Temple as Zechariah ben Jehoiada. See Origen, *Commentarius in Matthaeum* 10:18, concerning Matthew 13:57 (Griechischen christlichen Schriftsteller, Series Graeca 40, p. 609). This consideration, however, does not explain why *Targum Eikhah* also identifies the murder victim as Zechariah ben Berekhiah.

some Jewish and some Christian, identified this Zechariah as a specific individual from Israel's ancient or recent past.

Matthew 23:35, it will be recalled, reads as follows:

> Therefore I am sending you prophets and wise men and teachers. Some of them you will kill and crucify, others you will flog in your synagogues and pursue from town to town. And so upon you will come all the righteous blood that has been shed on earth, from the blood of righteous Abel to the blood of Zechariah son of Berekhiah, whom you murdered between the Temple and the altar.

Significantly, Luke 11:50–51 also mentions the murder of "Zechariah" in the Temple near the altar, but provides no patronymic, thereby precluding specification of which Zechariah he has in mind.

Matthew and the rabbis disagree about the chronology of events, but they agree that the murder of Zechariah led to the destruction of Jerusalem and the Temple. The rabbis have the first Temple in mind, however, and Matthew the second Temple.

Josephus, *Jewish War* 4.5.4, describes the murder in the Temple of yet another Zechariah, Zacharias son of Baris, who was murdered by the Zealots when he dared to dispute their trumped-up charges against him. According to Josephus, this murder did not directly lead to the destruction of the Temple, but it was one of many similar actions by the Judeans, and by the Zealots in particular, that had this disastrous effect.[77] Josephus, like Matthew but unlike the rabbis, depicts the murder of Zechariah taking place while the second Temple stood.

The *Protevangelium of James* 23–24, a Christian text probably composed during the second century,[78] describes the murder in the Temple of still another Zechariah, the father of John the Baptist.[79] Like the Zechariah of Matthew, Luke, and the rabbis, the *Protevangelist*'s Zechariah was murdered in a very sanctified part of the Temple, near the altar. In addition, in the

---

77. See also Josephus, *Antiquities* 11.7.1.

78. Dubois, "La mort de Zacharie," p. 23; Ronald F. Hock, ed. and trans., *The Infancy Gospels of James and Thomas* (Santa Rosa, CA: Polebridge Press, 1995), pp. 11–12; and J. Lionel North, "Reactions in Early Christianity to Some References to the Hebrew Prophets in Matthew's Gospel," *New Testament Studies* 54, no. 2 (2008): 260. For a translation, see Hock, *Infancy Gospels,* pp. 72–77.

79. See also John Chapman, "Zacharias, Slain between the Temple and the Altar," *Journal of Theological Studies* 13 (1912): 398. See also Epiphanius, *Panarion* 25.12 (Griechischen christlichen Schriftsteller, Series Graeca 25.290–92).

Protevangelium as in the rabbinic version, the blood of Zechariah figures very prominently, with its tangible presence remaining as a testament to the murderer's guilt, to be expunged only when the murder has been avenged. Interestingly, however, the *Protevangelist,* unlike Josephus, Matthew, Luke, and the rabbis, faults only specific individuals, namely, the king and his soldiers (who, of course, are doing the king's bidding), rather than the entire Israelite people. Finally, unlike the rabbinic versions and unlike Luke and Matthew and to a lesser extent Josephus, there is no indication in the *Protevangelium* that this murder will lead to the destruction of Jerusalem and the Temple.

The *Bordeaux Pilgrim,* who wrote in 333 C.E., also knows of a Zechariah murdered in the Temple, close to the altar. He likewise does not specify which Zechariah he has in mind. In this account as well, Zechariah's blood is a prominent motif and is a tangible presence centuries after it was shed. The blood does not bubble as in the rabbinic story, but neither has it coagulated or turned to stone as in several Christian versions. Instead, it looks like fresh blood, as if it had been "shed today."[80]

Another Christian version of the story, *Lives of the Prophets* 23:1, explicitly involves Zechariah ben Jehoiada, and this version likewise does not connect Zechariah's murder to the destruction of the Temple. There is controversy about the dating of *Lives of the Prophets,* but I am convinced by David Satran's claim that the text was composed in a late antique context, in the fourth or fifth century.[81] If Satran is correct, this text may indicate that it was not until the Byzantine period that the story about the murder of Zechariah in the Temple was taken to refer to Zechariah ben Jehoiada, and other identifications of Zechariah persisted long after this identification was made. The work of Sozomen, who flourished in the fourth century, provides a measure of confirmation of a fourth- or fifth-century origin of the identification of Zechariah as Zechariah ben Jehoiada. Sozomen describes the unearthing (in Caphar Zechariah, "the Village of Zechariah") of the relics of the martyr Zechariah ben Jehoiada. This discovery is accompanied by the discovery by a monk, also named Zechariah, the superior of a nearby monastery, of a "noncanonical" Hebrew book that described the

---

80. *Itinerarium Burdigalense* 589.7–592.7 (*apud* P. Geyer and O. Cuntz, eds., *Itineraria et alia geographica,* Corpus Christianorum, series Latina 175 [Turnhout: Brepols, 1965]), pp. 14–16.

81. David Satran, *Biblical Prophets in Byzantine Palestine: Reassessing the Lives of the Prophets* (Leiden: Brill, 1995), p. 118 and passim.

death of Joash's beloved son as punishment for his murder of the biblical Zechariah.[82]

The earliest reference to the murder of Zechariah in Mesopotamian Christian sources may be that of Ephrem, the fourth-century Mesopotamian Church Father, in his commentary on the *Diatessaron*.[83] This passage in Ephrem, however, is probably an interpolation.[84] The *Cave of Treasures* 47:12–17, composed in Mesopotamia, also narrates the murder in the Temple, near the altar, of Zechariah the father of John the Baptist, although the dating of this work is also the subject of controversy,[85] rendering it extremely unlikely that the tradition was current early enough in Mesopotamia to merit consideration as the source of the tradition in the Roman East.

Moving later and further east, to Baghdad in the ninth and tenth centuries, we find that Ṭabarī, who postdates the final compilation of the Bavli, transmits three versions of the tradition. He relates one version in the name of Ibn al-'Abbās, a second in the names of Ibn Mas'ūd, Ibn al-'Abbās and al-Suddi (see above), and a third version in the name of Ibn Isḥāq (d. 767).[86] According to all three versions reported by Ṭabarī, the Israelites murdered John the Baptist rather than his father, Zechariah. The version that Ṭabarī reports in the name of Ibn Isḥāq bears striking resemblances to the Babylonian rabbinic account, but also to the versions in Christian texts. Ṭabarī's affinities with the Babylonian rabbinic tradition are significant, since in this case as well the Palestinian rabbinic versions of a tradition appear to have made no impression on him:[87]

---

82. See Sozomen, *Ecclesiastical History* 9.17 (ed. Bidez/Hansen Griechischen christlichen Schriftsteller, Series Graeca 50). *Targum Sheni* to Esther 1:3 also identifies the murdered Zechariah as Zechariah ben Jehoiada, and while the dating of this Targum is uncertain, it is certainly not pre-Byzantine.

83. See Carmel McCarthy, *Saint Ephrem's Commentary on Tatian's Diatessaron: An English Translation of "Chester Beatty" Syriac Ms 709 with Introduction and Notes* (Oxford: Oxford University Press, 1993), pp. 62–63.

84. See Louis Leloir, *Éphrem de Nisibe: Commentaire de l'Évangile concordant ou Diatessaron* (Paris: Éditions du Cerf, 1966), p. 68. See also Schwemer, *Studien zu den frühjüdischen Propheten-legenden*, vol. 2, pp. 283–321, 73*–75*.

85. See James L. Kugel, *The Bible as It Was* (Cambridge, MA: Belknap Press of the Harvard University Press, 1997), p. 574.

86. See Perlmann, *History of al-Ṭabari*, vol. 4, pp. 103–11. See also Schützinger, "Die arabische Legende," pp. 113–41, esp. pp. 114–17, 128, 132–34; and Amikam Elad, *Medieval Jerusalem and Islamic Worship: Holy Places, Ceremonies, Pilgramage* (Leiden: Brill, 1995), pp. 122–23.

87. See Perlmann, *History of al-Ṭabari,* vol. 4, pp. 108–11. See also chapter 1.

(1) As for Ibn Isḥāq's version, we learned it from Ibn Humayd–Salamah–Muhammad ibn Isḥāq: When God took Jesus from their midst to heaven, they slew the Baptist. Some say when they killed the Baptist, God sent against them a Babylonian king called Khardūs.[88] He marched against them with a Babylonian host and entered Palestine. When he defeated them, he summoned one of his military chieftains, a man addressed as Nābuzarādhan the executioner, to whom he said, "I have sworn by my deity that if I defeat the people of Jerusalem, I shall kill them until their blood flows amidst my encampment, and until I find none to kill." The king commanded Nābuzarādhan to slay them until such was done.

(2) Nābuzarādhan entered the temple. He stood over the spot where they used to offer their sacrifices; and he found blood there that was boiling.

(3) He asked them, "O Children of Israel, why is this blood boiling? Tell me about it and do not conceal anything."

(4) They said, "It is the blood of a sacrifice which we had offered and which was not accepted from us; and therefore it is boiling, as you see. We have offered sacrifices for eight hundred years, and the sacrifice has always been accepted, except this one."[89]

(5) He said, "You have not told me the truth."

(6) They replied, "If things were as they used to be, it would be accepted; but we have been deprived of kingship, prophecy, and inspiration, and that is why this sacrifice of ours was not accepted."

(7) Nābuzarādhan slew 770 of their leaders on that spot, but the blood did not calm down. Upon his order seven hundred of their young men were brought and slaughtered over the blood, but it did not calm down. He ordered that seven thousand of their sons and their spouses be slain there, but the blood did not cool.

(8) When Nābuzarādhan saw that the blood was not calming down, he said to them, "O children of Israel, woe unto you. Tell me the truth, and endure for the sake of your Lord. For a long time you have been in possession of the land, acting in it as you please. [Tell me], before the last of you is slain, male or female."

(9) When they saw the gravity of the mayhem, they told him the truth: "This is the blood of a prophet of ours who often sought to forewarn us of divine wrath. Had we been obedient to him, he would have guided us. He used to

---

88. According to ibid., vol. 4, p. 109, n. 294, Khardūs is Herod.
89. Tabari's account here differs from both the Palestinian rabbinic versions and the Bavli's version. In this and in other contexts, the relationship between Tabari's account and the accounts of the rabbis is not entirely clear.

tell us about you, but we did not believe him. We killed him, and this is his blood."

(10) Nābuzarādhan then asked, "What was his name?"

(11) They answered, "John, the son of Zechariah."

(12) He exclaimed, "Now you have told me the truth. That is why your Lord is taking revenge upon you."

(13) When Nābuzarādhan perceived that they had told him the truth, he prostrated himself and said to those around him, "Lower the gates of the city, remove from it those who were here of the host of Khardūs."

(14) He remained with the Israelites. Then he exclaimed, "O John son of Zechariah, my Lord and your Lord knows the affliction suffered by your people on your account. Be calm now, by God's grace, before I exterminate your people."

(15) Then the Baptist's blood subsided so that Nābuzarādhan stopped the killing, saying, "I believe in the God of the Children of Israel. I sincerely believe in Him; I know for sure that He is the only God. No other deity can there be beside Him. Had He any associate, heaven and earth would not hold together. It would be wrong for Him to have a son. May He be blessed, sanctified, praised, glorified, the King of Kings who rules the seven heavens with knowledge and wisdom, strength and power; He who spread out the earth and set therein firm mountains for eternity. Thus it befits my Lord to be, and His realm to be."

(16) It was revealed to a leader of the remnant of the prophets that Nābuzarādhan was a sincere *habur*—*habur* in Hebrew is a new convert.[90]

(17) Nābuzarādhan told the Israelites, "Khardūs, the enemy of God, ordered me to slay so many of you that your blood should flow amid his encampment. I cannot disobey him."

(18) They told him, "Do as you were ordered."

(19) Upon his command, they dug a trench. He ordered that horses, mules, asses, cattle, sheep, and camels in their possession be placed there and slaughtered, and that blood be made to flow throughout the camp. Upon his order

---

90. Perlmann, *History of al-Tabari*, vol. 4, p. 110, n. 296, observes that the Arabic *habr* means a Jewish scholar. Geoffrey Herman informs me that when Tabarī writes that "*habur* in Hebrew is a new convert," he is probably not referring to *habr*—the common Arabic for a rabbi, since this is a well-known term. Rather, it appears that the diacritics of the Arabic have been incorrectly placed, and the root referred to is *gyr*, referring to *ger* or *giyura*, that is, a convert. The misplacement of diacritic vowels in "foreign" words in Arabic is a common phenomenon.

the corpses of the people who had been slain were thrown over the slaughtered animals, so that Khardūs was certain that the trench was filled with dead Israelites.

(20) When the blood reached his camp, he sent to Nābuzarādhan the message, "Stop, their blood has reached me. I have been revenged for what they have done."

(21) Whereupon he left for Babylonia after almost annihilating the Israelites. It was the last calamity that God brought upon them.

There are obvious differences between Tabarī's and the Bavli's versions, as well as between Tabarī's account and those in Christian sources, and it is difficult in many instances to determine whether these differences are due to deliberate tampering by Tabarī (or by the Muslim authors from whom he drew), or to the likelihood that he was drawing upon a partly shared but partly different fund of traditions and motifs.

Perhaps the most striking commonality between Tabarī and the rabbis, which distinguishes his version from most of the Christian versions,[91] is the fact that the blood boils. Tabarī's version, in contrast to both the rabbinic and the Christian versions, features John the Baptist's blood, and Zechariah figures hardly at all. It is likely that Tabarī took a tradition about Zechariah and turned it into a tradition about his much more prominent son, John the Baptist, whom his readers would more likely be familiar with.[92] Also distinctive to Tabarī's account is the fact that while the general is named Nābuzarādhan, in conformity with the rabbinic account, Tabarī's narrative is set during the time of King Herod and Jesus Christ, in conformity with most Christian versions. Tabarī's identification of John the Baptist's father as "the son of Iddo" may be an attempt by Tabarī to reconcile his account with the New Testament's tradition of the identity of Zechariah, since, as noted, Matthew's Zechariah is the son of Berekhiah, the minor prophet, who is said in Zechariah 1:1 to be the grandson of Iddo.

As noted, Tabarī's account resembles the Bavli a good deal more than the Palestinian version. The Palestinian version, it will be recalled, has the general kill eighty thousand young priests, and when that fails to stop the blood he rebukes Zechariah, which motivates God to apply an a fortiori argument to himself and to signal to the blood to stop boiling. According to the major-

---

91. The exceptions are the commentaries of Ibn al-Tayyib and the Ethiopian Christians. See above, and also Cowley, "The 'Blood of Zechariah,'" pp. 293, 298.

92. See also Schützinger, "Die arabische Legende," pp. 138–40.

ity of versions in the Bavli, in contrast, Nebuzaradan kills different groups of Israelites one after the other: (1) the Great Sanhedrin; (2) the Lesser Sanhedrin; (3) eighty thousand young priests; (4) children from the schoolhouse; (5) young boys and elders; and (6) "young men and virgins."[93] While Tabarī's list is not identical to either account, it clearly has more in common with the Bavli's, since according to Tabarī, Nābuzarādhan kills (1) "770 of their leaders"; (2) "seven hundred of their young men"; and (3) "seven thousand of their sons and spouses." The resemblance with the Bavli's version is even closer if we posit a mistake in the Arabic manuscripts before us. The number of leaders might have been seventy, which corresponds to the number of men comprising the Sanhedrin. This fits the parallel with the Bavli better and makes the numerical progression consistent, with the numbers steadily increasing, instead of decreasing and then increasing.[94] Also resembling the Bavli is Tabarī's assertion that Nābuzarādhan became a sincere convert, confessing his belief in the God of the children of Israel. Clearly, Tabarī's general is much more pious than the rabbis', and he is evidently a prototype of a righteous, orthodox Muslim, who becomes devoted to the God of the Israelites and knows that the Christians are wrong to assert that God has a son. But perhaps the most striking similarity between the Bavli and Tabarī is the fact that the blood stops boiling in response to the words of the Babylonian general rather than in response to a signal from God, as is the case in the Palestinian rabbinic versions.[95] True, in Tabarī's version, in part 15 above, the general beseeches the blood to "be calm now by God's grace,"

---

93. See our translation of the Bavli's version above. There are many manuscript variants of the Bavli's account of the victims of Nebuzaradan's slaughter. In b. Sanhedrin 96b the variants are as follows: (1) ms Munich 95: "our rabbis ... a total of ninety-four thousand"; (2) ms Karlsruhe-Reuchlin 2 reads like ms Munich 95, but adds "children *(dardekei)* of the schoolhouse" in the margin; (3) ms Florence II-I-9: "our rabbis ... children *(dardekei)* of the schoolhouse ... a total of ninety-one thousand"; (4) the Hebrew epitome of the story in ms JTS ENA 2089.6: "He brought the Great Sanhedrin and the Lesser Sanhedrin ... children *(tinokot)* of the schoolhouse ... young men and virgins"; and (5) the genizah fragment, T-S Misc. 26.55: "He brought the Great Sanhedrin ... the Lesser Sanhedrin ... children *(tinokot)* of the schoolhouse," followed by the slaughter of another group, whose identity cannot be determined since the text is illegible. In b. Gittin 57b the variants are as follows: (1) ms Vatican 140: "He brought the Great Sanhedrin and the Lesser Sanhedrin ... children *(tinokot)* of the schoolhouse"; (2) ms Munich 95: "the Great and Lesser Sanhedrin ... children *(tinokot)* of the schoolhouse"; (3) ms St. Petersburg-RNL Evr. I 187: "the Great and Lesser Sanhedrin ... young men and virgins ... children *(tinokot)* of the schoolhouse"; and (4) ms Vatican 130: "the Great and Lesser Sanhedrin ... young men and virgins."

94. I owe this observation to Geoffrey Herman.

95. See also Perlmann, *History of al-Tabari*, vol. 4, pp. 104–6.

according to which it is explicit that the general calls upon God to effectuate his plea that John's blood stop boiling, but we have seen that according to the Bavli God must be understood as active behind the scenes. In addition, it remains the case that the immediate impetus for the blood to rest is the general's plea rather than any explicit action on God's part, which conforms to the Bavli's version.

THE BABYLONIAN AND PALESTINIAN RABBINIC VERSIONS: THE CONVERSION MOTIF

As noted, among the most noticeable distinctions between the Babylonian and Palestinian versions of the Zechariah story is the conversion motif found only in the Bavli: "He fled, caused a split in his family, and converted."[96] Elsewhere in the Yerushalmi, however, we find a story about the Gibeonites and King Saul[97] with many of the same motifs as the Zechariah narrative, including that of conversion. This text, found in y. Kiddushin 4:1 (65b–c),[98]

---

96. See Sokoloff, *Dictionary of Jewish Babylonian Aramaic*, p. 932. In addition, in all versions of b. Gittin 57b and b. Sanhedrin 97b, immediately following the Zechariah story, a tradition describes Nebuzaradan as one of several enemies of the Jewish people who end up converting to Judaism. Anat Yisraeli-Taran, *Aggadot ha-Hurban: Mesorot ha-Hurban be-Sifrut ha-Talmudit* (Tel Aviv: Ha-Kibuz ha-Me'uhad, 1997), pp. 24–28 and 106–8, correctly observes, furthermore, that the motif of the murderous foreign leader who intends to destroy the Jews or the Israelites but ends up worshiping the Israelite God or converting to Judaism is characteristic of Babylonian Jewish literature, attested already in Daniel 2:46–47 and 3:31–33.

97. The rabbinic story develops the biblical account in 2 Samuel 21:1–14.

98. See also the parallel in y. Sanhedrin 6:4 (23d). This tradition is also paralleled in b. Yevamot 78b–79b. The relevant part of the Yerushalmi's version of this text is as follows:

> R. Abba bar Zemina in the name of R. Hoshaya, "Sanctification of [God's] Name is greater than profanation of [God's] name. Regarding profanation of [God's] name it is written, 'Do not leave [the executed criminal's] body hanging on a tree' (Deut 21:23). And regarding sanctification of [God's] name it is written, '... from the beginning of the harvest until rain from the sky fell on [the bodies]' (2 Sam 21:10). This teaches that [the sons of Saul] were hanging from the sixteenth of Nisan until the seventeenth of Marheshvan [that is, for five months]. And passers-by would say, 'What sin did these commit to warrant the suspension of the usual standards of justice [according to which a dead body cannot be left hanging overnight]?' And they would answer them, 'Because they mistreated insincere converts.' [The passers-by] would say, 'If they, who did not convert for the sake of heaven, see how the Holy One, blessed be He, demanded [recompense for] their blood, how much the more so for one who converts for the sake of Heaven. There is no God like your God and no nation like your nation. We must cleave to you [that is, we must convert to Judaism].' And many people converted at that time."

is similar to the Bavli's Zechariah narrative not only in ending with conversion, but also because it depicts those who convert doing so on the basis of an a fortiori argument. And even though the Palestinian Zechariah story does not end with conversion, it does, like the Bavli's narrative, end with an a fortiori argument (by God, who convinces Himself He should have compassion on the Israelites). Even further, the Yerushalmi's text about the Gibeonites depicts them seeking vengeance against the descendants of Saul, as "payment" for Saul's murder of seven Gibeonites, which corresponds to Zechariah seeking vengeance against the Israelites for murdering him.[99] The similarities do not end there, however. The rabbinic text about the Gibeonites clearly disapproves of their insistence on vengeance, depicting it as earning the disapproval of King David, Ezra, the rabbis, and God Himself, but at the same time, this text upholds the right of the Gibeonites to insist on vengeance, and to demand that it take the form of the death of several of Saul's descendants. Similarly, the Zechariah story in its Palestinian and Babylonian versions insists on Zechariah's prerogative to demand vengeance from the Israelites, depicting it as conforming to the will of God; and yet the story in both versions disapproves of his exercise of this prerogative, which earns him the rebuke of Nebuzaradan for his excessive harshness, a rebuke that God Himself endorses.[100] We observed above that the Ethiopian commentary on the book of Matthew makes it explicit that the actions of the Gibeonites vis-à-vis Saul serve as the prototype for Zechariah's vengeance against his murderers, evidence of a significant connection between the rabbinic and Ethiopian traditions, very likely mediated by Syriac and Arabic literature, although I have yet to find an explicit Syriac or Arabic parallel in the form of a tradition resembling the vengeance of the Gibeonites.

SUMMARY AND CONCLUSIONS

We concluded that the (hypothesized) original, Hebrew version of a story about the murder of a priest and prophet in the Temple was probably composed by nonrabbis, in all likelihood Christians, as indicated by its strikingly nonrabbinic conception of the relationship between the Jewish people and God and the numerous parallels in Christian sources. Earlier studies have

99. See the discussion of the Ethiopian version of the Zechariah story, above.
100. Either explicitly, in the Palestinian versions, or implicitly, in the Bavli's version.

yielded evidence of such receptivity to nonrabbinic traditions primarily in the Bavli, and it is significant that this chapter found evidence of it in Palestinian compilations.[101] The nonrabbinic tradition appears in rabbinic corpora with an Aramaic addition that softens somewhat its anomalous character, although even with this Aramaic addition its message can aptly be characterized as "stunning."

We observed that despite the claims of several modern scholars, there is no reason to assume that the Christian tradition postdates and is an adaptation of the rabbinic tradition of the murder of Zechariah. On the contrary, the rabbinic tradition in its present form is an adaptation of a Christian story, which in its "original" version dramatized God's abandonment of the Israelites. Our analysis of rabbinic versions of the Zechariah story, with special attention to language switching, revealed the presence of a later addition to the story that dramatically altered its meaning. The rabbis manipulated the story to teach a lesson about God's enduring *compassion* for the Israelites despite their murder of the prophets, which removed a divinely appointed check to His unrestrained fury in response to Israelite sins.

In two virtually identical Palestinian compilations, this addition was marked as an Aramaic addition to a Hebrew story,[102] and in the Bavli as a Hebrew addition to an Aramaic story. This chapter thus further proves that storytellers and tradents sometimes formulated later additions to Aramaic narratives in Hebrew to distinguish the editorial addition from the earlier Aramaic core of the text. Scholars have long been aware of this phenomenon in the case of *Megillat Ta'anit,* but its full extent has yet to be documented, and the present chapter is a step in that direction. The significance of the fact that in Palestine one Jewish language is the core and the other is the addendum while in Babylonia this situation is reversed is unclear at present, but hopefully future studies will enable us to explain this peculiar phenomenon.

We also found a surprising connection between rabbinic literature and Ethiopian Christian literature. While it is conceivable that the Ethiopians drew this material directly from Jewish sources, we concluded that it was more likely that their source for this material was Syriac and Arabic commentaries on the New Testament written in Persia, Mesopotamia, and Syria between the seventh and thirteenth centuries. The parallels between the

---

101. See also n. 3 of the introduction.
102. Y. Ta'anit 4:7 (69a–b) and *Pesikta de-Rav Kahana,* ed. Mandelbaum, pp. 257–58.

Jewish, Christian, and Muslim versions of the story, we concluded, were evidence of the porous boundaries between these groups, in late antiquity and into the Middle Ages.

We also found that Tabarī, a Muslim scholar from Baghdad who wrote in the ninth and tenth centuries, drew his rabbinic source material from the Babylonian Talmud, or from a source much closer to the Bavli than to the Yerushalmi, despite the fact that he spent part of his youth traveling in the vicinity of Palestine, where he might have had access to Palestinian rabbinic literature.

Finally, we found that analysis of these traditions in Jewish and non-Jewish traditions provides another example of a cultural current traveling from the eastern Roman provinces to Persia, throughout late antiquity and the early Middle Ages. The earliest attestation of the tradition in the Muslim world in what was formerly the Persian Empire was that of Tabarī, in the late ninth century or early tenth, who cites commentators on the Qoran who wrote no earlier than the mid-seventh century, contemporaneous with or shortly after the period of the Bavli's final redaction.

SIX

Pharisees

TRADITIONS ABOUT THE *PERUSHIM* (THE PHARISEES) in the Babylonian Talmud,[1] and analysis of parallel Christian traditions, will further illustrate the claims regarding the flow of nonrabbinic traditions from the Roman East to Mesopotamia and their incorporation into the Bavli. Important details of Babylonian rabbinic traditions about the Pharisees are without parallel in Palestinian rabbinic literature but have clear parallels in Josephus and the New Testament. Among the questions addressed in the ensuing discussion is whether the Bavli derives these details from the New Testament or from a source that the Bavli and the New Testament share in common, and we will conclude that the latter alternative is the more likely.

The Bavli's discussion is as follows:[2]

(1) Our rabbis taught [in a Baraita], there are seven *Perushim*: A *Parush Shikhmi;* a *Parush Nikhpi;* a *Parush Kizai;* a *Parush Medukhia;* a *Parush* "what is my obligation and I will do it?"; a *Parush* from love; and a *Parush* from fear.[3]

(2A–F) [The Talmud interprets the Baraita (part 1). Some of this interpretation is unattributed and some of it is attributed to Amoraim]:

---

1. For discussion of the problems involved in determining that the term *Perushim* refers to the second-Temple Jewish sect, the Pharisees, and is not an adjective meaning, for example, "abstemious" or "separatists," see, for example, Richard Kalmin, "The Pharisees in Rabbinic Literature," *Sidra* 24/25 (2010): vii–xxviii (the issue was edited by David Henschke). The text from the Bavli under discussion in this chapter (see immediately below) most likely uses the term *Perushim* to refer to the second-Temple sect.
2. See b. Sotah 22b.
3. See also Avot de-R. Natan, version A, chapter 37 (ed. Schechter, p. 104) and version B, chapter 45 (ed. Schechter, p. 124).

(2A) "A *Parush Shikhmi,*" this is someone who does the deed of Shechem [who performed a mitzvah for ulterior motives, namely, to marry Dinah the daughter of Jacob] (Gen 34:1–24).

(2B) "A *Parush Nikhpi,*" this is someone who knocks his feet together.[4]

(2C) "A *Parush Kizai,*" Rav Nahman bar Yizhak said,[5] "This is someone who lets blood [and it spatters] onto the walls."[6]

(2D) "A *Parush Medukhia,*" Rabbah bar Shila said, "Because he is slanted[7] like a pestle."

(2E) "A *Parush* 'what is my obligation and I will do it?'"

But this is a positive attribute!

Rather [the text] said, "What is my obligation *again* and I will do it?"[8]

(2F) "A *Parush* from love, a *Parush* from fear."

Abaye and Rava said to the *Tanna* [the professional "repeater" of rabbinic traditions], "Do not teach [in your version of the text] 'A *Parush* from love, a *Parush* from fear,' for Rav Yehudah said Rav said, 'A person should always engage in study of Torah and in the performance of mitzvot, even if not for their own sake, for by doing them not for their own sake one comes to do them for their own sake.'"[9]

(3) Rav Nahman bar Yizhak said, "That which is hidden is hidden. That which is revealed is revealed. The great [that is, heavenly] court will punish those who wrap themselves in cloaks."[10]

---

4. The meaning is uncertain. See, however, *Arukh ha-Shalem,* ed. Alexander Kohut (Vienna: Menorah, 1926), vol. 6, p. 451; and Jastrow, *Dictionary,* p. 934.

5. See *Dikdukei Soferim ha-Shalem,* ed. Avraham Liss, notes on line 5 and n. 22 for variants of the name.

6. The meaning here is also uncertain. See, however, *Arukh ha-Shalem,* ed. Kohut, vol. 6, p. 451; Jastrow, *Dictionary,* p. 932.

7. Or "bent over." See *Arukh ha-Shalem,* ed. Kohut, vol. 6, p. 451; and Sokoloff, *Dictionary of Jewish Babylonian Aramaic,* p. 1172.

8. The anonymous editorial voice of the Talmud clearly understands all of the items on this list to be negative, which forces him to emend or reinterpret the Baraita. The exact meaning of much of the Baraita, even following the emendation or reinterpretation, is not clear.

9. Abaye and Rava likewise assume that everything on the list is negative, which forces them to omit "a *Parush* from love, a *Parush* from fear," both of which are positive or lead to something positive.

10. My translation follows the explanation of Rashi, *Arukh ha-Shalem,* ed. Kohut, vol. 2, p. 317 (compare ibid., p. 463); and Jastrow, *Dictionary,* p. 223. Sokoloff, *Dictionary of Jewish Babylonian Aramaic,* p. 937, translates "May the great [that is, heavenly] court punish the ones who rub (?) g[undei],"and he understands "gundei" to mean "garments." See also

(4) Yannai the king said to his wife, "Do not fear the Pharisees, nor those who are not Pharisees. Rather, fear the hypocrites[11] who resemble Pharisees, for their deeds are the deeds of Zimri [that is, they are wicked] but they seek the reward of Pinhas [who killed Zimri and his Midianite paramour and thereby put an end to a divine plague against the Israelites]."[12]

The Baraita opening the discussion (part 1) corresponds almost word for word to a parallel Baraita recorded in y. Berakhot 9:5 (14b) and y. Sotah 5:5 (20c). Several of the interpretations in parts 2A–F are obscure,[13] but, from the statements that are clear (parts 2A, 2E, and 2F), it is evident that each item on the list was understood negatively in Babylonia. Judging from parts 2A and 2F, it is evident that the Babylonians understood the Baraita to refer to people who observe the commandments for improper motives.[14]

Rav Nahman bar Yizhak, or whoever placed his statement here ("That which is hidden is hidden. That which is revealed is revealed. The great [that is, heavenly] court will punish those who wrap themselves in cloaks"), appears to connect the term *Perushim* with hypocrisy, a charge against the Pharisees familiar to us from the New Testament.[15] An alternative version adds:

Sokoloff, *Dictionary of Jewish Babylonian Aramaic*, p. 478. It is unclear, however, why "the ones who rub garments" deserve punishment.

11. Literally, the "colored."

12. See Numbers 25:1–16.

13. For attempted explanations, see *Ozar ha-Geonim*, ed. Benjamin Lewin, vol. 11 (Jerusalem: Central Press, 1942), pp. 243 and 283–84.

14. It will be recalled that part 2A understands a *Parush Shikhmi* as "someone who does the deed of Shechem," that is, who performs the mitzvah of circumcision for ulterior motives. In addition, Abaye and Rava in part 2F remove a *Parush* from love and a *Parush* from fear from the list because such *Perushim* perform mitzvot for the proper reasons, implying that, in their view, only *Perushim* who perform mitzvot for the wrong reasons belong on the list.

15. See Mark 7:1–13; 12:13–17; Matthew 7:6; 12:15; 22:18; 23:1–29; Luke 11:37–44; 12:1; 16:15. See Shaye J. D. Cohen, "The Significance of Yavneh: Pharisees, Rabbis, and the End of Jewish Sectarianism," *Hebrew Union College Annual* 55 (1984): 40; and Alexander Guttmann, *Rabbinic Judaism in the Making* (Detroit: Wayne State University Press, 1970), pp. 165–67. See also Günther Stemberger, *Jewish Contemporaries of Jesus: Pharisees, Sadducees, Essenes*, trans. Allan W. Mahnke (Minneapolis: Fortress Press, 1995), pp. 26–27, for other possible parallels. See also Josephus, *Antiquities* 17:41, and Albert I. Baumgarten, "The Name of the Pharisees," *Journal of Biblical Literature* 102, no. 3 (1983): 415 and n. 16 there. Compare Stemberger, *Jewish Contemporaries of Jesus*, p. 45. David Flusser, "Perushim, Zedukim, ve-Essi'im be-Pesher Nahum," in *Sefer Zikaron le-Gedaliah Alon*, ed. Menahem Dormann, Shmuel Safrai, and Menahem Stern (Tel Aviv: Ha-Kibuz ha-Me'uhad, 1970), p. 136, claims that 4QpNahum[a] also criticizes the Pharisees as "hypocrites." Even if we accept, as do many scholars, that the term *dorshei halakot* in *Pesher Nahum* refers to Pharisees, it is not clear that the *Pesher* accuses

"Who say, 'Keep your distance! Don't come closer! For I am holier than you'" (Isa 65:5).[16] This reading changes the issue from hypocrisy to criticism of the Pharisees for their inflated view of themselves as holier than others, a criticism of the Pharisees that may also have precedent in the New Testament.[17] Given the New Testament's general hostility to Judaism, it is unlikely that the Bavli would have incorporated criticism of a Jewish group they tended to sympathize with (see below) directly from the New Testament. It is likely, therefore, that the New Testament and the Bavli independently received the "hypocrisy" and "holier than thou" motifs from an earlier source.[18] And since the New Testament comprises documents composed in Palestine and elsewhere in the eastern Roman provinces, it is likely that the Bavli inherited these traditions from these localities, either directly from the Roman East or indirectly via Syriac translations from Mesopotamia.

From the attribution of the statement under consideration to Rav Nahman bar Yizhak, it can be judged to have been placed in its present context no earlier than the mid-fourth century,[19] further evidence of the critical importance of this period for our investigation.

The story about Yannai and his wife, cited above (part 4), almost certainly uses the term *Perushim* to refer to Pharisees. Whoever put the Yannai story in its present context understood the Baraita and its anonymous editorial

---

them of hypocrisy. See, for example, Martin S. Jaffee, *Torah in the Mouth: Writing and Oral Tradition in Palestinian Judaism, 200 BCE–400 CE* (New York: Oxford University Press, 2001), pp. 41–42. Compare Anthony Saldarini, "Pharisees," in *The Anchor Bible Dictionary*, ed. David Noel Freedman (New York: Doubleday, 1992), vol. 5, pp. 300–301. See Lawrence II. Schiffman, "Pharisees and Sadducees in *Pesher Nahum*," in *Minhah le-Nahum: Biblical and Other Studies Presented to Nahum M. Sarna in Honour of his 70th Birthday* (Sheffield: Sheffield Academic Press, 1993), pp. 272–84 and 289–90; and Jaffee, *Torah in the Mouth*, pp. 43–44 and the references cited on p. 177, n. 14.

16. See *Dikdukei Soferim ha-Shalem*, ed. Liss, notes 50 on line 11.

17. See Matthew 9:10–13; Mark 2:16; Luke 5:30; 7:36–47; 15:1–2, and 18:9–14; and Anthony Saldarini, *Pharisees, Scribes and Sadducees in Palestinian Society* (Wilmington: Michael Glazier, 1988), pp. 176 and 179–80.

18. See, for example, Josephus, *Jewish War* 1:112. See also *Pseudo-Clementines Homiliae* II.29,1 (Griechischen christlichen Schriftsteller, Series Graeca 42.168). See also *Recognitions* 6.11.1 (Griechischen christlichen Schriftsteller, Series Graeca 51.194); and Albert I. Baumgarten, "Josephus and Hippolytus on the Pharisees," *Hebrew Union College Annual* 55 (1984): 13. See also Schäfer, *Jesus in the Talmud*, pp. 15–22 and 148–52; and Kalmin, "Review of Peter Schäfer's *Jesus in the Talmud*," pp. 107–12.

19. We can safely conclude this even if we doubt the reliability of the attribution. The later editor who (perhaps) falsely attributed the statement to Rav Nahman bar Yizhak obviously postdates the Amora himself.

commentary (parts 1–2) to refer to the Pharisees as well.[20] As Stemberger observes, "We probably ought to remember Josephus's report here, according to which the dying Alexander Jannaeus suggested [to his wife] a reconciliation with the Pharisees, since they would be able to cause much harm."[21] While we cannot speak of anything close to exact identity, the story unquestionably echoes the account in Josephus, *Antiquities* 13.398–404, with parallels that are too striking to be coincidental.[22] The story of Yannai and his wife also appears to know the motif of the Pharisees as hypocrites, although the Bavli gives the motif an unparalleled twist, in keeping with its tendency to sympathize with Pharisees and to equate them with sages, that is, rabbis.[23]

The most relevant section of Josephus is *Antiquities* 13.401–2:

> And then, [Alexander Jannaeus] said, on her return to Jerusalem as from a splendid victory, she should yield a certain amount of power to the Pharisees, for if they praised her in return for this sign of regard, they would dispose the nation favorably toward her. These men, he assured her, had so much influence with their fellow-Jews that they could injure those whom they hated and help those to whom they were friendly; for they had the complete confidence of the masses when they spoke harshly of any person, even when they did so out of envy; and he himself, he added, had come into conflict with the nation because these men had been badly treated by him.

In both the Josephan and the rabbinic accounts, a Hasmonean king gives advice to his wife about the Pharisees. In the Bavli the king is Yannai while in Josephus he is Alexander Jannaeus, but there is widespread agreement among scholars that these two names refer to the same person.[24] As noted, King Yannai in b. Sotah 22b advises his wife not to fear the Pharisees, which

---

20. Stemberger, *Jewish Contemporaries of Jesus*, p. 45. Stemberger correctly observes that "the redactor who had added this piece had connected the list with the Pharisees." When he states on the same page that "the text [is] completely without parallel," he apparently means that there is no parallel elsewhere in rabbinic literature. See also John Bowker, *Jesus and the Pharisees* (Cambridge: Cambridge University Press, 1973), pp. 36–37.

21. Stemberger, *Jewish Contemporaries of Jesus*, p. 45.

22. See the distinctions that Shaye Cohen draws between different kinds of parallels, with special reference to parallels between Josephus and the rabbis, in Cohen, "Parallel Traditions in Josephus and Rabbinic Literature," in *Proceedings of the Ninth World Congress of Jewish Studies* (Jerusalem: World Union of Jewish Studies, 1986), div. 2, vol. 1, pp. 7–14.

23. See the discussion below.

24. See, for example, Yisrael L. Levine, "Ha-Ma'avak ha-Politi bein ha-Perushim li-Zedukim bi-Tekufat ha-Hashmona'it," in *Perakim be-Toldot Yerushalayim bi-Yemei Bayit Sheni: Sefer Zikaron le-Avraham Shalit*, ed. Aharon Oppenheimer, Uriel Rapaport, and Menahem Stern (Jerusalem: Yad Yizhak Ben-Zvi, 1980), pp. 65–66.

has clear echoes in the message delivered by Alexander Jannaeus to his wife according to Josephus.

Clearly, there are important differences between the accounts of the king's words to his wife in Josephus and in the Bavli. In Josephus, the king instructs his wife about the measures she should take to ensure that the Pharisees do not use their very real powers to harm her. According to the Bavli, in contrast, the king simply asserts that the queen has nothing to fear from the Pharisees, clearly implying that they are not, in fact, harmful. This distinction between the Bavli's and Josephus's portrayal of the Pharisees, however, is in line with the Bavli's tendency to depict the Pharisees more favorably than they are depicted in Josephus.[25] This is due to the fact that the Bavli sometimes views the Pharisees as precursors to the rabbis, or views the terms *Perushim* and *hakhamim* ("sages," the rabbis' customary label for themselves) as synonymous.[26] When the Bavli concludes the story by having the king inform his wife that she should fear those who "are painted" (that is, disguised, hypocritical) and who therefore "resemble" the Pharisees, we apparently see another expression of the motif of association between the Pharisees and hypocrisy. The Bavli, however, defangs this as a criticism against the Pharisees, turning it instead into a criticism of those who pretend to be Pharisees. At the same time, we see there are clear limits to the extent to which the Bavli identifies rabbis and Pharisees, since b. Sotah 22b acknowledges that there are several kinds of *Perushim* with negative attributes.

Significantly, every post-Tannaitic tradition in b. Sotah 22b derives either from fourth-century Amoraim or from the Talmud's anonymous editors. As noted, the anonymous portions of the Talmud are generally considered to be a relatively late, if not the latest, layer of Talmudic discourse, deriving for the most part from the mid-fourth century and later.[27] It is likely, therefore, that the story about Yannai and his wife reached Babylonia from the Roman East, and was reworked and placed in its present context at the conclusion of this discussion—some time between the fourth century and the final redaction of the Bavli.

Clearly, in light of the negative attributes assigned to the *Perushim* in the discussion up until the concluding story, the Bavli did not uniformly view all

---

25. Kalmin, *Jewish Babylonia*, pp. 53–59.
26. See also Cohen, "Significance of Yavneh," p. 39; Jaffee, *Torah in the Mouth*, pp. 41, 52–55, and 60; and Kalmin, "Pharisees in Rabbinic Literature of Late Antiquity," pp. xvi–xvii and xxiv–xxviii.
27. See the Preface above and the literature cited there.

Perushim positively. To say that there are certain types of *Perushim* that have negative characteristics, however, is not to cast aspersions on the group as a whole. In fact, two of the comments, that by Abaye and Rava in part 2F and by the anonymous editors in part 2E, essentially mean that Pharisees out of love or fear and Pharisees who say "what is my responsibility and I will do it?" are positive, and precisely for that reason such Pharisees do not belong on the list. The term *Perushim* itself, therefore, is not necessarily a term of disapprobation, although the authors and transmitters of the tradition had no problem depicting *Perushim* negatively.

In order to see if it is possible that the commonalities between the Bavli and the New Testament were mediated to the Babylonians via the Yerushalmi, it is necessary to examine the Yerushalmi's discussion of the Baraita in some detail. We will see that while it is possible that the Yerushalmi also contains echoes of the New Testament's criticism of the Pharisees, there is no evidence that the Bavli inherited the motifs it shares with the New Testament from the Yerushalmi.

Y. Sotah 3:4 (19a) interprets the phrase "the blows of the Pharisees," found in m. Sotah 3:4, to refer to those who exploit legal technicalities to cause people hardship.[28] The Yerushalmi cites a story depicting heirs of an estate using halakhah to avoid their obligation to support their mother. They learn that if a woman requests her *ketubah,* she is no longer entitled to receive support from the estate.[29] The heirs trick their mother into requesting her *ketubah,* thereby forfeiting her right to maintenance. It is possible, although not necessary, to interpret the Yerushalmi as defining "the blows of the Pharisees" as hypocritical use of halakhah.

A second story in y. Sotah 3:4 (19a)[30] apparently interprets the mishnaic phrase the same way:

> A student of Rabbi [Yehudah Hanasi] had two hundred zuz minus one dinar [and thus was legally considered "poor" and was therefore entitled to receive the poor tithe]. Rabbi was accustomed to give him poor tithe once every three years. One time Rabbi's students gave him the evil eye and filled him [that is, they caused him to be worth a full two hundred zuz, disqualifying him

---

28. See also Baumgarten, "Name of the Pharisees," p. 420, n. 40. Compare Saldarini, *Pharisees, Scribes and Sadducees,* pp. 222–23.

29. See the reading of the Yerushalmi in *Arukh ha-Shalem,* ed. Kohut, vol. 6, p. 451. Compare *Penei Moshe* and *Korban ha-Edah.*

30. The story is paralleled in y. Peah 8:8 (21a).

from taking the poor tithe]. [Rabbi] came and wanted to give him charity as he was accustomed.

[The student] said to him, "Master, I have enough."

[Rabbi] said, "The blows of the Pharisees have struck you." He gestured to his students and they took him to a tavern and made him one *karat* poorer, and [Rabbi], as he was accustomed, gave him charity.

The second story, like the first, defines the term "the blows of the Pharisees" as the actions of people who exploit legal technicalities to cause people hardship, in this case to put the student just over the legal limit of poverty so he is no longer entitled to receive the poor tithe. Here as well, the New Testament accusation of Pharisaic hypocrisy may be related to the Yerushalmi's depiction of rabbis who cause others hardship by observing halakhah.

Y. Berakhot 9:5 (14b) preserves other motifs that may be paralleled in the New Testament, but it is likely that none of them gave rise to or served as the model for the Bavli's traditions that parallel the New Testament:[31]

(1) There are seven *Perushim*: a *Parush Shikhmi*, a *Parush Nikpi*, a *Parush Kizai*, a *Parush Mah Nekhiyah*, a *Parush* "I will know my obligation and do it," a *Parush* from fear, a *Parush* from love.

(2A) "A *Parush Shikhmi*." He carries his charitable deeds[32] on his shoulder.[33]

(2B) "A *Parush Nikpi*." "Lend to me on credit and I will give charity."[34]

(2C) "A *Parush Kizai*." He balances one sin against one good deed.[35]

(2D) "A *Parush Mah Nekhiyah*." "From what I have I deduct to give to charity."[36]

(2E) "A *Parush* 'I will know my obligation and do it.'" "What sin did I commit that I should give charity corresponding to it?"

(2F) "A *Parush* from fear." Like Job.

---

31. See also the parallel in y. Sotah 5:5 (20c), and *Arukh ha-Shalem*, ed. Kohut, vol. 6, p. 451. See also Steven Fraade, "Ascetical Aspects of Ancient Judaism," in *Jewish Spirituality from the Bible through the Middle Ages*, ed. Arthur Green (New York: Crossroad, 1986), p. 271.

32. Or his mitzvot. The term "mitzvah" can mean both "commandment" in general and "charity" in particular. It is not always clear which meaning is intended.

33. See Sokoloff, *Dictionary of Jewish Palestinian Aramaic*, p. 272.

34. Ibid., p. 361.

35. Ibid., p. 485.

36. Ibid., p. 350.

(2G) "A *Parush* from love." Like Abraham.

(2H) The most beloved of them all is the *Parush* from love, like Abraham.[37]

As noted, we are dealing here with *Perushim* who perform mitzvot, or more specifically give charity, for the wrong reasons or with improper motivation. The *Parush Shikhmi* (2A) is faulted either for flaunting the mitzvot he performs or for treating them like a burden.[38] If the criticism is that this Pharisee flaunts his performance of mitzvot, then we have a parallel to the New Testament's description in Matthew 23:4 of the Pharisees who "do all their deeds to be seen by men for they make their phylacteries broad and their fringes long," or in Luke 18:10–12 of the Pharisee who boasts that he fasts twice a week and tithes all of his possessions. The *Parush Kizai* is faulted for the grudging performance of mitzvot and for relying on the "credits" he has accumulated to give him the freedom to sin without punishment (he thinks), and, like the *Parush* "I will know my obligation and do it," he is faulted for doing only as many mitzvot as are necessary to counterbalance his sins and enable him to escape punishment. Here as well, the various examples of *Perushim* who perform mitzvot for ulterior motives or for the wrong reasons may be, but are not necessarily, related to the New Testament's denunciations of the hypocrisy of the Pharisees.

In any event, the traditions and motifs that the Bavli shares with the New Testament are significantly different from those that may be shared by the Yerushalmi and the New Testament. There is no reason to think that the Bavli inherited its motifs from the Yerushalmi, and it would appear that we are dealing with nonrabbinic literature deriving from the Roman East that has made its way into the Bavli.

The Yerushalmi, however, the only other post-Tannaitic, late antique rabbinic compilation that unquestionably mentions the Pharisees qua second-Temple Jewish sect, does not portray them as rabbis and does not portray them with special sympathy. Why is this so? I doubt the answer is that the Palestinian rabbis of the Yerushalmi omitted mention of the Pharisees in response to the harsh Christian rhetoric against them, for it is unlikely that we would find traditions critical of the *Perushim* in the Yerushalmi (see

---

37. For an attempt to clarify some of the obscurities of this passage, see Saul Lieberman, "Tikunei Yerushalmi 6 (Sof)," *Tarbiz* 5 (1934): 100–101; reprinted in *Mehkarim be-Torat Erez-Yisrael*, ed. David Rosenthal (Jerusalem: Magnes Press, 1991), pp. 203–4. See also Stemberger, *Jewish Contemporaries of Jesus*, pp. 44–45.

38. See Baumgarten, "Josephus and Hippolytus," pp. 11–12.

above) if the Palestinian rabbis were so sensitive about Christian attacks against them in the form of attacks against the Pharisees.[39] Explaining the Yerushalmi's attitudes toward Pharisees in terms of Christianity, therefore, raises a question no less serious than the one it attempts to resolve. More likely, the rabbis of the Yerushalmi do not portray the Pharisees as rabbis because the group ceased to exist and was therefore of no particular importance to them.

Why do the Babylonian rabbis sometimes use the terms "sages" and "Pharisees" interchangeably, however?[40] Why do stories about "sages" in Palestinian rabbinic compilations sometimes become stories about "Pharisees" in the Bavli? Why do stories in the Bavli tend to depict Pharisees more positively than do parallel versions in Palestinian rabbinic compilations[41] and in Josephus?

It is likely that the appearance in fourth-century Babylonia (and later) of Josephan or Josephus-like traditions, depicting Pharisees with features characteristic of rabbis, accounts for the differences between Babylonian and Palestinian rabbinic portrayals of a group that, according to all available evidence, had ceased to exist centuries earlier. I have shown elsewhere that traditions from Josephus or a Josephus-like source that depicted the Pharisees transmitting and adhering to "the traditions of the fathers" in addition to the traditions of Scripture[42] seem to have reached Babylonia and to have become incorporated into the Babylonian Talmud beginning in the fourth century, causing later Babylonian rabbis to esteem the Pharisees as protorabbis. These particular Josephan or Josephus-like traditions do not appear in Palestinian

---

39. Even if the term *Perushim* does not mean "Pharisees" in the Yerushalmi traditions, it could not have escaped the rabbis' attention that the term *Perushim* did sometimes refer to the second-Temple group in rabbinic literature itself. Attacking *Perushim,* therefore, would simply have been playing right into the hands of the Christians. It is possible, although unlikely, that the Palestinian rabbis were saying: "You Christians think Pharisees are so terrible? Well, we agree with you and we are not they." See Saldarini, "Pharisees," pp. 300–301.

40. Judging strictly by the number of traditions in which they figure prominently, however, it bears emphasizing that the Pharisees are not an issue of particular importance for the Babylonian rabbis either.

41. See also Cohen, "Significance of Yavneh," pp. 39–40.

42. For New Testament parallels to the portrayal of the Pharisees as the upholders of the "tradition of the fathers," see Mark 7:1-13 and Galatians 1:14. See also Albert I. Baumgarten, "The Pharisaic Paradosis," *Harvard Theological Review* 80, no. 1 (1987): 66–76; and Stemberger, *Jewish Contemporaries of Jesus,* p. 37. For relevant patristic literature, see Baumgarten, "The Pharisaic Paradosis," p. 66, n. 10. See also *Pseudo-Clementines Recognitions* I.54.6–7.

rabbinic compilations, and according to all available evidence they made no impression on Palestinian rabbis.[43]

We observed that Babylonian rabbis of the fourth century and later also inherited from the Roman East the motif of the Pharisees as hypocrites.[44] This motif would appear to gainsay the traditions portraying the Pharisees as protorabbis. The contradiction is hardly intolerable, however, since the very sources that criticize the Pharisees imply that there are good Pharisees as well as bad ones, and the name "Pharisee" itself is not a term of disapprobation. In addition, it is well documented that the Babylonian rabbinic movement was hardly monolithic, and also that these same rabbis were perfectly able to engage in self-criticism.[45] It is therefore not at all surprising that later Babylonian rabbis were able to portray the Pharisees as rabbis, while, at the same time, transmitting other texts criticizing the Pharisees.

---

43. See Kalmin, *Jewish Babylonia*, pp. 149–67 and 241–47. See also Jaffee, *Torah in the Mouth*, pp. 59–60. Regarding the peculiar fact that Eusebius, the late-third- and early-fourth-century Church historian who flourished in Palestine, made extensive use of Josephus, see Kalmin, *Jewish Babylonia*, p. 190, n. 11.

44. We were uncertain whether or not the Yerushalmi also preserved this motif.

45. To give only one example, see b. Gittin 56a.

SEVEN

Astrology

THIS CHAPTER FURTHER ADVANCES the central thesis of this book by demonstrating again that literature deriving from the Roman East was among the most important components of the Bavli. In addition, this chapter further supports my claim that the fourth century is an important turning point in Babylonian Jewish literature and history. Christian ideas and literary motifs figure prominently in the discussion below, but astrology was an international phenomenon, which requires us to exercise caution in distinguishing between the contribution of Christianity, Judaism, Zoroastrianism, and Greek and Roman paganism to Babylonian rabbinic attitudes toward astrology. Full discussion of Persian thought as a source of the late antique rabbinic traditions must await the examination of more material.[1]

Many modern scholars have discussed ancient rabbinic attitudes toward astrology. Some scholarly discussions have been hampered, however, by a lack of familiarity with the latest tools of modern critical scholarship on rabbinic literature,[2] and at times by an inability to understand rabbinic texts on

---

1. Preliminarily, see David Pingree, "Astrology and Astronomy in Iran" (ii. "Astronomy and Astrology in the Sasanian Period"), *Encyclopedia Iranica*, vol. 2, pp. 858–70; idem, "Classical and Byzantine Astrology in Sasanian Persia," *Dumbarton Oaks Papers* 43 (1989): 227–39.

2. To give just one example, see Kocku von Stuckrad, *Das Ringen um die Astrologie: Jüdische und Christliche Beiträge zum Antiken Zeitverständnis* (Berlin: Walter de Gruyter, 2000), pp. 496–97, who quotes b. Sukkah 29a incompletely, without the crucial statement that when Israel does the will of God it has no need to worry about the power of the luminaries. Von Stuckrad maintains incorrectly that the text supports the idea that astrology works for everyone, Jew and non-Jew alike. See also pp. 476–77, where he does not distinguish between the Hebrew statement attributed to Rav in b. Shabbat 156a and the anonymous editorial give-and-take (in Aramaic) based on Rav's statement.

their most basic level.³ A fresh look at the evidence is therefore a desideratum.

I confine the discussion to cases in which it is clear that the rabbis (a) divine God's will or the future based on the movements or appearance of heavenly bodies, or (b) acknowledge that heavenly bodies influence the course of events on earth.

The Hebrew and Aramaic words *mazal* and *mazla* are conventionally translated as "planet," "constellation," "heavenly body," "fortune," and even "guardian angel."⁴ Since it is impossible to capture all of these nuances with a single English word, I generally leave these words untranslated, either relying on context to convey the meaning or accompanying them with an explanation.

BAVLI SHABBAT 156A–B: AN ASTROLOGICAL MISCELLANY

My initial mode of entry into these issues will be a close reading of a series of stories in b. Shabbat 156a–b⁵ involving rabbis, all of whom ostensibly express the view that "Israel has no *mazal*," that is, astrological forces have no effect on Israel. The ensuing discussion argues that this expression or this idea reached Babylonia from the Roman East, including Roman Mesopotamia, apparently beginning in the fourth century. In the case of concern to us here, we find that the idea achieves literary expression in the Bavli and is expressed as fact by the anonymous editors. B. Shabbat 156a–b

---

3. Ibid., p. 460. In addition, ibid., p. 452, uses ancient and medieval rabbinic compilations indiscriminately, leading to distortions in his accounts of the late antique rabbinic views.

4. See Sokoloff, *Dictionary of Babylonian Jewish Aramaic,* pp. 653–54. Compare idem, *Dictionary of Palestinian Jewish Aramaic,* p. 298.

5. Compare Solomon Gandz, "The Origin of the Planetary Week *or* the Planetary Week in Hebrew Literature," *Proceedings of the American Academy of Jewish Research* 18 (1948–49): 213–67 (= *Studies in Hebrew Astronomy and Mathematics* [New York: Ktav, 1970], pp. 169–210); Von Stuckrad, *Das Ringen um die Astrologie,* pp. 460–80; Gregg Gardner, "Astrology in the Talmud: An Analysis of Bavli Shabbat 156," in *Heresy and Identity in Late Antiquity,* ed. Holger Zellentin and Eduard Iricinschi (Tübingen: Mohr/Siebeck, 2008), pp. 314–38 (my thanks to Professor Zellentin for making the page proofs available to me prior to publication); and Rubenstein, *The Culture of the Babylonian Talmud,* pp. 67–69; idem, "Talmudic Astrology," pp. 109–48; and idem, *Stories of the Babylonian Talmud,* pp. 150–81 and 273–85.

features Babylonian rabbinic editors incorporating the idea that "Israel has no *mazal*" into a collection of earlier traditions about astrology that originally bore no traces of this concept. The Bavli claims that the concept derived from earlier rabbis, but we will conclude that while it is possible that the concept was first formulated by Palestinian rabbis, it is at least as plausible that the concept was first formulated by Christians or nonrabbinic Jews from the eastern Roman provinces.

A story involving Shmuel and Avlat in b. Shabbat 156b will help illustrate the claim that "Israel has no *mazal*" is a later addition to a preexisting rabbinic discussion:

(1) Also from the incident involving Shmuel [we learn] that Israel has no *mazal*, for[6]

(2) Shmuel and Avlat[7] were sitting, and some people were going to the marsh. [Ms. Oxford-Bodl. heb. d. (2676)5 reads, "They saw children going (to look) for wood."][8]

(2A) Avlat said to Shmuel, "This man is going but he will not return."

(2B) Shmuel said to [Avlat], "If he is an Israelite he will go and return."

(2C) As they sat, [the man] went and returned. Avlat stood up and removed [the man's] burden. He found in it a snake that was cut and thrown in two pieces.[9]

(2D) Shmuel said to [the man], "What have you done?" [That is, what good deed have you done to merit your life being spared?]

(2E) [The man] said to [Shmuel], "Every day we used to throw the loaves together [for a common meal] and eat. [Ms. Oxford-Bodl. heb. d. 21 (2676)5 reads: "There were children with us who had no bread. Every day we took a piece and fed them."] Today there was one with us who did not have bread

---

6. Part 1 is an introduction to the story supplied by the anonymous editors rather than part of the story itself. See the discussion below.

7. See Jonas C. Greenfield and Michael Sokoloff, "Astrological and Related Omen Texts in Jewish Palestinian Aramaic," *Journal of Near Eastern Studies* 48 (1989): 213, who think that this name is derived from the ancient Akkadian name Uballit. See also Mark Geller, "The Last Wedge," *Zeitschrift für Assyriologie und Vorderasiatische Archäologie* 87 (1997): 57, n. 55.

8. *Menorat ha-Ma'or, Siman* 194, p. 409, reads: "They saw children going to the marsh." See the discussion below.

9. Several discussions in the Bavli refer to the cutting of reeds in a marsh. See b. Shabbat 95a, b. Sanhedrin 33a, b. Sanhedrin 82b, and b. Bekhorot 8b. The fact that the snake is cut in two is therefore not an argument in favor of the reading "going [to look] for wood."

with him, and he was ashamed. I said to my fellows, 'I shall get up and throw the bread for him.' When I came to his place, I pretended to take [it] from him so that he would not be ashamed."[10]

(2F) [Shmuel] said to [the man], "You have done a mitzvah."

(2G) Shmuel went out and expounded Scripture: "'Righteousness saves from death' (Prov 10:2; 11:4), and not [merely] from an unusual death but from death itself."

The first part of the story, up to and including part 2C, appears to illustrate the point that "Israel has no *mazal*," as the anonymous editors say explicitly in a brief introduction to the story (part 1). The second part of the story (parts 2D–2G), however, undercuts this point, since the explicit message of the second part is that the man who went to the marsh averted his fate not because he was Jewish, but because he was righteous and performed a mitzvah.

However, several manuscripts record Shmuel responding simply (at part 2B), "He will go and return," instead of the printed text's "If he is an Israelite he will go and return."[11] At first glance this reading appears to be simply wrong, since this reading implies that Shmuel assumes the man will return only if he has done good deeds, and also that Shmuel does not know at the outset that the man has done good deeds (as is indicated by his question later on in the story: "What have you done?" [part 2D]). If so, why is Shmuel sure the man will return and how does the story prove that Israel has no *mazal*?[12] As noted, the presence of manuscript variants is a sign of late composition, particularly when accompanied by other indications of lateness.[13]

Another indication that Shmuel's response (part 2B) is a late, probably post-Talmudic addition to the story is the fact that the Shmuel/Avlat story is paralleled by a narrative in y. Shabbat 6:9 (8d), and the version of the narrative in the Yerushalmi has no response to the astrologer's prediction. The response was probably added to the Bavli's version in an attempt to show how the story demonstrates the principle that "Israel has no *mazal*." Whoever

---

10. Sokoloff, *Dictionary of Jewish Babylonian Aramaic*, pp. 1087–88.
11. See *Dikdukei Soferim*, ed. Rabbinovicz, n. *het*.
12. It also bears mentioning that ms. Oxford-Bodl. heb. d. 21 (2676)5 reads part 2B as follows: "If he is a Jew, the matter does not depend on *mazal* but on merit." This reading is clearly an attempt to square the two halves of the story and turn it into a coherent, flowing narrative.
13. See Friedman, "Al Derekh Heker ha-Sugya," p. 30.

added Shmuel's response was unmindful, or unconcerned, about the fact that the story was rendered problematic thereby.

The parallel in the Yerushalmi reads as follows:

> Two of R. Hanina's students went out to chop wood. An astrologer saw them.
>
> [He said], "These two are going but they will not return."[14]
>
> When they went out, an elder encountered them.
>
> He said to them, "Obtain merit through me [by giving me charity], for it has been three days since I have eaten anything."
>
> They had with them one loaf. They cut it in half and gave it to him.[15] He ate it and prayed for them.
>
> He said to them, "May your lives be preserved this day as you have preserved my life this day."
>
> They went out in peace and returned in peace. And there were people there who heard his voice [that is, they heard the astrologer's prediction]."
>
> They said to him, "Didn't you say, 'These two are going but they will not return?'"
>
> He said, "Either I[16] am a liar or my[17] astrology is false."[18]
>
> Even so, they went and checked and found a snake, half in one's load and half in the other's load.
>
> They said to him, "What good deed did you do[19] this day?"
>
> [They] told him the story.[20]
>
> He said, "What can I[21] do when the God of the Jews is appeased with half a loaf?"

---

14. See Saul Lieberman, *Ha-Yerushalmi ki-Feshuto* (Jerusalem: Darom, 1934), p. 114.
15. Ibid.
16. Literally, "that man." The text employs the third person as a circumlocution.
17. See the previous note.
18. Lieberman, *Ha-Yerushalmi ki-Feshuto*.
19. Ibid.
20. It is not entirely clear whom the students are speaking to. According to the Aramaic text of the Yerushalmi, in the previous line they were addressed by unidentified speakers and in this line they respond to a single interlocutor, clearly the astrologer. Such small textual problems, however, are routine in the Leiden manuscript, and the basic meaning of the story is clear.
21. Literally, "he." See the notes above.

Despite the fact that the story in the Bavli is about Shmuel, a Babylonian rabbi, it is likely that it originated in the Yerushalmi and that Babylonian tradents changed it to a story about Shmuel, who was well known for his astrological/astronomical expertise.[22] Avlat was chosen as his interlocutor not because the Bavli knew that he was an astrologer, despite the claims of several modern scholars who wish to draw biographical conclusions about Avlat's identity as a Babylonian astrologer, but because the Bavli knows of several other dialogues between Shmuel and Avlat, a non-Jew. According to this understanding, the anonymous Babylonian editors took the statement that "Israel has no *mazal,*" which sounds like a general rule that admits of no exceptions, and made it the introduction to the story, thereby changing the statement's meaning. The message of the story and the statement combined is not that the stars have no power over Jews, but only that the stars have no power over a Jew who does righteous deeds.

In evaluating the connection of the second part of the Shmuel/Avlat story to the narrative in the Yerushalmi, it is important to note that a version of the Bavli's story preserved in a genizah fragment[23] has two children going out for wood and describes the good deed they perform as that of distributing food to poor people rather than saving someone from embarrassment. According to this version, the parallel to the Yerushalmi's story is even closer. Significant support for the reading of the genizah fragment is the fact that marshes were common in late antique Babylonia but wood was not.[24] It is likely that the reading of the genizah fragment was changed by later scribes in accordance with reality in Babylonia, yielding the reading of most manuscripts and printed editions.

The conclusion that the story originated in the Yerushalmi explains other anomalous features of the narrative as well.[25] The narrative's second half,

---

22. See, for example, b. Berakhot 58b and the parallel in y. Shabbat 9:2 (13c). The ancient world had no clear equivalent to the modern distinction between astrology and astronomy.

23. Ms Oxford-Bodl. Heb. D. (2676)5. See above.

24. See Moshe Beer, *Amoraei Bavel: Perakim be-Hayei ha-Kalkalah* (1974; Ramat-Gan: Bar-Ilan University Press, 1982), pp. 26–27, 68–69, 86, 99–100, 115, n. 48, and 230.

25. It is undeniable that several minor differences between the versions in the Yerushalmi and the Bavli are not obviously explicable as due to editorial revision in accordance with Babylonian culture. Perhaps the Babylonian and Palestinian Talmudic versions represent distinct oral performances of basically the same story, with shared motifs and didactic messages. We will see below that this is definitely true of the R. Akiba story vis-à-vis the Shmuel story in the continuation of b. Shabbat 156b. It is also possible that the Yerushalmi's version continued to evolve after an early version was transmitted to Babylonia,

parts 2D–2G, depicts Shmuel casually conversing with the Jew who performed the good deed, and this Jew is apparently not a rabbi. In addition, the second half also attributes a great deal of importance to mitzvot other than Torah study (the exclusive domain of rabbis), and values a mitzvah that can be performed by nonscholars as well, namely, giving charity to the poor or preserving one's fellow from embarrassment. As I have argued elsewhere, both of these motifs are characteristic of statements by and stories involving Palestinian Amoraim,[26] but are virtually nonexistent in statements by and stories about Babylonian rabbis prior to the fourth century. It is unexpected, therefore, to encounter a story depicting Shmuel, an early Babylonian Amora, (1) casually conversing with a nonrabbi, and (2) as the protagonist of a story that values mitzvot other than Torah study. According to our conclusions above, a later Babylonian editor has taken a story deriving from Palestine and has transformed it into a story about Shmuel, an early Babylonian rabbi.

A story involving R. Akiba immediately follows the Shmuel/Avlat story, and teaches the same lesson:

(1) Also from the incident involving R. Akiba [we learn] that Israel has no *mazal*, for

(2) R. Akiba had a daughter.

(2A) Chaldeans [that is, astrologers] said to him, "The day she enters the wedding chamber, a snake will bite her and she will die."

(2B) [R. Akiba] was very worried about this.

(2C) The day [she entered the bridal chamber] she took a twisted pin(?)[27] and stuck it into a crack [in the wall] and it happened that [the pin?] penetrated the snake's eye.[28] In the morning [when he removed it] the snake was adhering and following it.[29]

(2D) Her father said to her, "What have you done?" [That is, what good deed have you done to merit your life being spared?]

---

and it was this early version that was subjected to Babylonian editorial revision in b. Shabbat 156b. It is not necessary to decide between these two explanations since they are not mutually exclusive.

26. And Babylonian Amoraim of the fourth century and later. See Kalmin, *Jewish Babylonia*, pp. 173–86 and 249–54.

27. See Sokoloff, *Dictionary of Jewish Babylonian Aramaic*, p. 675.

28. Ibid., p. 1068.

29. Ibid., p. 832. Here Sokoloff seems to interpret *makhbanta* as a kind of garment. See also ibid., p. 345. Compare the previous two notes.

(2E) She said to him, "A poor man came in the evening [and] called at the door. Everyone was busy with the meal so no one heard him. I took a portion of food[30] and gave it to him."

(2F) He said to her, "You have done a mitzvah."

(2G) R. Akiba went out and expounded Scripture: "'Righteousness saves from death' (Prov 10:2; 11:4), and not [merely] from an unusual death but from death itself."

The anonymous editors introduce this story with the same expression ("Israel has no *mazal*") that they used to introduce Shmuel's statement (part 1). Once again the phrase "Israel has no *mazal*," which sounds like it means Israel is exempt from astrological influences, actually turns out to mean "astrology does have power over Israel, but this power will be neutralized if Jews perform mitzvot." Despite the differences in detail, the stories about R. Akiba and Shmuel are alternative versions of a single story.

A story involving Rav Nahman bar Yizhak, a mid-fourth-century Babylonian rabbi, concludes this collection:

(1) Also from the incident involving Rav Nahman bar Yizhak [we learn] that Israel has no *mazal*, for

(2) The mother of Rav Nahman bar Yizhak, Chaldeans said to her, "Your son will be a thief."

(2A) She said to [her son], "Cover your head so that the fear of heaven will be upon you, and ask for mercy [that is, pray]."

(2B) [Rav Nahman bar Yizhak] did not know why she said this to him. One day he was sitting and studying under a palm tree. The garment fell from his head. He lifted up his eyes and saw the palm tree. His inclination overpowered him, he ascended [the tree] and cut off the cluster [of dates] with his teeth.

It is likely that Rav Nahman bar Yizhak's actions at the conclusion of the story (part 2B: "His inclination overpowered him, he ascended [the tree] and cut off the cluster [of dates] with his teeth") demonstrate the truth of the Chaldeans' prediction.[31] The Rav Nahman bar Yizhak story, therefore, like

---

30. Ibid., p. 345.
31. Conceivably, we are to understand that the astrological prediction did not come true, since it is not stated explicitly that Rav Nahman bar Yizhak becomes a robber but only that he tears off a branch of dates with his teeth. Throughout the Talmud, however, the predictions of "Chaldeans" come true and they are never proven false, and several times it

the other stories in this collection, is in tension with the context supplied for it by the anonymous editors. Without this context, the point of the story is that astrology has much power over Jews, such that when the safeguards provided by mitzvot and proper piety toward God are removed, even momentarily, even a great rabbi performs an aggressive, presumably sinful act. The story emphasizes the need for constant vigilance if one is to counteract the forces of astrology. The previous two stories focused on the power of charity; this story focuses on study, prayer, and fear of heaven. In the Rav Nahman bar Yizhak story, we get no specification of Israel, although he overcomes the astrological prediction as long as he performs the rabbinically approved commandments of Torah study and prayer and maintains an attitude toward God that likewise conforms to rabbinic standards of proper piety.

We have in this collection of stories, therefore, two versions of a story that originated in Palestine, the first told about Shmuel and the second told about R. Akiba, and a third story about Rav Nahman bar Yizhak, a fourth-century Babylonian rabbi. For reasons to be expanded upon below, it is likely that the anonymous editors of this collection inherited the expression "Israel has no *mazal*" from the eastern Roman provinces, including one usage from Roman Mesopotamia, and transformed its meaning in a Babylonian rabbinic setting.

Having concluded that the concept "Israel has no *mazal*" was superimposed onto the collection of stories in b. Shabbat 156b at a relatively late date, we can suggest that another statement in the larger compilation of traditions composing b. Shabbat 156a–b probably received the same treatment at the hands of the anonymous Babylonian editors. I refer to a statement attributed to Rav immediately preceding this story collection:

(1) And Rav also thinks that Israel has no *mazal,* for

(2) Said Rav Yehudah said Rav, "What is the scriptural source [for the principle] that Israel has no *mazal*? As it is said, '[God] took [Abram] outside' (Gen 15:5). Said Abraham before the Holy One, blessed be He: 'Master of the world, "My steward will be my heir"' (Gen 15:3). [God] said to him, 'No. "None but your very issue [shall be your heir]"' (Gen 15:4). [Abram] said

---

is explicit that they conform to the will of God (see below). It is likely that the same is true in this story as well. See also b. Kiddushin 81b for another story, involving Rav Hiyya bar Ashi, in which a rabbi's impulse overpowers him and he climbs up to fetch fruit from the top of a date palm, and there it is clear that the rabbi is in the midst of committing a serious transgression.

before Him, 'Master of the world. I looked in my horoscope and I am not fit to father a son.' [God] said to him, 'Leave your horoscope, for Israel has no *mazal*.'"

(2A) What is your opinion, [Abram]? That Jupiter stands in the West? I will make [Jupiter] travel a circuit and place it in the East.[32] And this is [the meaning of] what is written, "Who has roused Jupiter to the East, summoned it to His service?" (Isa 41:2).[33]

This discussion attributes to Rav the statement "Israel has no *mazal*" (part 2), but in this case as well the phrase is suspicious. Supporting this contention is the fact that the anonymous Aramaic commentary based on Rav's statement implies that the stars have power over Israel, but that God has more power (part 2A). This idea is in tension with the idea that "Israel has no *mazal*," as were the stories in Shabbat 156b analyzed above. The anonymous commentary blunts the force of the statement attributed to Rav, making us understand it instead to mean that Israel *is* subject to astrological forces, but God, should He so choose, has the power to overcome these forces. It is possible that the word *Tzedek* in the anonymous editorial commentary based on Rav's statement, which means both "Jupiter" and "righteousness," indicates that God's decision to overturn the laws of astrology depends on the person's righteous behavior. If this is true, then the anonymous editors treat Rav's statement exactly as they treat the stories in the remainder of the collection.

In any event, while certainty on this subject is not possible, it is likely that Rav's statement originally did not contain explicit mention of the concept "Israel has no *mazal*," and it was to Rav's statement without this concept that part 2A was added, which yielded the message that God had the power to overcome the very real power of the stars over Israel. Later anonymous editors added the concept "Israel has no *mazal*" to Rav's statement, in line with their activity vis-à-vis the stories analyzed above. As noted, it is likely that the anonymous Babylonian editors inherited this concept from the Roman East and superimposed it onto a preexisting series of Amoraic and anonymous statements and stories, making it the prism through which later generations were to understand these traditions.

What is the basis for our contention that the concept "Israel has no *mazal*" derives from the Roman East? First, b. Shabbat 156a twice credits a

---

32. Sokoloff, *Dictionary of Jewish Babylonian Aramaic*, p. 366.
33. I have translated according to the midrashic meaning. JPS translates "Who has roused a victor from the East, summoned him to His service?"

Palestinian Amora, R. Yohanan, with the abstract declaration that "Israel has no *mazal*,"[34] although it is possible that R. Yohanan's statements were likewise reformulated by later Babylonian editors. The role of later Babylonian editors in reformulating R. Yohanan's statements is suggested by the fact that the second statement attributed to R. Yohanan in b. Shabbat 156a has a close parallel in *Bereshit Rabbah* 44:12,[35] and in this case as well the abstract declaration is absent from the Palestinian compilation.

The statement attributed to R. Yohanan in the Bavli is as follows:

> R. Yohanan said, "What is the scriptural source [for the principle] that Israel has no *mazal*? As it is said, 'Thus said the Lord, "Do not learn to go the way of the nations, and do not be dismayed by portents in the sky. Let the nations be dismayed by them"' (Jer 10:2). They will be dismayed but not Israel."

The relevant statement in *Bereshit Rabbah* is as follows:

> In the days of Jeremiah Israel wanted to engage in [astrology] and the Holy One blessed be He did not allow them. This is as it is written, "Thus said the Lord: 'Do not learn to go the way of the nations, and do not be dismayed by the portents in the sky; [Let the nations be dismayed by them]' (Jer 10:2). Abraham your father already wanted to engage in [astrology] but I did not allow him."[36]

Clearly this tradition is not an abstract statement about Israel's immunity to astrological forces. Instead, as noted, it asserts that God prohibited the Israelites of biblical times from engaging in astrology because biblical Israel has prophets, such as Abraham and Jeremiah, who are more effective than astrologers. Alternatively, Israel should not engage in astrology because it is beneath them, or simply inappropriate for them because it is a characteristically Gentile practice.[37] This polemic has abundant parallels in Christian and pagan sources from the eastern provinces of the Roman Empire.[38]

---

34. While R. Yohanan's statements may be Palestinian, we have no way of ascertaining when they arrived in Babylonia and were incorporated into this discussion.

35. *Bereshit Rabbah,* ed. Theodor and Albeck, pp. 433.

36. See also the statement attributed to R. Yonatan in *Mekhilta de-R. Yishmael, Pisha* 1:1 for another possible source reworked by the Bavli to form the statement before us. It is extremely common for the Bavli to attribute to R. Yohanan statements that in Palestinian compilations are attributed to other rabbis.

37. See, for example, Pesikta de-Rav Kahana, ed. Mandelbaum, p. 60; y. Shabbat 6:10 (8d) (twice); y. Rosh Hashanah 3:8 (59a); and y. Avodah Zarah 2:2 (41a).

38. See, for example, Origen, cited in Eusebius, *Praeparatio Evangelica* 6.11, and *Philocalia* 12.1–21. See also Nicola Denzey, "A New Star on the Horizon: Astral Christologies

It is possible, therefore, that the phrase "Israel has no *mazal*" was added to R. Yohanan's midrashic statement by later, Babylonian editors, in conformity with their treatment of the statements and stories in the collection examined above. This reading of the evidence is also in line with the conclusion of Leib Moscovitz that abstractions tend to be later, often anonymously formulated statements, and that early Amoraim tend to formulate their statements in casuistic or concrete terms.[39] The possibility cannot be excluded, however, that R. Yohanan himself added the abstract declaration to the midrash, and that this declaration, which forms the backbone of the second part of the Bavli's astrological miscellany, derives from Palestinian rabbinic culture.

Another indication that the phrase "Israel has no *mazal*" perhaps derives from Palestinian rabbinic culture is the presence of the phrase in a purportedly Tannaitic tradition preserved in *Midrash Tannaim* 18:14,[40] which states that Jews should not engage in astrology because the planets have no power over them *(she-Ein la-Hen le-Yisrael Mazal)*.

> Another interpretation: "[Those nations that you are about to dispossess do indeed resort to soothsayers and augurs]; to you, however, the Lord your God has not assigned the like" (Deut 18:14). For Israel does not have *mazal [she-Ein la-Hen le-Yisrael Mazal]*.

This statement, however, is also of uncertain Palestinian rabbinic provenance.[41] While much of the material in *Midrash Tannaim* is Tannaitic, at

---

and Stellar Debates in Early Christian Discourse," in *Prayer, Magic, and the Stars in the Ancient and Late Antique World*," ed. Scott Noegel, Joel Walker, and Brannon Wheeler (University Park: Pennsylvania State University Press, 2003), pp. 212–19.

39. Leib Moscovitz, *Talmudic Reasoning: From Casuistics to Conceptualization* (Tübingen: Mohr/Siebeck, 2002), passim.

40. *Midrash Tannaim*, ed. Hoffman, p. 111.

41. See most recently Michal Bar-Asher Siegal, "Parashat Ma'aserot (Devarim 14, 22–29) be-Mekhilta li-Devarim de-R. Yishmael: Bei'ur Tekstu'ali u-Feirush," MA thesis, Hebrew University, 2006. I thank Dr. Siegal for showing me her thesis in advance of its publication. In a private communication of October 8, 2008, Siegal wrote, "*Midrash Hagadol* uses authentically Tannaitic traditions from *Mekhilta li-Devarim*, but also reworks post-Tannaitic traditions, especially the Rambam, but the Bavli and Yerushalmi too, to appear Tannaitic." She labels *Midrash Tannaim* 18:14 "uncertain." She writes, "The Rambam, a usual suspect source in 'tannaitic-looking' paragraphs, has (in *Hilkhot Avodat Kokhavim* 11:15) Deuteronomy 18:14 with regards to the prohibition of following diviners, but does not specifically mention the phrase *Ein Mazal le-Yisrael*. In the Bavli (Shabbat 156a–b), where the phrase *Ein Mazal le-Yisrael* is mentioned, the Deuteronomy verse is not mentioned. One can easily see how

least some of it is suspected to be the product of later invention or tampering of earlier traditions based on the Bavli, since it is a work restored by David Zvi Hoffman in the nineteenth century based on texts found in *Midrash ha-Gadol,* a late medieval compilation. Hoffman argues convincingly that material in *Midrash ha-Gadol* that has no clear antecedents in prior midrash collections or other rabbinic works is likely to be Palestinian and Tannaitic, but obviously *Midrash Tannaim* has to be used with caution. Material in it that departs considerably from material of undoubted Palestinian, Tannaitic provenance and that conforms to the Bavli may have been emended based on the Bavli or on post-Talmudic texts.

There is no definitive proof, therefore, that the concept "Israel has no *mazal*" reached the Bavli from Palestinian rabbinic sources. Precisely this concept, however, if not precisely this expression, is attested in Christian and pagan sources from the Roman East, including a source composed in Syriac from Roman Mesopotamia, and as noted in the introduction, it is likely that Babylonian rabbis understood Syriac. Perhaps the Babylonian editors of b. Shabbat 156a–b derived the idea from these Christian and pagan sources, which certainly predate the Bavli's anonymous editors, especially given the fact that these anonymous editors superimpose the idea on a story involving Rav Nahman bar Yizhak, a mid-fourth-century Babylonian rabbi.

To be specific, we find the idea that Israel has no *mazal* expressed in Syriac by the second-century Christian author Bardaisan, who flourished in the Roman Mesopotamian city of Edessa. Bardaisan writes: "And the Jews ... the star that rules the climate they are in has no compulsive power over them."[42] Bardaisan, however, does not think that the Jews are unique,

---

the very short midrash in *Midrash Tannaim* could be created from a combination of the two. However, arguing in favor of a Tannaitic origin of *Midrash Tannaim* 18:14 is the fact that (1) the combination of *Ein Mazal le-Yisrael* and the Deuteronomy verse is unique and not found anywhere else; and (2) the precise grammatical construction of *she-Ein la-hem le-Yisrael Mazal* in *Midrash Tannaim* is also unprecedented. It comes down to the question of how much the author of *Midrash Hagadol* took the liberty to edit his sources. This has been debated in research, but I tend to be on the conservative side since I did not see any strong proof in my work that *Midrash Hagadol* made significant changes to his sources. It is debatable how significant would be the change in this particular case, and the fact that the midrash is very short and does not contain many unique terminologies or independent statements makes it harder to determine its origin."

42. See *The Book of the Laws of Countries: Dialogue of Fate of Bardaisan of Edessa,* ed. and trans. H. J. W. Drijvers, 2nd ed. (Piscataway, NJ: Van Gorcum, 2006), pp. 58–59. To be more precise, this work was probably composed by Bardaisan's pupil, Philip, and purports to represent Bardaisan's thought. Bardaisan is the protagonist of the book. See Sebastian

asserting that the stars do not rule over any country.[43] In addition, the second-century Syrian Christian apologist Tatian asserts that Christians are not subject "to the laws of astral fatalism, although these laws still bound their polytheist contemporaries.... Jesus Christ had abrogated destiny for all those to whom he had granted a new genesis through ... baptism."[44] The second-century Valentinian Christian author Theodotus writes that with the coming of Christ, those who believed in him were transferred from the domain of fate to the domain of Providence: "Until baptism, fate is real, but after it the astrologers are no longer right."[45] Hellenistic mystery cults attest a similar notion,[46] and Firmicus Maternus, a pagan author, asserts that Caesar is immune from astral determinism.[47]

CHALDEANS

Further support for the claim that the concept "Israel has no *mazal*" was superimposed at a relatively late date onto a preexisting discussion in the Bavli is the fact that this concept is diametrically opposed to Babylonian

---

Brock, "Bardaisan," in *Gorgias Encyclopedic Dictionary of the Syriac Heritage* (Piscataway, NJ: Gorgias Press, 2011), p. 56. Ephraim Urbach, *The Sages: Their Concepts and Beliefs*, trans. Israel Abrahams (Jerusalem: Magnes Press, 1979), p. 809, n. 66; and Saul Lieberman, *Greek in Jewish Palestine* (New York: Jewish Theological Seminary, 1942), pp. 99–100, mistakenly claim that Bardaisan asserts that the Jews are unique in this regard. For a nuanced discussion of Bardaisan's views on astrology, see Tim Hegedus, *Early Christianity and Ancient Astrology* (New York: Peter Lang, 2007), pp. 261–77.

43. See Hegedus, *Early Christianity and Ancient Astrology*, pp. 91–107.

44. See Tatian, *Oratio ad Graecos* 8:1, trans. Molly Whittaker (Oxford: Clarendon Press, 1982), p. 15. See also Denzey, "A New Star on the Horizon," p. 210.

45. See *Excerpta ex Theodoto* 74 and 78, ed. Robert Pierce Casey (London: Christophers, 1934), pp. 86 and 88, respectively; and notes on pp. 156 and 158. See also Urbach, *The Sages*, pp. 809–10, n. 68; and Denzey, "A New Star on the Horizon," pp. 211–13. Christian polemicists in the third and fourth centuries, however, began to assert that with the coming of Christ the power of the stars and planets was suspended altogether, and not just suspended only for Israel as in rabbinic polemics or for Christians as in pre-third-century Christian thought. See Denzey, "A New Star on the Horizon," pp. 218–19.

46. See, for example, Apuleius, *Metamorphosis* 11.15 and 11.25.2; and J.R. Bram, "Fate and Freedom: Astrology vs. Mystery Religions," *Society of Biblical Literature Seminar Papers, 1976* (Missoula, MT: Scholars Press, 1976), pp. 329–30.

47. *Matheseos* 2.30.5. See also Tamsyn Barton, *Ancient Astrology* (London: Routledge, 1994), pp. 65–66. See also Rubenstein, "Talmudic Astrology," p. 144; and idem, *Stories of the Babylonian Talmud*, pp. 172–73 and 281–82 for a discussion of relevant Christian and pagan attitudes.

rabbinic thought expressed elsewhere throughout the Talmud. Had the concept been introduced into Babylonia at an earlier date, it is likely that it would have gained greater currency in the Bavli, rather than achieve expression in no more than a single discussion, a discussion calculated, furthermore, to significantly neutralize the concept.

A glance at the term "Chaldaean," "astrologer," will illustrate the claim that the Bavli, in sharp contrast to Palestinian compilations, tends to depict astrologers as fully correct in their predictions.[48] In addition, the Bavli sometimes depicts the predictions of astrologers as conforming to the will of God. Not only does Israel have *mazal*, therefore, but even the fate of pious Jews and famous rabbis can be discerned by professional astrologers. The Bavli has no difficulty depicting righteous Jews, including rabbis, getting close enough to astrologers to be informed by them of their predictions for the future, although the Bavli never depicts them as actually *consulting* astrologers. A narrative in b. Shabbat 119a illustrates several of these points:

> Yosef Who Honors the Sabbath, there was a certain non-Jew in his neighborhood who had a lot of property.
>
> Chaldeans said to him, "Yosef Who Honors the Sabbath will consume all of your property."
>
> [The non-Jew] went and sold all of his property and bought with it a precious gem. He put it in his cap.[49] When he was crossing a bridge, a wind caused it to fly away and threw it into the water. A fish swallowed it. Someone lifted it up and brought [the fish] toward evening before the arrival of the Sabbath.
>
> They said, "Who will buy this now?"
>
> They said to them, "Go and bring it to Yosef Who Honors the Sabbath, who is accustomed to buying [things just before the Sabbath]."
>
> They brought it to him, he bought it and tore it open, and found in it the precious gem. He sold it for thirteen measures[50] of golden dinars.
>
> A certain elder encountered him.
>
> He said, "He who borrows [for the Sabbath], the Sabbath pays for him.

---

48. See also Richard Kalmin, "Problems in the Use of the Babylonian Talmud for the History of Late-Roman Palestine: The Example of Astrology," in *Rabbinic Texts and the History of Late-Roman Palestine,* ed. Martin Goodman and Philip Alexander (London: Oxford University Press, 2010), pp. 175–78.

49. See Sokoloff, *A Dictionary of Babylonian Jewish Aramaic,* p. 802.

50. Ibid., p. 855.

From the conclusion of this story, it is clear that Yosef receives the precious gem as a divine reward for honoring the Sabbath. The last two sentences are missing in several versions[51] and are therefore suspect as a later addition, but even without them the message is clear, first from Yosef's sobriquet ("Who Honors the Sabbath"), and second from his practice of buying expensive, perishable foods just before the Sabbath for the sole purpose of honoring the Sabbath. So apparently God is active behind the scenes, arranging for Yosef to be rewarded for his devotion to the Sabbath. The fact that there is conformity between the prediction of the astrologers and God's will serves to distinguish the Bavli's story from stories in Palestinian compilations. This story is one of many proofs that could be provided to illustrate the claim that the concept "Israel has no *mazal*" is atypical of the Bavli as a whole and is therefore likely to be a relatively late addition to b. Shabbat 156a–b, transformed, however, via its contact with Babylonian rabbinic culture.

B. Sanhedrin 95a preserves another tradition in which the prediction of the Chaldeans is correct and in conformity with God's will, and involves the Israelite people:

> (A) What is [the meaning of] "This same day at Nob [the king of Assyria] shall stand and wave his hand" (Isa 10:32)?
>
> (B) Said Rav Huna, "That day something remained of the sin of Nob (1 Sam 22:9–23) [when Saul commanded the execution of the priests of Nob and Doeg the Edomite carried out the command. If Sennacherib attacked Israel that day, God would see to it that he defeated them as punishment for the sin against the priests of Nob. If he did not, he would not succeed].
>
> "Chaldeans said to [Sennacherib], 'If you go now, you will defeat [Israel], but if not, no.'
>
> "A journey that should have taken ten days, [Sennacherib] walked it in one day. When they reached Jerusalem, [Sennacherib] threw down pillows until he ascended and sat above the wall and could see all of Jerusalem. When he saw it, it looked very small to him.
>
> "[Sennacherib] said, 'Is this not the city of Jerusalem, for which I set all my troops in motion and for which I captured the entire country? Is it not smaller and weaker than all of the cities of the nations that I captured with the strength of my hand?'

---

51. See *Dikdukei Soferim*, ed. Rabbinovicz, n. *het; Sheiltot* 1, ed. Mirsky, p. 15; *Midrash Aseret ha-Dibrot* (see *Beit ha-Midrash*, ed. Adolph Jellinek [1853–77; Jerusalem: Wahrmann Books, 1967], vol. 1, p. 75); mss Oxford, JTS ENA 2990.5–11; JTS ENA 2825.21; *Aggadot ha-Talmud*.

"[Sennacherib] arose, shaking his head and waving his hand to and fro against the Temple Mount in Zion and against the [Temple] court in Jerusalem.

"[His troops] said, 'Shall we attack it now?'

"[Sennacherib] said to them, 'You are now tired from your journey.[52] Each one of you should bring me tomorrow from [the wall of Jerusalem a piece the size of] a bulla.'[53]

"Immediately, 'That night an angel of the Lord went forth and struck down 185,000 in the Assyrian camp, and the following morning they were all dead bodies' (2 Kgs 19:35)."

(C) Said Rav Papa, "This is as people say, 'If the verdict is postponed overnight, it comes to naught.'"

As the discussion presently stands, the story about Sennacherib and the astrologers is linked to the statement of Rav Huna (part B). As such, the prediction of the Chaldeans conforms to the will of God, although there is no indication that the Chaldeans know that what they say conforms to God's will. Once again we search in vain for the idea that the predictions of the Chaldeans are inapplicable to Jews, or even for the idea that Jews can escape astrology's dictates through the performance of commandments.

Chaldeans also figure, to the same effect, in a statement attributed to Rav Hisda in b. Yevamot 21b:[54]

Said Rav Hisda, "This thing I heard from a great man (And who is it? R. Ami[55]): 'They only forbade a daughter-in-law on account of a daughter-in-law.' And Chaldeans said to me, 'You will be a teacher.' I said, 'If I will be a great man [that is, a prominent rabbi], I will explain [R. Ami's statement] on my own. If I will be a teacher of children, I will ask the rabbis who come to the synagogue.'"[56]

---

52. Sokoloff, *Dictionary of Jewish Babylonian Aramaic*, p. 1212. See Targum Yerushalmi to Isaiah 10:32.

53. Sokoloff, *Dictionary of Jewish Babylonian Aramaic*, p. 281.

54. The larger context of this statement is not significant for my purposes. I therefore confine the discussion to Rav Hisda's statement, leaving aside the abstruse halakhic background.

55. The brief question and answer in parentheses was probably added to Rav Hisda's statement by a later editor. How late the material was added is unclear, and the date of the addition is irrelevant for my purposes.

56. Mss Cambridge-T-S AS 75.86 and Günzburg read "house of study" *(bei midrasha)* instead of synagogue *(bei kenishta)*.

According to Rav Hisda the Chaldeans are once again correct, although the ambiguous nature of their prediction makes him uncertain exactly how his life will turn out. Rav Hisda's statement, however, is not a polemic against astrology, since the prediction is true; it is simply the case that Rav Hisda is not immediately able to interpret it. In addition, the prediction will eventually be shown to yield the truth when Rav Hisda correctly interprets R. Ami's statement. Finally, the prediction of the astrologers strikes to the very heart of the rabbinic movement, since they know the fate of one of the greatest Babylonian rabbis who ever lived.[57]

MORE ON *MAZLA* IN THE BAVLI AND ITS ANTECEDENTS IN THE ROMAN EAST

Further examination of the term *mazla* in the Bavli reveals a transformation of its meaning during and after the fourth century, unattested in earlier layers of the Bavli but with echoes in Palestinian rabbinic literature and, surprisingly, much stronger parallels in nonrabbinic and even non-Jewish literature deriving from the Roman Empire. These close parallels further support the theory that the fourth century was a turning point in the development of the literature and culture of Jewish Babylonia in response to cultural currents from the Roman East.[58]

---

57. See also the discussion of the story involving Rav Nahman bar Yizhak in b. Shabbat 156b above.

58. In addition to the traditions surveyed in detail below, see also b. Berakhot 55b (either Amemar, Mar Zutra, or Rav Ashi [see also the partial parallel in b. Nedarim 40a (Rava)]); b. Shabbat 61b (Rav Papa) and b. Shabbat 145b–146a (Rav Ashi); and b. Pesahim 110a (Abaye, according to mss JTS Rab. 1608 [ENA 850] and Vatican 109). See also the use of the term *benei hada mazla* in statements attributed to Rava and Rav Ashi in b. Baba Batra 12a–b; and see b. Bekhorot 8b for the term *bat mazla* in a story involving R. Yehoshua ben Hananiah and the sages of Athens. It is unlikely that the latter tradition, in Aramaic and without parallel in Tannaitic corpora, is actually Tannaitic. If it has roots in the Tannaitic period, however, then we find further support for the claim (see below) that the later Babylonian usage of *mazla* may derive from Palestine. In addition, one statement attributed to a mid-third-century rabbi in b. Baba Batra 98a reflects what is typically a later Babylonian rabbinic meaning of *mazla*. The statement is part of a discussion that reads as follows:

[Mishnah:] (1) One who sells wine to his fellow and it turned sour, he is not liable. But if his wine is known to turn sour, it is a sale in error.

[Talmud:] (2) Said R. Yosi b'R. Hanina, "They only taught [this Mishnah] when the bottles belong to the owner, but if the bottles belong to the seller, [the buyer] can say to [the seller], 'Here is your wine and here is your bottle.'"

It will be helpful to preface this discussion with a few words of definition. The ensuing discussion focuses on the term *mazla* when it designates a heavenly body that has a special connection to a particular individual, often serving to protect that individual from harm. The fates of the *mazla* and the individual are inextricably intertwined, such that the *mazla* becomes "impaired" or "lowered" when the individual suffers a reversal, and vice versa: the person suffers when his *mazla* loses potency. An individual's *mazla* can experience things on his behalf, producing an effect on the individual as if he had had the experience himself. A person's *mazla* comes into being when he is born, and although this is not stated explicitly, presumably it disappears when the person dies.

For example, we read in b. Megillah 3a:

(A) "I, Daniel, alone saw the vision. The men who were with me did not see the vision, yet they were seized with a great terror and fled into hiding" (Dan 10:7).

(B) ... Since they "did not see [the vision]," why were they frightened?

(C) Even though they did not see, their *mazla* saw.

(D) Said Ravina, "Derive from this that a man who is frightened, even though he doesn't see [anything frightening], his *mazla* sees."

....

(1) And [R. Yosi b'R. Hanina] disagrees with Rav Hiyya bar Yosef, for

(2) Said Rav Hiyya bar Yosef, "Wine, the *mazla* of its owner causes [it to be good or bad], as it is said, 'Even wine deals treacherously'" (Hab 2:5) (see *Yad Ramah*, s.v. *u-Mai*).

Rav Hiyya bar Yosef, however, lived in both Babylonia and Palestine (see Albeck, *Mavo la-Talmudim*, pp. 196–97), so it is difficult to know how to classify this statement. If we treat it as Palestinian, it can be added to the very slender evidence indicating that the Babylonian usage derives from Palestinian rabbis. If the statement is viewed as Palestinian, it must be admitted that we have no clear idea when this statement arrived in Babylonia, although it is interesting to note that Rav Hiyya bar Yosef's statement is introduced into the discussion by the anonymous editors, generally understood to represent a relatively late layer of Talmudic discourse.

If we view Rav Hiyya bar Yosef as Babylonian, however, then this single case challenges, but hardly negates, the fact that the bulk of the evidence supports a date in the mid-fourth-century C.E. for the introduction of this conception of *mazla* into the Bavli. It would not be at all unusual for later editors to reformulate an earlier Babylonian statement in accordance with later Babylonian conceptions.

The anonymous editors of this passage (part C) and Ravina[59] (part D) most likely date from the fourth century or later. According to both the later Amora and the anonymous editors, what the person's *mazla* "sees" or experiences produces an effect on the individual as if he or she saw or experienced it themselves.

B. Moed Katan 28a preserves another example:

> Rav Se'orim the brother of Rava sat before Rava. He saw that [Rava] was dying.[60]
>
> [Rava] said to [Rav Se'orim], "Let the master tell [the angel of death] not to cause us pain."
>
> [Rav Se'orim] said to [Rava], "Is not the master his close friend?"[61]
>
> [Rava] said to him, "Since my *mazla* has been lowered,[62] he pays no attention to me."
>
> [Rav Se'orim] said to him, "Appear to me [after your death]."
>
> He appeared to him.
>
> [Rav Se'orim] said to him, "Did the master have any pain?"
>
> [Rava] said to him, "Like the incision of a scalpel."[63]

This story, involving Babylonian Amoraim of the fourth century, supports my claim that a rabbi's *mazla* is closely linked to and may even be inseparable from his personal fate. Once Rava's *mazla* has been "lowered," presumably via his sickness, Rava no longer has any influence over the angel of death. The descent of the rabbi and his *mazla* occurs simultaneously.

B. Horayot 12a preserves a related usage:[64]

> (A) Said R. Ami ... "A person who wants to go on a journey and wants to know whether or not he will return home, let him stand in a dark place.[65] If he sees the shadow of a shadow, he will know that he will return home."[66]

---

59. Ms Göttingen 3 reads Rava instead of Ravina, which does not affect my claim about the relatively late date of the tradition. Mss London BL Harl. 5508 (400), Munich 95, Munich 140, Vatican 134, and Oxford Opp. Add. fol. 23 all read Ravina.
60. See Sokoloff, *Dictionary of Babylonian Jewish Aramaic*, p. 737.
61. Ibid., p. 1125.
62. Ibid., p. 693.
63. Ibid., p. 1072.
64. See also the parallel in b. Karetot 5b–6a.
65. See Sokoloff, *Dictionary of Jewish Babylonian Aramaic*, p. 280.
66. I have translated this statement as if it was the continuation of R. Ami's statement. It is possible that it is an anonymous addition, but this possibility has no impact on my findings.

(B) But no; this is without any basis. Perhaps he will become distraught and his *mazla* will be impaired.

In other words, the anonymous editorial statement in part B claims that the person who does not see "the shadow of a shadow" might fail to return home not because the unfavorable omen accurately forecasts the future, but because he will become distraught upon receiving what he has been made to *think* is an unfavorable omen. The person's negative state of mind has a negative impact on his *mazla*, which in turn has a negative impact on the person.[67] Once again the two mutually reinforce each other and lead to the downward spiral of both *mazla* and person.

Also revealing is a story in b. Hagigah 4b–5a:

(A) Rav Yosef, when he reached [the following] verse, he cried: "'Some are swept away without justice' (Prov 13:23).[68] Are there people who die before their time?"

(B) Yes, like this case:

(C) Rav Bibi bar Abaye, the angel of death was frequently with him. The angel of death said to his messenger, "Go, bring me *Miriam Megadla Neshaya* [that is, the plaiter of women's (hair)]."[69]

[The messenger] went and brought [to the angel of death] *Miriam Megadla Dardekei* [that is, the raiser of children].

[The angel of death] said to [the messenger], "I told you '*Miriam Megadla Neshaya*.'"

[The messenger] said to [the angel of death], "If so, I will return her."

[The angel of death] said to [the messenger], "Since you brought her, let her be counted [among the dead]."

[The angel of death said to the messenger], "How did you prevail over her?"

[The messenger said to the angel of death], "She was holding a rake in her hand and she was heating and raking the oven.[70] She took [the rake] and

---

67. See Rashi on b. Horayot 12a, s.v. *ve-Lav Milta Hi*.
68. I have translated according to the midrashic interpretation. JPS translates "But substance is swept away for lack of moderation."
69. Or "the raiser of women." The printed text reads *Megadla Se'ar Neshaya,* but none of the manuscripts has the word *se'ar* (hair). Nevertheless, the added word may have correctly captured the sense of the epithet. Compare Burton Visotzky, "Mary Maudlin among the Rabbis," in *Fathers of the World: Essays in Rabbinic and Patristic Thought* (Tübingen: Mohr/Siebeck, 1995), pp. 86–88.
70. Sokoloff, *Dictionary of Jewish Babylonian Aramaic*, p. 482.

placed it on top of her leg. The fire blazed up on her,[71] her *mazla* was impaired and I brought her."

Rav Bibi bar Abaye said to [the angel of death], "Do you [really] have permission to do this?"

[The angel of death] said to [Rav Bibi bar Abaye], "Is it not written, 'Some are swept away without justice'" (Prov 13:23)?

The fire causes Miriam's *mazla* to be weakened, initiating the downward spiral that culminates in her death.

Important information is also revealed in b. Baba Kamma 2b:

(A) What is the difference between [the verb used to describe the goring of] a person, where it is written, "When an ox gores *(Ki Yigah)* [a man or a woman to death]" (Ex 21:28), and a beast, where it is written, "When [an] ox gores *(Ki Yigof)* [his neighbor's ox and it dies]" (Ex 21:35)?

(B) [Regarding] a person, who has *mazla,* it is written *Ki Yigah*. [Regarding] an animal, which has no *mazla,* it is written *Ki Yigof*. And [Scripture] informs us in an incidental manner that [a beast that] has the presumption of goring a human being also has the presumption of goring a beast, but [a beast that] has the presumption of goring a beast does not have the presumption of goring a human being.

This anonymous discussion informs us that a human being has *mazla* but a beast does not, and that as a result, a beast is more likely to kill another beast than a human being. *Mazla* confers protection on a creature that is unavailable to one without *mazla*.

A discussion in b. Pesahim 2b provides additional information:

(A) What is [the meaning of] *Or,* [a term used in the Mishnah]?

(B) Rav Huna said, "Day."

(C) Rav Yehudah said, "Night."

(D) They objected [based on a tradition of higher authority], "Perish the day on which I was born.... May its twilight stars remain dark. May it hope for *Or* and have none. May it not see the glimmerings of the dawn" (Job 3:3, 9). Since Scripture says, "May it hope for *Or* and have none," this proves that *Or* is day.

(E) In that case [that is, in Job 3:3, 9), Job is cursing his *mazla,* saying, "May it be [God's] will that I[72] look for [a source of] light but not find it."[73]

---

71. Ibid., p. 983.
72. Literally, "that man," a circumlocution.
73. See Rashi, s.v. *Le-Nehora*.

According to the anonymous editors (section E in this passage), Job's *mazla* becomes his on the day of his birth.

All of the texts surveyed above derive from the fourth century or later.[74] A few traditions in post-Tannaitic Palestinian compilations reflect a similar conception of *mazla*, although we find significantly closer parallels in non-rabbinic literature. *Bereshit Rabbah* 10:4 preserves the most significant Palestinian rabbinic tradition:[75]

> Said R. Simon, "There is not a blade of grass that does not have a *mazal* in the heavens that strikes it and says to it, 'Grow!' This is what [is written], 'Do you know the laws of heaven or impose its authority on earth?'" (Job 38:33).

As noted, according to one discussion in the Bavli only human beings possess their own *mazla*.[76] Animals do not, and although it is not stated so explicitly, presumably plant life does not as well. According to this text in *Bereshit Rabbah*, in contrast, plant life, and perhaps only plant life, has its own *mazla*.

Two Palestinian Amoraic statements in the same context similarly affirm the power of heavenly bodies over plant life on earth,[77] although in contrast to R. Simon's statement in *Bereshit Rabbah* these two statements do not affirm the existence of a special connection between a particular *mazal* and a specific plant.

> (A) "Can you tie cords to Pleiades or undo the reins of Orion?" (Job 38:31).
>
> (B) R. Hanina bar Papa and R. Simon said, "Pleiades makes the fruits tender and Orion draws [the connection] between the stem [of the fruit] and the bottom [of the fruit]. This is [as it is written], 'Can you lead out *Mazzarot* in its season?'" (Job 38:32).
>
> (C) R. Tanhum b'R. Hiyya and R. Simon, "[*Mazzarot*] is a *mazal* that completes the ripening of the fruit."[78]

---

74. See, however, n. 58 above, regarding b. Bekhorot 8b and b. Baba Batra 98a.
75. *Bereshit Rabbah* 10:4, ed. Theodor and Albeck, pp. 78–79.
76. See the discussion of b. Baba Kamma 2b above.
77. *Bereshit Rabbah* 10:4, ed. Theodor and Albeck, p. 79.
78. See the commentary of Theodor and Albeck, p. 79. Compare Jastrow, *Dictionary*, p. 756. Other relevant passages, in later Palestinian compilations, are found in *Kohelet Rabbah* 7:15 (three times) and *Esther Rabbah* 7:10 (once), where the term *temi'a mazla*, "sunk *mazla*" (see Sokoloff, *Dictionary of Palestinian Jewish Aramaic*, pp. 226–27 and 298), associates *mazla* with the fortunes of particular wicked human beings. Although the later Palestinian

As noted, however, nonrabbinic sources from the Roman East provide much clearer parallels to the Bavli's conception of *mazla*. The Roman author Pliny the Elder in the first century C.E. asserts that every person has his or her own star, which rises with them at birth and falls with them at death, and varies in brightness corresponding to a person's fate in life.[79] In addition, according to the *Book of Hermes Addressed to Ammon*, a star causes an individual's illness "because it has suffered negative influence itself," and the star therefore needs strengthening by means of "sympathetic energy."[80] In addition, "In the *Sacred Book of Hermes Addressed to Asclepius*, the medical recipes clearly envisage strengthening the decan responsible for causing disease in a particular part of the body."[81] Barton characterizes the belief that each person has his or her own star as widespread throughout the Roman Empire.[82] Significantly, this conception, along with the term *mazal*, is attested in a Hebrew magical text, *Sefer Harazim*,[83] according to which it is likely that the concept penetrated Palestinian Jewish circles at some point in late antiquity and that the Babylonian rabbis could have easily inherited the concept from Palestinian Jews: "I adjure you to bring the planet of N and his *mazal* near to the *mazal* and planet of N, so his love will be tied with the heart of N son of N." These parallels from the Roman East are much closer to the Bavli's usage than to anything in a Palestinian rabbinic compilation. Here as well, however, the Bavli did not necessarily inherit the concept from a particular text, whether in Hebrew or in some other language, but rather, perhaps, as conventional wisdom deriving from multiple sources.

---

sources are confined to the wicked and are too brief to permit firm conclusions, they may provide an additional link to the concept as it developed in Babylonia.

79. See *Natural History* 2.5.23.

80. See *Physici et medici Graeci minores,* vol. 1, ed. Julius Ludwig Ideler (Berolini, 1841–42), pp. 387 and 430.

81. See C.E. Ruelle, "Hermès Trismégiste, le livre sacré sur les décans," *Revue de Philologie* 32 (1908): 252–53 and 258–59. Already Plato, *Timaeus* 41D–E, attests to this idea. See Barton, *Ancient Astrology*, pp. 190–91. For a discussion of "decans" in ancient astrological thought, see W. Gundel, *Dekane und Dekansternbilder: Ein Beitrag zur Geschichte der Sternbilder der Kulturvölker* (Glückstadt: J.J. Augustin, 1936).

82. Barton, *Ancient Astrology*, p. 113.

83. *Sefer ha-Razim*, ed. Bill Rebiger and Peter Schäfer (Tübingen: Mohr/Siebeck, 2009), pp. 28*–29*.

SUMMARY AND CONCLUSIONS

To summarize, the notion that "Israel has no *mazal*" reached Babylonia from Jewish, Christian, or pagan sources from the eastern Roman provinces (Palestine, Asia Minor, Syria, or Roman Mesopotamia) apparently during the fourth century. Confronted with the conception that "Israel has no *mazal*," the later editors of b. Shabbat 156a–b adopted a variety of strategies to blunt the force of several traditions that accepted the efficacy of astrology. These later editors asserted, with less-than-perfect consistency, (1) that traditions that appeared to express belief in determinism actually left substantial room for free will, and (2) that God had the power to overcome the power of the stars, either by virtue of His own free choice or by virtue of His decision to reward Jews who performed good deeds. The tendencies observable in the later layers of b. Shabbat 156a–b are not typical of the Bavli as a whole,[84] and hopefully future research will help us account for the lack of congruity between the attitudes of the later authors and editors of this extended miscellany and those found frequently in many other sources scattered throughout the Bavli.

In addition, the conception that the fate of individual human beings was linked to the regnant planets at the days or hours of their birth was a commonplace in Roman culture but had only faint echoes in Palestinian rabbinic literature. It is striking that the parallels to the popular Roman idea are much clearer in the Bavli than in Palestinian rabbinic compilations, although a clear attestation of the idea is preserved in a late antique Palestinian magical text.

As noted, astrology was an international phenomenon. The fact that this chapter documents several concepts that appear to have reached the Bavli from the Roman East does not negate the possibility that other Babylonian rabbinic conceptions reached the Bavli from a variety of other sources, including Zoroastrian Persia.

---

84. See Kalmin, "Problems in the Use of the Babylonian Talmud," pp. 175–78, and the discussion of Chaldeans above.

EIGHT

The Alexander Romance

MODERN SCHOLARS HAVE MADE MANY ATTEMPTS to interpret the traditions composing the Alexander compilation in Bavli Tamid, including several attempts to understand the message(s) of the compilation as a whole.[1] This chapter includes my own attempt, but it focuses primarily on the implications of the Alexander compilation for the major thesis of this book: that traditions from the Roman East are a crucially important constituent of the Babylonian Talmud.

There are many indications that these traditions reached rabbinic Babylonia from the eastern Roman provinces. First, as many scholars have shown, virtually all of the traditions that compose Tamid's compilation closely parallel traditions from the Alexander Romance, the earliest recension of which apparently derives from Alexandria in the third century C.E., but which incorporates a substantial amount of much earlier material.[2] There is scholarly controversy regarding the date of the traditions composing the Alexander Romance, as well as the date of compilation of its various

---

1. See, for example, E. E. Halevi, *Sha'arei ha-Aggadah* (Tel Aviv: n.p., 1963), pp. 115–37; Emmanuel Levinas, *New Talmudic Readings,* trans. Richard A. Cohen (Pittsburgh: Duquesne University Press, 1999), pp. 79–107; Admiel Kosman, *Masekhet Nashim* (Jerusalem: Keter, 2007), pp. 15–18; Ory Amitay, "Alexander in *Bavli Tamid:* In Search for a Meaning," in *The Alexander Romance in Persia and the East,* ed. Richard Stoneman, Kyle Erickson, and Ian Richard Netton (Groningen: Barkhuis, 2012), pp. 349–65; Dalia Marx, *Tractates Tamid, Midot and Qinnim* (Tübingen: Mohr/Siebeck, 2013), pp. 57–76; and Avi Friedman, "Hokhmato, Masaotav ve-Ozrotav shel Alexander Mokdon: Masekhet Tamid daf 31," www.daat.ac.il/chazal/maamar.asp?id = 323.
2. Richard Stoneman, "Naked Philosophers: The Brahmans in the Alexander Historians and the Alexander Romance," *Journal of Hellenic Studies* 115 (1995): 99, n. 1.

recensions,³ so crucial corroboration of its relevance to this chapter is the fact that many of the accounts in the earliest Greek biographers and historians of Alexander, of undoubted antiquity, likewise bear close resemblances to the Talmudic accounts. To name only one of the most striking parallels, Plutarch,⁴ *Alexander* 64, as well as several other ancient Greek and Latin accounts,⁵ preserves a riddling contest between Alexander and the Indian Gymnosophists (the "Naked Philosophers"), parallel to the riddling contest between Alexander and the Elders of the Negev in Bavli Tamid, and in both the rabbinic and the ancient Greek accounts Alexander threatens his interlocutors with death. Many other traditions and motifs in Bavli Tamid are paralleled in ancient Greek biographical and historical accounts, further indication of Babylonian rabbinic appropriation of earlier Greek accounts.⁶ We will see below that significant support for this conclusion is provided by the Berlin Papyrus of the first or second centuries B.C.E., the earliest surviving version of the dialogue between Alexander and the Indian Philosophers.⁷

Richard Stoneman is among the chief proponents of the scholarly consensus regarding the relationship between the Alexander Romance and Bavli Tamid, asserting that "Alexander's encounter with the Elders of the South [in Bavli Tamid] . . . is closely modeled on the encounter with the Brahmans in Ps.-Callisthenes [the Alexander Romance]."⁸ Along the same lines, Tal Ilan states that "there is little doubt that these stories belong to the grand 'Alexander Romance' traditions,"⁹ and Luitpold Wallach appropriately

3. See below.
4. Ca. 100 C.E.
5. Other ancient versions of the dialogue between Alexander and the Gymnosophists are found in the Berlin Papyrus (see below), the Metz Epitome, Anecdota Graeca, Iulius Valerius, and Clement of Alexandria, *Stromata*.
6. See, for example, Amitay, "Alexander in *Bavli Tamid*," pp. 353–61.
7. Berlin Papyrus 13044: Ulrich Wilcken (1923) = Fragmente der Griechischen Historiker (henceforth, FGrH) 153.9. English translation in Richard Stoneman, *The Legends of Alexander the Great* (London: J. M. Dent, 1994), pp. 77–78. See Ulrich Wilcken, "Alexander der Grosse und die indischen Gymnosophisten," *Sitzungsberichte der deutschen Akademie der Wissenschaften zu Berlin* (1923); Stoneman, *The Legends of Alexander the Great*, p. xi and passim; and Amitay, "Alexander in *Bavli Tamid*," p. 353. See also Lionel Pearson, *The Lost Histories of Alexander the Great* (New York: American Philological Association, 1960), p. 259.
8. See Richard Stoneman, "Jewish Traditions on Alexander the Great," *Studia Philonica Annual* 6 (1994), pp. 48–49.
9. See Tal Ilan, *Silencing the Queen: The Literary Histories of Shelamzion and Other Jewish Women* (Tübingen: Mohr/Siebeck, 2006), p. 5; and Richard A. Freund, "Alexander Macedon and Antoninus: Two Greco-Roman Heroes of the Rabbis," in *Crisis and Reaction:*

connects the ancient Greek account of Plutarch with the Talmudic compilation.¹⁰

Some scholars go beyond the evidence, however, claiming that the Talmud's account is a "literary reworking" of Alexander's dialogue with the Brahmans in the Romance.¹¹ All we can say for certain is that the Jewish and the Greek versions share several sources in common, and that both the Greek authors and the Babylonian rabbis adapted their sources for their own purposes. Perhaps the Talmudic account is based directly on one of the surviving Greek accounts, but this is impossible to prove definitively, and for our purposes it is not necessary to do so.

A variety of factors support the claim that the Alexander compilation was mediated to the Bavli via Greek sources. For example, according to some scholars of the ancient Greek versions, none of the versions of the frame story introducing the dialogue between Alexander and the Gymnosophists fits this dialogue very well, and these scholars speculatively attempt to reconstruct the "original" frame story on which the dialogue was based.¹² Other scholars contend that the dialogue between Alexander and the Gymnosophists was originally a "free-floating text," and was attached to the frame story after the fact.¹³ We will argue below that the dialogue between Alexander and the Elders of the Negev is similarly incongruous, and that the fact that in both the Talmudic and the Greek versions the relationship between the frame story and the dialogue is so similarly problematic is strong proof of a significant linkage between these two versions, since such a problematic relationship between frame and dialogue in parallel accounts preserved in different cultures is unlikely to be the result of sheer coincidence.¹⁴

The Heroes in Jewish History, ed. M. Mor (Omaha: Creighton University Press, 1995), pp. 22–47. See also Marx, *Tractates Tamid, Midot and Qinnim*, pp. 55–56.

10. Luitpold Wallach, "Alexander the Great and the Indian Gymnosophists in Hebrew Tradition," *Proceedings of the American Academy of Jewish Research* 11 (1941): 48–52. See also Freund, "Alexander Macedon and Antoninus," pp. 22–47; and Ilan, *Silencing the Queen*, pp. 5–7.

11. See, for example, Ilan, *Silencing the Queen*, p. 7.

12. See, for example, Helmut van Thiel, "Alexanders Gespräch mit den Gymnosophisten," *Hermes* 100 (1972): 343–58; and Philip R. Bosman, "The Gymnosophist Riddle Contest (Berol. P. 13044): A Cynic Text?" *Greek, Roman, and Byzantine Studies* 50 (2010): 181. See also the discussion below.

13. Stoneman, "Naked Philosophers," p. 113; and Bosman, "Gymnosophist Riddle Contest," p. 182.

14. See also Amitay, "Alexander in *Bavli Tamid*," pp. 357–58. It is likely that the disconnect between the text before us, where there is no indication that the king lied, is the reason why the reading "in blood," that is, in murder, came about. We have no explanation for

Several close parallels between the Talmudic and the Greek accounts further support the conclusion that the Talmud appropriated Greek versions of the traditions. As noted, a single parallel or a small number of parallels might be explicable as the result of coincidence or a shared folkloristic motif.[15] When virtually every scene in the Talmudic compilation has a close parallel in the Greek accounts,[16] explanation along such lines is very difficult.

For example, Alexander in Bavli Tamid is criticized for his unquenchable thirst to acquire more riches and more knowledge, well beyond what God had apportioned to him. This critique has ample precedent in the ancient Greek biographical and historical accounts of Alexander, as well as in the Alexander Romance. To give some representative examples, several ancient Alexander historians take the king to task for his insatiable desire for conquest and glory that drove him to embrace danger and to attempt to be the lord of all things.[17] In addition, Arrian, considered by modern scholars to be the most reliable ancient historian of Alexander, records vivid scenes in

---

the opposite process, namely, that a change from an original reading of "in blood" became the motiveless "in lies." Amitay, "Alexander in *Bavli Tamid*," asserts that other aspects of Alexander's dialogue with the Elders make sense only if we understand them as based on the ancient Greek accounts, but his arguments seem overly speculative.

15. Aleksandra Szalc argues that Indian riddle contests, the earliest records of which go back much earlier than the Greek variety, were an important inspiration for ancient Greek riddle contests. See Aleksandra Szalc, "Alexander's Dialogue with Indian Philosophers: Riddle in Greek and Indian Traditions," *Eos* 98 (2011): fasc. 1, pp. 7–25. See also Freund, "Alexander Macedon and Antoninus," p. 31. All of these parallels between the Indian question-and-answer texts and the ancient versions of Alexander's dialogues with the Gymnosophists, however, are too general to support such a claim. We cannot be absolutely certain that the Greek Alexander materials were not inspired in part by the Indian texts, or even vice versa, but the likelihood is slim. And even if we posit a direct link between the *Indian* and the *Greek* materials, the *Talmudic* texts are so similar to the *Greek* materials that it is unlikely that the Indian materials played a role in the creation and composition of the Talmudic compilation.

16. The major exceptions are Alexander's demand to be admitted to Paradise, the skull he receives as a gift, and his consultation with the rabbis.

17. Insatiable desire for conquest and glory: Arrian, *Anabasis* 6.13.4; desire to be lord of all things: Strabo, *Geography* 16.1.11 (741) FGrH 139 F 56; and Arrian, *Anabasis* 7.1.4–2.1 and 7.3.4. See also A.B. Bosworth, "Introduction," in *Alexander the Great in Fact and Fiction*, ed. A.B. Bosworth and E.J. Baynham (Oxford: Oxford University Press, 2000), p. 4. For basic works on the "Alexander historians," see Pearson, *Lost Histories of Alexander the Great*; Paul Pédech, *Historiens compagnons d'Alexandre* (Paris: Belles Lettres, 1984); A.B. Bosworth, *From Arrian to Alexander* (Oxford: Clarendon Press, 1988); and N.G.L. Hammond, *Three Historians of Alexander the Great* (Cambridge: Cambridge University Press, 1983); and idem, *Sources for Alexander the Great* (Cambridge: Cambridge University Press, 1993). See also Plutarch, *Alexander* 11.4; Diodorus, *Bibliotheca historica* 17.9.4; and Arrian, *Anabasis* 1.7.7–11, 1.8.1–2, 1.8.8.

which Alexander's generals reproach him for his excessive restlessness.[18] In addition, at the beginning of book 7 Arrian states that Alexander has an ambition for further conquest so extreme that if there were no one else to surpass, he would compete with himself.[19]

Arrian next relates three vignettes—the criticisms of Alexander by the Indian Gymnosophists, the king's meeting with Diogenes, and Megasthenes's account of Alexander's conversation with the Indian sage Dandamis—each of which supports the main theme: Alexander's failure to overcome his desire for fame.[20] Dandamis's warnings are an explicit commentary on the king's imperial ambitions, and form a bridge to the next episode in the history, the suicide of Calanus, who is portrayed as unconquerable in his resolution to die as Alexander is in his determination to achieve world Empire.[21]

We find other examples in rabbinic literature of Bavli Tamid's meditation on the futility of endless striving, as well as the purposelessness of travel to far-off places for conquest and acquisition. Significantly, however, the Tamid compilation sometimes critiques *any* sort of striving, and thus goes beyond what we find in other rabbinic texts. The story of Ashmedai's encounter with Solomon in Bavli Gittin 68a–b is a case in point.[22] The story teaches that Solomon, ruler of the world, was glorious enough without needing also to rule over the demonic realms. The Ashmedai story, however, is not saying that there is no gain *whatsoever* in striving and conquering. True, says Bavli

---

18. Arrian, *Anabasis* 6.12.1–3 and 6.13.4. For detailed discussion see A. B. Bosworth, *Alexander and the East: The Tragedy of Triumph* (Oxford: Clarendon Press, 1996), pp. 54–56; and Bosworth, "Introduction," p. 4.

19. Arrian, *Anabasis* 7.1.4. The general sentiment was expressed by Aristobulus (Strabo, *Geography*, ed. H. L. Jones (Cambridge, MA: Harvard University Press, 1917–32) 16.1.11 [741]), and Arrian, *Anabasis* 7.19.6, records it as his own view. See Peter Högemann, *Alexander der Grosse und Arabien* (Munich: C. H. Beck, 1985). In Arrian's concluding summary, he insists that Alexander was most continent with respect to bodily pleasures, but that with regard to fame he was completely insatiable. The lust for conquest was central in Arrian's picture of Alexander. See Bosworth, "Introduction," p. 5. Plutarch, *Alexander* 3, comments: "When he was still a boy, his self-control manifested itself in the fact that, though violent and impetuous in other respects, he was unmoved by the pleasures of the body and partook of such things very sparingly."

20. Arrian, *Anabasis* 7.1.5–2.1 (Gymnosophists), 7.2.1 (Diogenes), 7.2.2–4 = FGrH 715 F 34b (Dandamis). This last scene is also reported by Strabo, *Geography* 15.1.68 (718). On this episode see A. B. Bosworth, "Calanus and the Brahman Opposition," in *Alexander der Grosse: Eine Welteroberung und ihr Hintergrund*, ed. Wolfgang Will (Bonn: R. Habelt, 1998), pp. 181–90.

21. Arrian, *Anabasis* 7.3.4.

22. See the discussion of this story in chapter 4.

Gittin 68a–b, Solomon has no need for *endless* striving, but Solomon's conquests in this world are worth a great deal, as is shown by the lengths to which he goes to reacquire the throne and the absence of any criticism of him for his effort to do so. The unprecedented nature within rabbinic literature of this feature of Bavli Tamid's message may be further indication that the Alexander compilation reached the Bavli from sources outside rabbinic culture.

None of the scholars who commented upon the connection between the Greek and the Babylonian rabbinic Alexander material has noticed that the phenomenon is a routine feature of Babylonian rabbinic literature vis-à-vis the Roman East. This book has not attempted to provide statistical analysis of the frequency of the phenomenon, which, given the current state of our knowledge, would certainly be an exercise in futility, but hopefully the book will put the issue on the scholarly agenda, sensitize scholars of rabbinic literature to its importance for understanding rabbinic culture, and motivate scholars in related fields (for example, Mesopotamian Christian literature) to undertake comparable studies in order to improve our understanding of the history and literature of the entire region.[23]

WHAT IS THE ALEXANDER ROMANCE?

Elizabeth Baynham refers to "Alexander Romances" as a "generic term used to describe a miscellany of traditions derived from cultures and time periods as diverse as the ancient, medieval European, and Islamic worlds. These traditions were either derived from or related to a Greek prose biography of the

---

23. Perhaps the Greek Alexander Romance reached the Bavli via the Syriac translation that survives from late antiquity or the early Middle Ages, although there is scholarly difference of opinion about whether this Syriac translation derives from the Persian translation or vice versa. From Syriac to Persian: Richard Stoneman, *The Greek Alexander Romance* (New York: Penguin, 1991) p. 7; Richard Frye, "Two Iranian Notes," in *Papers in Honor of Mary Boyce* (Leiden: Brill, 1985), pp. 185–90; Claudia Ciancaglini, "Gli Antecedenti del *Romanzo Siriaco di Alessandro*," in *La diffusione dee'eredutà classica nell'età sardantica e medieval: Il "Romanzo di Alessanro" e altri scritti,* ed. Rosa Bianca Finazzi and Alfredo Valvo (Alexandria: Orso, 1998), pp. 55–93. From Persian to Syriac: Theodor Nöldeke, *Beiträge zur Geschichte des Alexanderromans* (Vienna, 1890), pp. 11–17; Kevin van Bladel, "The Sources of the Early Arabic Narratives of Alexander," in *Memory as History: The Legacy of Alexander in Asia,* ed. Himanshu Prabha Ray and Daniel T. Potts (New Delhi: Aryan Books International, 2007), pp. 61–64.

king. Known as Pseudo-Callisthenes, it was based very loosely around a quasi-historical framework consisting mostly of fabulous stories emphasizing Alexander's fabulous deeds and travels."[24] According to Baynham, "the earliest romances were not given form until possibly the second century A.D."[25]

According to Richard Stoneman, the basic components of the Alexander Romance were already in existence in Ptolemaic Egypt in the third century B.C.E., although many hands added to and molded the text in subsequent centuries.[26] Stoneman does not mean that the Romance qua completed compilation goes back to the third century B.C.E., but rather that many individual traditions or clusters of tradition are very early, and that the Romance qua compilation continued to take shape over the next several centuries and even continued to develop into the Middle Ages. Many of the Greek traditions and the earliest Greek version of the work as a whole precede the Bavli's version, perhaps by as much as several centuries.[27]

---

24. Elizabeth Baynham, *Alexander the Great: The Unique History of Quintus Curtius* (Ann Arbor: University of Michigan Press, 1998), p. 61. Compare Stoneman's dating, above and below.

25. Ibid., pp. 61–62. See also Reinhold Merkelbach, *Die Quellen der griecheschen Alexanderromans,* 2nd rev. ed., with Jürgen Trumpf (Munich: C. H. Beck, 1977).

26. See Stoneman, *Greek Alexander Romance,* pp. 7–9 and 28–32.

27. Most of the quotations from the Alexander Romance in this chapter are taken from the version referred in the literature as L (= Leiden Vulcanius 93), which Richard Stoneman, *Alexander the Great: A Life in Legend* (New Haven: Yale University Press, 2008), p. 231, characterizes as the most complete version of recension-*beta*. In relying on ms L, I follow the lead of Graham Anderson, "The *Alexander Romance* and the Pattern of Hero-Legend," in *The Alexander Romance in Persia and the East,* ed. Stoneman, Erickson, and Netton, p. 81, n. 1. Stoneman, *Greek Alexander Romance,* p. 28, claims that recension-*beta* was composed between the early fourth and the mid-sixth century, and in *Alexander the Great: A Life in Legend,* p. 191, Stoneman claims that ms L was composed in the eighth century. Both versions, he asserts, contain much material that precedes the final compilation by several centuries, a theory supported by the fact that many of the themes and traditions of these versions are closely paralleled by the undoubtedly ancient Greek historical and biographical accounts. The relatively late eighth-century date of this manuscript still makes it centuries earlier than the earliest manuscript of Bavli Tamid. (See Michael Krupp, "Manuscripts of the Babylonian Talmud," in *Literature of the Sages,* first part, *Oral Tora, Halakha, Mishna, Tosefta, Talmud, External Tractates,* ed. Shmuel Safrai [Assen: Van Gorcum, 1987], pp. 346–66.) For further discussion of the Romance's textual history, see David Flusser, *Sefer Yosippon* (Jerusalem: Mosad Bialik, 1978), vol. 2, pp. 236–41; and Stoneman, *Greek Alexander Romance,* pp. 8 and 28–32. Stoneman argues that the earliest recension of the Romance (conventionally referred to as *alpha*), no longer extant, is represented by ms A, which is extant but unfortunately in very poor shape. The *alpha*-recension was expanded to form the *beta*-recension and was further expanded to form the *gamma*-recension. Many scholars claim that the *gamma*-version has marked Jewish and Christian features and that Jews and Christians played an important

The present chapter focuses primarily on traditions found in undoubtedly ancient Greek biographical and historical accounts of Alexander, as well as on traditions found in ms L, the most complete version of recension-*beta* of the Alexander Romance.[28] When dealing with ancient texts, the line between history and biography on the one hand and fiction and romance on the other is often difficult to draw, and many of the motifs and traditions, including the most fantastic, that compose the Alexander Romance are also found in the undoubtedly early biographical and historical accounts.[29]

Other clues to the dating of the Greek compilation are provided by the fact that the earliest Latin translation dates from the fourth century and the Armenian translation is generally dated to the fifth century.[30]

THE BAVLI'S VERSION OF THE ALEXANDER ROMANCE (TAMID 31B–32B)

In the translation of the Talmudic Alexander compilation that follows, italicized passages denote Hebrew in the original, Roman text stands for Aramaic, and biblical quotations are in bold.[31] Hebrew questions and answers are introduced by the letter "H" (H1, H2, H3, and so on) and Aramaic questions and answers by the letter "A" (A1, A2, A3, and so on). After the series of questions and answers, I use Roman numerals to number the discrete sections of the compilation. Immediately following the translation of each section of text, I insert the heading "Commentary," separated from the translation by an ornamented break.[32] Manuscript variants are discussed in the notes.

---

role in its composition and transmission. See, for example, Friedrich Pfister, *Kleine Schriften zum Alexanderroman* (Meisenheim am Glan: Hain, 1976), pp. 95–103. The discussion in this chapter does not rely on the *gamma*-recension, since this recension was probably doctored, at least in part, on the basis of rabbinic sources.

28. *Leben und Taten Alexanders von Makedonien: Der griechische Alexanderroman nach der Handschrift L,* ed. Helmut van Thiel (Darmstadt: Wissenschaftliche Buchgessellschaft, 1974), III.5–6.

29. See also Anderson, *"Alexander Romance,"* pp. 95–103.

30. Stoneman, *Greek Alexander Romance,* p. 28.

31. Regarding the composite nature of this collection of narratives, see the appendix below.

32. The discussion that follows owes much to earlier scholarly discussions of these texts. See, for example, the literature cited in n. 1.

(H) *Alexander Macedon asked*[33] *the Elders of the Negev ten things:*

(H1) *[Alexander] said to them: "Is the distance greater from the sky to the earth or from east to west?"*

They said to him: "From east to west. Know [that we are right], for behold, when the sun is in the east, all look at it;[34] *when the sun is in the west, all look at it; when the sun is in mid-sky, none looks at it.*[35]

And the sages say: Both this and that are equal, as it is said: **For as the heaven is high above the earth . . . As far as the east is from the west** (Ps 103:11–12).

And if one of them were greater, would we write both like the one that is greater?

Now, when the sun is in mid-sky, why don't they look at it?

Because it stands openly, with nothing to cover it.[36]

---

33. Ms Florence II-I-7: "sent," with *"sha'al"* in the margin. Ms Oxford 370: "sent." Mss Munich 95 and Vatican 120: "asked," which works best with the rest of the text before us: *et ziknei ha-Negev*. Ms Oxford has *"the Elders of the Negev"* in the margin. According to the reading "sent," there is no face-to-face contact between Alexander and the Elders.

34. Mss Oxford 370 and Munich 95 end the response of the Elders of the Negev here. Ms Florence II-I-7 has the phrase "in mid-sky, none looks at it" in the margin.

35. Ms Oxford-Bodl. heb. d. 21 (2676) 10 reads this question and answer third. Mss Florence II-I-7, Oxford 370, Munich 95, and the printed edition read it first. See Simon Arazy, "Shtei Arikhot Kedumot shel Massekhet Tamid," *Tarbiz* 76 (2007): 266–67. On pp. 271–72, Arazy speculates that the placement of this question first is the work of a later editor who wanted to strengthen the connection of the Alexander material to the rest of tractate Tamid. Tamid before us lacks a clear connection between the Alexander material and the previous material. The later editor strengthened the connection of this statement to the preceding discussion, according to which the offering of the Tamid sacrifice was determined by the celestial location of the sun. Arazy's speculation, however, leaves unexplained the difference between the placement of question (A4) in the printed edition and most manuscripts on the one hand and its placement in the genizah fragment on the other, where it appears right after (H1). The order in which the various dialogue pairs appear in the various manuscripts is a mystery that has yet to be fully solved, although the fact that several questions are found in diverse contexts is a strong indication that they are later editorial additions to a preexisting compilation. Arazy further speculates that the Alexander compilation in Bavli Tamid was originally linked to the quotation of the story of Alexander's meeting with Shimon ha-Tzaddik and of the Jews' competition with the Samaritans (see Bavli Yoma 69a for the original context of this story in the Bavli), alluded to in the printed edition of Bavli Tamid.

36. Ms Oxford-Bodl. heb. d. 21 (2676) 10 reads the question and answer that compose part (A4) at this point: "He said to them: 'Is it better to dwell on the sea, or better to dwell on land?' They said to him: 'It is better to dwell on land, for all seafarers are ill at ease until they

. . .

Commentary: It is not entirely clear who the Elders of the Negev are supposed to have been, since the phrase appears nowhere else in rabbinic literature. The ensuing discussion argues that in certain respects the Elders behave like rabbis and in other respects they do not.[37] Are they rabbinized nonrabbis or unusual rabbis? In my view, it is impossible to answer this question,[38] and even if we successfully answered it we would not be in a better position to understand their encounter with Alexander.

It is not even clear that the Elders are Jews, an uncertainty that renders problematic the theory that the Tamid compilation was originally Alexandrian Jewish propaganda whose point was the superiority of Judaism to Greek culture.[39] Another significant argument against this theory is the fact that Alexander the Great has the last word vis-à-vis the Elders in one section of dialogue (see below), not to mention the fact that this theory raises the difficult question of why Alexandrian Jewish propaganda would have been incorporated into the Babylonian Talmud.

Without a doubt, however, "rabbis" speak twice in the Alexander compilation. Their status as rabbis is certain because they are referred to as *hakhamim* and *rabbanan,* terms used throughout rabbinic literature to refer exclusively to rabbis. This is one of several signs that the Alexander compilation distinguishes between full-fledged rabbis and "the Elders of the Negev," although the exact nature of that distinction is not entirely clear.

Another key to the identity of the Elders is the striking fact that in this compilation, Torah study is nowhere held up as an antidote to the problem

---

come up to land again.'" (H1), the first question-and-answer pair (the third according to the genizah fragment) is not concerned with the order of creation, unlike (H2) and (H3), the second and third (the first and second in the genizah fragment). (A4) is likewise not concerned with the order of creation. It may be for this reason that (H1) and (A4) were juxtaposed in the genizah fragment. (H1) and (A4) have in common that both deal with human behavior.

37. See also Amitay, "Alexander in *Bavli Tamid,*" p. 354; and Marx, *Tractates Tamid, Midot and Qinnim,* pp. 58–59. Richard Stoneman, "Who Are the Brahmans? Indian Lore and Cynic Doctrine in Palladius' *De Bramanibus* and Its Models," *Classical Quarterly* 44, no. 2 (1994); and idem, "Naked Philosophers," pp. 99–114, argues intriguingly, but in my view unconvincingly, that the Jewish character of Alexander's interlocutors according to the Talmud may be a reflection of the belief of some Hellenistic Greek writers that the Jews were in some way descendants of the Indian philosophers. Josephus, *Against Apion* 1.176–181, reports this view, attributing it to Clearchus of Soli.

38. The term "Elders" sometimes, but not always, refers to "rabbis" in rabbinic literature.

39. See, for example, Wallach, "Alexander the Great," pp. 62–63.

of the vanity of endless earthly striving. Biblical verses and rabbinic texts serve the Elders several times as responses to Alexander's questions, but at no point does the characteristically rabbinic, especially Babylonian rabbinic, activity of ceaseless striving in the realm of Torah serve as the solution to the problem of the vanity of *any* sort of earthly striving. This may be one of several indications that the Elders of the Negev take their inspiration from Mishnah Avot, for example, m. Avot 3:1: "Akaviah ben Mehalalel says, 'Contemplate three things and you will not sin: Know from where you came, and to where you are going, and before whom you will give an account. From where have you come? From a stinking drop. And to where are you going? To a place of dirt and worms. And before whom will you give an account? Before the king of kings of kings, the Holy One, blessed be He." This and similar statements in Mishnah Avot, however, are balanced by many more statements in this tractate that maintain the supreme value of Torah study and the importance of other forms of rabbinically approved behavior that neutralize or contextualize the statements that express the ultimate purposelessness of human life, forcing the audience to read them not as absolute declarations of despair, but as elements of the religious life of a righteous individual that help, for example, distance a person from sin.

On the one hand, the Elders of the Negev answer Alexander's questions (in parts A1–A3 below) via quotations of Mishnah Avot, a rabbinic text. The three questions and the second and third answers in (A1–A3) are attributed to Ben Zoma in m. Avot 4:1. On the other hand, as noted, undoubtedly nonrabbinic figures are sometimes depicted, particularly in the Bavli, as possessing knowledge of biblical and even rabbinic texts.[40] In addition, Mishnah Avot is the least rabbinic of rabbinic texts, since its maxims are often indistinguishable from international wisdom, although there is no unambiguous evidence that the classical rabbis were aware of this fact or that, if they were, they were prepared to acknowledge it or that it had the slightest impact on their evaluation of the rabbinic character of Avot. Interestingly, however, in parts A1–A3 the Elders do not cite the names of the rabbis they are quoting, which is a most unrabbinic mode of activity because of the premium rabbis placed on quoting statements in the rabbinic author's name.[41] Finally, the Elders' response to Alexander's ques-

---

40. See, for example, Ashmedai, king of the demons, in Bavli Gittin 68b; and Jesus in Bavli Avodah Zarah 16b–17a.

41. The Elders also take liberties with the text of Avot, since in Avot the answer to the first question ("Who is called wise?")—*"He who sees what is [being] born" [or: "what [has been] born]"*—is the response of R. Shimon to the instruction: "Go forth and see which

tion in A1 is the clearest proof yet that the Elders are not typical rabbis. For a typical rabbi, the answer to the question "who is called wise?" is obvious: he who is an expert in Torah study and has acquired much Torah knowledge.

. . .

(H2) *[Alexander] said to them: "Was the sky created first or the earth?"*

They said to him: "The sky was created first, as it is said: **In the beginning God created** the heaven and the earth" [Genesis 1:1].

. . .

Commentary: According to b. Hagigah 12a, Beit Hillel and Beit Shammai disagree about the answer to the question posed by Alexander here.[42] Despite the fact that Beit Shammai's opinion is typically ignored for purposes of determining the ultimate outcome of a debate, the Elders in Bavli Tamid answer in accordance with Beit Shammai. It is possible that the compilation in Tamid is unacquainted with the discussion in Bavli Hagigah, although the fact that the opinions of Beit Shammai and the Elders are phrased the same in the two contexts makes this possibility unlikely. There is also a distant possibility that the compilation in Tamid is unacquainted with the rule that in a dispute between Beit Hillel and Beit Shammai the decision is virtually always in accordance with Beit Hillel, since we find rare instances in the Bavli where the discussion ignores or is ignorant of this principle.[43] It is more likely, however, that this dialogue is another indication that the Elders of the Negev are not typical rabbis (if they are rabbis at all), since typical rabbis

---

is the way to which a person should cleave (m. Avot 2:9). On the other hand, it is likely that the authors of the Alexander compilation in Bavli Tamid avoided Avot's answer (the answer to the question "Who is called wise?" in m. Avot 4:1 is "He who learns from every man") because Alexander in Bavli Tamid fulfills that requirement, learning from the Elders and the African women. The authors of the Alexander compilation did not want to portray Alexander as "wise," so they found a different answer.

42. There is no mention of Alexander or the Elders of the Negev in Bavli Hagigah, however.

43. See, for example, David Halivni, *Mekorot u-Mesorot:* Yoma-Hagigah (Jerusalem: Jewish Theological Seminary, 1975), p. 281, n. 1. Ms Oxford 370 of Tamid is missing this question. The anonymous commentary in this manuscript based on the next question demands that this question was before the scribe, but he inadvertently omitted it. As noted, Ms Oxford-Bodl. heb. d. 21 (2676) 10 reads (H2) and (H3) before (H1), which is first in all of the other versions.

would have answered in accordance with Beit Hillel. It should also be noted that the Elders do not mention Beit Shammai by name, a most unrabbinic activity, since it is a truism among the rabbis that one who reports a statement in the name of its author "brings redemption to the world." We will find additional examples of this unrabbinic behavior below, buttressing our claim that the Elders are not typical rabbis.

. . .

(H3) [Alexander] said to them: "Was light created first, or darkness?" They said to him:[44] "This thing has no solution."

Now they might have told [Alexander]: *Darkness was created first, as it is written:* **And the Earth was without form, and void; and darkness [was over the surface of the deep]**, and then **God said: Let there be light! And there was light** (Gen 1:2–3).

They thought [they ought not to] lest he come to ask *what lies above and what below, what before and what behind.*[45]

But if so, they should not have told him about the sky either!

They [must have] thought initially that he was asking a random, general question. Yet once they saw his later question, they thought—we shall not tell him, lest he ask *what lies above and what below, what before and what behind.*

. . .

Commentary: There is no limit to what Alexander wants to know, but the Elders of the Negev inform him that there are, in fact, limitations to human knowledge, even to the knowledge of the greatest king who ever lived. The anonymous editors go on to say that the Elders knew the answer to Alexander's question but deliberately withheld it from him, which perhaps fuels Alexander's anger toward them later on in the compilation.

We have a similar portrayal of Alexander in the Alexander Romance:[46]

---

44. Ms Munich 95 reads "They said to him" in Aramaic. It is not surprising to find a lack of perfect consistency in all of the manuscripts where details such as language switching are concerned in a text transmitted imperfectly for as many centuries as was the Bavli.

45. This phrase is in Hebrew because it is borrowed from m. Hagigah 2:1, a Tannaitic tradition.

46. See Alexander Romance II.41; and Stoneman, *Greek Alexander Romance*, p. 123. This is a quotation from L (= Leiden Vulcanus 93), which, as noted, is the fullest version of recension-*beta*. See Stoneman, *Alexander the Great*, p. 231.

Then I [Alexander] began to ask myself again if this place was really the end of the world, where the sky touches the earth. I wanted to discover the truth, and so I gave orders to capture two of the birds that lived there.... I captured two of them and ordered them to be given no food for three days. On the third day I had something like a yoke constructed from wood, and had this tied to their throats. Then I had an ox-skin made into a large bag, [fixed it to the yoke,] and climbed in, holding two spears, each about ten feet long and with a horse's liver fixed to the point. At once the birds soared up to seize the livers, and I rose up with them into the air, until I thought I must be close to the sky.... Soon a flying creature in the form of a man approached me and said, "O Alexander, you have not yet secured the whole earth, and are you now exploring the heavens? Return to earth as fast as possible, or you will become food for these birds."...

Thus admonished by Providence above, I returned to earth, landing about seven days journey from my army. I was now frozen and half-dead with exhaustion.... Now I have decided to make no more attempts at the impossible. Farewell.

The message of the Romance and the Talmudic passage is the same: Alexander's desire to learn the truth goes beyond what is acceptable to human beings. Obviously the message is delivered in two very different ways in the two compilations, but in the discussion below we will document many instances in which other messages and formulations of messages are virtually identical in Greek and rabbinic literature.

. . .

(A1) *[Alexander] said to them:* "Who is called wise?"

They said to him: "He who sees what is [being] born" [or: "what (has been) born"].[47]

. . .

Commentary: Here we have the first Aramaic question, and after two additional Aramaic questions the text reverts to Hebrew. In the above and in the following two cases the responses by the Elders are in Hebrew, since they are quoting material from Mishnah Avot. It is unclear whether or not their first

---

47. The answers supplied by the Elders to the king's questions in sections (A1)–(A3) are paradoxical, at least at first glance. See Wallach, "Alexander the Great," p. 50.

answer is intended as a subtle rebuke of Alexander.[48] The two answers that follow (see [A2] and [A3]) clearly are.

We may find an interesting parallel to this portion of the dialogue in Arrian 7.28.1–2:

> According to Aristoboulos, [Alexander] ... was extremely adept at seeing immediately what had to be done when it was not yet obvious, and was exceptionally good at guessing what was likely to happen based on the available evidence.[49]

. . .

(A2) *[Alexander] said to them:* "Who is called a hero?"

They said to him: "He who conquers his desire."

(A3) *[Alexander] said to them:* "Who is called rich?"

They said to him: "He who is happy with his lot."[50]

. . .

Commentary: The responses in (A2) and (A3) are clearly directed at Alexander as lessons he needs to learn. These responses advocate doing exactly the opposite of what the king has spent his life doing. A hero, he learns, is not one who has been victorious in battle and who has distinguished himself as a conqueror, but one who has conquered his desire and has no need to accomplish anything beyond continued vigilance over his own self.[51] Similarly, one is rich not when one has acquired enormous wealth, but when one has learned to be satisfied with his allotted portion.

The responses of the Elders smack of Stoicism, with its emphasis on controlling the passions, which the text contrasts to Alexander's inability to

---

48. See Halevy, *Sha'arei ha-Aggadah*, p. 131.

49. See also Plutarch, *The Age of Alexander: Nine Greek Lives by Plutarch: Alexander*, trans. Ian Scott-Kilvert (London: Penguin, 1973), 4–5, pp. 255–56.

50. Ms Oxford-Bodl. heb. d. 21 (2676) 10 reads question (A5) here—"Who of you is wisest?"—together with the response found there. The connection is obvious, since (A1) asks for the definition of a wise man. As noted, the fact that several question-and-answer pairs are found in more than one context in the compilation is a significant indication that they are later editorial additions to a preexisting collection.

51. See also Halevy, *Sha'arei ha-Aggadah*, p. 131. Compare Alexander's characterization in Plutarch, *Age of Alexander* 21, pp. 275–78.

control his passions.⁵² Parallels can be found in rabbinic literature, however, so this response does not establish the Elders' identity as "Greeks."

We find an interesting parallel between this Talmudic passage and an account in Arrian:⁵³

> I surmise that one need look no further than Alexander's great successes for proof that neither physical strength nor illustrious birth nor uninterrupted success in war even greater than Alexander's—even if a man should circumnavigate Libya and Asia and conquer them, as Alexander meant to do, or add Europe, as the third part of his empire, to Asia and Libya—none of these things, I surmise, can gain a man happiness unless that man, whose achievements are seemingly so great, should at the same time possess the power to govern his passions.

And again in Arrian:⁵⁴

> I pity Alexander for his misfortune: he showed himself mastered on that occasion by two vices, namely, anger and drunkenness, neither of which should get the better of a sensible man.

And Arrian, *Anabasis* 6.13.4:

> But Alexander was mastered by passion for battle and lust for glory just as others are mastered by other pleasures, and he lacked the self-control to keep clear of danger.

We also find an interesting parallel in the Alexander Romance:⁵⁵

> Then Alexander said to them all, "Ask me for whatever you want and I will give it to you."
>
> At once they all burst out, "Give us immortality."
>
> But Alexander replied, "That is a power I do not have. I too am a mortal."
>
> Then they asked him, "Since you are a mortal, why do you make so many wars? When you have seized everything, where will you take it? Surely you will only have to leave it behind for others?"

---

52. See n. 19 above. In addition, see *Alexander the Great: Selections from Arrian, Diodorus, Plutarch, and Quintus Curtius,* ed. James Romm (Indianapolis: Hackett, 2005), p. xvii.
53. *Anabasis* 4.7.5.
54. *Anabasis* 4.9.1.
55. Alexander Romance III. 6 (ms L). See Stoneman, *Greek Alexander Romance,* p. 133.

"It is ordained by Providence above," replied Alexander, "that we shall all be slaves and servants of the divine will. The sea does not move unless the wind blows it, and the trees do not tremble unless the breezes disturb them; and likewise man does nothing except by the motions of divine Providence. For my part I would like to stop making war, but the master of my soul does not allow me...."

After this speech, Alexander gave Dandamis gold, bread, wine, and olive oil:

"Take these things, old man, in remembrance of me."

Dandamis laughed and said, "These things are useless to us. But in order not to appear proud, we will accept the oil."

Then, building a great pile of wood, he set it alight and poured the oil into the fire before Alexander's eyes.

And again in Arrian:[56]

It is with this in mind that I commend the Indian sages, some of whom Alexander reportedly encountered in the open air in a meadow where they were accustomed to pass their time in discussion. It is said that at the sight of Alexander and his army they merely stomped on the ground with their feet.

When Alexander inquired, through interpreters, what the gesture meant, they replied, "King Alexander, each man can have only so much land as this on which we are standing. You are human like the rest of us, except that in your restlessness and arrogance you travel so far from home, making trouble for yourself and others. Well, you will soon be dead and will have as much land as will suffice to bury your corpse."

At the time, Alexander praised the speakers and their remarks, though he acted otherwise and did the opposite of what he praised. Similarly, he is said to have admired Diogenes of Sinope. Coming upon Diogenes lying in the sun at the Isthmus, Alexander halted with his shield-bearers and infantry companions and asked the man if he needed anything. Diogenes replied that he needed nothing, other than for Alexander and his men to stand aside and stop blocking his sunlight. So Alexander was not wholly removed from a better way of thinking, but he was,to a great degree, overpowered by ambition. When he arrived in Taxila and saw the Indian sages who go naked, he was seized by a desire to have one of them join him, since he admired their endurance. The oldest sage, whose name was Dandamis (the others were his disciples), said that he would neither join Alexander himself nor allow the others to do so. He is said to have replied that if Alexander was really a son of Zeus, then so was he; that he needed nothing from Alexander but was

---

56. *Anabasis* 7.1.5–2.4.

content with his lot; and that, from what he could see, Alexander's men were wandering at length over land and sea for no good reason, nor was there any limit to their many wanderings. In any event, he desired nothing Alexander had the power to bestow, nor was he afraid to be deprived of anything under Alexander's control. While he lived, the land of India, bearing its fruit in season, was all he needed, and when he died, he would depart from his body as from an unseemly companion. The result was that Alexander did not after all try to coerce him, recognizing that the man was free.

The question of Alexander's lack of self-control is worked out even more explicitly in Palladius's *On the Races of India and the Brahmans*.[57] In sections 20–31, Palladius informs us that Alexander listened to Dandamis without anger because "the spirit of God was in him," but he was turned from Dandamis's advice "at the instigation of an evil demon." Palladius, therefore, may partially parallel the Bavli's claim that the Elders opposed Alexander because "Satan has won," depending on how we interpret that response (see below). Palladius follows by informing us that Alexander declined Dandamis's invitation to join the Brahmans because he was forced by circumstances to not follow the Gymnosophists' way of life, further proof that Alexander was not in control of himself. Finally, Palladius's Brahmans tell Alexander that "a philosopher is not restrained by another master, but masters himself."

. . .

(H4) *[Alexander] said to them: "What shall a man do and live?"*
They told him: "Kill himself."[58]
(H5) *"What shall a man do and die?"*
"Enliven himself."[59]

. . .

Commentary: The Elders' responses to Alexander's queries in (H4) and (H5) are the kind of paradoxes so favored by Cynic philosophers. They are

---

57. Palladius lived ca. 363–ca. 430 C.E. and was the bishop of Helenopolis in Turkey.
58. Ms Oxford-Bodl. heb. d. 21 (2676) 10 reads this and the following question and answer in Aramaic.
59. This question and answer are missing in ms Munich 95.

difficult, although not impossible, to square with rabbinic thought. Some commentators point out a parallel between the response in (H4)—"Kill himself"—and a statement by Resh Lakish in b. Berakhot 63b: "From where do we learn that words of Torah are firmly held by one who kills himself for it? As it is said, 'This is the Torah, when a man dies in a tent'" (Num 19:14). Resh Lakish's statement, however, emphasizes Torah study, which makes it acceptably rabbinic, whereas the response of the Elders appears to be a generalized call for extreme asceticism. While scholars have demonstrated that asceticism is by no means totally foreign to rabbinic thought, it rarely, if ever, takes the extreme form advocated by the Elders here.[60] A closer parallel seems to be provided by *Avot de-R. Natan*: "R. Yehudah Hanasi says, 'If you want to not die, then die before you die. If you want to stay alive, don't live while you are alive. It is preferable for you to die a death in this world, for you have no choice but to die, than to die in the future, for if you want you will not die.'"[61] The relevance of this parallel is not entirely clear, however, since *Avot de-R. Natan* is a problematic compilation, containing material from widely diverse time periods, from the Tannaitic period until the Middle Ages. The existence of a single parallel, furthermore, does not invalidate the claim that the Elders' response is strange in the mouth of a rabbi.

While the interpretation of the Elders' response in this context is not entirely clear, it is possible that they are advising Alexander not to strive at all, which, as noted, goes beyond anything we encounter in classical rabbinic literature, with the possible exception of the two statements cited immediately above, whose relevance to this discussion is not entirely clear.

Despite the fact that (problematic) parallels to the Elders' responses can be found in rabbinic literature and that there is no absolute need to say that they were borrowed directly from Greek and Roman sources, some of the Elders' responses sound more at home in Greek and Roman sources than in rabbinic literature, and are phrased as if they derived from Greek sources. The Elders' paradoxical answers about living and dying are far more amply paralleled in Hellenistic and Roman literature than in rabbinic literature. Already in the fourth century B.C.E., Diogenes Laertius recounted some Stoic doc-

---

60. See, for example, Eliezer Diamond, *Holy Men and Hunger Artists: Fasting and Asceticism in Rabbinic Culture* (New York: Oxford University Press, 2003), passim; and the references cited there.

61. *Avot de-R. Natan,* version B, ed. Schechter, p. 71. See also Halevy, *Sha'arei ha-Aggadah,* p. 132, n. 14.

trines concerning the permissibility of suicide.[62] Seneca and the later Stoic thinkers took this doctrine of rational suicide and transformed it from permissibility to near obligation. So we find in Seneca's *Epistula Morales* 104.21: "If you want to get rid of vice, you must retire from places where there are examples of vice. Cross over to the better people. Live with the Catos, with Laelius and Tubero. If you like to live with Greeks, join Socrates and Zeno. Socrates will teach you to die if necessity arise, Zeno before it arises."

Once again my claim is not that the Elders must be understood as Greeks, but rather that the greater ease with which they can be understood as Greeks rather than as rabbis supports the claim that the dialogue between Alexander and the elders originated in a Greek context, although it is "naturalizable" in a rabbinic context.[63]

. . .

(H6) *He said to them: "What shall a man do to become acceptable to people?"*

They said to him: "Let him hate kingship and government."[64]

[Alexander] said to them: "Mine is better than yours. *Let him love kingship and government,* and act kindly toward people."[65]

. . .

Commentary: The question and answer in (H6) is unique in this compilation in that Alexander is given the last word, suggesting that he wins this particular debate. The answers of both Alexander and the Elders might be true depending on the circumstances (for example, the nature of the ruler and the government), but this does not seem to be the conclusion that the authors of the compilation want the audience to reach.

    62. Diogenes Laertius, *Lives of Eminent Philosophers* 7.130.
    63. Compare Freund, "Alexander Macedon and Antoninus," p. 42.
    64. Ms Vatican 120 adds here, in Aramaic: "and act [most likely the *reish* at the end of the word *ya'avir* is a mistake for *ya'avid*] kindly toward people." Ms Oxford–Bodl. heb. d. 21 (2676) 10 reads the same phrase here, and has, correctly, *ya-avid*.
    65. Ms Oxford-Bodl. heb. d. 21 (2676) 10 reads all of part (H6) in Aramaic. Given the language change from Hebrew to Aramaic in most versions, it is possible that the phrase "and act kindly toward people" is a later addition to both the question and the answer. Ms Munich 95 lacks "He said to them, 'Mine is better than yours . . . and act kindly towards people.'" Most likely this variant is simply the result of homeoteleuton and it should not be taken seriously in our evaluation of the text.

Once again the response of the Elders marks them as atypical rabbis, if they are in fact rabbis at all. While there is certainly evidence that the rabbis were suspicious of kingship and government, and we apparently find a statement in m. Avot 1:10 to the effect that one should "hate authority," there is no indication that they would advocate declaring their hatred directly to a king. Also, m. Avot 1:10 might not be advocating "hating authority" in the sense of "hating people who have authority," but instead might mean that one should do all one can to distance oneself from a position of authority and to avoid seeking public office. After the disastrous revolts against the Romans in 66 C.E. and in the early second century C.E., the rabbis tended to advocate quietism, neither active hostility nor overly close relations with their Roman and Persian overlords.

While the answer of the Elders is very provocative, we have no indication that the king is angered by their response. It is conceivable that his anger later on is in part a response to the words of the Elders here, but it is not clear why Alexander waits until parts (A6) and (I), below, to express his anger, rather than doing so at the first available opportunity.

. . .

(A4) [Alexander] said to them: "Is it better to dwell on the sea or on land?"

They said to him: "It is better to dwell on land, for all seafarers are ill at ease until they come up to land again."[66]

. . .

Commentary: Here the text reverts again to Aramaic and continues in that language until the conclusion of the compilation. The Elders' response in this context can also be construed as provocative, since they may be telling Alexander that his mode of life, which involves constant travel over the sea (as well as the land), giving free reign to the expression of his *pothos*,[67] is inferior to a settled lifestyle, or to a mode of life in which conquest is con-

---

66. Ms Oxford-Bodl. heb. d. 21 (2676) 10 reads this question (A4) before ([A1]–[A3] and [H4]–[H5]). The first question (H1), which is the third in the genizah fragment, has in common with (A4) that the Elders answer both questions by appealing to knowledge of typical human behavior.

67. For other examples of Alexander's *pothos*, see, for example, Arrian, *Anabasis* 3.1.5; 5.2.1–2; 5.25.2; 5.26.1; 7.1.1; and 7.2.2; Victor Ehrenberg, "Pothos," reprinted in English

strained by the limits of human endurance.[68] Once again, however, the text supplies no indication at this point that Alexander takes offense.

. . .

(A5) [Alexander] said to them: "Who of you is the wisest?"

They told him: "All as one we are equal, for every question that you posed, we solved together."[69]

Commentary: The Elders' response here further reveals their atypical character, since typical rabbis draw rigid hierarchical distinctions between themselves. Rabbis typically attempt to outdo one another in an effort to establish themselves as superior, or else the hierarchical relationship between them is clear at the outset of their interaction and determines the way they behave toward one another.[70] Alexander's question here should probably be construed as deliberately provocative, as an attempt create discord among the Elders. If so, it fails utterly.

. . .

(A6) [Alexander] said to them: "What reason [do you have] for opposing us?"

They said to him: "Satan has won."[71]

. . .

Commentary: Alexander's question here and his threat in the very next statement clearly indicate his perception of conflict with the Elders. The response of the Elders is obscure, but it may indicate that they believe that Alexander is not in control of himself but rather has been mastered by an evil supernatu-

---

translation as chapter 2 of G. T. Griffith, ed., *Alexander the Great: The Main Problems* (Cambridge, MA: Heffer, 1966); and Romm, *Alexander the Great*, p. 22, n. 12.

68. See also Friedman, "Hokhmato, Masaotav ve-Ozrotav."

69. Mss Oxford 370 and Munich 95 read only "Every question that you posed, we solved together." Ms Florence II-I-7 reads the phrase "All as one we are equal" in the margin. This phrase might be missing in some of the manuscripts, however, due to homeoteleuton. Ms Oxford-Bodl. Heb. D. 21 (2676) 10 reads this question immediately after questions ([A1]–[A3]) (see above).

70. Kalmin, *Sages, Stories, Authors, and Editors*, pp. 175–212.

71. Ms Oxford-Bodl. heb. d. 21 (2676) 10 lacks "has won."

ral force and it is their responsibility to resist it. We observed above the parallel between the statement as thus interpreted and Palladius's *On the Races of India*. Alternatively, the Elders' response may be designed to admit to Alexander that they have, in fact, been opposing him, but to blame their behavior on an evil divine force and to absolve themselves of guilt.[72]

. . .

(I) [Alexander] said to them: "I will kill you by a royal decree!"

(II) They said to him: "Authority is in the hand of the kingdom, but a lie is not fitting for a kingdom."

(III) Immediately he dressed them in clothes of scarlet and threw necklaces of gold around their necks.

. . .

Commentary: In what may be a parallel to part (II), above, Arrian, *Anabasis* 1.2, states: "But, as narrators, Ptolemy and Aristoboulos impressed me as more reliable ... in Ptolemy's case not only because of his service under Alexander but also because it would have been more disgraceful for him to speak falsely than for another, given that he, too, was a king."

In part (II), the Elders are chastising Alexander for lying, but it is not at all clear what "lie" they are referring to. As noted, the Berlin Papyrus preserves the oldest extant Greek version of the dialogue between Alexander and the Gymnosophists, and it will be helpful to quote it here for purposes of comparison:[73]

"[Whomever] I command to judge, he shall be your moderator; if I decide that he has judged well, he alone shall be let off alive."

One of the Gymnosophists asked if they should set a penalty as well. This one having volunteered to go first, Alexander asked him whether he considered that the living were more numerous than the dead, or the reverse. He replied that the living were.

---

72. See Ilan, *Silencing the Queen*, p. 8, who suggests that the expression "Satan has won" means that "Alexander himself is compared to Satan," and by comparing Alexander to Satan they are explaining why they oppose him. For additional attempts to explain the expression, see Halevy, *Sha'arei ha-Aggadah*, pp. 130 and 133.

73. See n. 7.

"Is it not proper," he asked, "that those who exist should be more numerous than those who do not?"

Then he asked the next whether the earth [or the sea is greater]. The reply was that [the earth is greater] because the sea itself is beyond the earth.

He asked the third which he took to be the most cunning of all living creatures.

"That which no man has yet discovered."

He asked the fourth why he had incited Sabeilos to fight against him.

The reply came: "In order that he should succeed in either living nobly or dying nobly."

He ordered the fifth to state which came first, day or night.

He replied that the day came first, by a single night.

While Alexander was trying to work this out, the Indian noticed and remarked that the answers to riddling questions were likely to be just as riddling.

He asked the sixth what a man should do to make himself most loved by men.

He replied: "By being all-powerful yet frightening nobody."

He asked the seventh what a man should do in order to become a god.

He replied: "By doing what is impossible for a man to do."

He asked the eighth which is stronger, life or death.

He answered "Life, because it makes something that exists out of something that does not exist, whereas death makes something that does not exist out of what does."

He ordered the last to say how long it is good for a man to live.

He replied: "As long as [he does not regard death as better than life]."

There was now only one left, [Alexander] asked him to judge the answers, and to state which had given the worst answer. "I do not want you to think that I shall be neglectful in giving you your reward."

But the Indian did not want anyone to perish as a result of his answer, so he replied that each had answered worse than the other.

"Well then," said Alexander, "you shall all die, and you first because it was your judgment."

"But Alexander," replied the other, "it is not a kingly act to lie. You said, 'Whoever I shall [appoint judge], if I consider he has judged well, he shall live. . . . ' Your statement will . . . us. It is not for us to kill unjustly, but for you to preserve."

When Alexander heard that, he judged that the men were indeed wise. He ordered them all to be given a cloak and sent them away unharmed.

According to Van Thiel, if we understand the last Gymnosophist, that is, the judge, to include his own statement in his judgment, then he involves Alexander in a "liar's paradox." On the one hand, if the judge is correct, then Alexander *must* kill him, according to the original terms of their agreement, since the judge answered worse than all the others, just as they had all answered worse than him and than one another. On the other hand, if the judge is correct, then Alexander *cannot* kill him, as he promised at the outset, since Alexander promised to leave him alive if he answered correctly. Van Thiel also notes, however, that the judge's statement does not admit of this interpretation in its present form, since it is not at all clear as the text currently stands that the judge intended to include his own statement in his evaluation. Van Thiel, therefore, attempts to reconstruct the original dialogue.[74] Van Thiel's attempt is unconvincing, but his need to emend the text demonstrates the lack of congruity between the narrative frame and the dialogue, which, as noted, is matched in the case of the Alexander composition in the Talmud. It is difficult to view as sheer coincidence that the linkage between the frame story and the dialogue is problematic in the two literatures, and in both accounts the problem has to do with the nature of Alexander's lie. We therefore have further proof of a significant connection between the Greek and the rabbinic accounts.

The conclusion of both Tamid and the ancient Greek historical and biographical accounts is that Alexander is persuaded not to execute his interlocutors, and he instead gives them gifts and sends them on their way.

CONTINUATION OF BAVLI TAMID: ALEXANDER TRAVELS TO AFRICA

(IV) [Alexander] said to them: "I want to go to the country of Africa."

They said to him: "You cannot go, for mountains of darkness divide [here from there]."

[Alexander] said to them: "It is impossible for me not to go. Is this why I asked you? Rather, I asked you: 'What shall I do?'"

---

74. Van Thiel, "Alexanders Gespräch," pp. 346 and 352–53.

They said to him: "Fetch Libyan donkeys that can trek in the dark, and bring coils of rope, and tie [them] on this side, and when you return, hold them, and come back to your place."

. . .

Commentary: In response to the king's desire to travel to Africa, the Elders tell him that he cannot, repeating a motif reiterated throughout the first part of the compilation: that some destinations are off-limits to human beings. In addition, Alexander's insistence that he must go to Africa is in keeping with his portrayal in the Romance and in historical sources, where the theme of his *pothos* figures most prominently.

The Alexander Romance parallels the rabbinic account, although it is not stated in the Romance that the king needs to cross the Land of Darkness to reach the country of Africa but rather that he must cross the Land of Darkness to reach the Water of Life.

As noted by Avi Friedman, it is significant that according to the Talmud, Alexander asks the Elders how he can *travel to* the country of Africa and the Elders answer by telling him how he can *return* safely.[75] The Talmud's Alexander is concerned with constant discovery and forward progress, while the Elders are concerned with remaining closely tethered to civilization. In addition, Alexander once again reveals that he is not in control of himself when he says, "It is impossible for me not to go." He operates under a compulsion, which is paralleled in the Greek accounts of Alexander's encounter with the Gymnosophists. The strength of Alexander's compulsion is unique in the rabbinic corpus's portrayal of a non-Jewish king, further proof that it reached Bavli Tamid from a source external to rabbinic literature.

The Bavli's account of Alexander's desire to travel to Africa clearly echoes the Alexander of the Romance and of history, since it is well documented in both that Alexander made conquests in Africa.

The following text is the parallel in the Alexander Romance:[76]

> After we had marched for three days we came to a place filled with fog. Being unable to go further, because the land was without roads or paths, we pitched our tents there. The next day I took one thousand armed men with me and set off to see whether this was in fact the end of the world. We went toward

---

75. Friedman, "Hokhmato, Masaotav ve-Ozrotav."
76. Alexander Romance II.39–40 (recension L). See Stoneman, *Greek Alexander Romance,* pp. 120–22. See also Wallach, "Alexander the Great," p. 53.

the left, because it was lighter in that direction, and marched for half a day through rocky country full of ravines. I counted the passing of time not by the sun, but by measuring out the leagues we covered and thus calculating both the time and the distance. But eventually we turned back in fear because the way became impassable. So we decided to go instead to the right. The going was much smoother, but the darkness was impenetrable. I was at a loss, for my young companions all advised me not to go further into that region, for fear the horses should be scattered in the darkness over the long distance, and we should be unable to return.

Then I said to them, "You who are so brave in war, now you may see that there is no true bravery without intelligence and understanding. If there were an old man with us, he would be able to advise us how to set about advancing in this dark place. Who among you is brave enough to go back to the camp and bring me an old man? He shall be given ten pounds of gold."

The sons of the old man said to me, "Lord, if you will hear us without anger, we have something to say to you."

"Speak as you wish," I replied. "I swear by Providence above that I will do you no harm."

Then they told me all about their father, and how they had brought him along with them, and they ran and fetched the old man himself. I greeted him warmly and asked him for his advice.

"Alexander," the old man said, "it must be clear to you that you will never see the light of day again if you advance without horses. Select, then, mares with foals. Leave the foals here, and advance with the mares; they will without fail bring you back to their foals."

I sought through the whole army and found only one hundred mares with foals.

I took these, and one hundred selected horses besides, as well as further horses to carry our provisions. Then, following the old man's advice, we advanced, leaving the foals behind.

. . . .

I prayed, and then removed our guide and placed the mares at the head of the expedition. . . . Led by the voice of the foals, we arrived back at our camp after a journey of twenty-two days.

CONTINUATION OF BAVLI TAMID: ALEXANDER AND THE AFRICAN WOMEN

(V) So he did, and he went and arriving in that town where all were women, he wanted to make war against them.

They said to him: "If you kill us, they will say: 'He has killed women.' If we kill you, they will say: 'The king was killed by women!'"

(VI) [Alexander] said to them: "Bring me bread."

They brought him bread of gold on tables of gold.

He said to them: "Do people eat bread of gold?"

They said to him: "Was there no bread in your place to eat, that you came here?"

(VII) When he set out to return, he wrote on the gate of the town: "I, Alexander Macedon, had been a fool until I reached the African land of women, and took advice from women."[77]

. . .

Commentary: As noted by Tal Ilan, the women use precisely the same argument in both the Romance and the Talmud, even though the Talmud does not name them "Amazons." According to ms A of the Romance, undoubtedly a very early version, the Amazons' first words to Alexander are an attempt to dissuade him from attacking them: "If we conquer the enemy or put them to flight, that is regarded as a humiliation for them for the rest of time. But if they conquer us, it is only women that they have defeated."[78] The similarity between the Greek and the Hebrew and Aramaic accounts is obvious.[79]

Alexander's words to Darius in the Alexander Romance[80] provide another interesting parallel to the account in Tamid:

> Why did you write to me that you possess so much gold and silver? So that we should fight all the more bravely to win it? Well, if I conquer you, I shall be famous and a great king among both Greeks and barbarians for conquering a ruler as great as Darius. But if you defeat me, you will have done nothing

---

77. For close parallels in Palestinian rabbinic literature (but not involving a city of women), see y. Baba Mezia 2:3 (8c) and Vayikra Rabbah 27. The motif of Alexander being bested by women is a familiar one in world literature and folklore. Regarding the Amazons, see Tal Ilan, *Integrating Women into Second Temple History* (Tübingen: Mohr/Siebeck, 1999), pp. 129–32. See also Wallach, "Alexander the Great," p. 54.

78. Alexander Romance III.25 (ms L); see Stoneman, *Greek Alexander Romance*, p. 144.

79. It should not be overemphasized, however, since the story in the Romance ends with the Amazons submitting to Alexander's benevolent terms of surrender and paying him an annual tribute. See Ilan, *Silencing the Queen*, p. 6.

80. Alexander Romance I.38 (ms L); see Stoneman, *Greek Alexander Romance*, p. 72.

outstanding—simply defeated a bandit, as you wrote to me. I, however, shall be defeating the great king of kings and god, Darius.

Alexander in the Romance plays the role of the women in the Talmud, and Darius plays the role of Alexander.

. . .

(VIII) When [Alexander] came, he sat down at a spring; he was eating bread, and in his hand were salted fish. While he was whitening them, a spirit [or: a wind][81] fell on them [and they lived].[82] He said: "Learn from this: this spring comes from the Garden of Eden."[83]

. . .

Commentary: This scene and the next one are likewise closely paralleled in some versions of the Alexander Romance,[84] and in an early-sixth-century Syriac work by Jacob of Serug.[85] Both the Talmud and the Romance depict someone washing a salted fish in a spring or a body of water, although in the Talmud it is Alexander while in the Romance it is Alexander's cook. Both compilations depict the fish coming to life,[86] prompting Alexander to realize that he has come to the Waters of Life. In the Talmud the motif has been Judaized by having the waters come from the Garden of Eden. In addition, the peculiar detail in Tamid of Alexander "whitening" the fish at the Waters of Life appears to be paralleled in some versions of the Alexander Romance, where the Waters of Life are bathed in light, in contrast to the rest of the Land of Darkness.

81. The printed edition reads *reha*, "a scent." Mss Florence II-I-7, Oxford 370, Munich 95, and Oxford-Bodl. heb. d. 21 (2676) 10 read *ruha*, "a wind" or "a spirit." The meaning appears to be that the fish came to life. See the following note.

82. The phrase in brackets, "and they lived," is found in ms Oxford-Bodl. heb. d. 21 (2676) 10.

83. Stoneman, *Alexander the Great,* p. 191, observes that ms L is "the first that features the Water of Life tradition."

84. Alexander Romance III.40–41 (ms L). See Stoneman, *Greek Alexander Romance,* pp. 121–22.

85. E. A. W. Budge, *The History of Alexander the Great Being the Syriac Version of Pseudo-Callisthenes* (Cambridge, 1889), pp. 172–75; Jacob of Serug, lines 170–97. See also Budge, *History of Alexander the Great,* pp. 52–111, for an overview of the ancient sources about Alexander.

86. See, however, n. 82, above.

The account in the Romance is as follows:[87]

The old man had advised his sons to pick up anything they found lying on the ground after we had entered the Land of Darkness, and to put it in their knapsacks. These were 360 soldiers: I had the 160 unmounted ones go on ahead. So we went on for about fifteen leagues. We came to a place where there was a clear spring, whose water flashed like lightning, and some other streams besides. The air in this place was very fragrant and less dark than before. I was hungry and wanted some bread, so I called the cook Andreas by name and said, "Prepare some food for us." He took a dried fish and waded into the clear water of the spring to wash it. As soon as it was dipped in the water, it came to life and leapt out of the cook's hands. He was frightened, and did not tell me what had happened; instead, he drank some of the water himself, and scooped some up in a silver vessel and kept it. The whole place was abounding in water, and we drank of its various streams. Alas for my misfortune, that it was not fated for me to drink of the spring of immortality, which gives life to what is dead, as my cook was fortunate to do.

After we had eaten we went on for about another 230 leagues. Then we saw a light that did not come from the sun, moon, or stars. I saw two birds in the air: they had human faces and spoke in Greek. "Why, Alexander, do you approach a land which is god's alone? Turn back, wretch, turn back; it is not for you to tread the Islands of the Blessed. Turn back, O man, tread the land that has been given to you and do not lay up trouble for yourself."

CONCLUSION OF THE BAVLI TAMID ACCOUNT

(IX) [Alexander] took some water and spattered his face. It was revealed to him that this was the water of the Garden of Eden.[88]

(X) [Alexander] raised his voice: "Open the gate for me!"[89]

They said to him: **This is the gate of Yhwh [into which the righteous shall enter]** (Ps 118:20).

---

87. Alexander Romance II.39–41 (ms L); Stoneman, *Greek Alexander Romance*, pp. 120–22. For early Muslim parallels, see Mario Casari, "The King Explorer: A Cosmographic Approach to the Persian Alexander," in *The Alexander Romance in Persia and the East*, ed. Stoneman, Erickson, and Netton, pp. 182–83.

88. See Sokoloff, *Dictionary of Jewish Babylonian Aramaic*, pp. 287 and 517. I have translated this line according to the reading of ms Oxford-Bodl. heb. d. 21 (2676) 10. The text is problematic since we are informed twice that Alexander learns that the spring comes from the Garden of Eden.

89. Ms Oxford-Bodl. heb. d. 21 (2676) 10 reads: "He said to them, 'Let us enter!'"

He said to them: "I am a king! I am important [*arzanig*]!"⁹⁰

(XI) They gave him a skull. He came to weigh all of his gold and silver against it, and it did not weigh as much.

He said to the rabbis: "What is this?"

(XII) The rabbis said to him: "They gave⁹¹ the eyeball of a human being⁹² that is never satiated."

[Alexander] said to them: "How do you know that it is so?"

[They said to him]: "Take a speck of dirt and cover it."

[He did so] and it was immediately weighed. As it is written: **Hell and destruction are never full [so the eyes of man are never satisfied]** (Prov 27:20).

(XIII) It is taught in the house of Elijah, "Gehinnom is above the firmament. And some say it is behind the mountains of darkness."

. . .

Commentary: The king demands entrance through the gate blocking the way to the Garden of Eden. We see again his proverbial *pothos,* as well as the fact that he still has not truly internalized the lesson regarding the need for a person to be satisfied with the limits set for him by God.

When Alexander is informed (we are not told by whom) via a quotation of Psalms 118:20 that only the righteous are permitted entrance into the Garden of Eden, the king apparently demands entry because he is important.⁹³ Ilan comments appositely that "the answer [of the rabbis] alludes to Alexander's insatiable appetite for more wealth, which has led him on in his conquests."⁹⁴ Interestingly, however, the compilation in the Talmud does not suggest that Alexander is unique in this respect, or that he is particularly blameworthy. Rather, the implication is that all people behave this way, or that they would behave this way if they had the opportunity. Prior to this

---

90. For the Persian derivation of the word *arzanig*, found in ms Oxford-Bodl. heb. d. 21 (2676) 10, see David Rosenthal, "Arakhim Nosafim le-Milon ha-Talmudi [3]: 'Arzanig' (Bavli, Tamid 32b)," *Tarbiz* 61 (1992): 219–24. Regarding the translation of this passage, see ibid., p. 225.

91. See ibid., p. 223.

92. See Sokoloff, *Dictionary of Jewish Babylonian Aramaic*, p. 285.

93. See Rosenthal, "Arakhim Nosafim," p. 225.

94. Ilan, *Silencing the Queen*, p. 8.

point, Alexander has been portrayed as unique in the extreme nature of his desire for more.

Stoneman suggests that the story of the eye weighing down everything until it is covered with a bit of dirt may echo one of the sayings of Ahikar: "The eye of man is a fountain, and is never satisfied until it is filled with dust." He suggests that it may also echo sura 102 of the Qoran: "The emulous desire of multiplying riches occupies you, until you enter the grave."[95] While the similarities are undeniable, such parallels are general enough to reflect similar values of diverse civilizations and need not be the result of borrowing or appropriation.[96]

Several scholars have pointed out the similarity between Alexander's search for the Waters of Life in the Romance and in the Talmud and Gilgamesh's search for immortality in the Epic of Gilgamesh, composed in Babylonia.[97] Other scholars have noted that the parallel is not exact, since Gilgamesh on his own initiative searches for a plant that will confer upon him immortality, while in the Romance Alexander happens upon the Waters of Life.[98] The difference between the various accounts does not render impossible a literary relationship between them, although the precise nature of this relationship is not clear. And ultimately, positing a link between a Mesopotamian source and a rabbinic Babylonian tradition need not preclude the existence of a link between the Bavli's tradition and a Greek source from the Roman East, especially given the closer similarity between the Talmudic source and the Greek tradition, as well as the multiple parallels between the Greek and the Talmudic versions.

THE LESSONS OF BAVLI TAMID'S ALEXANDER COMPILATION

The major lesson imparted by virtually every discrete tradition in this compilation, including the anonymous commentary, is that a person should be

---

95. Stoneman, "Jewish Traditions on Alexander the Great," p. 48. See also F. Conybeare, J. R. Harris, and A. S. Lewis, *The Story of Ahikar* (Oxford, 1913), p. lxxxii.

96. See also Halevy, *Sha'arei ha-Aggadah*, p. 128, nn. 3 and 4; p. 129, n. 3; p. 130, n. 7, for additional examples.

97. See, for example, Stoneman, *Alexander the Great*, p. 21, and the literature cited in n. 57 there.

98. See, for example, Anderson, *"Alexander Romance,"* pp. 83–87 and the literature cited there.

satisfied with the portion that has been allotted to him by God. In the first section of the story, Alexander, the symbol of the man who has attained the most in the world, is forced to confront the limits of his ability to attain wealth, fame, territory, and wisdom and the ultimate uselessness of their acquisition by mere mortals.[99]

The first three question-and-answer pairs show that one should not investigate too deeply to uncover the mysteries of the cosmos. The Elders answer Alexander's questions with biblical verses that are straightforward responses to his questions, but they desist when they start to worry that his questions will be answerable only if they go beyond what is explicit in the Bible and will require them to investigate "what lies above and what below, what before and what behind." The next three question-and-answer pairs, borrowed from Mishnah Avot, also teach that a person should be satisfied with what God has allotted to him: "Who is wise? He who sees what is born." While this response admits of more than one interpretation, perhaps the meaning is: "Who is wise? He who has readily accessible knowledge, available to anyone." Alexander continues on to ask, "Who is a hero?"; the answer is not someone who distinguishes himself in battle or who conquers the world, but someone who is satisfied with his lot in life and does not strive to acquire more. The king next asks, "Who is rich?"; the answer is in keeping with the theme of the compilation: someone who is satisfied with what God has apportioned to him.

The next question is, "What shall a man do and live?" The answer is not "eat, drink, and be merry" or "carpe diem" or some similar response. Instead, the answer is "kill himself." In a rabbinic compilation, this response is probably not meant to be taken literally (although if the text originated in a Stoic or Cynic context, that might have been its meaning); rather, it is meant as the advice that a person lives best and longest if he lives ascetically and satisfies himself with little. The next question and answer is simply the mirror image of the previous one, expressing the view that the man who constantly indulges his appetites will end up dying a premature death or living a life not worth living.

The answers to the next several questions likewise fit the central theme of the compilation. Alexander first asks the Elders, "What shall a man do to become acceptable to people?" Their answer is "let him hate kingship and government." Their answer is certainly provocative, and their bravery, even

---

99. See also W. Jac. Van Bekkum, "Alexander the Great in Medieval Hebrew Literature," *Journal of the Warburg and Courtland Institutes* 49 (1986): 226; and Sulochana Asirvatham, "Alexander the Philosopher in the Greco-Roman, Persian and Arabic Traditions," in *The Alexander Romance in Persia and the East,* ed. Stoneman, Erickson, and Netton, pp. 311–18.

foolhardiness, is striking in expressing such sentiments in the presence of a man who rules the world. Surprisingly, instead of threatening them with death, or even executing them on the spot, Alexander simply asserts that his answer is better than theirs, and in fact, his response does have a good deal to recommend it—"Let him love kingship and government, and act kindly toward people"—especially given the rabbis' tendency to discourage open rebellion after the failure of the revolt of 70 C.E. and the Bar Kokhba rebellion. Here as well, the lesson is that a person should be satisfied with the status quo, and this time Alexander delivers the message. After this exchange, the following one seems to be anticlimactic: "Is it better to dwell in the sea, or better to dwell on land?" This question-and-answer pair perhaps fits the compilation as a whole in that the Elders are advocating a life not of restless conquest in far-off lands, but of stability and settlement.

Alexander's next question is perhaps designed to sow discord between the Elders of the Negev: "Who of you is the wisest?" If so, they overcome the challenge by answering, and providing good proof, that they are all equal. Once again we see that the ideal is stasis and stability rather than striving for superiority. As noted, Alexander's next question ("Why did you oppose us?"), together with the response ("Satan has won"), is extremely obscure. It may be a claim that Satan has conquered Alexander such that he is no longer in control of his actions, leaving the Elders no choice but to resist him so that he does not become a disruptive force in the world. On the other hand, perhaps the lesson here is that there are limits to the Elders' firmly held conviction that it is desirable to maintain the status quo, namely, when Satan himself controls the authorities in power. The next statement by Alexander is his most confrontational, since he threatens to kill the Elders, who answer in a manner that expresses their fealty to the king and again maintains the status quo: "Authority is in the hand of the kingdom." Along the same lines, in response to Alexander's request for help in traveling to Africa, at first the Elders claim that it is impossible, but when he insists, they give him instructions on how to return home safely. When Alexander encounters the city of women and demands bread, they convince him of the folly of his travels to far-off places, since there is nothing in his new locality that is not also found in his original locality. The next episode takes place at the entrance to the Garden of Eden, where once again he learns the lesson of the folly of his relentless striving, since his life will soon be over and all of his acquisitions and accomplishments will count for nothing.[100]

100. See also Friedman, "Hokhmato, Masaotav ve-Ozrotav."

Rabbis routinely strive for as much knowledge of the Torah as possible, and this knowledge confers upon them power, prestige, and a higher place in the rabbinic hierarchy. Given that Tamid's Alexander compilation is preserved in a rabbinic source, one might expect the lesson of the Alexander material to be that striving after greatness in Torah study can be a this-worldly good just like striving after gold, and can be just as vain in the grand scheme of things as Alexander's hunger for conquest, territory, and domination over subject peoples. Alexander is the fitting example of such striving, because no one in antiquity had achieved and acquired as much as he did. He represents the most that a human being could accomplish; since even he was not satisfied with all he had, the same had to be true of all other human beings. To suggest this as the compilation's message is to indulge in pure speculation, however, for despite the fact that rabbis speak and are quoted several times, the compilation has nothing to say about rabbinic study, either to critique its abuse, which the rabbis certainly were capable of doing,[101] or to articulate the conception that knowledge of Torah is exceptional and satisfies an individual's craving and supplies meaning even though all else fails. Perhaps the absence of any commentary about rabbinic study, anomalous in a rabbinic text, is further evidence that the compilation comes to Babylonian rabbinic culture from an outside source, although we must be wary of putting undue weight on an argument from silence.

APPENDIX: THE COMPOSITE NATURE OF THE BAVLI'S ALEXANDER ROMANCE

The Bavli's Alexander compilation shows definite signs of being a composite and of possessing a complicated prehistory that yields no simple answer to the question of its provenance. First, there is no scholarly agreement regarding the dialect of Aramaic in which it was composed,[102] and Y. N. Epstein and David Rosenthal have observed that the manuscripts do not preserve a consistent picture.[103] Second, the compilation alternates between Hebrew and

---

101. That is, rabbis were capable both of abusing Torah study and of critiquing its abuse. See, for example, chapter 2.

102. See, for example, Israel Levi, "La légende d'Alexandre dans le Talmud," *Revue des études Juives* 2 (1881): 293–300; and Rosenthal, "Arakhim Nosafim," pp. 221–25, and the literature cited there.

103. See Y. N. Epstein, *Mevo'ot le-Sifrut ha-Amoraim* (Jerusalem: Magnes Press, 1962), pp. 54, 72, 74, and 142. See also Rosenthal, "Arakhim Nosafim," pp. 222–23.

Aramaic, with all of the Hebrew coming at the beginning of the compilation,[104] giving way to the Aramaic in the latter part. Finally, much of the composition is presented as a dialogue between the Elders of the Negev and Alexander, which has multiple parallels in ancient non-Jewish accounts. The remainder is (1) a dialogue between Alexander and the women, which also has multiple ancient non-Jewish parallels; (2) Alexander's journey to find the Waters of Life, paralleled in the Alexander Romance and in an early-sixth-century Syriac source;[105] and (3) two unparalleled statements attributed to "sages," referred to at the beginning of the compilation as *hakhamim,* and at the conclusion as *rabbanan.*

---

104. There is some Aramaic in this part of the text, however: a thin layer of anonymous editorial Aramaic commentary, and three questions addressed by Alexander to the Elders of the Negev in Aramaic.

105. See n. 85.

Summary and Conclusions

THIS BOOK ARGUED THAT A significant cultural change is discernible in fourth-century Babylonia and later, due to the incorporation into the Bavli of nonrabbinic and even non-Jewish traditions from the eastern Roman provinces as well as traditions deriving from and information concerning Christian and pagan cultures east of Syria. The textual analyses undertaken throughout this book supported the thesis that it is critically important to study the Bavli in light of multiple cultural contexts, particularly the eastern provinces of the Roman Empire.

This book focused in detail on several rich narratives, or, to be more precise, on several passages and motifs, most of them clearly of nonrabbinic and even non-Jewish origin, which are first attested in the Bavli by the latest Babylonian rabbis. Since we confined the discussion to parallel words, motifs, and clusters of motifs, that is, to very specific narrative details, rather than to more general patterns that could be dismissed as the result of coincidence or as the independent incorporation of folk motifs, the commonalities we observed were very likely attributable to the intermingling of cultures, to the appropriation of aspects of one literature by a contemporaneous literature via historical contacts, whether direct or indirect.

Given the present state of our knowledge, we found that it is often difficult to know whether traditions deriving from the Roman East reached Babylonia directly from the eastern Roman provinces or were instead mediated to the rabbis via the Syriac-speaking Christian and pagan communities of Mesopotamia and its environs. Whether the parallels between Babylonia and the Roman East were direct or indirect, however, the literary analyses in this book supported the claim that traditions from the Roman East achieved literary expression in the Bavli during the fourth century, a phenomenon that continued for two or more centuries thereafter. It is important, furthermore, to continue the search for evidence of the extent and nature of cultural contacts between Jewish, Christian, and pagan cultures east of Byzantium, since these cultures have traditionally been studied in blissful isolation from one another. It is hoped that the present book is a modest corrective to this scholarly tendency, and demonstrates in small ways the rewards of studying these cultures in light of one another.

This book raises several significant historical questions, some of which we were able to answer, but others of which we were not. First, when one finds a parallel between Persian literature and the Bavli, or between Mesopotamian culture and the Bavli, is one's work over or has one's work just begun? This book argued that one's work has just begun and that one must examine whether the parallel is symptomatic of a special relationship between two particular cultures or is symptomatic instead of late antiquity in general.

Second, what are we to conclude when traditions attributed to a Palestinian rabbi in the Bavli are unparalleled by traditions preserved in Palestinian rabbinic corpora? Are we to assume that the traditions in the Bavli are Persian or Mesopotamian, or is it equally plausible that they derive from the Roman East and tell us about provincial Roman culture rather than or in addition to Babylonian, Mesopotamian, or Persian culture? We argued that both conclusions are possible, in contrast to scholars who conclude without further ado that such materials must be products of Mesopotamian or Persian culture. Such scholars have given insufficient attention to nonrabbinic literature from the Roman East, which, we found, frequently reveals close parallels to the rabbinic material preserved only in the Bavli. Such material, we concluded, very likely derived from the Roman East, but for reasons that are often not clear was not preserved in Palestinian rabbinic compilations. We concluded that it is unlikely that in each one of these cases, Palestinian rabbinic literature was the true source of the tradition in the Bavli, and that it is simply a historical accident that the traditions are missing from Palestinian rabbinic compilations. In a small number of cases such an explanation would be reasonable; in the presence of so many cases such an explanation is untenable, since it compels us to seek multiple explanations for the absence of the traditions from Palestinian compilations.

Third, the conclusions of this book force us to speculate about how traditions traveled from one locality to the other, from the Roman East to Babylonia, and why the geographically distant Roman Empire contributed so much to rabbinic Babylonia. We suggested one possibility: the periodic wars of conquest of the Persians deep into Roman territory and the resettlement of Jewish, Christian, and pagan populations in Mesopotamia, eastern Syria, and western Persia. But are other explanations equally plausible? Fourth, what does it say about relationships between Mesopotamian Jews and Christians that they might have contributed so little to each other's culture? Or is their apparent isolation from each other due to a studied "rhetoric of insularity"?[1]

Fifth, perhaps the conclusions of this book shed light on the much-debated question of the extent to which Persian culture appropriated from Greek and Roman culture rather than vice versa, since each of the literary studies in this book concluded that traditions traveled from the eastern Roman provinces to Mesopotamia, and only subsequently to Persia.

This book also demonstrated the importance of language switching in narratives as a tool for uncovering the thematic and chronological layering that gives new meaning to the Bavli and reveals its independence in reinterpreting its narrative sources. The attention paid to language switching was one objective factor supporting our contention that many earlier scholars have overestimated the degree to which rabbinic narratives are the unified product of later editors or storytellers smoothing out the seams separating the discrete traditions that compose their compositions. These scholars, we contended, did not do justice to the rough spots and ungrammaticalities that usually remain when ancient authors stitch together diverse sources to form a larger whole, and failure to attend to these ungrammaticalities frequently leads to serious misunderstandings of the sources under discussion.

Undoubtedly, however, attentiveness to language switching is not *always* an effective tool in uncovering the seams in rabbinic narratives. It is hoped that future studies will improve our ability to explain why this criterion is sometimes helpful and other times not.

Finally, the role of Persian literature in the development of the Babylonian rabbinic stories examined in this study was not extensive, and the Persian versions of these texts were almost without exception late and derivative. While the cultural connection between Persia and the Bavli is real, extensive, and extremely important—perhaps *the* most important connection between the rabbis and others in late antiquity—we found few traces of it in the mate-

---

1. Albert De Jong, "Zoroastrian Religious Polemics and Their Contexts: Interconfessional Relations in the Sasanian Empire," in *Religious Polemics in Context,* ed. A. van der Kooij and T. L. Hettema (Assen: Van Gorcum, 2004), p. 58.

rial examined in this book. Perhaps this fact suggests that the role of Persia in the formation of the Bavli is not as all-pervasive as some of its most enthusiastic claimants would have us believe. It should be noted preliminarily that some important prior research on the subject of "how much Persian is in the Babylonian Talmud" has demonstrated that a substantial amount of the rabbis' creativity with respect to Persia had to do with resisting elements in Jewish society that attempted to cultivate Persian norms.[2] Perhaps, therefore, some Babylonian rabbis deliberately downplayed the impact of Persian culture, and what we find in the Bavli is not an accurate reflection of the importance of Persia for Babylonian Jewish culture. This issue, however, must be left for future studies, and I offer it merely as one possible implication of our findings.

---

2. See, for example, Elman, "Middle Persian Culture and Babylonian Sages," pp. 192–94; and Herman, *Prince without a Kingdom,* pp. 239–57.

BIBLIOGRAPHY

PRIMARY SOURCES

Apocrypha and Pseudepigrapha

Barton, J. M. T. "The Ascension of Isaiah." In *The Apocryphal Old Testament,* edited by H. F. D. Sparks, 784–94. Oxford: Clarendon Press, 1984.

Charles, R. H. *The Ascension of Isaiah.* London: Adam and Charles Black, 1900.

Delatte, A. "Testament de Salomon." *Anecdota Atheniensia* 36 (1927): 211–27.

Duling, D. C., trans. "Testament of Solomon." In *The Old Testament Pseudepigrapha,* vol. 1, *Apocalyptic Literature and Testaments,* edited by James H. Charlesworth, 960–87. Garden City, NY: Doubleday, 1983.

Geoltrain, Pierre, and Jean-Daniel Kaestli, eds. *Écrits apocryphes chrétiens.* Vol. 2. Paris: Gallimard, 2005.

Hammershaimb, Erling, trans. "Das Martyrium Jesajas." In *Jüdische Schriften aus hellenistisch-römischer Zeit,* vol. 2, pt. 1, edited by Werner Georg Kümmel and Christian Habicht, 23–32. Gütersloh: Gerd Mohn, 1973.

Hare, D. R. A., ed. "Lives of the Prophets." In *The Old Testament Pseudepigrapha,* vol. 2, edited by James Charlesworth, 373–400. Garden City, NY: Doubleday, 1985.

Hock, Richard F., ed. and trans. *The Infancy Gospels of James and Thomas.* Santa Rosa, CA: Polebridge Press, 1995.

James, M. R., trans. and notes. "Gospel of Bartholomew." In *The Apocryphal New Testament.* Oxford: Clarendon Press, 1924.

Knibb, Michael A., trans. "Martyrdom and Ascension of Isaiah." In *The Old Testament Pseudepigrapha,* vol. 2, edited by James H. Charlesworth, 156–76. Garden City, NY: Doubleday, 1985.

Kraft, Robert A., and Ann-Elizabeth Purintum, trans. *Paraleipomena Jeremiou.* In *Texts and Translations 1: Pseudepigrapha Series 1,* 46–47. Missoula, MT: Scholars Press for the Society of Biblical Literature, 1972.

Lipsius, Richard A. *Die apokryphen Apostelgeschichten und Apostellegenden.* 2 vols. 1883–90; Amsterdam: APA Philo Press, 1976.

McCown, C. C., ed. *The Testament of Solomon*. Leipzig, 1922.
Wright, W. *Contributions to the Apocryphal Literature of the New Testament*. Oxford: Clarendon Press, 1865.

Texts from the Nag Hammadi Library

Bethge, Hans-Gebhard, Bentley Layton, and Societas Coptica Hierosolymitana, trans. "On the Origin of the World." In *The Nag Hammadi Library in English*, rev. ed., edited by James M. Robinson. Leiden: Brill, 1988.
Giverson, S., and Birger A. Pearson, trans. "The Testimony of Truth (IX,3)." In *Nag Hammadi Library in English*, rev. ed., edited by James M. Robinson, 449. Leiden: Brill, 1988.

Armenian

Garitte, Gérard. *La narratio de rebus armeniae*. Leuven: L. Durbecq, 1952.
Leloir, Louis, ed. *Écrits apocryphes sur les apôtres: Traduction de l'édition arménienne de Venise*. Vol. 4. Turnhout: Brepols, 1992.

Georgian

Les versions géorgiennes d'Épiphane de Chypre, traité des poids et des mesures. Vol. 2. Edited and Translated by Michel-Jean van Esbroeck. Leuven: Peeters, 1984.

Magical Texts

Montgomery, James A. *Aramaic Incantation Texts from Nippur*. Philadelphia: University Museum, 1913.
Sefer ha-Razim. Edited by Bill Rebiger and Peter Schäfer. Tübingen: Mohr/Siebeck, 2009.

Ethiopic

Wängel Qəddus. Addis Ababa, 1916.

Greek and Latin Authors

Aelian. *On the Characteristics of Animals*. Edited and translated by Alwyn Faber Scholfield. Loeb Classical Library 448. Cambridge, MA: Harvard University Press, 1959.
Aeschylus. *Choephori*. Edited by A. F. Garvie. Oxford: Oxford University Press, 1986.

Ammianus Marcellinus. *The History*. Edited by J. C. Rolfe. Loeb Classical Library 331. Cambridge, MA: Harvard University Press, 1950.

Apuleius. *Metamorphoses (The Golden Ass)*. Edited and translated by J. Arthur Hanson. Loeb Classical Library 453. 1915; Cambridge, MA: Harvard University Press, 1996.

Arrian. *Anabasis Alexandri*. Edited and translated by P. A. Brunt. Rev. ed. 2 vols. Loeb Classical Library 269. Cambridge, MA: Harvard University Press, 1983.

Derrett, J. D. M., ed. "Palladius: De vita bragmanorum narratio, alias palladii de gentibus indiae et bragmanibus commonitorii necnon arriani opusculi versio ornatior." *Classica et Mediaevalia* 21 (1960): 108–35.

Diodorus. *Library of History*. Edited by C. H. Oldfather. Loeb Classical Library 279. Cambridge, MA: Harvard University Press, 1935.

Diogenes Laertius. *Lives of Eminent Philosophers*. Edited and Translated by R. D. Hicks. Cambridge, MA: Harvard University Press, 1979–80.

Hadas, Moses, ed. and trans. *Aristeas to Philocrates: Letter of Aristeas*. New York: Harper, 1951.

Hammond, N. G. L., trans. and comm. *Three Historians of Alexander the Great*. Cambridge: Cambridge University Press, 1983.

———, trans. and comm. *Sources for Alexander the Great*. Cambridge: Cambridge University Press, 1993.

Ideler, Julius Ludwig. *Physici et medici graeci minores*. Berolini, 1841–42.

Jacoby, Felix, ed. Strabo. Fragmente der griechische Historiker, 139, 741. Leiden: Brill, 1923.

Plato. *Timaeus*. Edited by G. P. Goold. Translated by R. G. Bury. Loeb Classical Library 234. 1999; Cambridge, MA: Harvard University Press, 1929.

Pliny. *Natural History*. Edited by E. H. Waemington. Translated by H. Rackham. Loeb Classical Library 352. Cambridge, MA: Harvard University Press, 1942.

Plutarch. *The Age of Alexander: Nine Greek Lives*. Translated by Ian Scott-Kilvert. London: Penguin, 1973.

Procopius. *History of the Wars, Books 1–2, The Persian War*. Vol. 1, edited by H. B. Dewing. Loeb Classical Library 48. Cambridge, MA: Harvard University Press, 1914.

Romm, James, ed. *Alexander the Great: Selections from Arrian, Diodorus, Plutarch, and Quintus Curtius*. Indianapolis: Hackett, 2005.

Ruelle, C. E. "Hermès Trismégiste, le livre sacré sur les décans." *Revue de Philologie* 32 (1908): 247–77.

Seneca. *Epistulae Moralas ad Lucilium*. Edited and translated by Richard Mott Gummere. 3 vols. Loeb Classical Library 75–77. Cambridge, MA: Harvard University Press, 1917–25.

Stern, Menahem. *Greek and Latin Authors on Jews and Judaism*. 3 vols. Jerusalem: Israel Academy of Arts and Sciences, 1974–80.

Stoneman, Richard, trans. *The Greek Alexander Romance*. New York: Penguin, 1991.

———, trans. *The Legends of Alexander the Great*. London: J. M. Dent, 1994.

Strabo, *Geography*. Edited and Translated by H. L. Jones. Cambridge, MA: Harvard University Press, 1917–32.
Suetonius. *Caligula*. In *The Lives of the Caesars,* vol. 1, edited by K. R. Bradley, translated by J. C. Rolfe. Loeb Classical Library 31. Cambridge, MA: Harvard University Press, 1914.
van Thiel, Helmut, ed. *Leben und Taten Alexanders von Makedonien: Der griechische Alexanderroman nach der Handschrift L.* Darmstadt: Wissenschaftliche Buchgesellschaft, 1974.
Wendland, Paul, ed. *Aristeae ad Philocratem epistula cum ceteris de origine versionis LXX interpretum testimoniis.* Leipzig: Teubner, 1900.
Wilcken, Ulrich, ed. "Berlin Papyrus 13044." In Fragmente der griechische Historiker 153.9. Leiden: Brill, 1923.

Early Christian Works

Casey, Robert Pierce, ed. *Excerpta ex Theodoto.* London: Christophers, 1934.
Cyril of Jerusalem. *Discourse on the Cross.* In *Miscellaneous Coptic Texts in the Dialect of Upper Egypt,* edited and translated by E. A. Wallis Budge. New York: AMS Press, 1915. This edition was reprinted in 1977.
Didymus. *Commentarius in Psalmos.* In *Papyrologische Texte und Abhandlungen* 8.354–357, Tura-Papyrus III.218.3–14. Bonn: Habelt, 1969.
Epiphanius. *Panarion.* Edited by Frank Williams. Leiden: Brill, 1994.
Esbroeck, Michel-Jean, ed. and trans. *Les versions géorgiennes d'Épiphane de Chypre, traité des poids et des mesures.* Leuven: Peeters, 1984.
Eusebius, *Ecclesiastical History*. Edited and Translated by Kirsopp Lake. Loeb Classical Library. 1926; Cambridge, MA: Harvard University Press, 1998.
———. *Praeparetio Evangelica.* Edited and Translated by Karl Meas. 2 vols. Griechischen christlichen Schrifsteller. Berlin: Akademie Verlag, 1982–83.
Geyer, P., and O. Cuntz, eds. *Itinerarium Burdigalense* 589.7–592.7. In *Itineraria et alia geographica,* 14–16. Corpus Christianorum, series Latina 175. Turnhout: Brepols, 1965.
Jerome. *Commentarii in Isaiam.* Corpus Christianorum, series Latina 73.16. Turnhout: Brepols, 1953.
———. *Epistulae* XLVI. Edited and Translated by F. A. Wright. Loeb Classical Library. Cambridge, MA: Harvard University Press, 1933.
———. *Hieronymi presbyteri opera.* Pars I,6, *Commentarii in prophetas minores.* Corpus Christianorum, series Latina 76A. Turnhout: Brepols, 1969.
———. *Prologus in Pentateucho.* In *Biblia Sacra Vulgata,* edited by Robert Weber, 364–66. Stuttgart: Deutsche Bibelgesellschaft, 1983.
Justin Martyr. *Dialogue with Trypho.* In *Philosophia Patrum,* vol. 1, edited by J. H. Waszink and J. C. M. van Winden. Leiden: Brill, 1971.
Lawlor, Hugh Jackson, and John Ernest Leonard Oulton, trans. and eds. Eusebius, Bishop of Caesarea. *Ecclesiastical History and the Martyrs of Palestine.* Vol. 1. London: Society for Promoting Christian Knowledge, 1927.

Origen. *Commentarii in Matthaeum*. Edited by R. Girod. Sources chrétiennes 162. Paris: Éditions du Cerf, 1970.

———. *Homiliae in Isaiam*. Edited by W. A. Baehrens. Griechische Christlichen Schriftsteller 33. Leipzig: J. C. Hinrichs, 1925.

Pseudo-Chrysostom. *Opus Imperfectum in Matthaeum, Homily 33 to Matthew 19.20*. Edited by J. P. Migne. Patrologiae cursus completus, series Graeca 56.808. Paris, 1859.

Pseudo-Clementines. Homilies II.29,1. Edited by Bernhard Rehm and George Strecker. Griechische christliche Schriftsteller 42.168. Berlin: Akademie Verlag, 1992.

Pseudo-Justin. *Cohortatio ad Graecos*. Edited by M. Marcovich. PTS 32. Berlin: Walter de Gruyter, 1990.

Sozomen. *Ecclesiastical History*. Edited by J. Bidez. Rev. ed. by G. C. Hansen. Griechische christliche Schriftsteller New Series 4. Berlin: Walter de Gruyter, 1995.

Stevenson, J., ed. *A New Eusebius: Documents Illustrative of the History of the Church to A.D. 337*. London: Society for Promoting Christian Knowledge, 1960.

Tatian. *Oratio ad Graecos*. Translated by Molly Whittaker. Oxford: Clarendon Press, 1982.

Tertullian. *De patientia*. Edited by Jean-Claude Fredouille. Sources chrétiennes 310. Paris: Les Éditions du Cerf, 1984.

———. *Scorpiace*. Edited by Giovanna Azzali Bernardelli. Biblioteca Patristica 14. Florence: Nardini, 1990.

Theodotus. *Interpretatio in Ezechielem*. Edited by John Migne. Patrologia Graeca 81. Paris: Garnier Fratres, 1862.

Zeno. *Tractatus*. Edited by John Migne. Patrologia Latina 11. Paris: Garnier Fratres, 1862.

Syriac

Abramowski, L., and A. E. Goodman, ed. and trans. *A Nestorian Collection of Christological Texts*. Cambridge University Library MS, Oriental 1319, 2 vols.

Bonnet, Max, ed. *Passio sancti Bartholomaei apostoli*. In *Acta apostolorum apocrypha*, vol. 2. Leipzig, 1891–1903.

Budge, E. A. Wallis. *Cave of Treasures*. London: Religious Tract Society, 1927.

———. *The History of Alexander the Great Being the Syriac Version of Pseudo Callisthenes*. Cambridge: Cambridge University Press, 1889.

———, ed. and trans. *The Book of the Bee*. Oxford: Clarendon Press, 1886.

Cureton, William, trans. and ed. *The Acts of Sharbil in Ancient Syriac Documents*. Amsterdam: Oriental Press, 1864. The book was reprinted in 1967.

Drijvers, H. J. W., ed. and trans. *The Book of the Laws of Countries: Dialogue of Fate of Bardaisan of Edessa*. 2nd ed. Piscataway, NJ: Van Gorcum, 2006.

Hamilton, F. and Brooks, E. W., trans. *The Syrian Chronicle Known as That of Zachariah of Mitylene*. London: Methuen, 1899.

Leloir, Louis. *Éphrem de Nisibe: Commentaire de l'Évangile concordant ou Diatessaron.* Paris: Éditions du Cerf, 1966.

McCarthy, Carmel. *Saint Ephrem's Commentary on Tatian's Diatessaron: An English Translation of "Chester Beatty" Syriac Ms 709 with Introduction and Notes.* Oxford: Oxford University Press, 1993.

Olinder, G., ed. *Iacobi Sarugensis epistulae quotquot supersunt.* Corpus scriptorum Christianorum Orientalium, Scriptores Syri 57. Leuven: Brill, 1952.

Pratten, B. P., trans. *Memoirs of Edessa, and Other Ancient Syriac Documents: Acts of Sharbil.* Grand Rapids, MI: William B. Eerdmans, 1951.

Reitzenstein, R., ed. *Poimandres: Studien zur griechisch-ägyptischen und frühchristlichen Literatur.* Darmstadt: Wissenschaftliche Buchgesellschaft, 1966.

Roberts, Alexander, and James Donaldson, ed. *The Acts of Sharbil.* In The Ante-Nicene Fathers, vol. 8, edited by A. Cleveland Coxe, 676–84. London: T & T Clark, 1980.

Scott, W., and A. S. Ferguson, trans. *Hermetica IV: Testimonia.* Oxford: Oxford University Press, 1936.

Zosimus of Panoplis, "Mystery of the Nine Letters of Solomon." In *Histoire des sciences: La chimie au moyen age,* vol. 2, edited by M. Berthelot, 264–65. Paris: Imprimerie Nationale, 1893.

Persian

Darmesteter, James, trans. *The Zend-Avesta.* In The Sacred Books of the East, Vol. 23. Oxford: Clarendon Press, 1883.

Ferdowsi. *Shahnameh: The Persian Book of Kings.* Translated by Dick Davis. New York: Viking, 2006.

Mackenzie, D. A. "Kerdir's Inscription," in *Iranische Denkmäler,* fasc. 13, "The Sasanian Rock Reliefs at Naqsh-I Rustam," pp. 35–72. Berlin: Dietrich Reimer, 1989.

Sachau, C. Eduard, ed. and trans. *The Chronology of Ancient Nations.* 1879; Whitefish, MT: Kessinger, 2006.

West, E. W., trans. *The Bundahisn.* In The Sacred Books of the East, vol. 5. Oxford: Clarendon Press, 1880.

———, trans. *Dadestan i denig.* In The Sacred Books of the East, vol. 18. Oxford: Clarendon Press, 1882.

———, trans. *Denkard.* In The Sacred Books of the East, vol. 37. Oxford: Clarendon Press, 1892.

———, trans. *Videvdat.* In The Sacred Books of the East, vol. 5. Oxford: Clarendon Press, 1880.

Muslim

Brinner, William M., trans. *The History of al-Tabari.* Vol. 3, *The Children of Israel.* Albany: SUNY Press, 1991.

Perlmann, Moshe, trans. *The History of al-Tabari.* Vol. 4, *The Ancient Kingdoms.* Albany: SUNY Press, 1987.

Post-Talmudic Rabbinic Compilations

Hildesheimer, Ezriel, ed. *Halakhot Gedolot.* Vol. 2. Berlin, 1892.
Jellinek, Adolph, ed. *Bet ha-Midrasch.* 3rd ed. 1853–79; Jerusalem: Wahrmann Books, 1967.
Kohut, Alexander, ed. *Arukh ha-Shalem.* Vol. 2. 1878–92; Vienna: Menorah, 1926.

SECONDARY SOURCES

Alibert, Dominique, Michèle Brossard-Dandre, and Simon Mimouni. "Actes Apocryphes des Apôtres de la collection dite du Pseudo-Abdias." In *Écrits apocryphes chrétiens,* vol. 2, ed. Pierre Geoltrain and Jean-Daniel Kaestli. Paris: Gallimard, 2005.
Allen, Pauline. "Zachariah Scholasticus and the Historia Ecclesiastica of Evagrius Scholasticus." *Journal of Theological Studies* 31 (1980): 471–88.
Amaru, Betsy. "The Killing of the Prophets: Unraveling a Midrash." *Hebrew Union College Annual* 54 (1983): 153–80.
Amit, Aaron. "A Rabbinic Satire on the Last Judgment." *Journal of Biblical Literature* 129 (2010): 679–97.
Amitay, Ory. "Alexander in *Bavli Tamid:* In Search for a Meaning." In *The Alexander Romance in Persia and the East,* edited by Richard Stoneman, Kyle Erickson, and Ian Richard Netton, 349–65. Groningen: Barkhuis, 2012.
Anderson, Graham. "The *Alexander Romance* and the Pattern of Hero-Legend." In *The Alexander Romance in Persia and the East,* edited by Richard Stoneman, Kyle Erickson, and Ian Richard Netton, 81–102. Groningen: Barkhuis, 2012.
Aptowitzer, Avigdor. "Die rabbinischen Berichte über die Entstehung der Septuaginta." *Ha-Kedem* 2 (1908): 11–27 and 102–22 and 3 (1909): 4–17.
Arazy, Simon. "Shtei Arikhot Kedumot shel Massekhet Tamid." *Tarbiz* 76 (2007): 265–72.
Asirvatham, Sulochana. "Alexander the Philosopher in the Greco-Roman, Persian and Arabic Traditions." In *The Alexander Romance in Persia and the East,* edited by Richard Stoneman, Kyle Erickson, and Ian Richard Netton, 311–26. Groningen: Barkhuis, 2012.
Assemani, Giuseppe S. *Bibliotheca Orientalis Clementino-Vaticana.* Vol. 3, pt. 2. Hildesheim: G. Olms, 2000.
Bacher, Wilhelm. "La légende de l'exorcisme d'un démon par Simon b. Yohaï." *Revue des études juives* 35 (1897): 285–87.
Bakhos, Carol, and Rahim Shayegan, ed. *The Talmud in its Iranian Context.* Tübingen: Mohr/Siebeck, 2010.
Bar, Oded. "Rabbi Shimon bar Yohai u-Mekomo be-Hayei ha-Hevrah." PhD diss., Tel Aviv University, 2002.

Bar-Asher Siegal, Michal. *Early Christian Monastic Literature and the Babylonian Talmud.* Cambridge: Cambridge University Press, 2014.

———. "Hafikhat Rav le-Nazir: Ha-Reka le-Masoret R. Shimon bar Yohai ba-Me'arah." *Zion* 76, no. 3 (2011): 279–304.

———. "Parashat Ma'aserot (Devarim 14:22–29) be-Mekhilta li-Devarim de-R. Yishmael: Bei'ur Tekstu'ali u-Feirush." MA thesis, Hebrew University, 2006.

Barb, A. A. "St. Zacharias the Prophet and Martyr: A Study in Charms and Incantations." *Journal of the Warburg and Courtland Institutes* 11 (1948): 35–67.

Bar-Ilan, Meir. "Gerush Shedim al Yedei Rabanim: Mashehu al Isukam shel Hakhmei ha-Talmud bi-Keshafim." *Da'at* 34 (1995): 17–31.

Barton, Tamsyn. *Ancient Astrology.* London: Routledge, 1994.

Bassiouney, Reem. *Arabic Sociolinguistics: Topics in Diglossia, Gender, Identity, and Politics.* Washington, DC: Georgetown University, 2009.

Baumgarten, Albert I. "Josephus and Hippolytus on the Pharisees." *Hebrew Union College Annual* 55 (1984): 1–25.

———. "The Name of the Pharisees." *Journal of Biblical Literature* 102, no. 3 (1983): 411–28.

———. "The Pharisaic Paradosis." *Harvard Theological Review* 80, no. 1 (1987): 63–77.

Baynham, Elizabeth. *Alexander the Great: The Unique History of Quintus Curtius.* Ann Arbor: University of Michigan Press, 1998.

Becker, Adam. "Beyond the Spatial and Temporal 'Limes': Questioning the 'Parting of the Ways' outside the Roman Empire." In *The Ways That Never Parted: Jews and Christians in Late Antiquity and the Early Middle Ages,* edited by Adam Becker and Annette Yoshiko Reed, 373–92. Tübingen: Mohr/Siebeck, 2003.

———. "The Comparative Study of 'Scholasticism' in Late Antique Mesopotamia: Rabbis and East Syrians." *Association for Jewish Studies Review* 34, no. 1 (2010): 91–113.

———. *Fear of God and the Beginning of Wisdom: The School of Nisibis and the Development of Scholastic Culture in Late Antique Mesopotamia.* Philadelphia: University of Pennsylvania Press, 2006.

Becker, Hans-Jürgen. "Die Zerstörung Jerusalems bei Matthäus und den Rabbinen." *New Testament Studies* 44, no. 1 (1998): 59–73.

Beer, G. "Das Martyrium Jesajae." In *Die Apokryphen und Pseudepigraphen des Alten Testaments,* vol. 2, edited by E. Kautzsch. Tübingen: Mohr/Siebeck, 1900.

Beer, Moshe. *Amoraei Bavel: Perakim be-Hayei ha-Kalkalah.* 1974; Ramat-Gan: Bar-Ilan University Press, 1982.

Ben-Amos, Dan. *Folktales of the Jews: Tales from the Sephardic Dispersion.* Philadelphia: Jewish Publication Society, 2006.

Ben-Dov, Yonatan. "Ha-Ketivah ba-Aramit u-va-Ivrit be-Megilot Qumran u-va-Sefarim ha-Hizonim: Ha-Reka ba-Olam he-Atik ve-ha-Hipus Ahar Samkhut Yehudit Ketuvah." *Tarbiz* 78, no. 1 (2008): 27–60.

Berger, K. "Hellenistische Gattungen im neuem Testament." In *Aufstieg und Niedergang der römischen Welt* 2:25/2 (1984): 1031–432.

Bernheimer, Richard. "The Martyrdom of Isaiah." *Art Bulletin* 34, no. 1 (1952): 19–34.

Bickerman, Elias J. "Zur Datierung des Pseudo-Aristeas." *Zeitschrift für die neutestamentliche Wissenschaft* 20 (1930): 280–98. Reprinted, in revised form, in *Studies in Jewish and Christian History*, vol. 1, 109–36. Leiden: Brill, 1976.

Blank, Sheldon H. "The Death of Zechariah in Rabbinic Literature." *Hebrew Union College Annual* 12/13 (1937–38): 327–46.

Bock, V. *Archéologie de l'Egypte chrétienne.* Paris, 1901.

Bohak, Gideon. *Ancient Jewish Magic: A History.* Cambridge: Cambridge University Press, 2008.

Bokser, Baruch M. "Wonder-Working and the Rabbinic Tradition: The Case of Hanina ben Dosa." *Journal for the Study of Judaism* 16 (1985): 42–92.

Bosman, Philip R. "The Gymnosophist Riddle Contest (Berol. P. 13044): A Cynic Text?" *Greek, Roman, and Byzantine Studies* 50 (2010): 175–92.

Bosworth, A. B. *Alexander and the East: The Tragedy of Triumph.* Oxford: Clarendon Press, 1996.

———. "Calanus and the Brahman Opposition." In *Alexander der Grosse: Eine Welteroberung und ihr Hintergrund,* edited by Wolfgang Will, 181–90. Bonn: R. Habelt, 1998.

———. *From Arrian to Alexander.* Oxford: Clarendon Press, 1988.

———. "Introduction." In *Alexander the Great in Fact and Fiction,* edited by A. B. Bosworth and E. J. Baynham, 1–22. Oxford: Oxford University Press, 2000.

Boustan, Ra'anan S. "The Spoils of the Jerusalem Temple at Rome and Constantinople: Jewish Counter-Geography in a Christianizing Empire." In *Antiquity in Antiquity: Jewish and Christian Pasts in the Greco-Roman World,* edited by Gregg Gardner and Kevin L. Osterloh 327–72. Tübingen: Mohr/Siebeck, 2008.

———. "The Study of Hekhalot Literature: Between Mystical Experience and Textual Artifact." *Currents in Biblical Research* 6 (2007): 130–60.

Bowker, John. *Jesus and the Pharisees.* Cambridge: Cambridge University Press, 1973.

Bowman, John. "Solomon and Jesus." *Abr-Nahrain* 23 (1984–85): 1–13.

Boyarin, Daniel. *Border Lines: The Partition of Judaeo-Christianity.* Philadelphia: University of Pennsylvania Press, 2004.

———. *Carnal Israel: Reading Sex in Talmudic Culture.* Berkeley: University of California Press, 1990.

———. *Dying for God: Martyrdom and the Making of Christianity and Judaism* Stanford: Stanford University Press, 1999.

———. *Socrates and the Fat Rabbis.* Chicago: University of Chicago Press, 2009.

Bram, J. R. "Fate and Freedom: Astrology vs. Mystery Religions." In *Society of Biblical Literature Seminar Papers, 1976,* 326–30. Missoula, MT: Scholars Press, 1976.

Breuer, Yohanan. "Gadol mei-Rav Rabbi, Gadol mei-Rabbi Rabban, Gadol mei-Rabban Shemo." *Tarbiz* 66, no. 1 (1997): 41–59.

Brock, Sebastian P. "Bardaisan." In *Gorgias Encyclopedic Dictionary of the Syriac Heritage,* 56–57. Piscataway, NJ: Gorgias Press, 2011.

———. *A Brief Outline of Syriac Literature*. Kottayam: St. Ephrem Ecumenical Research Institute, 1997.

Brody, Robert. "Stam ha-Talmud ve-Divrei ha-Amoraim." In *Ha-Mikra ve-Olamo: Sifrut Hazal u-Mishpat Ivri u-Mahshevet Yisrael*, edited by Baruch Schwartz, Abraham Melamed, and Aharon Shemesh, 213–32. Jerusalem: Ha-Igud ha-Olami le-Mada'ei ha-Yahadut, 2008.

Brossard-Dandré, Michéle. "La collection du Pseudo-Abdias: Approche narrative et coherence interne." *Apocrypha* 11 (2000): 195–205.

Brown, Peter. "Arbiters of the Holy: The Christian Holy Man in Late Antiquity." In *Authority and the Sacred: Aspects of the Christianization of the Roman World*, 55–78. Cambridge: Cambridge University Press, 1995.

———. "The Diffusion of Manichaeism in the Roman Empire." *Journal of Roman Studies* 59 (1969): 92–103.

———. "The Rise and Function of the Holy Man in Late Antiquity." *Journal of Roman Studies* 61 (1971): 80–101. This is included, with important additions, in *Society and the Holy in Late Antiquity*. Berkeley: University of California Press, 1982, 103–52.

———. "Town, Village and Holy Man: The Case of Syria." In *Society and the Holy in Late Antiquity*, 153–65. Berkeley: University of California Press, 1982.

Bundy, David. "Early Asian and East African Christianities." In *Cambridge History of Christianity*, vol. 2, *Constantine to ca. 600*, edited by A. Casiday and F. W. Norris, 118–48. Cambridge: Cambridge University Press, 2008.

Campenhausen, H. F. "Das Martyrium des Zacharias, seine früheste Bezeugung in zweiten Jahrhundert." *Historisches Jahrbuch* 77 (1958): 302–7.

Canepa, Matthew P. "Distant Displays of Power: Understanding Cross-Cultural Interaction among the Elites of Rome, Sasanian Iran, and Sui-Tang China." In *Theorizing Cross-Cultural Interaction among the Ancient and Early Medieval Mediterranean, Near East and Asia*, edited by Matthew P. Canepa, special issue, *Ars Orientalis* 38 (2010): 121–54.

———. *The Two Eyes of the Earth: Art and Ritual of Kingship between Rome and Sasanian Iran*. Berkeley: University of California Press, 2009.

Caquot, A. "Bref commentaire du Martyre d'Isaïe." *Semitica* 23 (1973): 65–93.

Carroll, Scott T. "The *Apocalypse of Adam* and Pre-Christian Gnosticism." *Vigiliae Christianae* 44 (1990): 263–79.

Casari, Mario. "The King Explorer: A Cosmographic Approach to the Persian Alexander." In *The Alexander Romance in Persia and the East*, edited by Richard Stoneman, Kyle Erickson, and Ian Richard Netton, 175–203. Groningen: Barkhuis, 2012.

Chapman, John. "Zacharias, Slain between the Temple and the Altar." *Journal of Theological Studies* 13 (1912): 398–410.

Chaumont, M. L. *La christianisation de l'empire iranien des origenes aux grandes persécutions du IVe siècle*. Leuven: Peeters, 1988.

Christensen, Arthur. *Les typos du premier Homme et du premier Roi dans l'histoire légendaire des Iraniens*. Vol. 2. Leiden: Brill, 1934.

Ciancaglini, Claudia. "Gli antecedenti del *Romanzo* Siriaco di Alessandro." In *La diffusione dee'eredutà classica nell'età sardantica e medieval: Il "Romanzo di Alessandro" e altri scritti,* edited by Rosa Bianca Finazzi and Alfredo Valvo, 55–93. Alexandria: Orso. 1998.

Cohen, Shaye J. D. "Antipodal Texts: B. Eruvin 21b–22a and Mark 7:1–23 on the Tradition of the Elders and the Commandment of God." In *Envisioning Judaism: Studies in Honor of Peter Schäfer on the Occasion of his Seventieth Birthday,* edited by Ra'anan Boustan, Klaus Herrmann, Reimund Leicht, Annette Yoshiko Reed, and Giuseppe Veltri, 965–83. Tübingen: Mohr/Siebeck, 2013.

———. "Parallel Traditions in Josephus and Rabbinic Literature." In *Proceedings of the Ninth World Congress of Jewish Studies,* div. 2, vol. 1, 7–14. Jerusalem: World Union of Jewish Studies, 1986.

———. "Patriarchs and Scholarchs," *Proceedings of the American Academy of Jewish Research* 48 (1981): 57–85.

———. "The Significance of Yavneh: Pharisees, Rabbis, and the End of Jewish Sectarianism." *Hebrew Union College Annual* 55 (1984): 27–53.

Conybeare, F. "Christian Demonology." *Jewish Quarterly Review* 9 (1897): 444–70.

Conybeare, F., J. R. Harris, and A. S. Lewis. *The Story of Ahikar.* Oxford: Clarendon, 1913.

Cowley, Roger W. "The 'Blood of Zechariah' (Mt. 23:35) in Ethiopian Exegetical Tradition." In *Studia Patristica* 18, vol. 1, *Papers of the Ninth International Conference of Patristic Studies, Oxford, 1983,* edited by Elizabeth A. Livingstone, 293–302. Kalamazoo, MI: Cistercian Publications, 1985.

———. *Ethiopian Biblical Interpretation: A Study in Exegetical Tradition and Hermeneutics.* Cambridge: Cambridge University Press, 1988.

———. *The Traditional Interpretation of the Apocalypse of St John in the Ethiopian Orthodox Church.* Cambridge: Cambridge University Press, 1983.

Daniel, R. "The Testament of Solomon xviii 27–28, 33–40." In *Festschrift zum 100-jährigen Bestehen e34 Papyrussammlung der österreichlische Nationalbibliothek: Papyrus Erzherzog Rainer,* vol. 1, 294–304. Vienna: Brüder Hollinek, 1983.

Davies, W. D., and D. C. Allison. *A Critical and Exegetical Commentary on the Gospel According to Saint Matthew.* Vol. 3. Edinburgh: T & T Clark, 1997.

Davies-Browne, B. P. "The Significance of Parallels between the Testament of Solomon and Jewish Literature of Late Antiquity (between the Closing Centuries B.C.E. and the Talmudic Era) and the New Testament." PhD diss., St. Andrews, Scotland, 2003.

Denzey, Nicola. "A New Star on the Horizon: Astral Christologies and Stellar Debates in Early Christian Discourse." In *Prayer, Magic, and the Stars in the Ancient and Late Antique World,* edited by Scott Noegel, Joel Walker, and Brannon Wheeler, 207–21. University Park: Pennsylvania State University Press, 2003.

Diamond, Eliezer. *Holy Men and Hunger Artists: Fasting and Asceticism in Rabbinic Culture.* New York: Oxford University Press, 2003.

Dignas, Beate, and Engelbert Winter. *Rome and Persia in Late Antiquity: Neighbors and Rivals.* Cambridge: Cambridge University Press, 2007.

Dochhorn, Jan. "Die Ascensio Isaiae." In *Jüdische Schriften aus hellenistisch-römischer Zeit,* vol. 6, pt. 1, edited by Gerbern S. Oegema, 1–48. Gütersloh: Gütersloher Verlagshaus, 2005.

Drijvers, H. J. W. *Cults and Beliefs at Edessa.* Leiden: Brill, 1980.

Dubois, Jean-Daniel. "La mort de Zacharie: Mémoire juive et mémoire chrétienne." *Revue des Études Augustiennes* 40 (1994): 23–38.

Duling, D. C. "The Eleazar Miracle and Solomon's Magical Wisdom in Flavius Josephus's *Antiquitates Judaicae* 8.42–49." *Harvard Theological Review* 78 (1985): 1–25.

———. Introduction to *Testament of Solomon.* In *The Old Testament Pseudepigrapha,* vol. 1, edited by James H. Charlesworth, 935–59. Garden City, NY: Doubleday, 1983.

———. "The Testament of Solomon: Retrospect and Prospect." *Journal for the Study of the Pseudepigrapha* 2 (1988): 87–112.

Ehrenberg, Victor. "Pothos." Reprinted in English translation as chapter 2 of *Alexander the Great: The Main Problems,* edited by G. T. Griffith, 74–83. Cambridge, MA: Heffer, 1966.

Elad, Amikam. *Medieval Jerusalem and Islamic Worship: Holy Places, Ceremonies, Pilgramage.* Leiden: Brill, 1995.

Elman, Yaakov. "Middle Persian Culture and Babylonian Sages: Accommodation and Resistance in the Shaping of Rabbinic Legal Tradition." In *The Cambridge Companion to the Talmud and Rabbinic Literature,* edited by Charlotte E. Fonrobert and Martin S. Jaffee, 165–97. Cambridge: Cambridge University Press, 2007.

Elwell, Walter A., and Philip Wesley Comfort. *Tyndale Bible Dictionary.* Wheaton, IL: Tyndale House, 2001.

Engel, H. *Die Susanna-Erzählung. Einleitung, Übersetzung und Kommentar zum Septuagint Text und zur Theodotion-Bearbeitung.* Freiburg: Universitätsverlag Neukirchener, 1985.

Epstein, Y. N. *Mevo'ot le-Sifrut ha-Amoraim.* Jerusalem: Magnes Press, 1962.

Evans, Craig A. "Scripture Based Stories in the Pseudepigrapha." In *Justification and Variegated* Nomism, vol. 1, edited by A. Carson, Peter T. O'Brien, and Mark A. Seifrid, 57–72. Tübingen: Mohr/Siebeck, 2001.

Farmer, D. H., ed. "Bartholomew." In *Oxford Dictionary of Saints,* 5th ed. New York: Oxford University Press, 2004.

Faultless, Julian. "The Two Recensions of the Prologue to John in ibn al-Tayyib's Commentary on the Gospels." In *Christians at the Heart of Islamic Rule: Church Life and Scholarship in 'Abbasid Iraq,* edited by David Richard Thomas, 177–98. Leiden: Brill, 2003.

Fiey, J. M. *Jalons pour une histoire de l'église en Iraq.* Leuven: Secrétariat du Corpus SCO, 1970.

Finkelstein, Louis. *Akiba: Scholar, Saint, and Martyr.* 1936; New York: Atheneum, 1970.

Flusser, David. "Perushim, Zedukim, ve-Essi'im be-Pesher Nahum." In *Sefer Zikaron le-Gedaliah Alon,* edited by Menahem Dormann, Shmuel Safrai, and Menahem Stern, 133–68. Tel Aviv: Ha-Kibuz ha-Me'uhad, 1970.

———. *Sefer Yosippon.* Vol. 2. Jerusalem: Mosad Bialik, 1978.

Foley, J. M. "Word-Power, Performance and Tradition," *Journal of American Folklore* 105 (1992): 275–301.

Ford, James Nathan, and Alon Ten-Ami. "Ke'arat Hashba'ah al shem Rav Mesharshia bar Qaqay." *Tarbiz* 80, no. 2 (2012): 219–30.

Fowden, Elizabeth K. *The Barbarian Plain: Saint Sergius between Rome and Iran.* Berkeley: University of California Press, 1999.

Fowden, Garth. *Empire to Commonwealth: Consequences of Monotheism in Late Antiquity.* Princeton: Princeton University Press, 1993.

Fraade, Steven. "Ascetical Aspects of Ancient Judaism." In *Jewish Spirituality from the Bible through the Middle Ages,* edited by Arthur Green, 53–88. New York: Crossroad, 1986.

Fraenkel, Yonah. *Darkhei ha-Aggadah ve-ha-Midrash.* Givatayim, Israel: Yad La-Talmud, 1991.

———. "Kavim Boltim be-Toldot Masoret ha-Text shel Sippurei ha-Aggadah," In *Divrei ha-Kongress ha-Olami ha-Shevi'it le-Mada'ei ha-Yahadut: Studies in Talmud, Halachah, and Midrash,* 5–70. Jerusalem: Ha-Igud ha-Olami le-Mada'ei ha-Yahadut, 1981.

Freund, Richard A. "Alexander Macedon and Antoninus: Two Greco-Roman Heroes of the Rabbis." In *Crisis and Reaction: The Heroes in Jewish History,* edited by M. Mor, 19–72. Omaha: Creighton University Press, 1995.

Friedman, Avi. "Hokhmato, Masaotav ve-Ozrotav shel Alexander Mokdon: Masekhet Tamid daf 31." www.daat.ac.il/chazal/maamar.asp?id = 323.

Friedman, Shamma. "Al Derekh Heker ha-Sugya." In *Perek ha-Ishah Rabbah ba-Bavli,* 7–45. Jerusalem: Jewish Theological Seminary, 1978.

———. "Ketiv ha-Shemot 'Rabbah' ve-'Rava' ba-Talmud ha-Bavli." *Sinai* 55 (1992): 140–64.

———. *Talmud Arukh: Bavli Bava Mezi'a VI.* Vol. 2. New York: Jewish Theological Seminary, 1996.

Frye, Richard. "Two Iranian Notes." In *Papers in Honor of Mary Boyce,* 185–90. Leiden: Brill, 1985.

Gafni, Yeshayahu. "Ha-Yeshivah ha-Bavlit la-Or B. Q. 111a." *Tarbiz* 49 (1980): 292–301.

———. "Le-Heker ha-Khronologiah be-Igeret Rav Sherira Gaon." *Zion* 52 (1987): 1–24.

———. *Yehudei Bavel bi-Tekufat ha-Talmud: Hayyei ha-Hevrah ve-ha-Ruah.* Jerusalem: Zalman Shazar Center for Jewish History, 1990.

———. "'Yeshiva' u-'Metivta.'" *Zion* 43 (1978): 12–37.

Gager, John H. "The Dialogue of Paganism with Judaism: Bar Cochba to Julian." *Hebrew Union College Annual* 45 (1973): 89–118.

Gandz, Solomon. "The Origin of the Planetary Week *or* the Planetary Week in Hebrew Literature." *Proceedings of the American Academy of Jewish Research* 18

(1948–49): 213–67. Also published in *Studies in Hebrew Astronomy and Mathematics,* 169–210. New York: Ktav, 1970.

Gardner, Gregg. "Astrology in the Talmud: An Analysis of Bavli Shabbat 156." In *Heresy and Identity in Late Antiquity,* edited by Holger Zellentin and Eduard Iricinschi, 314–38. Tübingen: Mohr/Siebeck, 2008.

Garsoïan, Nina. "Byzantium and the Sasanians." In *Cambridge History of Iran,* vol. 3, pt. 1, edited by Ehsan Yarshater, 568–75. Cambridge: Cambridge University Press, 1983.

Geiger, Bernard. *Tosafot he-Arukh ha-Shalem.* Vienna: Alexander Kohut Memorial Foundation, 1937.

Geller, M. J. "The Last Wedge." *Zeitschrift für Assyriologie und Vorderasiatische Archäologie* 87 (1997): 43–95.

———. "Two Incantation Bowls Inscribed in Syriac and Aramaic." *Bulletin of the School of Oriental and African Studies* 39 (1976): 422–27.

Giversen, S. "Solomon und die Dämonen." In *Essays on the Nag Hammadi Texts in Honour of Alexander Böhlig,* edited by M. Krause, 16–21. Leiden: Brill, 1972.

Gnoli, Gherardo. "Questioni comparative sull'*Ascensione d'Isaia*: La tradizine iranica." In *Isaia, il diletto e la Chiesa: Vision ed esegesi profetica cristiano-primitiva nell'Ascensione di Isaia,* edited by Mauro Pesce, 117–32. Brescia: Paideia, 1983.

Goldberg, Avraham. "The Babylonian Talmud." In *The Literature of the Sages: Oral Tora, Halakha, Mishna, Tosefta, Talmud, External Tractates,* Compendia Rerum Iudaicarum ad Novum Testamentum, pt. 1, sec. 2, vol. 3, edited by Shmuel Safrai, 323–45. Assen: Van Gorcum, 1987.

Goodlbatt, David. "The Babylonian Talmud." In *The Study of Ancient Judaism,* vol. 2, edited by Jacob Neusner, 20–99. New York: Ktav, 1981.

———. "Hitpathuyot Hadashot be-Heker Yeshivot Bavel." *Zion* 43 (1978): 14–38.

———. *Rabbinic Instruction in Sasanian Babylonia.* Leiden: Brill, 1975.

Gray, Alyssa. *A Talmud in Exile: The Influence of Yerushalmi Avodah Zarah on the Formation of Bavli Avodah Zarah.* Providence, RI: Brown University Press, 2005.

Green, William Scott. "Palestinian Holy Men: Charismatic Leadership and Rabbinic Tradition." In *Aufstieg und Niedergang der römischen Welt* 19:2/2 (1979): 619–47.

Greenfield, Jonas. "Ratin Megusha." In *Exploring the Talmud,* vol. 1, edited by Haim Z. Dimitrovsky, 63–69. New York: Ktav, 1974.

Greenfield, Jonas C., and Michael Sokoloff, "Astrological and Related Omen Texts in Jewish Palestinian Aramaic." *Journal of Near Eastern Studies* 48 (1989): 201–14.

Grelot, P. "Deux tosephtas targoumiques inedites sur Isaie LXVI." *Revue Biblique* 79 (1972): 511–43.

Gruen, Erich. *Heritage and Hellenism: The Reinvention of Jewish Tradition.* Berkeley: University of California Press, 1998.

Gruenwald, Itamar. "Ha-Polmos be-Inyan Targum ha-Torah le-Yevanit." In *Te'udah,* vol. 4, edited by Mordechai Friedman and Moshe Gil, 65–78. Tel Aviv: University of Tel Aviv, 1986.

Gundel, W. *Dekane und Dekansternbilder: Ein Beitrag zur Geschichte der Sternbilder der Kulturvölker.* Glückstadt: J. J. Augustin, 1936.

Guttmann, Alexander. *Rabbinic Judaism in the Making.* Detroit: Wayne State University Press, 1970.

Halbertal, Moshe, and Shlomo Naeh. "Ma'ayanei ha-Yeshuah: Satirah Parshanit u-Teshuvat ha-Minim." In *Higayon L'Yona: New Aspects in the Study of Midrash, Aggadah, and Piyut in Honor of Professor Yona Fraenkel,* edited by Joshua Levinson, Yaakov Elboim, and Galit Hasan-Rokem, 179–97. Jerusalem: Magnes Press, 2006.

Halevi, E. E. *Sha'arei ha-Aggadah.* Tel Aviv: n.p., 1963.

Halevy, J. "Ben-Thymelion et Bartholomée." *Revue des études juives* 10 (1885): 60–65.

Halivni, David. *Mekorot u-Mesorot:* Yoma-Hagigah. Jerusalem: Jewish Theological Seminary, 1975.

Hall, Robert G. "*The Ascension of Isaiah:* Community Situation, Date, and Place in Early Christianity." *Journal of Biblical Literature* 109, no. 2 (1990): 289–306.

———. "Isaiah's Ascent to See the Beloved: An Ancient Jewish Source for the *Ascension of Isaiah?*" *Journal of Biblical Literature* 113, no. 3 (1998): 463–84.

Hanhart, Robert. "Fragen um die Entstehung der LXX." *Vetus Testamentum* 12 (1962): 139–63.

Harari, Yuval. *Ha-Kishuf ha-Yehudi ha-Kadum: Mehkar, Shitah, Mekorot.* Jerusalem: Mosad Bialik, 2010.

Harding, James, and Loveday Alexander. "Dating the Testament of Solomon." 1999. www.st-andrews.ac.uk/divinity/rt/otp/guestlectures/harding.

Harvey, Susan Ashbrook. "The Edessan Martyrs and Ascetic Tradition." In *V Symposium Syriacum, 1988,* edited by René Lavenant, 195–206. Rome: Pont. Institutum Studiorum Orientalium, 1990.

Hasan-Rokem, Galit. *Web of Life: Folklore and Midrash in Rabbinic Literature.* Stanford: Stanford University Press, 2000.

Hegedus, Tim. *Early Christianity and Ancient Astrology.* New York: Peter Lang, 2007.

Heinemann, Yosef. *Aggadot ve-Toldoteinhen.* Jerusalem: Keter, 1974.

Hengel, Martin. *The Septuagint as Christian Scripture: Its Prehistory and the Problem of Its Canon.* Edinburgh: T & T Clark, 2002.

Herman, Geoffrey. "Ahasuerus, the Former Stable-Master of Belshazzar and the Wicked Alexander of Macedon: Two Parallels between the Babylonian Talmud and Persian Sources." *Association for Jewish Studies Review* 29, no. 2 (2005): 283–97.

———. *A Prince without a Kingdom.* Tübingen: Mohr/Siebeck, 2012.

———. "Rashut ha-Golah be-Vavel bi-Tekufat ha-Talmud." PhD diss., Hebrew University, 2005.

———. "The Story of Rav Kahana (BT Baba Qamma 117a-b) in Light of Armeno-Persian Sources." In *Irano-Judaica,* vol. 6, edited by Shaul Shaked and Amnon Netzer, 53–80. Jerusalem: Yad Yizhak Ben-Zvi, 2008.

Hezser, Catherine. "Die Verwendung der hellenistischen Gattung im frühen Christentum und Judentum." *Journal for the Study of Judaism* 27 (1996): 371–439.

———. *Jewish Literacy in Roman Palestine.* Tübingen: Mohr/Siebeck, 2001.

———. *Jewish Travel in Antiquity*. Tübingen: Mohr/Siebeck, 2011.
Himmelfarb, Martha. "The Mother of the Messiah in the Talmud Yerushalmi and Sefer Zerubbabel." In *The Talmud Yerushalmi and Graeco-Roman Culture*, vol. 3, edited by Peter Schäfer, 369–89. Tübingen: Mohr/Siebeck, 2002.
Högemann, Peter. *Alexander der Grosse und Arabien*. Munich: C. H. Beck, 1985.
Holmberg, Bo. "A Reconsideration of the Kitāb al-Maǧdal." *Parole de l'Orient* 18 (1993): 255–73.
Houtman, Alberdina. "The Targumic Versions of the 'Martyrdom of Isaiah.'" In *Studies in Hebrew Literature and Jewish Culture*, edited by Martin F. J. Baasten and Reinier Munk, 189–201. Dordrecht: Springer, 2007.
Hoyland, Robert G. *Seeing Islam as Others Saw It*. Princeton: Darwin Press, 1999.
Ilan, Tal. *Integrating Women into Second Temple History*. Tübingen: Mohr/Siebeck, 1999.
———. *Silencing the Queen: The Literary Histories of Shelamzion and Other Jewish Women*. Tübingen: Mohr/Siebeck, 2006.
Ilan, Yaakov David, ed. *Shitah Mekubetzet im Kuntres Acharon: Massekhet Meilah*. Benei Berak, Israel: Makhon Keneset ha-Rishonim, 1977.
Jackson, H. M. "Notes on the Testament of Solomon." *Journal for the Study of Judaism* 19 (1988): 19–60.
Jaffee, Martin S. *Torah in the Mouth: Writing and Oral Tradition in Palestinian Judaism, 200 BCE–400 CE*. New York: Oxford University Press, 2001.
Jastrow, Marcus. *A Dictionary of the Targumim, Talmud Babli, Yerushalmi, and Midrashic Literature*. 1886–1903. New York: Judaica Press, 1971.
Jellicoe, Sidney. *The Septuagint and Modern Study*. Oxford: Oxford University Press, 1968.
Johnston, Sarah Iles. "The Testament of Solomon from Late Antiquity to the Renaissance." In *The Metamorphosis of Magic from Late Antiquity to the Early Modern Period*, edited by Jan N. Bremmer and Jan R. Veenstra, 36–49. Leuven: Peeters, 2002.
Kafir, Zivya. "Yannai ha-Melekh ve-Shimon ben Shetach: Aggadah Amora'it be-Tahposet Historit." *Tura* 3 (1994): 85–97.
Kahana, Menahem. *Midrash Zuta Devarim*. Jerusalem: Magnes, 2002.
Kalimi, Isaac. *The Retelling of Chronicles in Jewish Tradition and Literature*. Winona Lake, IN: Eisenbrauns, 2009.
———. "The Story about the Murder of the Prophet Zechariah in the Gospels and Its Relation to Chronicles." *Revue Biblique* 116, no. 2 (2009): 246–61.
Kalmin, Richard. "Christians and Heretics in Rabbinic Literature of Late Antiquity." *Harvard Theological Review* 87, no. 2 (1994): 155–69.
———. "The Formation and Character of the Babylonian Talmud." In *The Cambridge History of Judaism*, vol. 4, *The Late Roman-Rabbinic Period*, 840–76. Cambridge: Cambridge University Press, 2006.
———. "Hillel and the Soldiers of Herod: Sage and Sovereign in Ancient Jewish Society." In *Jewish Religious Leadership: Image and Reality*, vol. 1, edited by Jack Wertheimer, 91–126. New York: JTS Press, 2004.

———. "Holy Men, Rabbis, and Demonic Sages in Late Antiquity." In *Jewish Culture and Society under the Christian Roman Empire,* edited by Richard Kalmin and Seth Schwartz, 213–49. Leuven: Peeters, 2003.

———. "Jesus in Sasanian Babylonia." Review essay of Peter Schäfer's *Jesus in the Talmud. Jewish Quarterly Review* 99, no. 1 (2008): 107–12.

———. *Jewish Babylonia between Persia and Roman Palestine.* New York: Oxford University Press, 2006.

———. "Language Switching." In *Critical Terms in Jewish Language Studies.* Frankel Institute Annual, 2011:18–20.

———. "'Mekorot Arzi'yisre'elim' u-'Mekorot Bavli'im.'" *Zion* 66, no. 2 (2001): 227–30.

———. "The Modern Study of Ancient Rabbinic Literature: Yonah Fraenkel's Darkhei ha'aggadah vehamidrash." *Prooftexts* 14 (1994): 189–204.

———. "The Pharisees in Rabbinic Literature." *Sidra* 24/25 (2010): vi–xxviii. The issue was edited by David Henschke.

———. "Problems in the Use of the Babylonian Talmud for the History of Late-Roman Palestine: The Example of Astrology." In *Rabbinic Texts and the History of Late-Roman Palestine,* edited by Martin Goodman and Philip Alexander, 165–83. London: Oxford University Press, 2010.

———. "Rabbinic Traditions about Roman Persecutions of the Jews: A Reconsideration." *Journal of Jewish Studies* 54, no. 1 (2003): 21–50.

———. *The Sage in Jewish Society of Late Antiquity.* London: Routledge Press, 1999.

———. *Sages, Stories, Authors, and Editors in Rabbinic Babylonia.* Atlanta: Scholars Press, 1994.

———. "Targum in the Babylonian Talmud." In *Envisioning Judaism: Studies in Honor of Peter Schäfer on the Occasion of his Seventieth Birthday,* edited by Ra'anan Boustan, Klaus Herrmann, Reimund Leicht, Annette Yoshiko Reed, and Giuseppe Veltri, 501–25. Tübingen: Mohr/Siebeck, 2013.

———. "Zechariah and the Bubbling Blood: An Ancient Tradition in Jewish, Christian, and Muslim Literature." In *Jews and Christians in Sasanian Babylonia,* edited by Geoffrey Herman. Piscataway, NJ: Gorgias Press, forthcoming.

Kasher, Rimon. *Toseftot Targum la-Nevi'im.* Jerusalem: Ha-Igud ha-Olami le-Mada'ei ha-Yahadut, 1996.

Kaufman, S. A. "A Unique Magic Bowl from Nippur." *Journal of Near Eastern Studies* 32 (1973): 170–74.

Kent, R. G. *Old Persian: Grammar, Texts, Lexicon.* New Haven: American Oriental Society, 1953.

Kettenhofen, Erich. "Deportations II: In the Parthian and Sasanian Period." *Encyclopaedia Iranica.* www.iranicaonline.org/articles/deportations#pt.2.

Kiperwasser, Reuven, and Serge Ruzer. "Zoroastrian Proselytes in Rabbinic and Syriac Christian Narratives: Orality-Related Markers of Cultural Identity." In *History of Religions* 51, no. 3 (2012): 197–218.

Klutz, Todd. *Rewriting the "Testament of Solomon": Tradition, Conflict and Identity in a Late Antique Pseudepigraphon.* London: T & T Clark, 2005.

Knibb, Michael A. "Isaianic Traditions in the Apocrypha and Pseudepigrapha." In *Writing and Reading the Scroll of Isaiah*, vol. 2, edited by Craig C. Broyles and Craig A. Evans, 633–50. Leiden: Brill, 1997.

———. "The Martyrdom of Isaiah." In *Outside the Old Testament*, edited by Marinus de Jonge, 178–92. Cambridge: Cambridge University Press, 1985.

Kohut, Alexander, ed. *Arukh ha-Shalem*. 8 vols. 1878–92. Vienna: Menorah, 1926.

Koltun-Fromm, Naomi. *Jewish-Christian Conversation in Fourth-Century Persian Mesopotamia*. Piscataway, NJ: Gorgias Press, 2011.

Kosman, Admiel. *Masekhet Nashim*. Jerusalem: Keter, 2007.

Krappe, Alexander H. "Solomon and Ashmodai." *American Journal of Philology* 54, no. 3 (1933): 260–68.

Kraus, Matthew. "Zechariah's Blood and the Destruction of the Temple: An Anthropological Reading of Lamentations Rabbah 23." Paper delivered at the Society of Biblical Literature Conference in San Diego, 2007.

Krupp, Michael. "Manuscripts of the Babylonian Talmud." In *The Literature of the Sages: Oral Tora, Halakha, Mishna, Tosefta, Talmud, External Tractates*, Compendia Rerum Iudaicarum ad Novum Testamentum, pt. 1, sec. 2, vol. 3, edited by Shmuel Safrai, 346–66. Assen: Van Gorcum, 1987.

Kugel, James L. *The Bible as It Was*. Cambridge, MA: Belknap Press of the Harvard University Press, 1997.

Kushelevsky, Rella. "Pe'arim bein Girsa'ot ke-Mekhonenei Teima." In *Ma'aseh Sipur: Mehkarim be-Siporet ha-Yehudit Mugashim le-Yoav Elstein*, 221–41. Ramat Gan: Bar Ilan University Press, 2006.

Kutscher, E. Y. "Aramaic." In *Encyclopaedia Judaica*, vol. 3 (1971): col. 259–87.

Labendz, Jenny. "The Book of Ben Sira in Rabbinic Literature." *Association for Jewish Studies Review* 30, no. 2 (2006): 347–92.

Lang, J., P. T. Craddock, and St J. Simpson. "New Evidence for Early Crucible Steel." *Journal of the Historical Metallurgy Society* 32, no. 1 (1998): 7–14.

Larionoff, S. "Histoire du Roi Djemchid et des Divs." *Journal Asiatique* 14 (1889): 59–83.

Lee, A. D. *Information and Frontiers: Roman Foreign Relations in Late Antiquity*. Cambridge: Cambridge University Press, 1993.

Levene, Dan. *A Corpus of Magic Bowls: Incantation Texts in Jewish Aramaic from Late Antiquity*. London: Kegan Paul, 2003.

———. "'A Happy Thought of the Magicians,' The Magical *Get*." In *Shlomo: Studies in Epigraphy, Iconography, History and Archaeology in Honor of Shlomo Moussaieff*, edited by Robert Deutsch, 175–83. Tel Aviv: Archaeological Center Publication, 2003.

Levi, Israel. "Encore un mot sur la legende de Bartalmion." *Revue des études juives* 10 (1885): 66–73.

———. "La légende chrétienne de Bartholomée dans le Talmud." *Revue des études juives* 8 (1884): 200–202.

———. "La légende d'Alexandre dans le Talmud." *Revue des études Juives* 2 (1881): 293–300.

Levinas, Emmanuel. *New Talmudic Readings.* Translated by Richard A. Cohen. Pittsburgh: Duquesne University Press, 1999.

Levine, Yisrael L. "Ha-Ma'avak ha-Politi bein ha-Perushim li-Zedukim bi-Tekufat ha-Hashmona'it." In *Perakim be-Toldot Yerushalayim bi-Yemei Bayit Sheni: Sefer Zikaron le-Avraham Shalit,* edited by Aharon Oppenheimer, Uriel Rapaport, and Menahem Stern, 61–83. Jerusalem: Yad Yizhak Ben-Zvi, 1980.

Levinson, Joshua. "The Cultural Dignity of Narrative." In *Creation and Composition: The Contribution of the Bavli Redactors (Stammaim) to the Aggada,* edited by Jeffrey L. Rubenstein, 361–81. Tübingen: Mohr/Siebeck, 2005.

Levy, Jacob. *Wörterbuch über die Talmudim und Midraschim.* Vol. 3. Berlin: Benjamin Harz, 1924.

Lezer, Aron. *Me'il Aharon.* Brooklyn: A. Lezer, 2004.

Lieberman, Saul. *Greek in Jewish Palestine.* New York: Jewish Theological Seminary, 1942.

———. *Ha-Yerushalmi ki-Feshuto.* Jerusalem: Darom, 1934.

———. "Roman Legal Institutions in Early Rabbinics and in the *Acta Martyrum.*" In *Texts and Studies,* 57–111. New York: Ktav, 1944.

———. "Tikunei Yerushalmi 6 (Sof)." *Tarbiz* 5 (1934): 100–101. The text is reprinted in *Mehkarim be-Torat Erez-Yisrael,* edited by David Rosenthal, 203–4. Jerusalem: Magnes Press, 1991.

Lieu, S. N. C. "Captives, Refugees and Exiles: A Study of Cross-Frontier Civilian Movements and Contacts between Rome and Persia from Valerian to Jovian." In *The Defence of the Roman and Byzantine East,* edited by P. Freeman and D. Kennedy, 475–505. Oxford: B. A. R., 1986.

Linder, Amnon. *Ha-Yehudim ve-ha-Yahadut be-Hukei ha-Keisarit ha-Romit.* Jerusalem: Ha-Akademiyah ha-Le'umit ha-Yisre'elit le-Mada'im, 1983.

Lövestam, E. "Jésus Fils de David chez les Synoptiques." *Studia Theologica* 28 (1974): 97–109.

Mackenzie, D. N. "Bundahisn." In *Encyclopaedia Iranica,* vol. 4, edited by Ehsan Yarshater, 547–49. Boston: Routledge & Kegan Paul, 1990.

Mandel, Pinhas. "Ha-Sipur be-Midrash Eikhah: Nusah ve-Signon." MA thesis, Hebrew University, 1983.

———. "Midrash Eikhah Rabati: Mavo u-Mahadurah Bikortit la-Parashah ha-Shelishit." 2 vols. PhD diss., Hebrew University, 1997.

Margaliot, Eliezer. "Ivrit ve-Aramit ba-Talmud u-va-Midrash." *Leshonenu* 27/28 (1963–64): 20–33.

Martin, Dale B. "When Did Angels Become Demons?" *Journal of Biblical Literature* 129, no. 4 (2010): 657–77.

Marx, Dalia. *Tractates Tamid, Midot and Qinnim.* Tübingen: Mohr/Siebeck, 2013.

McCown, C. C. "The Christian Tradition as to the Magical Wisdom of Solomon." *Journal of the Palestine Oriental Society* 2 (1922): 1–24.

Mclynn, N. "A Self-Made Holy Man: The Case of Gregory Nazianzen." *Journal of Early Christian Studies* 6 (1998): 462–64.

Merkati, G. "Un supposto framento di Origene." *Revue Biblique* 7 (1910): 76–79.

Merkelbach, Reinhold. *Die Quellen der griecheschen Alexanderromans.* 2nd rev. ed. with Jürgen Trumpf. Munich: C. H. Beck, 1977.

Metzger, David, ed. *Mafteah ha-Talmud le-Rav Nisim Gaon: Shabbat.* Jerusalem: Makhon Lev Sameach, 1995.

Millar, Fergus. *The Roman Near East, 31 BC–AD 337.* Cambridge, MA: Harvard University Press, 1993.

———. "A Rural Jewish Community in Late Roman Mesopotamia, and the Question of a 'Split' Jewish Diaspora." *Journal for the Study of Judaism* 42 (2011): 351–74.

Montgomery, James A. *Aramaic Incantation Texts from Nippur.* Philadelphia: University Museum, 1913.

Morony, Michael G. *Iraq after the Muslim Conquest.* Princeton: Princeton University Press, 1984.

———. "Population Transfers between Sasanian Iran and the Byzantine Empire." In *Convengo Internazionale La Persia e Bisanzio, Roma: 14–18 ottobre 2002,* 161–79. Rome: Accademia Nazionale dei Lincei, 2004.

Moscovitz, Leib. *Talmudic Reasoning: From Casuistics to Conceptualization.* Tübingen: Mohr/Siebeck, 2002.

Moss, Charlene McAfee. *The Zechariah Tradition and the Gospel of Matthew.* Berlin: Walter de Gruyter, 2008.

Müller, Karlheinz. "Die rabbinischen Nachrichten über die Entstehung der LXX." In *Wort, Lied und Gottespruch: Beiträge zur Septuaginta, Festschrift Josef Ziegler,* vol. 1, edited by Josef Schreiner, 527–36. Würzburg, 1972.

Müller, Mögens. *The First Bible of the Church: A Plea for the Septuagint.* Sheffield: Sheffield Academic Press, 1996.

Müller-Kessler, Christa. "The Earliest Evidence for Targum Onqelos from Babylonia and the Question of Its Dialect and Origin." *Journal for the Aramaic Bible* 3 (2001): 181–98.

Naeh, Shlomo. "Freedom and Celibacy: A Talmudic Variation on Tales of Temptation and Fall in Genesis and its Syrian Background." In *The Book of Genesis in Jewish and Oriental Christian Interpretation,* edited by Judith Frishman and Lucas van Rompay, 73–89. Leuven: Peeters, 1997.

Naveh, Joseph, and Shaul Shaked. *Amulets and Magic Bowls.* Jerusalem: Magnes Press, 1985.

Neusner, Jacob. *Judaism: The Classical Statement: The Evidence of the Bavli.* Chicago: University of Chicago Press, 1986.

———. *The Rabbinic Traditions about the Pharisees before 70. Part 1, The Masters.* 1971; Atlanta: Scholars Press, 1999.

Nickelsburg, George W. E. "Stories of Biblical and Early Post-Biblical Times." In *Jewish Writings of the Second Temple Period: Apocrypha, Pseudepigrapha, Qumran Sectarian Writings, Philo, Josephus: The Literature of the Jewish People in the Period of the Second Temple and the Talmud.* Compendia Rerum Iudaicarum ad Novum Testamentum, edited by Michael E. Stone, sec. 2, 33–87. Assen: Van Gorcum, 1984.

Niditch, Susan. *Underdogs and Tricksters: A Prelude to Biblical Folklore.* San Francisco: Harper & Row, 1987.

Nikiprowetzky, Valentin. "Pseudépigraphes de l'ancien testament et manuscript de la mer morte." *Revue des Études Juives* 128 (1969): 5–40.

Nöldeke, Theodor. *Beiträge zur Geschichte des Alexanderromans.* Vienna, 1890.

Norelli, Enrico. *Ascension du prophète Isaïe.* Turnhout: Brepols, 1993.

North, J. Lionel. "Reactions in Early Christianity to Some References to the Hebrew Prophets in Matthew's Gospel." *New Testament Studies* 54, no. 2 (2008): 254–74.

Omidsala, M. "Jamsid." In *Encyclopedia Iranica*, section 2, Jamsid. www.iranicaonline.org/articles/jamsid-ii.

———. "Of the Usurper's Ears, the Demon's Toes, and the Ayatollah's Fingers." *Psychoanalytic Study of Society* 18 (1993): 105–18.

Oppenheimer, Aharon. "Contacts between Eretz Israel and Babylonia at the Turn of the Period of the *Tannaim* and the *Amoraim*." In *Between Rome and Babylon*, 417–32. Tübingen: Mohr/Siebeck, 2005.

Orlinsky, Harry. "The Septuagint and Its Hebrew Text." In *The Cambridge History of Judaism*, vol. 3, *The Early Roman Period*, edited by W. D. Davies and Louis Finkelstein, 534–62. Cambridge: Cambridge University Press, 1989.

Parpola, Simo. "Excursus: The Substitute King Ritual." In *Letters from Assyrian Scholars to the Kings Esarhaddon and Assurbanipal*, xxii–xxxiv. Kevelaer: Butzon & Bercker, 1970–83.

Pearson, B. A. "Jewish Haggadic Traditions in *The Testimony of Truth* from Nag Hammadi (CG IX,3)." In *Ex Orbe Religionum: Studia Geo Widengren oblata*, edited by J. Bergmann, K. Drynjeff, and H. Ringgren, 457–70. Leiden: Brill, 1972.

Pearson, Lionel. *The Lost Histories of Alexander the Great.* New York: American Philological Association, 1960.

Pédech, Paul. *Historiens compagnons d'Alexandre.* Paris: Belles Lettres, 1984.

Pesce, Mauro. "Presupposti per l'utilizzazione storica dell'*Ascensione di Isaia*." In *Isaia, il diletto e la Chiesa: Visione ed esegesi profetica cristiano-primitiva nell'Ascensione di Isaia*, edited by Mauro Pesce, 13–69. Brescia: Paideia, 1983.

Peterson, William L. *Tatian's Diatessaron: Its Creation, Dissemination, Significance, and History in Scholarship.* Leiden: Brill, 1993.

Pfister, Friedrich. *Kleine Schriften zum Alexanderroman.* Meisenheim am Glan: Hain, 1976.

Philonenko, M. *Pseudépigraphes de l'ancien Testament et Manuscrits de la Mer Morte*, vol. 1. Paris: Presses Universitaires de France, 1967.

Pines, Shlomo. "Wrath and Creatures of Wrath in Pahlavi, Jewish and New Testament Sources." In *Irano-Judaica: Studies Relating to Jewish Contacts with Persian Culture throughout the Ages*, edited by Shaul Shaked and Amnon Netzer, 76–82. Jerusalem: Ben-Zvi Institute, 1982.

Pingree, David. "Astrology and Astronomy in Iran" (ii. "Astronomy and Astrology in the Sasanian Period."). *Encyclopedia Iranica*, vol. 2, 858–70.

———. "Classical and Byzantine Astrology in Sassanian Persia." *Dumbarton Oaks Papers* 43 (1989): 227–39.

Piovanelli, Perluigi. "Bartholomew," "Bartholomew, Gospel [Questions] of," and "Bartholomew the Apostle, Book of the Resurrection of Christ by." In *The New Interpreter's Dictionary of the Bible*, vol. 1, edited by Katherin Doob Sakenfeld. Nashville, TN: Abingdon Press, 2006.

Porton, Gary G. "Isaiah and the Kings: The Rabbis on the Prophet Isaiah." In *Writing and Reading the Scroll of Isaiah*, vol. 2, edited by Craig C. Broyles and Craig A. Evans, 693–716. Leiden: Brill, 1997.

Preisendanz, Karl. "Salomo." In *Paulys Real-Encyclopädien der classischen Altertumswissenschaft*. Suppl. 8. (1956) col. 660–704.

Raschke, Manfred. "New Studies in Roman Commerce with the East." In *Aufstieg und Niedergang der römischen Welt* 2:19/2 (1978): 604–1361.

Rose, Els. *Ritual Meaning: The Apocryphal Acts and Liturgical Commemoration in the Early Medieval West, c. 500–1215*. Leiden: Brill, 2009.

Rosenthal, David. "Arakhim Nosafim le-Milon ha-Talmudi [3]: 'Arzanig' (Bavli, Tamid 32b)." *Tarbiz* 61 (1992): 219–25.

———."Arikhot Kedumot ba-Talmud ha-Bavli." In *Mehkerei Talmud*, vol. 1, edited by David Rosenthal and Yaakov Sussmann, 155–204. Jerusalem: Magnes Press, 1990.

Rosenthal, E. S. "La-Milon ha-Talmudi." *Tarbiz* 40 (1971): 178–200.

Rubenstein, Jeffrey L. *The Culture of the Babylonian Talmud*. Baltimore: Johns Hopkins University Press, 2003.

———. "Talmudic Astrology: *Bavli Šabbat* 156a–b." *Hebrew Union College Annual* 78 (2007): 109–48.

———. *Talmudic Stories: Narrative Art, Composition, and Culture*. Baltimore: Johns Hopkins University Press, 1999.

———. *Stories of the Babylonian Talmud*. Baltimore: Johns Hopkins University Press, 2010.

Russell, James R. "The *Ascensio Isaiae* and Iran." In *Irano-Judaica*, vol. 3, edited by Shaul Shaked and Amnon Netzer, 63–71. Jerusalem: Yad Izhak Ben-Zvi, 1994.

———. "God Is Good: On Tobit and Iran." *Iran and the Caucasus* 5 (2001). Reprinted in *Armenian and Iranian Studies*, 1131–33. Cambridge, MA: Harvard University Department of Near Eastern Languages and Literatures, 2004.

Sabato, Mordechai. *Ketav-Yad Temani le-Massekhet Sanhedrin (Bavli) u-Mekomo bi-Mesoret ha-Nusah*. Jerusalem: Yad Yizhak Ben-Zvi, 1998.

Sack, Ronald Herbert. *Images of Nebuchadnezzar: The Emergence of a Legend*. Selinsgrove, PA: Susquehanna University Press, 2004.

Saldarini, Anthony. "Pharisees." In *The Anchor Bible Dictionary*, vol. 5, edited by David Noel Freedman, 289–303. New York: Doubleday, 1992.

———. *Pharisees, Scribes and Sadducees in Palestinian Society*. Wilmington: Michael Glazier, 1988.

Särkiö, Pekka. "Salomo und die Dämonen." In *Verbum et Calamus: Semitic and Related Studies in Honour of the Sixtieth Birthday of Professor Tapani Harviainen*, edited by Hannu Juusola, 305–22. Helsinki: Finnish Oriental Society, 2004.

Sartre, Maurice. *The Middle East under Rome*. Translated by Catherine Porter and Elizabeth Rawlings. Cambridge, MA: Harvard University Press, 2005.

Sasson, Gilad. "Be-Ikvot ha-Masoret al Shlomo ha-Magikan be-Sifrut Hazal." *Jewish Studies Internet Journal* 6 (2007): 37–53.

———. "Melekh ve-Hedyot—Yahasam shel Hazal le-Shlomo ha-Melekh." PhD diss., Bar Ilan University, 1995.

Satran, David. *Biblical Prophets in Byzantine Palestine: Reassessing the Lives of the Prophets*. Leiden: Brill, 1995.

Schäfer, Peter. *Jesus in the Talmud*. Princeton: Princeton University Press, 2007.

———. *The Jewish Jesus: How Judaism and Christianity Shaped Each Other*. Princeton: Princeton University Press, 2012.

Schiffman, Lawrence H. "Pharisees and Sadducees in *Pesher Nahum*." In *Minhah le-Nahum: Biblical and Other Studies Presented to Nahum M. Sarna in Honour of His 70th Birthday*, 272–90. Sheffield: Sheffield Academic Press, 1993.

Schoeps, Hans J. "Die jüdischen Prophetenmorde." In *Aus frühchristlicher Zeit: Religionsgeschichte Untersuchungen*, 126–43. Tübingen: Mohr/Siebeck, 1950.

Scholter, David Milton. "Israel Murdered Its Prophets: The Origins and Development of the Tradition in the Old Testament and Judaism." Doctor of Theology diss., Harvard Divinity School, 1980.

Schremer, Adiel. Review of Kalmin, *The Sage in Jewish Society of Late Antiquity*. *Zion* 60, no. 2 (2000): 229–35.

Schürer, Emil. *The History of the Jewish People in the Age of Jesus Christ*. Vol. 3, pt. 1, revised and edited by Geza Vermes, Fergus Millar, and Martin Goodman. Edinburgh: T & T Clark, 1986.

Schützinger, Heinrich. "Die arabische Legende von Nebukadnezar und Johannes dem Täufer." *Der Islam* 40 (1965): 113–41.

Schwartz, Daniel. "Ha-Im Hayah Rabban Yohanan ben Zakkai Kohen?" *Sinai* 88, nos. 1/2 (1981): 37–39.

Schwartz, Joshua. "The *Encaenia* of the Church of the Holy Sepulchre, Temple of Solomon and the Jews." *Theologische Zeitschrift* 43, no. 3 (1987): 266–79.

Schwarz, Sarah. "Building a Book of Spells: The So-Called *Testament of Solomon* Reconsidered." PhD diss., University of Pennsylvania, 2005.

———. "Reconsidering the *Testament of Solomon*." *Journal for the Study of the Pseudepigrapha* 16, no. 3 (2007): 203–37.

Schwemer, A. M. *Studien zu den frühjüdischen Prophetenlegenden Vitae Prophetarum*. 2 vols. Tübingen: Mohr/Siebeck, 1995–96.

Secunda, Shai. *The Iranian Talmud: Reading the Bavli in Its Sasanian Context*. Philadelphia: University of Pennsylvania Press, 2013.

———. "Reading the Bavli in Iran." *Jewish Quarterly Review* 100, no. 2 (2010): 310–42.

Shaked, Shaul. *Dualism in Transformation: Varieties of Religion in Sasanian Iran*. London: School of Oriental and African Studies, 1994.

———. "First Man, First King: Notes on Semitic-Iranian Syncretism and Iranian Mythological Transformations." In *Gilgul: Essays on Transformation, Revolution and Permanence in the History of Religions,* edited by Shaul Shaked, David D. Shulman, and Gedaliahu Stroumsa, 238–45. Leiden: Brill, 1987.

———. "A Persian House of Study, a King's Secretary: Irano-Aramaic Notes." *Acta Orientalia Academiae Scientiarum Hungaricae* 48 (1995): 171–86.

———. "The Zoroastrian Demon of Wrath." In *Tradition and Translation: Zum Problem der interkulturellen übersetzbarkeit religiöser Phänomene,* edited by Christoph Elsas and Carsten Colpe, 285–91. Berlin: Walter de Gruyter, 1994.

Shinan, Avigdor. "Ivrit ve-Aramit be-Sifrut Beit-ha-Keneset." *Tura* 1 (1999): 224–32.

———. "The Late Midrashic, Paytanic, and Targumic Literature." In *The Cambridge History of Judaism,* vol. 4, *The Late Roman-Rabbinic Period,* edited by Steven T. Katz, 678–98. Cambridge: Cambridge University Press, 2006.

Skjaervo, Prods O. "DIV." In *Encyclopedia Iranica.* www.iranicaonline.org/articles/div.

———. "Jamsid-i." In *Encyclopedia Iranica.* www.iranicaonline.org/articles/jamsid-i.

Smelik, William F. "The Aramaic Dialect(s) of the Toldot Yeshu Fragments." *Aramaic Studies* 7 (2009): 39–73.

Sokoloff, Michael. "The Date and Provenance of the Aramaic *Toledot Yeshu* on the Basis of Aramaic Dialectology." In *Toledot Yeshu ("The Life Story of Jesus") Revisited,* edited by Peter Schäfer, Michael Meerson, and Yaakov Deutsch, 13–26. Tübingen: Mohr/Siebeck, 2011.

———. *A Dictionary of Jewish Babylonian Aramaic of the Talmudic and Geonic Periods.* Ramat-Gan, Israel: Bar-Ilan University Press, 2002.

———. *A Dictionary of Jewish Palestinian Aramaic of the Byzantine Period.* Ramat-Gan, Israel: Bar Ilan University Press, 1992.

———. *Kitei Bereshit Rabba min ha-Genizah.* Jerusalem: Ha-Akademi'ah ha-Le'umit ha-Yisre'elit le-Mada'im, 1982.

Steck, Odil Hannes. *Israel und das gewaltsame Geschick des Propheten: Untersuchungen zur Überlieferung des deuteronomistischen Geschichtsbildes im Alten Testament, Spätjudentum und Urchristentum.* Neukirchen-Vluyn: Neukirchener Verlag, 1957.

Steiner, Richard. "Semitic Names for Utensils in the Demotic Word-List from Tebtunis." *Journal of Near Eastern Studies* 59, no. 3 (2000): 191–94.

Stemberger, Günther. *Jewish Contemporaries of Jesus: Pharisees, Sadducees, Essenes.* Translated by Allan W. Mahnke. Minneapolis: Fortress Press, 1995.

Stoneman, Richard. *Alexander the Great: A Life in Legend.* New Haven: Yale University Press, 2008.

———. *The Greek Alexander Romance.* New York: Penguin, 1991.

———. "Jewish Traditions on Alexander the Great." *Studia Philonica Annual* 6 (1994): 37–53.

———. "Naked Philosophers: The Brahmans in the Alexander Historians and the Alexander Romance." *Journal of Hellenic Studies* 115 (1995): 99–114.

———. "Who Are the Brahmans? Indian Lore and Cynic Doctrine in Palladius' *De Bramanibus* and its Models." *Classical Quarterly* 44, no. 2 (1994): 500–10.
Swartz, Michael D. "Bubbling Blood and Rolling Bones: Agency and Teleology in Rabbinic Myth." In *Antike Mythen: Medien Transformationen und Konstruktionen,* edited by Ueli Dill and Christine Walde, 224–41. Berlin: Walter de Gruyter, 2009.
———. *The Signifying Creator: Non-Textual Sources of Meaning in Ancient Judaism.* New York: New York University Press, 2012.
Szalc, Aleksandra. "Alexander's Dialogue with Indian Philosophers: Riddle in Greek and Indian Traditions." *Eos* 98, fasc. 1 (2011): 7–25.
Thompson, Stith. *Motif-Index of Folk Literature.* Bloomington: Indiana University Press, 1966.
Thornhill, R. "The Paraleipomena of Jeremiah." In *The Apocryphal Old Testament.* Oxford: Clarendon, 1984.
Torijano, Pablo A. *Solomon the Esoteric King: From King to Magus, Development of a Tradition.* Leiden: Brill, 2002.
Tov, Emanuel. *The Greek and Hebrew Bible: Collected Essays on the Septuagint.* Leiden: Brill, 1999.
———. "The Rabbinic Tradition concerning the 'Alterations' Inserted into the Greek Pentateuch and Their Relation to the Original Text of the LXX." *Journal for the Study of Judaism* 15 (1984): 65–89.
———. "Review of G. Veltri, *Eine Tora für den König Talmai*." *Scripta Classica Israelica* 14 (1995): 178–83.
———. "The Septuagint." In *Mikra: Text, Translation, Reading and Interpretation of the Hebrew Bible in Ancient Judaism and Early Christianity,* Compendia Rerum Iudaicarum ad Novum Testamentum, vol. 1, sec. 2, edited by Martin J. Mulder, 161–88. Assen: Van Gorcum, 1990.
Urbach, Ephraim. *The Sages: Their Concepts and Beliefs.* Translated by Israel Abrahams. Jerusalem: Magnes Press, 1979.
van Bekkum, W. Jac. "Alexander the Great in Medieval Hebrew Literature." *Journal of the Warburg and Courtland Institutes* 49 (1986): 218–26.
van Bladel, Kevin. "The Sources of the Early Arabic Narratives of Alexander." In *Memory as History: The Legacy of Alexander in Asia,* edited by Himanshu Prabha Ray and Daniel T. Potts, 61–64. New Delhi: Aryan Books International, 2007.
van Esbroeck, Michael. "La naissance du culte Barthélémy en Arménie." *Revue des études Arméniennes* 17 (1983): 171–85.
———. "The Rise of Saint Bartholomew's Cult in Armenia from the Seventh to the Thirteenth Centuries." In *Medieval Armenian Culture,* edited by Thomas Samuelian and Michael Stone, 161–78. Chico, CA: Scholars Press, 1984.
van Henten, Jan Willem. "The Story of Susanna as a Pre-Rabbinic Midrash to Dan. 1:1–2." In *Variety of Forms: Dutch Studies in Midrash,* edited by A. Kuyt, E. G. L. Schriver, and N. A. van Uchelen, 1–14. Amsterdam: Publications of the Juda Palache Institute, 1990.

van Henten, Jan Willem, and Friedrich Avemarie. *Martyrdom and Noble Death.* London: Routledge, 2002.

van Thiel, Helmut. "Alexanders Gespräch mit den Gymnosophisten." *Hermes* 100 (1972): 343–58.

Veltri, Giuseppe. *Eine Tora für den König Talmai: Untersuchungen zum Übersetzungsverständnis in der jüdisch-hellenistischen und rabbinischen Literatur.* Tübingen: Mohr/Siebeck, 1994.

———. *Libraries, Translations, and "Canonic" Texts: The Septuagint, Aquila and Ben Sira in the Jewish and Christian Tradition.* Leiden: Brill, 2006.

Vidas, Moulie. "Greek Wisdom in Babylonia." In *Envisioning Judaism: Studies in Honor of Peter Schäfer on the Occasion of his Seventieth Birthday,* edited by Ra'anan Boustan, Klaus Herrmann, Reimund Leicht, Annette Yoshiko Reed, and Giuseppe Veltri, 287–305. Tübingen: Mohr/Siebeck, 2013.

Visotzky, Burton. *Golden Bells and Pomegranates: Studies in Midrash Leviticus Rabbah.* Tübingen: Mohr/Siebeck, 2002.

———. "Mary Maudlin among the Rabbis." In *Fathers of the World: Essays in Rabbinic and Patristic Thought,* 85–92. Tübingen: Mohr/Siebeck, 1995.

von Stuckrad, Kocku. *Das Ringen um die Astrologie: Jüdische und Christliche Beiträge zum Antiken Zeitverständnis.* Berlin: Walter de Gruyter, 2000.

Wallach, Luitpold. "Alexander the Great and the Indian Gymnosophists in Hebrew Tradition." *Proceedings of the American Academy of Jewish Research* 11 (1941): 47–83.

Ward-Perkins, J. B. "The Roman West and the Parthian East." *Proceedings of the British Academy* 51 (1985): 174–99.

Wasserstein, Abraham. "On Donkeys, Wine and the Uses of Textual Criticism: Septuagintal Variants in Jewish Palestine." In *Ha-Yehudim ba-Olam ha-Hellenisti ve-ha-Romi: Mehkarim le-Zikhro shel Menahem Stern,* edited by Aharon Oppenheimer, Yeshayahu M. Gafni, and Daniel Schwartz, 119–41. Jerusalem: Zalman Shazar Center for Jewish History, 1996.

Wasserstein, Abraham, and David J. Wasserstein. *The Legend of the Septuagint: From Classical Antiquity to Today.* Cambridge: Cambridge University Press, 2006.

Wheeler, Brannon N. *Prophets in the Quran: An Introduction to the Quran and Muslim Exegesis.* New York: Continuum, 2002.

Wiesehöfer, Josef. *Ancient Persia from 550 BC to 65 AD.* Translated by Azizeh Azodi. London: Tauris, 1996.

Wilcken, Ulrich. "Alexander der Grosse und die indischen Gymnosophisten." *Sitzungsberichte der deutschen Akademie der Wissenschaften zu Berlin* (1923): 150–83.

Yahalom, Joseph. "Angels Do Not Understand Aramaic: On the Literary Use of Palestinian Aramaic in Late Antiquity." *Journal of Jewish Studies* 47 (1996): 33–44.

Yasif, Eli. *The Hebrew Folktale: History, Genre, Meaning.* Bloomington: Indiana University Press, 1999.

———. "Iyunim be-Sippurei Kishuf be-Aggadat Hazal." In *Sefer Yitshak Bakon*, edited by Aharon Komem. Beer-Sheva: Ben Gurion University, 1992.

———. *Sipur ha-Am ha-Ivri: Toldotav, Sugav u-Mashma'uto*. Jerusalem: Mosad Bialik, 1994.

Yisraeli-Taran, Anat. *Aggadot ha-Hurban: Mesorot ha-Hurban be-Sifrut ha-Talmudit*. Tel Aviv: Ha-Kibuz ha-Me'uhad, 1997.

Yuval, Israel. *Two Nations in Your Womb: Perceptions of Jews and Christians in Late Antiquity and the Early Middle Ages*. Translated by Barbara Harshav and Jonathan Chipman. Berkeley: University of California Press, 2006.

Zellentin, Holger. *Rabbinic Parodies of Jewish and Christian Literature*. Tübingen: Mohr/Siebeck, 2011.

Zender, Matthias. "Bartholomaeus." In *Lexicon des Mittelalters*, vol. 1, col. 1491. Munich: Artemis, 1977.

GENERAL INDEX

Abaye, 165, 170
R. Aha, 70
R. Akiba, 78, 181–83
Abel, murder of, 142–43
Alexander the Great: and the Amazons, 226–28; anger of, 212, 217, 220; in the Babylonian Talmud, 200–205, 207–15, 217–35; desire of, to go beyond the limits of human knowledge, 212–13, 232; excessive ambition of, 203–4, 210, 212, 214–18, 220–21, 225, 230–34; inability of, to control his passions, 214–17, 225; and the Elders of the Negev, 201–2, 208–15, 217–22, 224–25, 233–35; Greek biographies of, 201–7, 212–31; and the Indian Philosophers, 201–2, 204, 216–17, 222–25
Alexander Romance: origins of, 200–201, 205–7; relationship of, to the Alexander compilation in Bavli Tamid, 201–4, 212–13, 224–25, 227–231, 234–35; textual history of, 206n27, 207
Alexandria, 5, 84, 90, 200, 209; library of, 87–88
R. Ami, 191–92, 194
anchorites. *See* Asceticism; desert fathers; holy men
angel of death, 195–96
angels, 24, 57, 65, 71, 115; and demons, 102–4, 107–11
Aramaic: dialects of, 9, 13, 234; and Hebrew, in rabbinic literature, 15–20, 23–24, 26–28, 64–66, 71–72, 76, 130–32, 137–40, 147–51, 162, 207, 213, 220, 234–35; as a medium for cultural transfer between Babylonia and the Roman East, 12–13, 74–75. *See also* literature, Palestinian rabbinic, language switching in; Talmud, Babylonian, language switching in
Armenia. *See* Christianity, Armenian
Arrian, 203–4, 214–16
Ascension of Isaiah, 30–38, 41–42, 44–45, 48–52; "the Beloved" (Jesus) in, 32, 35, 41
asceticism, 97, 218, 232
Rav Ashi, 80–81
Ashmedai (Asmodeus), 96–129, 204–5; anger of, 111–12, 115, 118, 121; portrayal of, as a holy man, in the Babylonian Talmud, 97, 110, 116–20, 210n40; riddles of, 100, 102, 109–10, 117, 121
astrology: Babylonian rabbinic attitudes toward, 175–99; Christian attitudes toward, 187–88; as a means of determining God's will, 176, 189–92; prohibition of, in some rabbinic traditions, 185–86. *See also* Chaldaeans; *mazal (mazla)*
attributions: importance of, in rabbinic culture, 60–62, 67, 70, 210; in rabbinic literature, xi–xii, 11–12, 34n15
Avlat, 177–81

Baraita, 90–91
Bartholomew, the Apostle, 72–77
Barton, Tamsyn, 198

Baynham, Elizabeth, 205–6
Beit Hillel, 211–12
Beit Shammai, 211–12
Beliar. *See* Satan
Ben Thalamion, 57–58, 60, 62–64, 66–69, 72–73, 75–78
Benaiah ben Jehoiada, 99–102, 109–10, 112, 117, 119, 121
Bernheimer, Richard, 50
Rav Bibi bar Abaye, 195–96
blood, 68; innocent, avenging of, 141–45, 154, 161; of Isaiah, 42–43; motif of, as evidence of a unified rabbinic composition, 54, 57–58, 63, 66, 68. *See also* Abel, murder of; Zechariah (priest), murder of
bowls, magic, 14–15, 96, 122–23, 125, 128–29
Boyarin, Daniel, 8–10, 38n25

Celsus, 4–5
Chaldaeans (astrologers), 188–92
Christianity: Armenian, 1–2, 8–9, 14, 53, 74–77, 88–89, 207; Ethiopic, and rabbinic literature, 130–31, 142–46, 162–63; Georgian, 88–90; Mesopotamian, and Babylonian rabbis, 3–6, 8–10, 13–14, 29, 52–53, 80, 83–84, 91–94, 236, 238; Mesopotamian, and Eastern Roman Christianity, 3–6, 80. *See also* Rabbis, Babylonian, connections with Christians in the Roman East; Rabbis, Babylonian, connections with Mesopotamian Christians
Church Fathers, 30, 33, 36, 42, 51–52
circumcision, 55–56, 58–59, 66
code switching. *See* literature, Palestinian rabbinic, language switching in; Talmud, Babylonian, language switching in
conversion, of enemies of the Jews, 149, 151, 157–61
Cowley, Roger, 143, 146
curses, of rabbinic sages, 60, 63–64, 66–67, 73
Cynicism, 217–18, 232

Dandamis, 204, 216–17
Darius the Great, 105, 227–28
David, King, 145–46

decrees (of persecution). *See* Roman Empire, decrees of, against Jewish ritual practice
demons, 95–125; power of, 99–104, 107–11, 127–28; sinfulness of, 115–16, 119–20; subjugation of, by Solomon, 99–103, 106–15, 119–22, 124–26, 204–5; as sympathetic figures, 97, 116–21. *See also* angels; Ashmedai (Asmodeus); Ben Thalamion; Satan
desert fathers, 118–19. *See also* asceticism; holy men
Diatessaron, 8–9, 77, 155

Eden, Garden of, 228–31
R. Elazar bar R. Yosi, 55–70, 72–73
Elders of the Negev, 201–2, 208–15, 217–22, 224–25, 233–35; identity of, 209–12, 215, 218–21
Eliezer (biblical), 70
Elijah the Prophet, 60
Emden, Yaakov, 94
Emperor, Roman, 118; in the Babylonian Talmud, 58, 60–66, 68, 73, 76
Enoch, 142
Epiphanius, 88–90, 134n13
Epstein, Y. N., 234
Ethiopia. *See* Christianity, Ethiopic
Exilarchs, 27–28

folklore, xiv, 3, 11, 76, 96, 105–6, 117, 203, 236
Fraenkel, Yonah, 18–20, 68
Friedman, Avi, 225
Friedman, Shamma, 16n35, 65

Georgia. *See* Christianity, Georgian
Gnoli, Gherardo, 46
God: compassion of, for the Jewish people, 130, 135, 137–41, 159–62; and divine punishment, 18–20, 29, 138–41, 145, 156–58; and divine revelation, 30, 86; intervention of, 82, 85–86, 88–89, 93, 137–40, 143–45; name of, 35, 38, 107, 121–22; special relationship of, with the Jewish people, 30, 41–42, 130, 135, 140–41. *See also* astrology, as a means of determining God's will

Greek (language), 12–13; translation of the Torah into, 81, 83, 85, 87–88, 91–94. *See also* Hebrew, and the translation of the Septuagint; Septuagint, legend of the composition of

Gymnosophists. *See* Alexander, and the Indian Philosophers

Hagar, 57n16, 66, 70–71, 77–78
Hasmoneans. *See* kings, Hasmonean; Talmud, Babylonian, and Hasmonean kings; Yannai, King
Hebrew: and Aramaic, in rabbinic literature, 15–20, 23–24, 26–28, 64–66, 71–72, 76, 131–35, 137–41, 147–51, 161–62, 207, 213, 234–35; and cultural transfer between Mesopotamia and the Roman East, 12–13; and the translation of the Septuagint, 83, 85, 88, 90–91; and the writing of Torah scrolls, 80–81. *See also* Aramaic, and Hebrew, in rabbinic literature; literature, Palestinian rabbinic, language switching in; Septuagint, legend of the composition of; Talmud, Babylonian, language switching in
Heinemann, Joseph, 132
Hekhalot literature, 22–23
Herod, 24–26, 142–43, 156–58
Rav Hisda, 191–92
R. Hiyya, 71
Hoffman, David Zvi, 187
holy men: as antagonists of conventional religious and political figures, 118–19, 122–23; "rabbinization" of, in the Babylonian Talmud, 97, 116–19, 122–23. *See also* Ashmedai, portrayal of, as a holy man, in the Babylonian Talmud
Rav Huna, 191

Ibn Daud, Abraham, 93–94
Ibn al-Tayyib, Abū al Faraj 'Abd Allāh, 143–44
Ilan, Tal, 201, 227, 230
Isaiah: criticism of, in the Babylonian Talmud, 37–38, 40–44; evaluation of, in comparison to Moses, 29, 31, 34–38, 40–44, 46; execution of, in ancient Christian literature, 29–33, 35–42, 44–45, 48–52; execution of, in the *Ascension of Isaiah,* 30–33, 35–38, 41–42, 44–45, 48–52; execution of, in the Babylonian Talmud, 29–30, 33–48, 51–52; execution of, motif of speech and, 38–40; execution of, in the Palestinian Talmud, 42–44, 48, 51–52; execution of, parallels to, in Iranian literature, 45–48, 51–52; as a rabbi, in Babylonian rabbinic literature, 38, 40–41; as a stand-in for Jesus, 29–30
Israel, people of: implication of, in the murder of Isaiah, 41–42, 47; implication of, in the murder of Zechariah, 133–40, 148–49, 156–57, 161–62; sinfulness of, 133–34, 138–40, 162; supersession of, in Christian thought, 30, 130–31, 140. *See also* God, special relationship of, with the Jewish people

Jamshed, King, 46–47, 106. *See also* Yima
Jannaeus, Alexander. *See* Yannai, King
Jerome, 30
Jesus, 118, 156, 188; in the *Ascension of Isaiah,* 32, 35, 41; in the Babylonian Talmud, 4–5, 20, 29–30, 123–25, 210n40
Joash, King, 135–36, 155
John the Baptist, 131–32, 143–44, 153, 155–60
Johnston, Sarah Iles, 107–8
Josephus: appearance of traditions from, in fourth-century Babylonia, 173–74; parallels with the Babylonian Talmud, 24–26, 86, 88, 153–54, 164, 168–69, 173–74; and the Pharisees, 164, 168–69, 173–74
Justin, 51

Kahana, Menahem, 24
Kavad I, 6
Khusrau I, 6
Khusrau II, 6
kings: Davidic, 27–28; Hasmonean, 24–28. *See also* David, King; Herod; Solomon, King; Yannai, King
Kushelevsky, Rella, 104–5

language switching. *See* Aramaic; Hebrew; literature, Palestinian rabbinic, language switching in; Talmud, Babylonian, language switching in

literature, Palestinian rabbinic, ix–x; language switching in, 137–40, 150–51, 162; receptivity of, to nonrabbinic material, 21–22, 52, 59, 83, 90–91, 131, 142–46, 162. *See also* Talmud, Babylonian, Palestinian rabbinic traditions in

magicians, 97, 107, 122–25; Jesus as, 4–5, 124–25; Solomon as, 97, 112, 124–25. *See also* bowls, magic
mamzer (child born of a forbidden sexual union), 34
Manasseh, 29, 31–38, 41–44, 46, 49
Mandel, Pinhas, 132–33
martyrdom, 38–40, 50, 73, 75
R. Matya ben Heresh, 54–55, 61–62, 67, 70
mazal (*mazla*): of animals and plants, 196–97; definition of, 176, 193–96; in Palestinian rabbinic literature, 197–99; and the rabbinic expression "Israel has no *mazal*," 176–89, 199; of rabbis, 194; transformation of the meaning of, in fourth-century Babylonia, 192–99
Megillat Ta'anit, 162
menstruant women, prohibition of intercourse with, 55–56, 58–59, 66, 103, 119
Millar, Fergus, 13
miracles: rabbis and, 56–57, 60, 62–64, 73, 77–78; translation of the Septuagint as, 88–89, 92–93
mitzvot, 165–66, 170–71; ability of, to neutralize power of astrology, 178–84, 191, 199
monasticism, 4n3. *See also* asceticism; holy men
Moscovitz, Leib, 186
Moses, 29–31, 34–38, 40–44, 46, 78; as lawgiver, 81, 83; as a rabbi, in Babylonian rabbinic literature, 37, 40, 81

Naeh, Shlomo, 9
Nag Hammadi library, 113–14
Rav Nahman bar Yizhak, 165–67, 182–83, 187

nahotei (rabbis who traveled between Palestine and Babylonia), 6n8
Nahum Ish Gamzu, 60–61
Nebuzaradan, 134–35, 137–41, 143, 147–51, 156–61; conversion of, 149, 151, 157–61
New Testament, 118, 130; and the Babylonian Talmud, 4–5, 8–9, 53, 75–77, 158; Pharisees in, 164, 166–67, 170–72
niddah (laws of menstrual purity). *See* menstruant women, prohibition of intercourse with
Nisibis, School of, 4n3

Origen, 30, 36, 51
Ornias, 107–8

Rav Papa, 191
persecution. *See* Roman Empire, decrees of, against Jewish ritual practices
Persian Empire: invasions of Roman territory in the third- through sixth-centuries, 5–6, 237–38; resettlement of Eastern Roman populations in Mesopotamia, 5–6, 238
Pharisees: in the Babylonian Talmud, 164–70, 172–74; "blows of," 170–7; in Christian sources, 164, 166–67, 170–73; criticism of, for hypocrisy, 166–67, 169–72, 174; in Josephus, 164, 168–69, 173–74; reasons of, for performing mitzvot, 165–66, 170–71; as sages or protorabbis, 168–69, 172–74; in the Yerushalmi, 166, 170–74
Philo, 84–88
philosophy, Greco-Roman. *See* Cynicism; Stoicism
Plutarch, 201–2
polemic, 3, 10, 29, 77, 91–92, 123–24, 132
pothos. *See* Alexander, excessive ambition of
priests, rabbinic criticism of, 133
prophets, biblical, 40–44, 185; in Christian theology, 29–30, 91; condemnation of the Israelites by, 37, 41, 46, 130, 134, 148, 156–57; intercession of, on behalf of Israel, 139–40, 162. *See also* Isaiah; Zechariah (priest), as a prophet
Pseudo-Abdias, 73–75
Ptolemy, King, 81–83, 86–88, 90, 92–94

Rabbi (Yehudah Hanasi), 170–71, 219
rabbis: conflict among, 66–69, 77; hierarchical relationships among, 61–62, 66–67, 78, 221, 234; relationships with Romans, 67–69, 77, 79, 220
rabbis, Babylonian: and anti-Christian polemic, 10, 19–20, 77, 79, 123–24; attitudes of, toward biblical law, 78; attitudes of, toward kingship and government, 219–20; attitudes of, toward nonrabbis, x–xi, 78, 97, 116–19, 122–25, 181, 209–12; awareness of Christianity, 10, 19–20, 77, 91–92; connections with East, 3–7, 9–10, 13–14, 28–29, 53, 75, 80, 107–14, 122, 126, 131, 147, 164, 167, 169, 172, 175–77, 185–88, 192, 198–200, 205, 231, 236–38; connections with Mesopotamian Christians, 3–6, 8–10, 14, 29, 52–53, 80, 91–94; emphasis of their own importance, 106, 151; encounters of, with non-Jews, 58, 60–66, 68, 73, 76, 177–80; the fourth century as a transitional period among, xiii, 5–7, 12, 28–29, 52, 94, 167, 169, 173–76, 181, 192, 236; and the New Testament, 4–5, 8–9, 53, 75–77, 158; and Palestinian rabbis, 21–22; Persian context of, 20–21, 104–6, 122, 237–39; position of, within Babylonian Jewish community, ix, 96–97, 116–25; reading of biblical figures as rabbis, 40, 96–97, 116, 120–21; self-perception of, in relation to biblical figures, 78–79; and the value of Torah study, ix, 181, 183, 209–11, 218, 234
Rav, 18–19, 165, 183–84; attribution of statements to, in the Babylonian Talmud, 34n15, 183–84
Rava, 34, 36–37, 48, 78, 165, 170; death of, 194; problems with attribution of statements to, in the Babylonian Talmud, 34n15
Ravina, 193–94
Resh Lakish, 218
R. Reuven ben Istrobli, 55–56, 59–60, 63–64, 66–68
revelation. *See* God, and divine revelation
riddle contests, 201–3, 211, 222–23
Roman Empire: cultural exchange with Persia, 5–7; decrees of, against Jewish ritual practice, 55–61, 66; destruction of the Second Temple, 49, 113; portrayal of, in the Babylonian Talmud, 67–69. *See also* Emperor, Roman
Rosenthal, David, 234
Russell, James, 45

Sabbath, observance of, 55, 58–59
sacrifice: 134, 147–48, 156; pagan, 39, 74
Sanhedrin, 103, 148, 151, 159
Sasanians. *See* Persian Empire
Sasson, Gilad, 124–25
Satan, 31–32, 35, 37, 47–49, 51, 221–22, 233
Satran, David, 154
Saul, King, 145–46, 160–61, 190
Schäfer, Peter, 8–10, 59
Schwarz, Sarah, 95, 126
Sennacherib, 190–91
Septuagint, legend of the composition of: in Babylonian rabbinic sources, 81–94; in Christian sources of the Roman East, 83–84, 86–88, 90–91, 94; in Hellenistic Jewish sources, 84–87, 92–94; in Mesopotamian Christian sources, 88–92, 94. *See also* Hebrew, and the translation of the Septuagint
Shahdost of Tirhan, 89–90
Shahnameh, 46–47, 106
Shapur I, 5–6; transfer of populations from the Roman East, 5–6
Shapur II, 6
Shemira (Shamir), 98, 101, 107, 112–13, 115, 120–21
Shimon ben Shetach, 23–24, 26–27
R. Shimon ben Yohai, 54–73, 78
Shmuel (amora), x, 177–83; astrological expertise of, 180
R. Simon, 197
Solomon, King, 95–109, 111–16, 119–28; criticism of, in the Babylonian Talmud, 96–97, 115–16, 119–25, 204–5; ring of, 99, 103, 107, 112, 121–22; use of demons to build the Temple, 98–102, 106–8, 112–16, 120–21, 126
Stemberger, Günther, 168
Stoicism, 214–15, 218–19, 232
Stoneman, Richard, 201, 206, 231
Suicide, 218–19

GENERAL INDEX · 273

Syriac: and Ethiopic Christian literature, 143, 145–46, 161–62; as a medium for cultural transfer between Babylonia and the Roman East, 4, 8–10, 13, 84, 89–90, 94, 130–31, 167, 187, 236; parallels between the Babylonian Talmud and, 29, 38, 77, 80, 88, 114, 130–31, 187, 228, 235

Tabarī, 47–48, 51, 155–60, 163
Talmud, Babylonian: abstraction as a sign of lateness in, 186; anonymous portions of, xi, 37, 41, 80–82, 167–70, 176–87, 194–97, 231–32; anthological nature of, 15–17; appropriation of Eastern Roman culture, 3–7, 9, 13–14, 20–21, 48, 51–52, 75, 80, 83–84, 95–96, 107–14, 122, 126, 131, 147, 164, 167, 169, 172, 175–76, 184–85, 187–88, 192–93, 197–205, 218–19, 231, 236–37; and Arabic literature, 47–48, 130–31, 143–45, 155–60, 163; attitudes of, toward earthly striving, 204–5, 209–10, 212–14, 218, 220–21, 225–34; composite nature of longer narratives in, 53–54, 59–66, 68–69; cultural context of, ix, 2–3, 20–22; incorporation of nonrabbinic material, 3, 5, 11, 14, 20–22, 28, 35–42, 48, 51–52, 75–77, 80, 83–91, 96, 104–115, 130–31, 145, 162, 164, 173–74, 197–98, 200–205, 234, 236–37; language switching in, 15–20, 23–24, 28, 53, 64–66, 71–72, 76, 130–31, 147–51, 162, 213, 220, 234–35, 238; "narrativization" of nonnarrative material, 59, 71; overemphasis of the Persian cultural context of, 20–21, 104–6, 122, 237–39; Palestinian rabbinic traditions in, xii–xiii, 21–22, 27–28, 42–44, 51, 59, 70–71, 90–91, 96, 131, 147–51, 180–87, 197–98, 237; redaction of, xii, 12, 15–17, 19–20, 28, 53–54, 59–66, 68–69, 89, 96, 106, 150, 163, 169; relationship of, to Armenian culture, 8–9, 14, 53, 74–77; relationship of, to Christian Mesopotamian culture, 3–6, 8–10, 13–14, 29, 52, 80, 83–84, 89–91, 236; relationships between parents and children in, 66–68, 71
Talmud, Palestinian. *See* literature, Palestinian rabbinic
Temple: attitudes toward, in the Babylonian Talmud, 115–16; First, destruction of, 133–35, 136, 147, 153–54; Second, destruction of, 18–20, 111, 113, 153–54
Tertullian, 51
Testament of Solomon, 13, 95–96, 105, 107–13; composition of, 125–26, 128
Titus, 142–44
Torah scrolls, 80–81
Torah study. *See* Rabbis, Babylonian, and the value of Torah study
Translation, 4, 13, 81–93. *See also* Septuagint, legend of the composition of
trickster, in rabbinic literature, 38

Van Esbroeck, Michael, 74–75
Van Thiel, Helmut, 224
Veltri, Giuseppe, 83–84nn11–13, 89, 92

Wallach, Luitpold, 201–2

Yannai, King, 23–24, 26–27; and the Pharisees, 166–69
R. Yehudah, 81
Yima, 45–48. *See also* Jamshed, King
R. Yohanan, 185–86
Rav Yosef, 195
R. Yosi, 56–57, 60–61, 65–67
R. Yosi b'R. Hanina, 71
Yuval, Israel, 10

Zechariah (the priest); identification of, 135–37, 141, 152–55, 158; murder of, 131–55, 158–63; name of, 136; as a prophet, 134–35, 139–40, 148, 156–57
Zoroastrianism, 21, 45–47, 106, 175, 199
Zosimus of Panoplis, 114–15

INDEX OF PRIMARY SOURCES

HEBREW BIBLE

Genesis

1:1, 82, 211
1:2–3, 212
1:26, 82
2:2, 82
5:2, 82
15:3, 183
15:4, 183
15:5, 183
18:12, 82
34:1–24, 165
49:6, 82

Exodus

4:20, 82
12:40, 82
21:28, 196
21:29, 23
21:35, 196
23:26, 34
24:5, 82
24:11, 82
33:20, 31, 34, 36

Leviticus

11:6, 82
11:29, 55, 57, 62, 70
17:13, 133–34

Numbers

12:8, 43–44
16:15, 82
19:14, 218
24:8, 102

Deuteronomy

4:7, 34–35
4:19, 82
4:31, 135, 137–38
14:7, 82
17:3, 82
18:14, 186
19:17, 24, 26
21:23, 160n98

Judges

13:22, 71

1 Samuel

22:9–23, 190

2 Samuel

21:1–14, 145, 160–61

1 Kings

6:7, 98, 121

2 Kings

19:35, 191
20:6, 34
21:16, 43–44

Isaiah

6:1, 31, 34–36, 42
6:5, 35, 37–38
10:32, 190
41:2, 184
55:6, 34–35
65:5, 167

Jeremiah

10:2, 185
17:1, 112–13

Ezekiel

3:9, 112–13
24:7–8, 134

Hosea

4:11, 99

Amos

1:3, 50

Micah

2:2, 17–19

Zechariah

1:1, 158
7:11–12, 112–13

Psalms

103:11–12, 208
104:15, 99
118:20, 229–30
129:1–2, 94

Proverbs

10:2, 178, 182
11:4, 178, 182
13:23, 195–96
20:1, 99
25:15, 100
27:20, 230

Job

3:3, 196
3:9, 196
16:18, 141
38:31, 197
38:32, 197
38:33, 197

Song of Songs

3:7–8, 104, 129

Ecclesiastes

1:3, 103
1:12, 103
2:8, 98

Daniel

10:7, 193

2 Chronicles

24:17–22, 135–36
24:23–25, 136
33:11, 31
33:13, 42

APOCRYPHA AND PSEUDEPIGRAPHA

1 Enoch

22:6–7, 142

Ascension of Isaiah

1:7–10, 31
3:6–10, 31, 36–37
5:1–2, 32
5:6–7, 32
5:11, 32
5:13–16, 32, 37
11:41, 32

Lives of the Prophets

23:1, 154

Obsequies of the Holy Virgin

pp. 42–43 (ed. Wright), 127–28

Paraleipomena of Jeremiah

9:19–21, 33n13

Protevangelium of James

23–24, 153–54

Testament of Solomon

2:9–3:1, 129
5:1–5, 111

10:4–7, 112
15:7–12, 111–12
20:1–17, 108–10, 127–28

NEW TESTAMENT

Matthew

10:1, 75
10:3, 73n49
10:5–8, 75
23:4, 172
23:35, 142, 152–54

Mark

3:15, 75n58
3:18, 73n49
6:7, 75n58

Luke

6:14, 73n49
9:1, 75n58
11:50–51, 153–54
18:10–12, 172

John

1:43–51, 73

TEXTS FROM THE NAG HAMMADI LIBRARY

Testimony of Truth

9:3, 113–14, 116

GEORGIAN TEXTS

Epiphanius (Georgian translation)

On Weights and Measures, 88–90

ETHIOPIC TEXTS

Wängel Qəddus

p. 163, 142–46, 161

GREEK AND LATIN AUTHORS

Alexander Romance

I.38, 227–28
II.39–41, 212–13, 225–26, 228–29
III.6, 215–16
III.25, 227
III.40–41, 228

Apuleius

Metamorphosis
11.15, 188n46
11.25.2, 188n46

Arrian

Anabasis
1.2, 222
1.7.7–11, 203n17
1.8.1–2, 203n17
1.8.8, 203n17
4.7.5, 215
4.9.1, 215
6.12.1–3, 204
6.13.4, 203–4, 215
7.1.4–2.1, 203–4
7.1.5–2.4, 216–17
7.2.1, 204
7.2.2–4, 204
7.3.4, 203–4
7.19.6, 204n19
7.28.1–2, 214

Diodorus

Bibliotheca historica
17.9.4, 203n17

Diogenes Laertius

Lives of Eminent Philosophers
7.130, 218–19

Firmicus Maternus

Matheseos
2.30.5, 188

Pliny the Elder

Natural History
2.5.23, 198

Plutarch

Alexander
3, 204n19
11.4, 203n17
64, 201–2

Seneca

Epistula Morales
104.21, 219

Strabo

Geography
15.1.68 (718), 204n20
16.1.11 (741), 203, 204n19

Suetonius

Caligula
27:3, 50

JEWISH AUTHORS IN GREEK AND LATIN

Josephus

Antiquities
11.297–301, 136n22

13.398–404, 168–69
14.168–177, 25–28

Jewish War
1.204–212, 25–26
4.5.4, 153–54

Philo

De Vita Mosis
2.36–40, 84–87, 92

EARLY CHRISTIAN WORKS

Didymus

Commentarius in Psalmos
34.19, 36n23

Epiphanius

Panarion
26.12.1–4, 134n13

Eusebius

Ecclesiastical History
2.23.11–18, 136n22
5.8.11–15, 87n24

Irenaeus

Against Heretics
3.21.2–3, 86–87, 92

Itinerarium Burdigalense
589.7–592.7 (ed. Geyer and Cuntz, pp. 14–16), 154

Jerome

Commentarii in Isaiam
1.1.10, 36n23

Justin

Dialogue with Trypho
120.5, 33n13

Origen

Homiliae in Isaiam
1.5, 36

Palladius

On the Races of India and the Brahmans
20–31, 217, 222

Pseudo-Justin

Cohortatio ad Graecos
14 (ed. Marcovich, pp. 4–6), 84, 87–90

Sozomen

Ecclesiastical History
9.17, 154–55

Tatian

Oratio ad Graecos
8:1, 188

Tertullian

De patientia
14.1, 33n13

Theodotus

Excerpta ex Theodoto
74 (ed. Casey, p. 86), 188
78 (ed. Casey, p. 88), 188

SYRIAC TEXTS

Acts of Sharbil

vol. 8, p. 684 (ANF), 39–40, 48, 51

Bardaisan

Book of the Laws of Countries
pp. 58–59 (ed. Drijvers), 187–88

Cave of Treasures

47:12–17, 155

Shahdost of Tirhan

pp. 56–57 (ed. Abramowski and Goodman, text volume), 89–90

Zosimus of Panoplis (Syriac translation)

"Mystery of the Nine Letters of Solomon"
vol. 2, pp. 264–65 (ed. Bertholet), 114

RABBINIC LITERATURE

Mishnah

Sotah
3:4, 170

Sanhedrin
2:2, 24, 27–28
10:2, 37

Avot
1:10, 220
3:1, 210
4:1, 210

Tosefta

Yoma
1:12, 133

Mekhilta

Bo, Pisha, Parashah 14 (ed. Lauterbach, pp. 111–12; ed. Horowitz and Rabin, pp. 50–51), 83n11

Sifrei Zuta Devarim

pp. 282–86 (ed. Kahana), 24, 26–27

Avot de-R. Natan

version B, p. 71 (ed. Schechter), 218

Bereshit Rabbah

10:4 (ed. Theodor and Albeck, 78–79), 197
15:7 (ed. Theodor and Albeck, pp. 140–41), 35n17
44:12 (ed. Theodor and Albeck, p. 433), 185
45:7 (ed. Theodor and Albeck, p. 455), 71
60:8 (ed. Theodor and Albeck, p. 650), 70–71, 78
65:22 (ed. Theodor and Albeck, pp. 741–42), 49–50

Pesikta de-Rav Kahana

pp. 257–58, 133, 141, 150, 162
pp. 385–86 (ed. Mandelbaum), 104n28

Palestinian Talmud

Berakhot
9:5 (14b), 166, 171–72

Shabbat
6:9 (8d), 178–81

Ta'anit
4:7 (69a–b), 133–51, 155, 158–63

Megillah
1:8 (71d), 83n11

Sotah
3:4 (19a), 170–71
5:5 (20c), 166, 171–72

Kiddushin
4:1 (65b–c), 160–61

Sanhedrin
10:2 (28c), 42–44, 48, 51–52

Babylonian Talmud

Berakhot
63b, 218

Shabbat
12b, 64–65
119a, 189–90
156a–b, 176–88, 190, 199

Pesahim
2b, 196–97

Ta'anit
21a, 60–61, 72n46

Megillah
3a, 193–94
8a–9a, 80–93

Moed Katan
28a, 194

Hagigah
4b–5a, 195–96
12a, 211

Yevamot
21b, 191–92
49b–50a, 33–52

Nedarim
25a, 72n46

Sotah
22b, 164–70
33a, 64–65

Gittin
57b, 159n93
58a, 17–20
68a–b, 95–96, 98–129, 204–5

Kiddushin
81b, 9

Baba Kamma
2b, 196

Baba Batra
3b–4a, 26
98a, 192n58

Sanhedrin
19a–b, 23–24, 26–28
95a, 190–91
96b, 147–52, 155, 158–63
101a, 35n17
103b, 43–44

Makkot
22b, 78

Horayot
12a, 194–95

Menahot
29b, 78

Meilah
17a–b, 53–79

INDEX OF PRIMARY SOURCES · 281

Tamid

31b–32b, 200–25, 227–35

Midrash Tannaim

18:14 (ed. Hoffman, p. 111), 186–87

Pesikta Rabbati

41a–b (ed. Ulmer, pp. 540–41), 72

PERSIAN TEXTS

Avesta Yast

19.49, 45–46

History of King Jamshed and the Demon

pp. 64–65 (ed. Larionoff), 46–48

MUSLIM TEXTS

The History of al-Tabari

vol. 4, p. 41 (ed. Perlmann), 47–48, 51
vol. 4, p. 103–11 (ed. Perlmann), 155–60, 163

Abū-Raihūn Muhammad ibn Ahmad al-bīrūnī

The Chronology of Ancient Nations
p. 297 (ed. Sachau), 144–45